HITOS

Noun - Place thing verb.
adj - modpies nour — blu con
verb - samthing oido - e.

English Grammar and Composition

Third Course

John E. Warriner

FRANKLIN EDITION

626

HBJ

Harcourt Brace Jovanovich, Publishers

Orlando   New York   Chicago   Atlanta   Dallas

THE SERIES:

English Grammar and Composition: First Course
English Grammar and Composition: Second Course
English Grammar and Composition: Third Course
English Grammar and Composition: Fourth Course
English Grammar and Composition: Fifth Course
English Grammar and Composition: Complete Course
Test booklet and teacher's manual for each above title.

CORRELATED SERIES:

English Workshop: First Course
English Workshop: Second Course
English Workshop: Third Course
English Workshop: Fourth Course
English Workshop: Fifth Course
English Workshop: Review Course

Composition: Models and Exercises, First Course
Composition: Models and Exercises, Second Course
Composition: Models and Exercises, Third Course
Composition: Models and Exercises, Fourth Course
Composition: Models and Exercises, Fifth Course
Advanced Composition: A Book of Models for Writing, Complete Course

Vocabulary Workshop: First Course
Vocabulary Workshop: Second Course
Vocabulary Workshop: Third Course
Vocabulary Workshop: Fourth Course
Vocabulary Workshop: Fifth Course
Vocabulary Workshop: Complete Course

John E. Warriner taught English for thirty-two years in junior and senior high schools and in college. He is chief author of the *English Grammar and Composition* series, coauthor of the *English Workshop* series, general editor of the *Composition: Models and Exercises* series, and editor of *Short Stories: Characters in Conflict*. His co-authors have all been active in English education.

Printed in the United States of America
ISBN 0–15–311882–2

To the Student

The title of this textbook is *English Grammar and Composition*. Let's consider briefly the meaning of the two words *grammar* and *composition*.

Grammar is a description of the way a language works. It explains many things. For example, grammar tells us the order in which sentence parts must be arranged. It explains the work done by the various kinds of words – the work done by a noun is different from the work done by a verb. It explains how words change their form according to the way they are used. Grammar is useful because it enables us to make statements about how to use our language. These statements we usually call rules.

The grammar rule that the normal order of an English sentence is subject-verb-object may not seem very important to us, because English is our native tongue and we naturally use this order without thinking. But the rule would be very helpful to people who are learning English as a second language. However, the rule that subjects and verbs "agree" (when the subject is plural, the verb is plural), and the rule that some pronouns (I, he, she, we, they) are used as subjects while others (me, him, her, us, them) are used as objects – these are helpful rules even for native speakers of English.

Such rules could not be understood – in fact, they could not be formed – without the vocabulary of grammar. Grammar, then, helps us to state how English is used and how we should use it.

The word *composition* means "putting together." When you speak and write, you are putting words together to express your ideas. You compose sentences in this way, and you compose essays and stories by grouping sentences.

Much in this book will help you to speak better, but another important purpose of this book is to help you to write better. Unlike speaking, which you learned even before you went to school, writing is something that you learned only in school, where you first encountered the need for it. To learn how to write, you must study and practice. Written sentences must be more carefully composed than spoken ones. Writing requires more careful organization than informal speaking. You are not aware of paragraphs and paragraph structure when you carry on a conversation, but you must understand the structure of a paragraph if you are to write clearly. Writing requires other skills — punctuation, capitalization, and spelling, for example.

With the aid of the grammar explained in this book, the rules of composition, and the practice exercises provided, you will be able to improve your English.

J.W.

Contents

Preface   **iii**

PART ONE: Grammar

1. The Parts of Speech   3
The Work That Words Do

The Noun   3
Common and Proper Nouns   4
Compound Nouns   6
The Pronoun   6
Personal Pronouns   8
Other Commonly Used Pronouns   8
The Adjective   10
Pronoun or Adjective?   11
Nouns Used as Adjectives   11
Articles   12
Adjectives in Sentences   12
The Verb   15
Action Verbs   16
Linking Verbs   17
Verb Phrases   20
The Adverb   22
Adverbs Modifying Verbs   22
Adverbs Modifying Adjectives   23
Adverbs Modifying Adverbs   25
Forms of Adverbs   26
The Preposition   29
The Conjunction   31

The Interjection 33
Determining Parts of Speech 34
Summary of Parts of Speech 35

2. The Parts of a Sentence　　38
Subject, Predicate, Complement

The Sentence 39
Subject and Predicate 40
The Simple Subject 42
The Simple Predicate 43
Finding the Subject 45
The Subject in an Unusual Position 48
The Understood Subject 50
Compound Subjects 51
Compound Verbs 52
Diagraming Sentences 55
Diagraming Subject and Verb 55
Diagraming Adjectives and Adverbs 58
Complements 62
The Subject Complement 66
Objects 67
Diagraming Complements 71
Classifying Sentences by Purpose 75

3. The Phrase　　78
Prepositional and Verbal Phrases,
Appositive Phrases

Prepositional Phrases 79
The Adjective Phrase 81
The Adverb Phrase 83
Diagraming Prepositional Phrases 85
Verbals and Verbal Phrases 88

The Participle 88
The Participial Phrase 91
The Gerund 93
The Gerund Phrase 95
The Infinitive 97
The Infinitive Phrase 98
The Infinitive with *to* Omitted 98
Diagraming Verbals and Verbal Phrases 99
Appositives and Appositive Phrases 102

4. The Clause 106
Independent and Subordinate Clauses

Kinds of Clauses 106
The Uses of Subordinate Clauses 108
The Adjective Clause 109
Relative Pronouns 109
The Adverb Clause 113
Subordinating Conjunctions 114
The Noun Clause 115
Diagraming Subordinate Clauses 117
**Sentences Classified According to
  Structure 120**

PART TWO: Usage

5. Agreement 129
Subject and Verb, Pronoun and
Antecedent

Agreement of Subject and Verb 130
The Compound Subject 137
Other Problems in Agreement 140
Agreement of Pronoun and Antecedent 147

6. The Correct Use of Verbs 153
Principal Parts, Regular and
Irregular Verbs

Principal Parts of Verbs 153
Regular Verbs 154
Irregular Verbs 155
Tense 162
Consistency of Tense 164
Active and Passive Voice 166
Special Problems with Verbs 168
Lie and *Lay* 168
Sit and *Set* 171
Rise and *Raise* 173

7. The Correct Use of Pronouns 179
Nominative and Objective Uses

The Case Forms of Personal Pronouns 180
The Nominative Case 181
The Objective Case 184
Special Pronoun Problems 190
Who and *Whom* 190
The Pronoun in an Incomplete Construction
196

8. The Correct Use of Modifiers 202
Comparison and Placement

Comparison of Modifiers 202
Regular Comparison 203
Irregular Comparison 205
Use of Comparative and Superlative
Forms 206

Dangling Modifiers 210
Correcting Dangling Modifiers 211
Misplaced Modifiers 214
Misplaced Phrase Modifiers 214
Misplaced Clause Modifiers 216

9. A Glossary of Usage   220

PART THREE: Sentence Structure

10. Writing Complete Sentences   243
Sentence Fragments and Run-on Sentences

The Sentence Fragment 243
Common Types of Sentence Fragments 246
The Run-on Sentence 254
Correcting Run-on Sentences 255

11. Sentence Combining and Revising   259
Achieving Sentence Variety

Sentence Combining 259
Avoiding Stringy Sentences 277
Varying Sentence Beginnings 278
Varying Sentence Structure 286

PART FOUR: Composition

12. Writing Paragraphs   293
Structure and Development
of Paragraphs

The Structure of a Paragraph   293
The Topic Sentence   294
The Development of a Paragraph   299
Ways of Developing a Paragraph   303
Coherence   311
Arrangement of Ideas   311
Connecting Sentences   316
Types of Paragraphs   325
Narrative   325
Descriptive   327
Expository   328

13. Writing Compositions   332

The Materials of Writing   333
Your Own Experiences   333
Experience of Others   336
Two Model Compositions   337
Bringing Material into Focus   340
Planning Your Composition   344
Making an Outline   348
Outline Form   349
Writing the Composition   353
Connecting Paragraphs   358
Achieving Emphasis in the
    Composition   363
**Summary of Steps in Writing a
Composition**   364
Checklist for Writing Compositions   366
Suggested Topics for Composition   367

14. Manuscript Form 371
Standards for Written Work

15. Writing Summaries and Reports 376

Writing a Summary 376
A Report Based on Several Sources 387
Choosing Your Subject and Source 387
Reading and Taking Notes for the Report 391
Writing the Report 395
Checklist for Writing Reports 397
Sample Report with Bibliography 397

16. Writing Stories 403
Essential Elements in Narratives

The Setting 404
The Characters 404
The Situation or Conflict 404
The Action 405
The Climax 405
The Outcome 405
Planning a Short Story 406
Writing the Story 409
A Model Narrative 416

17. Making Writing Interesting 419
Words and Their Use

The Sounds of Words — Onomatopoeia 419
Sound and Meaning 421
Beauty in Words 423
Word Histories — Derivation 424

Sources of English Words   425
New Words   427
The Denotative and Connotative Meanings
   of Words   428
Loaded Words   431
Formal Words and Informal Words   432
Slang   433
Degrees of Formality Among Synonyms   434
Appropriate Words   435
Tired Words   436
General Words and Specific Words   438
Summary   439
Composition Assignment—Specific
   Verbs   440

18. The Business Letter   444

Some Tips on Writing Letters   444
The Business Letter—Standard Practices
   445
Stationery and Appearance   446
Letter Form   447
Request Letters   453
Order Letters   454
Adjustment Letters   455
The Envelope   457
Checklist for Writing Letters   460

PART FIVE: Mechanics

19. Capital Letters   465

The Rules for Capitalization

Summary Style Sheet   481

20. End Marks and Commas 483
Periods, Question Marks,
Exclamation Points, Commas

End Marks 483
Commas 487
Summary of Uses of Comma 509

21. Semicolons and Colons 513

Semicolons 513
Colons 523

22. Italics and Quotation Marks 527

Italics 527
Quotation Marks 529

23. Apostrophes 540
Possessive Case, Contractions,
Plurals

24. Other Marks of Punctuation 553
Hyphens, Dashes, Parentheses

Hyphens 553
Dashes 556
Parentheses 557

PART SIX: Aids to Good English

25. The Library 565

Location and Arrangement of Facilities

Know Your Library 565
Arrangement of Books 566
Fiction 567
Nonfiction 568
The Card Catalogue 570
The Title Card 571
The Author Card 571
The Subject Card 572
"See" and "See Also" Cards 572
Summary of Card Catalogue 574
Reference Books 575
The *Readers' Guide* 576
Vertical File 579
Other Reference Books 579

26. The Dictionary 590

Arrangement and Content of Dictionaries

Kinds of Dictionaries 590
The Unabridged Dictionary 591
The College Dictionary 594
The School Dictionary 594
Kinds of Information in Dictionaries 598
Pronunciation 606
Consonant Sounds 607
Vowel Sounds 608
Accent Marks 611
Words Commonly Mispronounced 613

27. Vocabulary   615
Context Clues, Synonyms, Word Analysis

Diagnostic Test   615
Ways to Learn New Words   618
Determining the Part of Speech   622
Using the Right Word   626
Prefixes and Roots   631
Vocabulary List   639

28. Spelling   643
Improving Your Spelling

Good Spelling Habits   643
Spelling Rules   648
Adding Prefixes and Suffixes   649
The Plural of Nouns   655
Words Often Confused   659
Spelling Words   673

PART SEVEN: Speaking and Listening

29. Speaking Before Groups   679
Preparing for and Delivering Various Kinds of Speeches

Preparing a Speech   679
Delivering a Speech   685
Nonverbal Communication   686
Pronunciation and Enunciation   687
Kinds of Speaking Situations   693
Talking About an Experience or Telling a
    Story   693

Talking About Current Events 695
Talking About Books, Movies, and Television
Shows 697

30. Listening 700
Sharpening Listening Skills

Purposeful Listening 700
Listening to Speeches 703

Index 709
Tab Key Index 729

Grammar

PART ONE

Chapter 1

The Parts of Speech

The Work That Words Do

When you speak or write, you express your thoughts in words. Sometimes you may use only one word, such as *Quiet!* or *Hello.* Usually, however, you use groups of words that make statements, ask questions, or give instructions or directions. Every word you speak or write has a definite use in expressing a thought or idea. The way the word is used determines what *part of speech* that word is. There are eight parts of speech:

nouns	verbs	conjunctions
pronouns	adverbs	interjections
adjectives	prepositions	

As you study this chapter, learn to recognize the parts of speech, the eight ways that words work for you as you communicate your thoughts and ideas to others.

THE NOUN

Perhaps the words most frequently used are those by which we identify someone or something. These labels, or name words, are called *nouns.*

1a. A *noun* is a word used to name a person, place, thing, or idea.

Persons	Celia, Mr. Tompkins, hair stylist, fire-fighter, women, Americans
Places	Chicago, Alaska, Europe, Bryant Park, kitchen, suburbs
Things	money, poem, pencils, airplanes, merry-go-round
Ideas	perfection, strength, happiness, obedience, liberty

EXERCISE 1. Copy each of the following words on your paper. After each, tell whether it names a person, a place, a thing, or an idea. If the word does not name, write *not a noun*.

1. novelist
2. biscuits
3. sharpen
4. sharpener
5. gratitude
6. gratify
7. loses
8. silly
9. plumber
10. patriotism
11. believe
12. belief
13. across
14. for
15. Midwest
16. advertise
17. supposedly
18. faith
19. file clerk
20. joy

Common and Proper Nouns

There are two classes of nouns, *proper nouns* and *common nouns*. A proper noun names a particular person, place, or thing, and is always capitalized. A common noun names any one of a group of persons, places, or things, and is not capitalized.

COMMON NOUNS	PROPER NOUNS
inventor	Thomas A. Edison, Sarah Boone
woman	Pearl Bailey, Hannah Arendt, Dr. Alvarez, Maria Tallchief
city	Boston, Des Moines, Salt Lake City

non - samting - verb.
adjitic -

school	Lincoln High School, Harvard University
state	Georgia, Tennessee, Utah, Pennsylvania
river	Mississippi River, Colorado River
month	January, April, August, November

EXERCISE 2. There are fifty nouns in the following paragraph. As you list the nouns on your paper, circle all the proper nouns. A name is counted as one noun, even if it has more than one part.

1. In our living language, proper nouns occasionally change to common nouns. 2. Losing their value as names of particular people, these words become names for a general class of things. 3. For example, during the nineteenth century, Samuel A. Maverick was unique among ranchers in Texas. 4. Maverick did not regularly brand his calves. 5. Therefore, neighbors on other ranches began to call any unbranded, stray yearling a "Maverick." 6. For these ranchers, a *maverick* soon became a common name for a certain kind of calf, and now *maverick* is standard English for any unbranded animal or motherless calf. 7. Many other words have similar origins. 8. The term *pasteurization* is named after Louis Pasteur, and *mesmerism* comes from F. A. Mesmer. 9. From John L. McAdam, a Scottish engineer, comes the word *macadam*, referring to a pavement made of crushed stones. 10. Although they were once names of particular people, *silhouette, macintosh,* and *watt* have undergone similar changes and no longer begin with capital letters.

EXERCISE 3. Study the nouns listed below. In class, be prepared to (1) identify each noun as a common or a proper noun, and (2) if the noun is a common noun, name a corresponding proper noun; if the noun is proper, name a corresponding common noun. Remember that capitalization is one of the signals of a proper noun.

1. woman	6. city	11. college	16. holiday
2. month	7. lake	12. Dallas	17. teacher
3. Peru	8. actor	13. Kansas	18. Mt. Fuji
4. singer	9. Ohio	14. street	19. river
5. Athena	10. ocean	15. Aunt Jo	20. team

Compound Nouns

By now, you have probably noticed that two or more words may be used together as a single noun. In the examples below rule 1a on page 4, you find *hair stylist* and *Mr. Tompkins* in the list of persons, *Bryant Park* in the list of places, and *merry-go-round* in the list of things. These word groups are called *compound nouns.*

As you see, the parts of a compound noun may be written as one word, as two or more words, or may be hyphenated. Here are some other commonly used compound nouns.

EXAMPLES   prizefighter, volleyball, newsstand, news room, commander in chief, beach ball, home economics, sister-in-law, baby-sitter, Stratford-on-Avon

If you are in doubt as to how to write a compound noun, you should consult your dictionary. Some dictionaries may give two correct forms for a word; for example, you may find *vice-president* written both with and without the hyphen. As a rule, it is wise to use the form the dictionary lists first.

THE PRONOUN

1b. A *pronoun* is a word used in place of one or of more than one noun.

One way to refer to something is to use the noun that names it. We usually have to do this to make clear what we mean. However, once we have made clear the identity of the person or thing we are talking about, we can make other references without having to give the name each time.

EXAMPLE　Gloria stepped back from the picture and looked at **it.**

It would be awkward and unnecessary to repeat *the picture* in the last part of this sentence. The pronoun *it* does the job better by simply taking the place of the noun *picture*.

In the following sentences a number of different pronouns are used. Notice that they all take the place of a noun the way *it* does in the example above.

EXAMPLES　Where is Lois? **She** said **she** would be here on time. [The pronoun *she*, used twice, takes the place of *Lois* in the second sentence.]

Our teacher and Mrs. Barnes said **they** would go to the meeting. [The pronoun *they* takes the place of two nouns: *teacher* and *Mrs. Barnes*.]

As these examples show, pronouns almost always refer to a word mentioned earlier. This noun on which the pronoun depends for its meaning is called the *antecedent,* which simply means "something going before." In the following examples, the arrows point from the pronouns to their antecedents.

EXAMPLES　Jill opened her **book** and read from **it.**

The coach showed the **players** how **they** should throw the ball.

Janet took **her** dog to the veterinarian.

Personal Pronouns

The pronouns that have appeared in the examples so far are called *personal* pronouns. In this use, *personal* does not have its common meaning of "private or having to do with a person." Instead it refers to one of the three possible ways of making statements: The persons speaking can talk about themselves (first person: *I, we*) or they can talk about the persons spoken to (second person: *you*) or they can talk about anyone or anything else (third person: *he, she, it, they*). The few pronouns in English that have different forms to show person are called *personal pronouns*.

Personal Pronouns

	SINGULAR	PLURAL
First person (the person speaking)	I, my,[1] mine, me	we, our, ours, us
Second person (the person spoken to)	you, your, yours	you, your, yours
Third person (some other person or thing)	he, his, him she, her, hers it, its	they, their, theirs, them

Other Commonly Used Pronouns

Here are some other kinds of pronouns that you will encounter as you study this textbook:

REFLEXIVE PRONOUNS   (the *–self, –selves* forms of the personal pronouns)

---

[1] The possessive forms *my, your, her,* etc., are called pronouns in this book. (See page 11.)

myself	ourselves
yourself	yourselves
himself, herself, itself	themselves

► **NOTE**   Never write or say *hisself* or *theirselves.*

RELATIVE PRONOUNS (used to introduce adjective clauses; see pages 109–10)

who   whom   whose   which   that

INTERROGATIVE PRONOUNS   (used in questions)

Who...?   Whose...?   What...?
Whom...?   Which...?

DEMONSTRATIVE PRONOUNS   (used to point out a specific person or thing)

this   that   these   those

INDEFINITE PRONOUNS   (not referring to a definite person or thing; frequently used without antecedents)

all	each	more	one
another	either	most	other
any	everybody	much	several
anybody	everyone	neither	some
anyone	everything	nobody	somebody
anything	few	none	someone
both	many	no one	

EXERCISE 4. Number 1–20 on your paper. List in order the twenty pronouns in the following sentences.

1. Angela has an interesting hobby. She writes down the first and last lines of her favorite works of literature.
2. "Everyone knows the opening sentence of *Moby Dick,*" she said to me, "but few can recall the last sentence."

3. "The book opens," she continued, "with 'Call me Ishmael.' It ends with 'Now small fowls flew screaming over the yet yawning gulf; a sullen white surf beat against its steep sides; then all collapsed, and the great shroud of the sea rolled on as it rolled five thousand years ago.' "
4. I replied, "That is the ending of the story but not of the epilogue, which reads, 'On the second day, a sail drew near, nearer, and picked me up at last. It was the devious-cruising *Rachel,* that in her re-tracing search after her missing children, only found another orphan.' "

EXERCISE 5. Copy the following paragraph and fill in the twenty blanks with appropriate pronouns.

—— main objection to mystery stories is the effect that —— have on —— peace of mind. When reading —— of ——, —— imagine that —— is in the closet or just outside the window. Whether the author chooses to have a victim poisoned or to have —— strangled, —— always has —— murdered. In a story that —— read recently, a murderer overpowers a millionaire, twisting and bruising —— body and cast-ing —— into the cage of a gorilla. Unlike ——, Helen, —— likes mystery stories as a means for escape, par-ticularly enjoys reading —— just before —— goes to sleep. —— favorite stories include —— —— cause terrible nightmares.

THE ADJECTIVE

Sometimes we wish to describe, or make more defi-nite, a noun or pronoun we use. We then *modify* the word by using an adjective.

1c. An *adjective* modifies a noun or a pronoun.

To *modify* a word means to describe the word or to

make its meaning more definite. An adjective modifies a noun or a pronoun by answering one of these questions: *What kind? Which one? How many?* Notice how the bold-faced adjectives which follow answer these questions about the nouns modified.

WHAT KIND?	WHICH ONE?	HOW MANY?
white car	**this** road	**one** minute
nylon rope	**last** week	**three** girls
wise person	the **first** day	**few** people
big desk	the **other** man	**several** days

Pronoun or Adjective?

Notice that in the phrases above, *one, this, other, few,* and *several* — words which may also be used as pronouns — are adjectives, because they modify the nouns in the phrases rather than take the place of the nouns.

The words *my, your, his, her, its, our,* and *their* are called pronouns throughout this book; they are the *possessive* forms of personal pronouns, showing ownership or relationship. Some teachers, however, prefer to think of these words as adjectives because they tell *Which one?* about nouns: *my* sister, *your* book, *our* team, *their* tents. Often they are called *pronominal adjectives.*

Nouns Used as Adjectives

Sometimes you will find nouns used as adjectives.

NOUNS	NOUNS USED AS ADJECTIVES
large **table**	**table** leg
expensive **dinner**	**dinner** table
next **Sunday**	**Sunday** dinner

Notice in the last example above that a proper noun, *Sunday,* is used as an adjective. Here are some other proper nouns used as adjectives:

Florida coast   **Navaho** tradition
Norway pine   **Joplin** song

When you find a noun used as an adjective, your teacher may prefer that you call it an adjective. If so, proper nouns used as adjectives will be called *proper adjectives*. In any exercises you do, follow your teacher's directions in labeling nouns used as adjectives.

Articles

The most frequently used adjectives are *a, an,* and *the*. These little words are usually called *articles*.

A and *an* are indefinite articles; they refer to one of a general group.

EXAMPLES   **A** woman arrived.
                An automobile went by.
                She waited **an** hour.

A is used before words beginning with a consonant sound; *an* is used before words beginning with a vowel sound. Notice in the third example above that *an* is used before a noun beginning with the consonant *h,* because the *h* in *hour* is not pronounced. *Hour* is pronounced as if it began with a vowel (like *our*). Remember that the *sound* of the noun, not the spelling, determines which indefinite article will be used.

The is a definite article. It indicates that the noun refers to someone or something in particular.

EXAMPLES   **The** woman arrived.
                The automobile went by.
                The hour passed quickly.

Adjectives in Sentences

In all the examples you have seen so far, the adjective

comes before the noun modified. This is its usual position.

Mrs. Russell gave **each** boy here **hot** tea and **apple** pie.

The **ancient, battered** manuscript was found in her desk.

Sometimes, however, adjectives follow the word they modify.

Magazines, **old** and **dusty,** cluttered her desk.

Other words may separate an adjective from the noun or pronoun modified.

Anna seemed **unhappy.** She was not **optimistic.**

Courageous in battle, he deserved his medals.

EXERCISE 6. Copy the following sentences onto your paper, and fill in the blanks with adjectives. (Do not use articles.) Answer the questions *What kind? Which one? How many?* Draw an arrow from each adjective to the noun or pronoun modified.

1. My family visited the —— zoo on Sunday.
2. —— monkeys were chattering in their —— cages.
3. My sister heard the —— lion roaring and immediately became ——.
4. She laughed, though, when she saw the —— birds with —— feathers on their heads.
5. The —— birds made —— squawks.
6. The seals, —— and ——, performed stunts.
7. The —— elephants appeared —— for our peanuts.
8. The bears were begging for food on their —— feet.
9. By —— afternoon the sky was becoming ——.

10. After a —— day, we finally arrived home, ——
and ——.

EXERCISE 7. Except for articles, the sentences be-
below contain no adjectives. Using a separate sheet
of paper, revise the sentences by supplying interesting
adjectives to modify the nouns or pronouns. Underline the adjectives.

1. Winds uprooted trees, leveled houses, and swept
   cars off the streets.
2. All during the night in the forest, the campers heard
   noises, cries of birds and beasts.
3. Without money, I strolled down the midway at the
   fair and watched the crowds at the booths and on
   the rides.
4. At Linda's party, the guests were served sandwiches, meatballs, salad, and later, fruit, cake, and
   ice cream.
5. Everybody at the party received a gift, such as
   stationery, jewelry, soap, or a book.

EXERCISE 8. Look for adjectives as you read a newspaper or a magazine. Find a section containing at
least twenty adjectives, not counting articles. Clip it
out and paste it onto your paper. Underline the adjectives.

REVIEW EXERCISE A. List on your paper the *italicized* words in the following sentences. Before each
word, write the number of its sentence, and after the
word, write whether it is a noun, a pronoun, or an
adjective.

EXAMPLE 1. *This* article tells about Shakespeare's
life.
1. *This, adjective*
1. *life, noun*

1. Most high school *students* read at least one *play* by William Shakespeare.
2. *Shakespeare,* the most *famous* playwright of *all* time, was born in Stratford-on-Avon in 1564.
3. He was baptized in the *small* church at Stratford shortly after *his* birth.
4. *He* was buried in the *same* church.
5. On the stone above his grave, *you* can find an inscription which places a *curse* upon *anyone* who moves his bones.
6. Out of *respect* for his wish or because of fear of his curse, *nobody* has disturbed the grave.
7. *This* explains why his body was never moved to Westminster Abbey, where many *other English* writers are buried.
8. Besides seeing the church, the visitor in *Stratford* can see the house in *which* Shakespeare was born.
9. *One* can walk through the home of the *parents* of Anne Hathaway, the *woman* whom Shakespeare married.
10. Inside the thatch-roofed cottage a person can see a very *uncomfortable* bench on which William and *Anne* may have sat when he called on *her.*
11. At *one* time visitors could also see the *large* house which Shakespeare bought for *himself* and his *family.*
12. When he retired from the *theater* he lived there, and there he also died.
13. Unfortunately, the house was destroyed by a *later* owner *who* did not want to pay taxes on *it.*

THE VERB

A noun or a pronoun, no matter how many modifiers it may have, cannot make a sentence. The noun or pronoun must act in some way, or something must be said about it. The part of speech that performs this function is the *verb.*

1d. A *verb* is a word that expresses action or otherwise helps to make a statement.

Action Verbs

Words such as *do, come, go,* and *write* are action verbs. Sometimes action verbs express an action that cannot be seen: *believe, remember, know, think,* and *understand.*

EXERCISE 9. Make a list of twenty action verbs not including those listed above. Include and underline at least five verbs that express an action that cannot be seen.

There are two large classes of action verbs — transitive and intransitive. A verb is *transitive* when the action it expresses is directed toward a person or thing named in the sentence.

EXAMPLES   Neil **sliced** the pie. [The action of the verb *sliced* is directed toward *pie.* The verb is transitive.]

                Tina **mailed** the package.

In these examples the action passes from the doer — the subject — to the receiver of the action. Words that receive the action of a transitive verb are called *objects.*

A verb is *intransitive* when it expresses action (or helps to make a statement) without reference to an object.[1] The following sentences contain intransitive verbs.

EXAMPLES   Last Saturday we **stayed** inside.

                The children **laughed.**

                The train **arrived** on time.

[1] Linking verbs (*be, seem, appear,* etc.) are usually considered to be *intransitive verbs.* See pages 17–19.

The same verb may be transitive in one sentence and intransitive in another. A verb that can take an object is often used intransitively when the emphasis is on the action rather than on the person or thing affected by it.

EXAMPLES Daisy **speaks** French. [transitive]
Daisy **speaks** fluently. [intransitive]
The speaker **answered** many questions. [transitive]
The speaker **answered** angrily. [intransitive]

EXERCISE 10. Some of the action verbs in the following sentences are transitive and some are intransitive. Write the verb of each sentence after the proper number and label it as a dictionary would — *v.t.* for transitive, *v.i.* for intransitive.

1. The festival judges selected Robert Hayden.
2. Architects like I. M. Pei sometimes charge high fees for their designs.
3. The army retreated to a stronger position.
4. The club finally voted funds for the picnic.
5. Even good friends sometimes disagree.
6. At the last moment, Miguel remembered his friend's warning.
7. The rain lasted all afternoon.
8. June practices in the afternoon for an hour.
9. On the opening night of the class play, Carlos got a standing ovation.
10. During vacation, time passes rapidly.

Linking Verbs

Some verbs help to make a statement, not by expressing an action but by serving as a link between two words. These verbs are called *linking verbs* or *state-of-being verbs*.

The most commonly used linking verbs are forms of the verb *be*. You should become thoroughly familiar with the verbs in the following list.

be	shall be	should be
being	will be	would be
am	has been	can be
is	have been	could be
are	had been	should have been
was	shall have been	would have been
were	will have been	could have been

Any verb ending in *be* or *been* is a form of the verb *be*.

Here are some other frequently used linking verbs:

appear	grow	seem	stay
become	look	smell	taste
feel	remain	sound	turn

Notice in the following sentences how each verb is a link between the words on either side of it. The word that follows the linking verb fills out or completes the meaning of the verb and refers to the word preceding the verb.

The sum of two and four **is** six. [sum = six]

Sue **could have been** a carpenter. [Sue = carpenter]

That roast beef **smells** good. [good roast beef]

The light **remained** red. [red light]

▶ **NOTE** Many of the linking verbs listed can be used as action (nonlinking) verbs as well.

The movie star **appeared** nervous. [linking verb —nervous movie star]

The movie star **appeared** in a play. [action verb]

The soup **tasted** good. [linking verb—good soup]

The cook **tasted** the soup. [action verb]

Even *be* is not always a linking verb. It may be followed by only an adverb: I was *there*.[1] To be a linking verb, the verb must be followed by a word that names or describes the subject.

EXERCISE 11. Copy the following sentences, supplying a linking verb for each blank. Use a different verb for each blank.

1. My dog's name —— Jim Dandy.
2. I —— tired.
3. Pine trees —— tall.
4. She —— a good Samaritan.
5. Did she eventually —— a physician or a researcher?
6. My face —— red.
7. All morning the baby —— quiet.
8. This soup —— good.
9. Paul —— lucky.
10. She always —— happy.

EXERCISE 12. Using the linking verb given in italics, change each word group below to a sentence. Write the sentence on your paper and underline the linked words.

EXAMPLES
1. *became* one impatient clerk
1. One <u>clerk</u> *became* <u>impatient</u>.
2. *is* Dr. Alford, our family doctor
2. <u>Dr. Alford</u> *is* our family <u>doctor</u>.

1. *was* the lukewarm coffee
2. *had been* Billie Holiday, a singer of blues
3. *looks* the frightened animal
4. *grew* the restless audience
5. *tastes* that bitter medicine
6. *is* Arthur Ashe, a tennis player
7. *remained* the calm lake
8. *seems* their odd behavior
9. *may become* one daughter, a famous pianist
10. *looks* that expensive watch

[1] See pages 22–26 for a discussion of adverbs.

EXERCISE 13. For each noun in the list below, write a sentence in which the noun is followed by an action verb. Then write another sentence using the same noun with a linking verb.

EXAMPLE 1. sister
1. *My sister helped me with my math homework.* [action verb]
My sister is an avid football fan. [linking verb]

1. brother
2. Dolores
3. meteors
4. farmer
5. actress

Verb Phrases

Parts of the verb *be* may serve another function besides that of linking verb. They may be used as *helping verbs* (sometimes called *auxiliary verbs*) in *verb phrases*. A *phrase* is a group of related words. A verb phrase consists of a main verb preceded by one or more helping verbs. Besides all forms of the verb *be*, helping verbs include the following:

has	can	might
have	may	must
had	should	do
shall	would	did
will	could	does

These helping verbs work together with main verbs as a unit. The helping verbs are in bold-faced type in the following examples.

is leaving	**may** become	**might have** remained
had seemed	**should** move	**must have** thought
shall be going	**could** jump	**does** sing

Sometimes the parts of a verb phrase are interrupted by other parts of speech.

EXAMPLES   She **had** always **been thinking** of her
future.

Her book **may** not **have been stolen**
after all.

They **should** certainly **be arriving** any
minute.

Parts of verb phrases are often separated in questions.

EXAMPLES   **Did** you **see** Bill Cosby's film?

Can her sister **help** us?

Has the girl next door **been collecting**
the records of José Feliciano?

EXERCISE 14. List on your paper the verbs and verb
phrases in the following sentences. Be sure to include
all helping verbs, especially when the parts of a verb
phrase are separated by other words. Some sentences
contain two verbs. There are twenty-five verbs and
verb phrases.

EXAMPLE   1. We will go to the concert if we can get
tickets.
1. *will go, can get*

1. Mr. Jensen always sweeps the floor first.
2. Then he washes the chalkboards.
3. He works slowly but steadily.
4. Thieves had broken into the office.
5. They did not find anything of value.
6. The intruders were probably looking for cash.
7. The weather report had confidently predicted
rain.
8. All morning the barometer was dropping rapidly.
9. The storm was slowly moving in.
10. Although the food tasted good, it was not very
good for you.
11. Your dog will become fat if you feed it too much.
12. Dogs will usually eat everything you give them.
13. Cats will stop when they have had enough.

14. You should have told us where you were going.
15. After the team has had more practice, they will surely play better.
16. Because we had always lived in the South, we had never seen snow.
17. We liked the snow, but we hated the cold.

THE ADVERB

You know that nouns and pronouns are modified by adjectives. Verbs and adjectives may have modifiers, too, and their modifiers are called *adverbs*. Adverbs may also modify other adverbs.

1e. An *adverb* is a word used to modify a verb, an adjective, or another adverb.

Adverbs Modifying Verbs

Sometimes an adverb modifies (makes more definite the meaning of) a verb. Study the adverbs in bold-faced type below. Notice that they modify verbs by answering one of these questions: *Where? When? How? To what extent* (*how long or how much*)?

WHERE?

I moved **forward.**
Sleep **here.**
Did you go **there?**

WHEN?

I moved **immediately.**
Sleep **later.**
Did you go **daily?**

HOW?

I **gladly** moved.
Sleep **well.**
Did you go **quietly?**

TO WHAT EXTENT?

I **barely** moved.
She **scarcely** sleeps.
Did you go **far?**

Adverbs may precede or may follow the verbs they modify, and they sometimes interrupt the parts of a verb phrase. Adverbs may also introduce questions.

19. Find and list the ten adverbs that mod-
adverbs in the following sentences. After
rb, give the adverb modified.

ges in our economy have occurred somewhat
lly.
cer research has advanced rather dramatically
e last few years.
reached the meeting too late to hear the com-
te discussion.
ou handle this material very carefully, you will
in no danger.
o our surprise, Father took the news quite calmly.
e always completely rewrites the first draft of
er novels.
We all finally agreed that Earl Campbell had done
extremely well.
Usually it seems that each month goes more
rapidly than the month before.
Arguments on both sides were most cleverly presented.
Although they are extremely young, these students measure up surprisingly well.

Forms of Adverbs

You have probably noticed that many adverbs end in
–ly. You should remember, however, that many adjectives also end in –ly: the *daily* newspaper, an *early*
train, an *only* child, her *untimely* death, a *friendly*
person. Moreover, words like *now, then, far, wide,
fast, high, already, somewhat, not,* and *right,* which
are often used as adverbs, do not end in –ly. In order
to identify a word as an adverb, do not depend entirely
upon the ending. Instead, ask yourself: Does this word
modify a verb, an adjective, or another adverb? Does
it tell *when, where, how,* or *to what extent?*

EXAMPLE **How** on earth will we **ever** finish our w
on time? [The adverb *how* modifies the
verb phrase *will finish*. Notice, too, the
adverb *ever,* which interrupts the verb
phrase and also modifies it.]

EXERCISE 15. Number your paper 1–10. After the
appropriate number, write an adverb to fill each blank
in the sentence. Following each adverb, write what the
adverb tells: *where* the action was done, *when* the
action was done, *how* it was done, or *to what extent*
it was done.

1. Play ——.
2. I can swim ——.
3. Mr. Thomas —— changes his opinions.
4. Does your sister practice ——?
5. Around the campfire we —— told spooky stories.
6. They won ——.
7. I —— want to send letters, but I —— like to get
them.
8. Could she listen ——?
9. The girl rowed —— and yelled ——.
10. He sighed —— as he —— waited for the telephone
to ring.

EXERCISE 16. Write ten sentences describing an incident at a ball game, in the classroom, or at a party.
Use at least ten adverbs modifying verbs. Underline
the adverbs, and draw arrows from them to the verbs
they modify.

Adverbs Modifying Adjectives

Sometimes an adverb modifies an adjective.

EXAMPLES Ruth is an **unusually** good goalie.
[The adjective *good* modifies the noun

goalie. The adverb *unusually* modifies the adjective *good,* telling "how good."]

During the burglary our dog stayed strangely silent. [The adverb *strangely* modifies the adjective *silent,* which in turn modifies the noun *dog.*]

Probably the most frequently used adverbs are *too* and *very.* In fact, these words are overworked. Try to avoid overusing them in speaking and particularly in writing; find more precise adverbs to take their place.

The following adverbs frequently modify adjectives:

extremely	entirely	unusually
dangerously	rather	especially
definitely	completely	surprisingly
quite	terribly	dreadfully

EXERCISE 17. Give one adverb modifier for each of the italicized adjectives below. Use a different adverb in each item; do not use *too* or *very.*

1. a *clever* remark
2. *beautiful* sunsets
3. an *easy* question
4. *dangerous* waters
5. a *sharp* blade
6. Toni seemed *happy.*
7. My allowance is *small.*
8. Robert became *sick.*
9. Had Clara been *safe?*
10. The test was *difficult.*

EXERCISE 18. Find and list the ten adverbs that modify adjectives in the following sentences. After each adverb, give the adjective modified.

1. Plato, a Greek philosopher, wrote a book called the *Republic* nearly three thousand years ago.
2. In the *Republic,* Plato describes the organization of a perfectly just government.

3. Plato's governm[...] such as the city [...] Greece in his time [...]
4. But his ideas are [...] apply to larger gove[...]
5. Each citizen of Plato [...] of three completely [...] military, or rulers.
6. All citizens study mu[...] most promising studen[...] cation.
7. Guardians who protect t[...] state are trained to be alwa[...]
8. A definitely important co[...] is that women and men are [...]
9. Women receive an education [...] and fight alongside men in wa[...] states.
10. Does this extremely brief des[...] state persuade you to accept o[...] of government?

Adverbs Modifying Other Adverbs

Sometimes an adverb modifies another a[...] in the first column below that each itali[...] modifies a verb or an adjective. In the sec[...] each added word in bold-faced type is an [...] modifies the italicized adverb.

EXAMPLES

Roy is *always* hungry.   Roy is **almost** *always* h[...]

They had met *before.*   They had met **long** *bef[...]*

She saw it *recently.*   She saw it **rather** *recentl[...]*

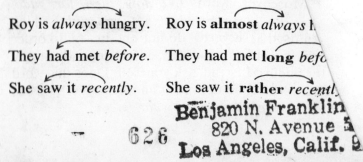

626

EXERCISE 20. Number your paper 1–20, and list after the proper number the adverbs in each sentence. After each adverb, write the word or expression it modifies. Be able to tell whether the word or expression modified is a verb, an adjective, or another adverb.

1. People who travel abroad usually visit the Tower of London.
2. The Tower, which was first built by William the Conqueror, is one of the most famous landmarks in London.
3. The Tower formerly served as a fortress, and troops are still stationed in it today.
4. A special ceremony called "The Ceremony of the Keys" is performed nightly.
5. The three gates of the Tower are securely locked by the Chief Warder, and an escort is especially assigned for the ceremony.
6. The Chief Warder and the escort promptly report to the front of the Tower.
7. The sentry immediately challenges them: "Halt! Who comes there?"
8. The Chief Warder quickly responds, "The Keys."
9. The sentry then asks, "Whose keys?" and the Warder replies distinctly, "Queen Elizabeth's Keys."
10. The Chief Warder then calls solemnly, "God preserve Queen Elizabeth."
11. And all the guards respond together, "Amen."
12. Finally the Chief Warder carries the keys to the Queen's House, and they remain there for the night.
13. The Ceremony of the Keys is not the only pageantry associated with the Tower.
14. Royal salutes are often fired from the Tower in recognition of particularly important occasions.
15. At the coronation of a king or queen, a sixty-two-gun salute is traditionally fired.

16. A royal birth is appropriately proclaimed by a forty-one-gun salute.
17. The oldest residents of the Tower of London are ravens; they have probably always been at the Tower.
18. Legend claims that the Tower will fall if the ravens ever leave.
19. So that ravens are always there in the Tower, the guards clip their wings.
20. The ravens are not unhappy; their needs are well supplied by the weekly rations that they receive from the state.

EXERCISE 21. Rewrite each of the following sentences by adding at least one adverb. Avoid using the adverbs *too* or *very*.

1. Angelo promised me that he would try to meet the train.
2. My coat was torn during the long hike, and Barbara lent me her poncho.
3. Engineering degrees are popular with students because job opportunities are good.
4. The Wallaces are settled into a new house, which they built by themselves.
5. When the baseball season begins, I will be attending games every day.
6. Ronald dribbled to his left and threw the ball into a crowded defensive zone.
7. Visits to national monuments and parks remind us that our country has an exciting history.
8. We returned the book to Marcella, but she had planned her report without it.
9. Georgia O'Keeffe displayed her paintings and received the admiration of a large audience.
10. The recipe calls for two or three eggs, but I did not have time to buy any at the store.

THE PREPOSITION

Certain words function in a sentence as relaters. They relate nouns and pronouns to other nouns and pronouns, to verbs, or to modifiers. These words are called *prepositions*.

1f. A *preposition* is a word that shows the relationship of a noun or a pronoun to some other word in the sentence.

The relationship shown by the preposition is an important one. In the examples below, the prepositions in bold-faced type make a great difference in meaning as they relate *house* to *walked* and *Douglass* to *book*.

I walked **to** the house.

I walked **around** the house.

I walked **through** the house.

The book **by** Douglass is new.

The book **about** Douglass is new.

The book **for** Douglass is new.

The following words are commonly used as prepositions. You should study the list and learn to recognize the words.

Commonly Used Prepositions

aboard	behind	during
about	below	except
above	beneath	for
across	beside	from
after	besides	in
against	between	inside
along	beyond	into
among	but (meaning *except*)	like
around	by	near
at	concerning	of
before	down	off

on	throughout	until
out	till	up
over	to	upon
past	toward	with
since	under	within
through	underneath	without

▶ **NOTE** Many words in this list can also be adverbs. To distinguish between adverbs and prepositions, ask yourself whether the word relates a following noun or pronoun to a word that precedes. Compare the following:

> Look **around**. [adverb]
> Look **around** the corner. [preposition]

There are also compound prepositions, having more than one word. Here are some that are frequently used.

Compound Prepositions

according to	in addition to	next to
as of	in front of	on account of
aside from	in place of	out of
because of	in spite of	owing to
by means of	instead of	prior to

The preposition and the noun or pronoun that follows combine to form a *prepositional phrase*. (For a discussion of prepositional phrases, see page 79.)

EXERCISE 22. Number your paper 1–10. Write in order after the proper number appropriate prepositions or compound prepositions to fill the blanks.

1. Recently I have learned a great many facts —— animals.
2. A whale cannot stay —— the water long because it must breathe air.

3. Though a whale may live a hundred years, a horse is old —— the age —— thirty, and a dog usually dies before it reaches twenty.
4. The deafness —— insects may surprise you.
5. —— their blindness, bats depend greatly —— their voices and ears.
6. Equipped —— a type —— radar, a blind bat squeaks —— a high-pitched voice, listens —— the echo, and detects and dodges obstacles.
7. The ears —— both bats and dogs can detect sounds that cannot be heard —— human ears.
8. Owls may see rays —— light which are invisible —— human eyes.
9. It is, —— course, a tragedy when a person loses an arm or a leg —— an automobile accident.
10. Yet, if —— chance a starfish should lose arms, new arms would grow; if one type —— flatworm should get its head chopped off, it would —— time grow a new head.

THE CONJUNCTION

1g. A *conjunction* joins words or groups of words.

There are three kinds of conjunctions: *coordinating* conjunctions, *correlative* conjunctions, and *subordinating* conjunctions. Since you will study subordinating conjunctions in connection with subordinate clauses in Chapter 4, at present you need to concern yourself only with the first two kinds of conjunctions:

COORDINATING CONJUNCTIONS	CORRELATIVE CONJUNCTIONS
and	both . . . and
but	not only . . . but also
or	either . . . or
nor	neither . . . nor
for	whether . . . or
yet	

Coordinating conjunctions may join single words, or they may join groups of words. They always connect items of the same kind:

EXAMPLES   baseball **and** tennis [two nouns]

at home **or** in the library [two prepositional phrases]

Kate has arrived, **for** I saw her in the garden. [two complete ideas]

Correlative conjunctions also connect items of the same kind. However, unlike coordinating conjunctions, correlatives are always used in pairs.

EXAMPLES   **Both** Jim Thorpe **and** Roberto Clemente were athletes.

The freshmen asked **not only** for a big celebration **but also** for a special holiday. [two prepositional phrases]

Either you must wash the dishes, **or** you will have to clean the bedroom. [two complete ideas]

EXERCISE 23. Number your paper 1–10. Write all the correlative and coordinating conjunctions from the same sentence after the corresponding number on your paper. (Separate the conjunctions by commas.) Be prepared to tell whether they are correlative or coordinating conjunctions.

EXAMPLE   1. Both her mother and she played tennis in high school and in college.
       1. *both — and, and*

1. I have fished in the Colorado River many times, but I never caught any fish there.
2. Not only have I tried live bait, but I have also used artificial lures.
3. Whether I go early in the morning or late in the

afternoon, the fish either are not hungry or will not eat.

4. Using both worms and minnows, I have fished for perch and bass, but I have usually caught turtles or eels.
5. The guide told me last winter that my poor luck was caused neither by my lack of skill nor by my choice of the wrong bait.
6. He advised me to fish at either Lake Travis or Marshall Creek, for there, he said, the fish are more plentiful.
7. He also suggested that I buy a spinning reel and a special kind of lure.
8. I saved my money and bought both the reel and the lure, for I was determined to make a big catch.
9. January 2 was very cold, but I decided to try my luck at Lake Travis; I caught nothing.
10. An old man and his companion told me that my new lure was made only for white bass and should be used only in early spring; the man started to tell me a different way to catch fish, but I didn't stay to listen.

THE INTERJECTION

Sometimes we use a word like *Ouch! Whew! Ahem!* or *Well!* to show anger, surprise, or some other sudden emotion. These words are called *interjections*.

1h. An *interjection* is an exclamatory word that expresses emotion. It has no grammatical relation to the rest of the sentence.

Interjections are not connectives or modifiers. Since they are unrelated to other words in the sentence, they are set off from the rest of the sentence. They are usually followed by an exclamation point. Sometimes, however, when the exclamation is mild, the interjection may be followed by a comma.

EXAMPLES   **Ugh!** The milk tastes sour.
              Terrific! We won!
              Wow! It worked.
              Well, forget it.
              Oh, all right.

DETERMINING PARTS OF SPEECH

It is easy to identify a word like *oh* as an interjection. However, the part of speech of a word is not always so simply determined. You must see how the word is used in the sentence.

1i. What part of speech a word is depends upon how the word is used.

The same word may be used as different parts of speech.

EXAMPLES   1. The quarterback made a first **down.** [noun]
             2. She made a small **down** payment. [adjective]
             3. You must **down** the spoonful of medicine. [verb]
             4. She glanced **down.** [adverb]
             5. She glanced **down** the hall. [preposition]

To determine what part of speech *down* is in each sentence, you must first read the entire sentence. What you are doing is studying the *context* of the word—how the word is used in the sentence. From the context, you can identify the part of speech that *down* is.

    The following summary will help you identify parts of speech in context:

SUMMARY

Rule	Part of Speech	Use	Examples
1a	noun	names	**Martha** likes **fish.**
1b	pronoun	takes the place of a noun	**You** and **I** must change **this.**
1c	adjective	modifies a noun or a pronoun	What a **hot** day! They were **angry.**
1d	verb	shows action or helps to make a statement	They **played** and **sang.** She **is** a senior.
1e	adverb	modifies a verb, an adjective, or another adverb	We **soon** left. I am **very** sad. It happened **quite** suddenly.
1f	preposition	relates a noun or a pronoun to another word	Two **of** the gifts **under** the Christmas tree had my name **on** them.
1g	conjunction	joins words	Jo **or** Sue won.
1h	interjection	expresses strong emotion	**Wow! Ouch! Oh,** I don't mind.

EXERCISE 24. Number 1–20 on your paper. Study the use of each italicized word in the following sentences. Place beside the proper number the part of speech of the italicized word. Be able to justify your answer by giving the *use* of the word in the sentence. Use the following abbreviations:

n.	noun	*adv.*	adverb
pron.	pronoun	*prep.*	preposition
v.	verb	*conj.*	conjunction
adj.	adjective	*interj.*	interjection

1. *Light* the oven now.
2. A *light* rain fell.
3. A red *light* flashed.
4. Cars whizzed *by.*

5. Pam went *by* air.
6. Look *up*.
7. Sail *up* the river.
8. Can you *top* that?
9. Lock the *top* drawer.
10. We climbed to the *top*.
11. *Shoo!* Get out of here!
12. I *shooed* the hen away.

13. *That* looks beautiful.
14. *That* cat is smart.
15. He did it *for* you.
16. I slept, *for* I was tired.
17. We must soon *part*.
18. One *part* is missing.
19. It may *snow* tonight.
20. We saw *snow* there.

EXERCISE 25. Write twenty short sentences using each of the following words as two different parts of speech. Underline the word, and give its part of speech in parentheses after the sentence.

EXAMPLE 1. on
      1. *We drove <u>on</u>.* (*adverb*)
        I sat <u>on</u> his hat. (*preposition*)

1. off	3. over	5. near	7. out	9. above
2. run	4. like	6. ride	8. love	10. paint

REVIEW EXERCISE B. Number 1–33. After each number, give the part of speech of the italicized word following that number in the paragraph below. Be able to explain its use in the sentence.

(1) *One* of the most (2) *popular* animal fables is a story (3) *about* an owl who (4) *becomes* a god (5) *to* its fellow creatures. Because the owl can see in the (6) *dark* (7) *and* can (8) *answer* questions with a few pat phrases, the (9) *other* animals decide (10) *it* is the wisest creature in the world. They (11) *follow* in the owl's footsteps and (12) *mimic* its (13) *every* action. When it bumps (14) *into* a tree, they (15) *do* the same. And when it staggers down the (16) *middle* of the highway, they follow the owl's (17) *lead*. They do

(18) *not* realize that their (19) *idol* cannot see (20) *during* the daytime. Because the owl fails to see a truck that (21) *is* approaching, it marches (22) *straight* ahead, and the other animals follow (23) *behind* it, thinking that it is (24) *very* (25) *brave* and that it will protect them from (26) *harm*. Naturally the owl is (27) *no* help to them when they are in the path of a fast-moving truck. The truck proves (28) *beyond* question that the owl (29) *is* (30) *not* a god, but (31) *this* lesson comes too (32) *late*. The (33) *foolish* animals are all killed by the truck. They followed their leader without question.

Chapter 2

The Parts of a Sentence

Subject, Predicate, Complement

As you study this chapter and do the exercises in it, you will become familiar with the structure of a sentence. You will learn how a given part of speech functions as part of a sentence—how a noun functions as a subject or a complement, for example. You will then be able to develop or fortify your "sentence sense." This means that you will learn to recognize what a sentence is and how its parts fit together to communicate a complete thought. This understanding of sentence structure will help you to speak and to write more effectively.

In your everyday conversations, you frequently do not use complete sentences. You might say something like the following:

Nice weather for this time of year.
Hi, Jane.

Your meaning here is perfectly clear. In *written* English, however, you should express your ideas in clear, complete sentences.

EXAMPLE   Although it was still February, the weather was turning warm, promising an early spring.

THE SENTENCE

Although you use sentences constantly in speaking and writing, you may not be able to say exactly what a sentence is.

2a. A *sentence* **is a group of words expressing a complete thought.**

As the basic unit of written expression, a sentence must express a complete thought.

SENTENCE	We peered into the room.
NOT A SENTENCE	the room with the high ceiling
SENTENCE	The thief was waiting by the door.
NOT A SENTENCE	waiting by the door
SENTENCE	Who has finished the test?
NOT A SENTENCE	after you have finished the test

If a group of words does not express a complete thought, it is a *fragment,* or piece of a sentence, not a sentence.

FRAGMENTS	chicken and rice
	from August through October
	the president of our club
	doing well in school

These groups of words can become sentences only when other words are added to make the thoughts complete:

SENTENCES	I enjoy a meal of chicken and rice.
	The rainy season lasts from August through October.
	Florence was elected president of our club.
	Most of us are doing well in school.

EXERCISE 1. Number 1–20 on your paper. Decide whether each group of words is a sentence or only a

fragment. If the word group is a sentence, write *S* after the proper number. If the word group is a fragment, change it to a sentence by adding one or more words to make the thought complete, and write the sentence. As you turn the fragments into sentences, remember to begin the first word with a capital letter and to insert a mark of punctuation after the last word.

1. on Monday or later this week
2. patiently waiting for the mail carrier
3. will you be there tomorrow
4. four people in a small car
5. just yesterday I discovered
6. two strikes and no one on base
7. it runs smoothly
8. leaning far over the railing
9. two doves and a swan
10. all during the movie and then later at home
11. she sauntered in alone
12. at the corner we spotted
13. either bean sprouts or alfalfa
14. noticed my new jogging shoes
15. neither of them would have wanted
16. while playing the videotape recorder
17. Ray turned pale
18. performed an entire symphony
19. give me a hand
20. a firm understanding of decimals

SUBJECT AND PREDICATE

2b. A sentence consists of two parts: the *subject* and the *predicate*. The *subject* of the sentence is the part about which something is being said. The *predicate* is the part which says something about the subject.

In the following examples, the subjects are separated from the predicates by vertical lines.

Seagulls | were flying around the pier.
The members of the club | arrived.
The person in the first row | is my sister.

As you see, the subject and the predicate may be only one word each, or they may be more than one word.

In the previous examples, the words to the left of the vertical line make up the *complete subject*. The words to the right of the vertical line make up the *complete predicate*. Often, however, the subject can be in the middle of or at the end of a sentence. Notice the complete subjects, which are in bold-faced type, in the examples below.

On rainy mornings, is **your bus** usually late?
In the desk were **the red pencils**.
Do **your parents** mind your getting home late?

EXERCISE 2. Number your paper 1–10. After the corresponding number on your paper, write the complete subject of each sentence.

1. Some large animals can move very quickly.
2. The rhinoceros, one of the world's largest animals, can charge with great speed and change direction rapidly.
3. Its big, bulky body makes it a fearsome sight.
4. Animals such as the water buffalo and the elephant are more dangerous, however.
5. The legs of a rhinoceros are rather stout and short and end in broad feet.
6. Jutting from its upper lip is a large, heavy horn.
7. Other mammals have horns in more appropriate locations.
8. Doesn't the rhinoceros charge at the slightest disturbance?
9. Its eyesight is very poor, however.
10. Swarms of bloodsucking parasites crawl all over its back.

EXERCISE 3. Add complete predicates to the following complete subjects to make complete sentences.

1. they
2. honesty
3. her nickname
4. good intentions
5. my best friend
6. all kinds of fireworks
7. a lantern and a hatchet
8. a basket of peaches
9. one girl near me
10. a trip to Utah or Ohio

The Simple Subject

Within the complete subject, every sentence has a *simple subject.*

2c. The *simple subject* is the main word or group of words in the complete subject.

To distinguish the simple subject from the complete subject, you select the most important word in the complete subject. This word names the person, place, thing, or idea being talked about.

EXAMPLE   Successful executives budget their time wisely.
Complete subject   Successful executives
Simple subject   executives

EXAMPLE   The venturous Langston Hughes called his autobiography *The Big Sea.*
Complete subject   The venturous Langston Hughes
Simple subject   Langston Hughes

► **NOTE** Compound nouns, such as *Langston Hughes* in the example, are considered one noun.

From the examples above, you can see that the complete subject consists of the simple subject and all the words that belong with it. Adjectives and prepositional phrases that modify the simple subject are included in the complete subject.

Hereafter in this book, the term *subject*, when used in connection with the sentence, refers to the simple subject, unless otherwise indicated.

EXERCISE 4. On a separate sheet of paper, fill in each of the following blanks with a subject plus any other words needed to complete the thought.

1. —— may soon wither.
2. —— will rearrange the furniture.
3. —— is an interesting conversationalist.
4. Had —— eaten a green persimmon?
5. —— scooted over to the curb.
6. —— glittered in the moonlight.
7. —— flippantly tossed a coin to the beggar.
8. Next in line was ——.
9. Lying beside the wrecked car was ——.
10. On the other side of the fence stood ——.

The Simple Predicate

2d. The *simple predicate*, or *verb*, is the main word or group of words within the complete predicate.

The essential word (or words) in the complete predicate is always the simple predicate, usually referred to as the *verb*. The other words in the complete predicate may affect the meaning of the verb in various ways, often by making it more definite, but it is the verb that is essential in completing the statement.

EXAMPLE   The Canadian hockey player flicked the puck deftly past the goalie and into the net. [Complete predicate: *flicked the puck deftly past the goalie and into the net.* Verb: *flicked.*]

The simple predicate may consist of a single verb or of a verb phrase. In the latter, the verb will be more than one word: *will sing, has been broken, may have been trying,* etc.

When you are asked to pick out the simple predicate in a sentence, be sure to include all parts of a verb phrase. In doing so, keep in mind the various helping verbs that are commonly used as parts of verb phrases: *shall, will, has, have, had, do, does, did, may, might, must, can, could, should, would, am, is, are, was, were, be,* and *been.*

Study the following examples, noticing the difference between the complete predicate and the verb.

EXAMPLE Douglas had thoroughly scrubbed the dingy walls.

Complete predicate had throughly scrubbed the dingy walls

Verb had scrubbed

EXAMPLE My aunt was sitting on the sofa.

Complete predicate was sitting on the sofa

Verb was sitting

Hereafter throughout this book, the word *verb* will be used to refer to the simple predicate, unless otherwise indicated.

EXERCISE 5. Make two columns on your paper. Label one of them *Complete predicate* and the other *Verb*. From the following sentences, copy the complete predicates and the verbs in the appropriate columns. If you find a verb phrase, be sure to include all helpers.

1. Many writers' first novels are autobiographical.
2. *Look Homeward, Angel,* the first novel of Thomas Wolfe, was written about his early life in Asheville, North Carolina.
3. In the novel appear the people and scenes of Wolfe's youth.

4. His mother, father, and brother Ben will always be remembered because of Wolfe's book.
5. The boyhood home of Wolfe is still standing in Asheville.
6. The house and its furnishings are carefully described by Wolfe in *Look Homeward, Angel.*
7. A trip to the Asheville library supplies one with many facts about Wolfe.
8. In the library can be found all the newspaper clippings about Wolfe's life and works.
9. At first an outcast in Asheville, Wolfe was later revered by the town's citizens.
10. The whole town mourned the early death of its most famous son.

Now that you have learned about subjects and predicates, you should be able to distinguish sentences from fragments more easily.

EXERCISE 6. Remembering that a sentence must have a subject and a predicate, revise the following fragments to make the thoughts complete. Number your paper 1–10 and write each complete thought after the proper number.

1. my bruised toes
2. food for the puppies
3. seems unnecessary
4. a wasp on the back of your neck
5. flashing neon signs
6. rolled down the mountainside
7. dropped thirty degrees during the night
8. a capsized canoe
9. completely destroyed the old building
10. soared high above the dark clouds

Finding the Subject

The best way to find the subject of a sentence is to

find the verb first. After you have found the verb, ask "Who?" or "What?" in connection with the verb.

EXAMPLES   There we can wade across the Mississippi River. [The verb is *can wade*. Who can wade? The answer is *we,* the subject.]

Around the bend roared a freight train. [The verb is *roared*. What roared? The *train* roared; therefore, *train* is the subject.]

The road to the lake has big holes in it. [The verb is *has*. What has? *Road* is the subject.]

EXERCISE 7. Find the subject of each of the following sentences by first finding the verb and then by asking "Who?" or "What?" in front of the verb. After numbering 1–10, list on your paper each verb and its subject. Be sure to include all parts of a verb phrase.

1. Before the equal rights movement, American women became leaders in their professions.
2. Evangeline Booth was General of the International Salvation Army from 1934 to 1939.
3. The Salvation Army has always treated men and women equally.
4. Have you heard of Nellie Bly, the famous newspaper reporter?
5. In 1890 she traveled alone around the world.
6. Her travels were reported in the *New York World.*
7. Nellie Bly's investigative reporting showed courage and cleverness.
8. In 1876 Melville Bissell invented the carpet sweeper.
9. After the death of her husband in 1888, Anne Bissell managed his company for forty years.
10. Under her management as corporation president, the company sold millions of carpet sweepers.

2e. The subject of a verb is never in a prepositional phrase.

You will remember that a prepositional phrase begins with a preposition and ends with a noun or a pronoun: *to the bank, by the door, in the picture, of a book, on the floor, after class, at intermission, for them, except him.* (For a full discussion of prepositional phrases, see page 79). Since the prepositional phrase contains a noun or a pronoun, and since it often comes before the verb, you may make the mistake of thinking that the noun following a preposition is the subject.

EXAMPLE   One **of the girls** helped us.

When you ask "Who helped?" you may be tempted to answer, "Girls helped." But on second thought you realize that the sentence does not say the *girls helped;* it says only *one* of the girls *helped.* The fact is that a word in a prepositional phrase is never the subject. *Girls* is in the phrase *of the girls.*

Prepositional phrases can be especially misleading when the subject follows the verb.

EXAMPLE   **In the middle of the lake** is a small island.

Neither *middle* nor *lake* can be the subject because each word is part of a prepositional phrase. The subject of *is* has to be *island.*

EXERCISE 8. Copy the following sentences onto your paper. Cross out each of the prepositional phrases. Underline each verb twice and its subject once.

1. That house near the railroad tracks is my home.
2. My aunt on my father's side willed it to us last year.

3. Everything about the house except its location is very satisfactory.
4. Every hour or so trains of all shapes and sizes roar through our backyard.
5. The vibrations of the heavy freight trains cause the most damage.
6. Sometimes a picture on the living-room wall crashes to the floor.
7. The oven door of the gas range habitually snaps open.
8. Yesterday at breakfast, a piece of plaster from the ceiling fell into Mom's coffee.
9. The thunderous clanking of the trains completely absorbs the sound of our television.
10. Each of the advertisers on the screen seems to speak without saying a thing.

The Subject in an Unusual Position

Sentences that ask questions and sentences that begin with *there* or *here* have a word order which places the subject in an unusual position.

Sentences That Ask Questions

Questions often begin with a verb or with a verb helper. They also frequently begin with words such as *what, when, where, how,* or *why.* Either way, the subject ordinarily *follows* the verb or verb helper.

EXAMPLES How is she now?
Does the novel have a happy ending?

In questions that begin with a helping verb, like the second example above, the subject always comes between the helper and the main verb. You can also find the subject by turning the question into a statement, finding the verb, and asking "Who?" or "What?" in front of the verb.

EXAMPLES Was the door open? *becomes* The door was open. [What was open? *Door.*]
Did she tell you the news? *becomes* She did tell you the news. [Who did tell? *She.*]

Sentences Beginning with *There*

There is never the subject of a sentence, except when spoken of as a word, as in this sentence. However, this word often appears in the place before a verb where we would expect to find a subject. *There* can be used to get a sentence started when the real subject comes after the verb. In this use, *there* is called an *expletive*. (The verb and its subject are labeled for you in the sentences below.)

EXAMPLES
$$\overset{\text{V}}{\text{There is}} \text{ a } \overset{\text{S}}{\text{log cabin}} \text{ in the clearing.}$$

$$\overset{\text{V}}{\text{There are}} \overset{\text{S}}{\text{oranges}} \text{ in the refrigerator.}$$

To find the subject in such a sentence, omit *there* and ask "Who?" or "What?" before the verb.

There is someone in the phone booth. [Who *is? Someone.* Therefore, *someone* is the subject.]

With *there* omitted, these sentences read as follows:

A log cabin is in the clearing.
Oranges are in the refrigerator.
Someone is in the phone booth.

EXERCISE 9. Numbering your paper 1–20, list the subjects and verbs in the following sentences after the proper numbers. Write subjects first, verbs second.

1. There are many questions on American history in my book.

2. Naturally, there are answers, too.
3. Under whose flag did Columbus sail?
4. Where is Plymouth Rock?
5. How much do you know about the Lost Colony?
6. What does "squatter's rights" mean?
7. In what area did most of the early Dutch colonists settle?
8. Was there dissension among settlers in Massachusetts?
9. What kinds of schools did the colonists' children attend?
10. How did one travel in colonial America?
11. Were there any sports?
12. When were the famous Salem witch trials?
13. Why did such a tragedy occur?
14. Can you name the three oldest colleges in America?
15. Were there many great American writers during the colonial period?
16. For what inventions is Benjamin Franklin remembered?
17. Why were the colonists dissatisfied with England?
18. How did the Americans proclaim their independence?
19. Did all of the colonists fight against England?
20. How many of the leaders of the Revolution can you identify?

The Understood Subject

In a request or a command, the subject of a sentence is usually not stated. In such sentences, the person spoken to is understood to be the subject.

EXAMPLES   Please close the door.
            Listen carefully to these instructions.

In the first sentence, a request, *who* is to close the door? *You* are — that is, the person spoken to. In the second sentence, a command, *who* is to listen? Again, *you* are. In each sentence, then, *you* is the understood subject.

Sometimes a request or command will include a name.

EXAMPLES   **Phyllis,** please close the door.
Listen carefully to these instructions, **students.**

Neither *Phyllis* nor *students* is the subject of its sentence. These words are called nouns of *direct address*. They *identify* the person spoken to. *You,* however, is still the understood subject of each sentence.

Phyllis, (you) please close the door.

Compound Subjects

2f. A *compound subject* **consists of two or more subjects joined by a conjunction and having the same verb.**

The conjunctions most commonly used to connect the words of a compound subject are *and* and *or*. Study these sentences:

EXAMPLES   **Antony** baked the bread [Who baked the bread? Antony baked it. *Antony* is the simple subject.]
Antony and **Mae** baked the bread. [Who baked the bread? Antony baked it. Mae baked it. *Antony* and *Mae*, then, form the compound subject.]

When more than two words are included in the compound subject, the conjunction is generally used only between the last two words. Also, the words are separated by commas.

EXAMPLE   Antony, Mae, **and** Pamela baked the bread. [Compound subject: *Antony, Mae, Pamela*]

Correlative conjunctions may be used with compound subjects.

EXAMPLE   **Either** Antony **or** Mae baked the bread. [Compound subject: *Antony, Mae*]

EXERCISE 10. Number your paper 1–10. Find and list the compound subjects as well as the verbs in the following sentences.

EXAMPLE   1. Broken mirrors and black cats are often associated with bad luck.
1. *mirrors, cats — are associated*

1. Hurricanes and earthquakes are two kinds of natural disasters.
2. The hero of the novel and a student in my class have similar personalities.
3. Venus, Juno, and Minerva were three famous Roman goddesses.
4. Do you or he know the origin of the word *bedlam?*
5. *Frankenstein* and *Dracula* were both written during the nineteenth century.
6. Either a parrot or a crow may outlive its owner.
7. Into the room swept Queen Bess and her companion.
8. There have always been optimists and pessimists.
9. Both poets and royalty are buried in Westminster Abbey.
10. Where are the dictionaries and other reference books located?

Compound Verbs

2g. A *compound verb* consists of two or more verbs joined by a conjunction and having the same subject.

The following sentences show how verbs may be compound:

EXAMPLES   Sojourner Truth **traveled** and **lectured** much of her life.
We **searched** the attic but **found** nothing.
The children **skated, rode** bicycles, and **played** hopscotch.
Mother **will rent** or **sell** the house.

Notice in the last sentence that the helping verb *will* is not repeated before *sell,* though it is understood: Mother *will rent* or *will sell* the house. In compound verbs consisting of verb phrases, the helper may or may not be repeated before the second verb if the helper is the same for both verbs. Often the helper is not repeated when there is a correlative conjunction:

EXAMPLE   I **will** not only **scrub** the floor but also **wax** it.

EXERCISE 11. After numbering 1–10, make a list of the compound verbs in these sentences. Be sure to include verb helpers.

1. Stop, look, and whistle.
2. During the class Walter stretched, yawned, and sighed.
3. At the rodeo Vaughan leaped upon the wild steer and stayed on it for four full minutes.
4. Must you always worry or complain?
5. My hound can bark, sit up, or lie down.
6. Pauline can neither sing nor dance.
7. Between two and three o'clock I will either be studying in Room 17 or be reading in the library.
8. Can you type a letter or take shorthand?
9. Jeff rewound the cassette and then pressed the playback button.
10. The ball lingered for a few seconds on the edge

of the basket and then dropped through for a score.

Both the subject and the verb may be compound.

EXAMPLES The **boys** and **girls** | **played** games and **sang** songs.
Either **Karen** or **Fran** | **will rent** the tape recorder and **reserve** the auditorium. [Notice that with the second verb, *reserve*, the helper *will* is understood.]

REVIEW EXERCISE A. Try to make a perfect score on this exercise, which is a mastery test on subjects and verbs. After you have copied the sentences below, your job is this:

1. Cross out all prepositional phrases so that you can isolate the verb and the subject.
2. Cross out a *here* or *there* at the beginning of a sentence, thus eliminating these words as possible subjects.
3. Underscore all verbs twice; be sure to include all helpers and all parts of a compound verb.
4. Underscore all subjects once; be sure to underscore all parts of a compound subject.

EXAMPLES 1. *At our school, ballads have become very popular.*

2. *There are individual singers and group singers on the music program tonight.*

1. There are ballads for different tastes and for different occasions.
2. Ballads tell simple stories and create strong moods.
3. In ballads people live, work, love, and die.
4. The words of ballads were written by the common

people and therefore relate the concerns of the common people.

5. In one ballad can be heard a jilted lover's complaints.
6. In another is found the lament of a mother for her dead son.
7. The death of a dog and the heroism of a coal miner are related in still other ballads.
8. How can anyone resist the appeal of such simple tales?
9. Everyone at some time or other has felt the emotions of the characters in ballads.
10. Here, then, are some of the reasons for the popularity of ballads since the Middle Ages.

DIAGRAMING SENTENCES

In order to write good sentences, you should have in your mind a clear picture of the ways in which sentences are built. Many students find that they can understand a sentence better when they use a diagram. A diagram is a quick picture of how the parts of a sentence fit together and how the words in a sentence are related.

Diagraming the Subject and the Verb

A diagram begins with a straight horizontal line. This line is for the main parts of the sentence. Crossing it approximately in the center is a short vertical line. This vertical line divides the complete subject from the complete predicate. On the horizontal line the simple subject is placed to the left of the vertical line, the verb to the right of it.

PATTERN

subject	verb

EXAMPLE   Students voted.

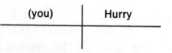

If the sentence has an understood subject, place *you* in parentheses on the subject line.

EXAMPLE   Hurry!

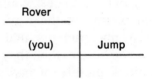

Nouns of direct address are placed on a separate horizontal line above the understood subject.

EXAMPLE   Jump, **Rover!**

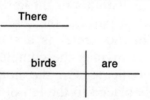

The expletive *there* is also placed on a separate horizontal line. (Modifiers have been omitted from the following diagram.)

EXAMPLE   **There** are three birds in the tree.

There
_____

birds | are
_____|_____
      |

When the sentence has a compound subject, diagram it as in the following example. Notice the position of the coordinating conjunction on the broken line.

EXAMPLE **Arthur** and **Lewis** are studying.

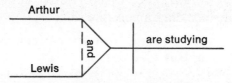

If the verb is compound, it is diagramed in this way:

EXAMPLE **We** **live** and **learn**.

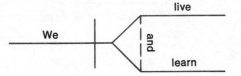

A sentence with both a compound subject and a compound verb is diagramed in this way:

EXAMPLE **Students** and **teachers** **shouted** and **waved**.

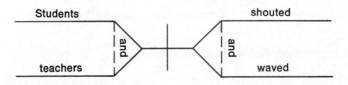

Notice how a compound verb is diagramed when the helping verb is not repeated:

EXAMPLE They **were screaming** and **crying**.

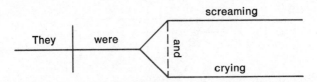

Since *were* is the helper for both *screaming* and *crying*, it is placed on the horizontal line, and the conjunction *and* joins the main verbs *screaming* and *crying*.

Sometimes parts of a compound subject or a compound verb will be joined by correlative conjunctions. Correlatives are diagramed like this:

EXAMPLE **Both** Miriam **and** Ernest can **not only** sing **but also** dance.

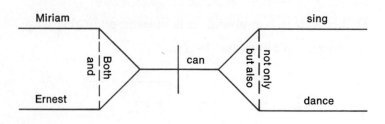

EXERCISE 12. Diagram the following sentences.

1. Vesuvius erupted.
2. Look, Mario!
3. James and he are sleeping.
4. Soldiers fought and died.
5. Both Ellen and Camille have finished and gone.

Diagraming Adjectives and Adverbs

Adjectives modify nouns or pronouns, and adverbs modify verbs, adjectives, or other adverbs. Both adjectives and adverbs are written on slanted lines connected to the words they modify.

PATTERN

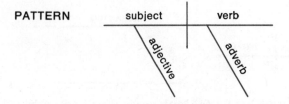

EXAMPLE **Our new** sofa has **not** arrived.

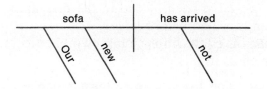

An adverb that modifies an adjective or an adverb is placed on a line connected to the adjective or adverb modified, as follows:

EXAMPLE   That **extremely** lazy dog **almost** never barks.

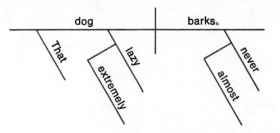

Notice the position of the modifiers in the following example:

EXAMPLE   **Tomorrow** Charlotte and **her** mother will write or will telephone.

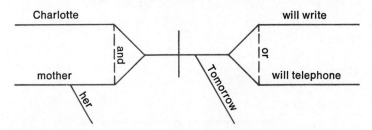

Her modifies only one part of the compound subject: *mother. Tomorrow* modifies both parts of the compound verb: *will write* and *will telephone.* Where would *will* have been placed in the diagram if it had not been repeated before *telephone?*

When a conjunction joins two modifiers, it is diagramed as in this example:

EXAMPLE   The French **and** German dancers twirled rapidly **and** extremely gracefully.

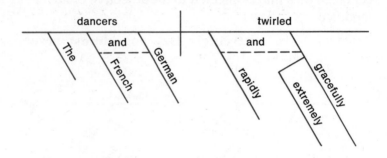

EXERCISE 13. Diagrams for the following sentences have been provided for you. Copy them on your paper, and fill them in correctly.

1. Each boy listened attentively.

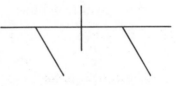

2. Do not leave now.

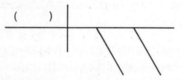

3. The scouts arose very early.

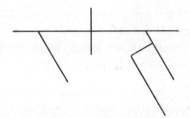

4. An extremely interesting book nearly always sells.

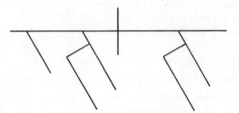

5. The big airliner landed safely and quite smoothly.

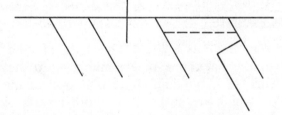

REVIEW EXERCISE B. Diagram each of the following sentences.

1. Leon and Tom win occasionally.
2. There was much hubbub.
3. Rosalie graciously smiled and bowed.
4. There were many unpopular and seemingly sense-less regulations.
5. The fire flickered weakly and then died.
6. Father and Uncle Edmund are hammering and sawing enthusiastically.
7. Menacingly the white and red horse snorted and stamped.

8. Here come Dr. Bradford and her intelligent assistant.
9. Sit quietly and concentrate hard.
10. Both Elise and her brother can read and write rather well.

REVIEW EXERCISE C. Write five separate sentences, using an example of each of the following; underline what is asked for.

EXAMPLE   1. a prepositional phrase
            1. *We ate at the drugstore.*

1. a verb phrase
2. a compound verb
3. a compound subject
4. an understood subject
5. an adverb modifying an adjective

COMPLEMENTS

Every sentence has a *base*. This base may be compared to the backbone of an animal or to the main framework of a building. It is that part of the sentence on which are suspended all other parts. A sentence base may consist of only the subject and the verb; for many sentences nothing else is needed.

EXAMPLES   Flowers died.

              One girl from Oklahoma was yodeling.

Frequently the sentence base will have not only a subject and a verb but also a completer, or *complement*.

2h. A *complement* completes the meaning begun by the subject and the verb.

It is possible for a group of words to have a subject

and a verb and not express a complete thought. Notice how the following word groups need other words to complete their meaning.

EXAMPLES   Those clothes look
She may become
I said

If you add words to complete the meaning, the sentences will make sense.

EXAMPLES   Those clothes look **clean.**
She may become **an engineer.**
I said **that.**

The words *clean, engineer,* and *that* are complements; they complete the thought of the sentence. The complement may be a noun, a pronoun, or an adjective.

Study the structure of these sentences. The base of each sentence — subject, verb, complement — is labeled.

EXAMPLES

                    S   V   C
A stranger approached me.

                    S   V   C
The man in the moon looks friendly.

                        S   V   C
At that time labor was very cheap.

                    S   V   C
Roberta will be a lawyer.

                    S   V   C
A recording provided background music.

The complement is never in a prepositional phrase. Look at these sentences:

EXAMPLES   Later she consulted the other students.
Later she consulted with the other students.

In the first sentence, *students* is the complement. In the second sentence, *students* is the object of the preposition *with;* the prepositional phrase *with the other students* modifies the verb *consulted.*

EXERCISE 14. Add a complement to each of the following items.

1. Carol brought
2. Jim usually seems
3. Tomorrow the class will hear
4. That broiled fish looks
5. The student in front of me raised
6. Last week our class visited
7. Do you have
8. At the end of the meal, we left
9. A noun is
10. The word *mobility* means

EXERCISE 15. Write five sentences using the following sentence bases. Do not be satisfied with adding only one or two words. Make *interesting* sentences.

	Subject	*Verb*	*Complement*
1.	underdogs	upset	champions
2.	impact	shattered	glass
3.	girls	feel	responsible
4.	people	desire	peace
5.	recreation	can become	work

EXERCISE 16. Make three columns on your paper. Label the first *subject,* the second *verb,* and the third *complement.* Find the base of each sentence and enter the parts in the appropriate column.

1. The history of the English stage is very interesting.

2. In the beginning churches gave plays for instruction.
3. The stories of early English drama were usually biblical ones.
4. The plays, however, eventually became too irreverent for religious instruction.
5. Clergymen then recommended the abolition of acting within the churches.
6. At the same time, they encouraged the performance of religious drama in courtyards near the churches.
7. The actors presented their plays on wagons in the open air.
8. The top of the wagon soon became a convenient place for "heaven."
9. There the "angels" in the play could address the "sinners" on earth below.
10. In Shakespeare's time, the upper stage was an important part of the theater.
11. It was especially useful for eavesdroppers and critics.
12. Shakespeare used the upper stage for the famous balcony scene in *Romeo and Juliet*.

EXERCISE 17. Using each word in the list below as a complement, write ten sentences. Underscore the subject once, the verb twice, and the complement three times.

EXAMPLE 1. glint
          1. *Thomas* then *noticed* the *glint* in Susan's eye.

1. pencil   6. sluggish
2. bellhop   7. fable
3. groceries   8. clown
4. pilot   9. skeleton
5. shrewd   10. inevitable

The Subject Complement

2i. A *subject complement* is a noun, pronoun, or adjective that follows a linking verb.[1] It describes or explains the simple subject.

EXAMPLES   Mark Twain's real name was **Clemens.**
The sea grew **calm.**

In the first sentence, the complement *Clemens* explains the subject *name.* In the second, the complement *calm* describes the subject *sea.*

(1) A *predicate nominative* is one kind of subject complement. It is a noun or pronoun that explains or identifies the subject of the sentence.

EXAMPLES   Angela will be our **soloist.**
The mayor is **she.**
A whale is a **mammal.**

(2) A *predicate adjective* is another kind of subject complement. It is an adjective that modifies the subject of the sentence.

EXAMPLES   That soil looks **dry.** [dry soil]
The soup is too **hot.** [hot soup]
She looks **capable.** [capable she]

Subject complements may be compound.

EXAMPLES   The class officers are **Gina** and **Calvin.**
[compound predicate nominatives]
The corn tastes **sweet** and **buttery.**
[compound predicate adjectives]

EXERCISE 18. In the sentences of Exercise 16 (page 64) there are six subject complements. List them on your paper. After each noun or pronoun, write *predicate nominative;* after each adjective, *predicate adjective.*

[1] Linking verbs are discussed on pages 17–19.

EXERCISE 19. Read the following groups of words aloud, making sentences by using nouns, pronouns, or adjectives as subject complements. Use five compound complements. Tell whether each complement is a predicate nominative or a predicate adjective.

1. Detours are often
2. This is
3. Ms. White seemed
4. They may be
5. The berries taste
6. Were they
7. The shark appears
8. The river looks
9. Manny had been
10. Does she sound

Objects

Objects are complements that do not refer to the subject.

EXAMPLE   Lee Trevino sank the **putt.**

In this sentence, the object *putt* does not explain or describe the subject *Lee Trevino,* and *sank* is an action verb rather than a linking verb.

There are two kinds of objects: the *direct object* and the *indirect object.* Neither is ever in a prepositional phrase.

2j. The *direct object* of the verb is a noun or pronoun that receives the action of the verb or shows the result of the action. It answers the question "What?" or "Whom?" after an action verb.

EXAMPLES   Ruth defeated **Nate** in straight sets.
            Her essay won a **prize.**

In the first sentence, *Nate* receives the action expressed by the verb *defeated* and tells *whom* Ruth defeated; therefore, *Nate* is the direct object. In the second sentence, *prize* names the result of the action expressed by the verb *won* and tells *what* her essay won; *prize* is the direct object.

As you study the following sentences, observe that each object answers the question "Whom?" or "What?" after an action verb.

```
  S     V      O
```
Vivian moved furniture.
```
  S      V     O
```
Sarcasm annoys me.
```
  S     V         O
```
We were singing songs.
```
       S     V          O
```
The police were expecting trouble.

EXERCISE 20. Number your paper 1–10 and write after the appropriate number the direct object for each sentence.

1. This article gives many interesting facts about libraries.
2. Alexandria, in Egypt, had the most famous library of ancient times.
3. This library contained a large collection of ancient plays and works of philosophy.
4. The Roman emperor Augustus founded two public libraries.
5. Fire later destroyed these buildings.
6. Readers could not take books from either the Roman libraries or the library in Alexandria.
7. The monastery library of the Middle Ages first introduced the idea of a circulating library.
8. In the sixth century, everyone in the Benedictine monasteries borrowed a book from the library for daily reading.
9. Today, the United States has thousands of circulating libraries.
10. Readers borrow millions of books from them every year.

EXERCISE 21. There are twenty direct objects in the following quotations. Number your paper 1–11 and write the direct objects after the appropriate numbers. Some sentences contain two or more direct objects.

1. Wit has truth in it.—DOROTHY PARKER
2. A generous heart repairs a slanderous tongue. —HOMER
3. The clearsighted do not rule the world, but they sustain and console it.—AGNES REPPLIER
4. One must never . . . turn his back on life. —ELEANOR ROOSEVELT
5. We may give advice, but we do not inspire conduct. —LA ROCHEFOUCAULD
6. Vanity plays lurid tricks with our memory. —JOSEPH CONRAD
7. One half of the world cannot understand the pleasures of the other.—JANE AUSTEN
8. The wise make proverbs, and fools repeat them. —ISAAC D'ISRAELI
9. If you once forfeit the confidence of your fellow citizens, you can never regain their respect and esteem.—ABRAHAM LINCOLN
10. Poetry ennobles the heart and the eyes and unveils the meaning of all things. . . . It discovers the secret rays of the universe and restores to us forgotten paradises.—DAME EDITH SITWELL
11. But through all my changes I still see myself. —SIMONE DE BEAUVOIR

2k. The *indirect object* of the verb is a noun or pronoun that precedes the direct object and usually tells "to whom" or "for whom" (or "to what" or "for what") the action of the verb is done.

DIRECT OBJECTS   Lisa sent a **telegram.**
Don will sing a **ballad.**

INDIRECT OBJECTS Lisa sent **Dorothea** an urgent telegram.

Don will sing **us** a ballad.

In the sentences above, *telegram* and *ballad* are direct objects answering the question "What?" after action verbs. Lisa sent a telegram *to whom? Dorothea,* the answer, is an indirect object. Don will sing a ballad *for whom? Us* is the indirect object.

The indirect objects in the sentences below are boldfaced. Each tells *to whom* or *for whom* something is done.

EXAMPLES He showed **her** the lantern.

The doctor gave **Mother** good advice.

I bought **her** a new baseball bat.

My cousin left **Denise** a message.

If the word *to* or *for* is used, the word following it is part of a prepositional phrase, not an indirect object.

PREPOSITIONAL PHRASES I sold tickets **to the class.**

Kathy saved some cake **for me.**

INDIRECT OBJECTS I sold the **class** tickets.

Kathy saved **me** some cake.

Both direct and indirect objects may be compound.

EXAMPLES Donna showed **snapshots** and **slides.** [compound direct object]

Donna showed **Oscar** and **me** some pictures. [compound indirect object]

EXERCISE 22. Number your paper 1–10, and list the indirect and direct objects in the following sentences. After each, write in parentheses *i.o.* (for indirect object) or *d.o.* (for direct object). You will not find an indirect object in every sentence.

1. According to Greek mythology, Daedalus, a famous artist and inventor, built the king of Crete a mysterious building known as the labyrinth.
2. The complicated passageways of this building give us our word for "a confusing maze of possibilities."
3. After the completion of the labyrinth, the king imprisoned Daedalus and his son, whose name was Icarus.
4. In order to escape, Daedalus made Icarus and himself wings out of feathers and beeswax.
5. He gave Icarus careful instructions not to fly too near the sun.
6. But Icarus soon forgot his father's advice.
7. He flew too high, and the hot sun melted the wax in the wings.
8. Daedalus used his wings wisely and reached Sicily in safety.
9. Mythology tells us many other stories of Daedalus' fabulous inventions.
10. Even today, the name Daedalus suggests almost superhuman ingenuity.

Diagraming Complements

As a part of the sentence base, the subject complement is placed on the horizontal line with the subject and verb. It comes after the verb. A line *slanting toward the subject,* drawn upward from the horizontal line, separates the subject complement from the verb.

PATTERN

| subject | verb | subject complement |

PREDICATE NOMINATIVE Shrews are tiny **creatures.**

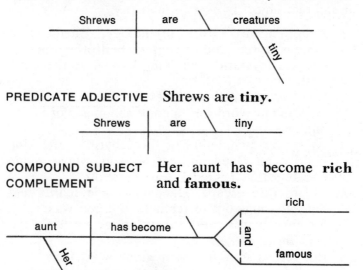

PREDICATE ADJECTIVE Shrews are **tiny.**

| Shrews | are \ tiny |

COMPOUND SUBJECT Her aunt has become **rich**
COMPLEMENT and **famous.**

EXERCISE 23. Diagram the following sentences.

1. Superstitions are illogical beliefs.
2. A black cat is a bad sign.
3. A broken mirror remains an unlucky omen.
4. Such notions seem both childish and foolish.
5. Superstitious beliefs are still common.

The *direct object* is diagramed in much the same manner as the predicate nominative. The only difference is that the line separating the direct object from the verb is vertical, not slanting.

PATTERN

| subject | verb | direct object |

EXAMPLE Everyone played **games.**

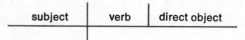

| Everyone | played | games |

The compound direct object is diagramed in this way:

EXAMPLE   They sell **bicycles** and **sleds.**

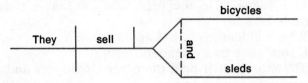

The *indirect object* is diagramed on a horizontal line beneath the verb.

EXAMPLE   Randy tossed **Elmer** an apple.

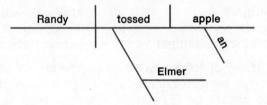

Note that the slanting line from the verb extends slightly below the horizontal line for the indirect object.

The compound indirect object is diagramed in this way:

EXAMPLE   Ray gave the **dogs** and **cats** some hamburger.

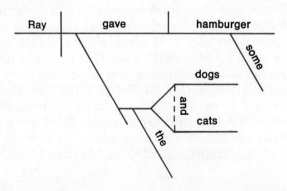

EXERCISE 24. Diagram the following sentences.

1. The traitor sold the enemy important secrets.
2. Mr. Tseng gave the team and the fans a memorable lesson.
3. Who will lend us a tent and a canoe?
4. Karen gave us a confident wave.
5. The storekeeper paid the other employees and me our wages and a bonus.

REVIEW EXERCISE D. Identify the italicized words in the passage below. (The italicized letters *X* and *O* are not words.) Use the following abbreviations:

s.	subject	*p.a.*	predicate adjective
v.	verb	*d.o.*	direct object
p.n.	predicate nominative	*i.o.*	indirect object

(1) *Many* of Edgar Allan Poe's stories do not deal with horror or terror. Not (2) *all* of his main characters are ghosts or (3) *devils.* Poe has written many comic (4) *tales.* For instance, "X-ing a Paragraph" or "Loss of Breath" (5) *gives* the (6) *reader* a (7) *chance* for hearty laughter.

"X-ing a Paragraph" (8) *is* the (9) *story* of a feud between two newspaper editors. Mr. Bullethead (10) *had moved* to a small town in the West, hoping to become its only newspaper editor. Much to his surprise, the (11) *town* already (12) *had* an (13) *editor,* Mr. John Smith, who (14) *published* the daily (15) *Gazette.* Bullethead, however, stubbornly (16) *refused* to move. (17) *He* published a competing (18) *paper* and in its first issue satirically (19) *attacked* Mr. Smith's (20) *style* of writing. Mr. Smith soon (21) *replied* with his own biting sarcasm, making fun of the letter *O*'s in Bullethead's prose. Mr. Bullethead (22) *became* so (23) *incensed* over the sarcasm that (24) *he* foolishly (25) *prepared* to print a paragraph filled with *O*'s. When the paragraph (26) *appeared,* however, (27) *it* was (28) *Mr. Smith* who (29) *had* the last laugh. Apparently, someone had stolen (30) *all* of the *O*'s from Mr. Bullethead's printer. The (31) *printer,* therefore, (32) *substituted* an *X* wherever an *O* (33) *was supposed* to appear. The resulting (34) *paragraph* was (35) *impossible* to read. (36) *Townspeople* knew that Mr. Smith (37) *had played* an X-cellent (38) *joke* on his rival.

In "Loss of Breath" is another amusing (39) *character.* The (40) *author* saw the (41) *humor* of the expression, "I've lost my breath." He (42) *based* a (43) *story* on it. The main (44) *character* in "Loss of Breath" (45) *is* (46) *Mr. Lackobreath.* Angry with his wife, he (47) *argues* furiously and loses his breath. Then the unhappy husband begins a long (48) *search* for his lost breath. Finally he finds it. On the very day of the argument, a (49) *man* by the name of Mr. Windenough had "caught his breath." The end of the story is a happy (50) *one.*

CLASSIFYING SENTENCES BY PURPOSE

Sentences may be classified according to the kinds of messages they express. This method of classifying, which distinguishes between questions, statements, commands or requests, and exclamations, reflects the purpose of the speaker or writer.

2I. Sentences may be classified as *declarative, imperative, interrogative,* **or** *exclamatory.*

(1) A *declarative* **sentence makes a statement.**

Declarative sentences make assertions or state ideas without expecting a reply. Most sentences are declarative. All declarative sentences are followed by periods.

EXAMPLE   Dr. Rosalyn Yalow won a Nobel Prize in medicine in 1977.

(2) An *imperative* sentence gives a command or makes a request.

A command or a request has the understood subject *you.* Like the declarative sentence, the imperative sentence is usually followed by a period. Very strong commands, however, may take an exclamation point.

EXAMPLES   Go to the storm cellar now.
             Be courteous to other drivers.
             Run!

(3) An *interrogative* sentence asks a question.

To *interrogate* means to "ask." An interrogative sentence is followed by a question mark.

EXAMPLES   Wasn't her joke funny?
             Why didn't she and Jan carry Susan?

(4) An *exclamatory* sentence expresses strong feeling. It exclaims.

An exclamatory sentence is always followed by an exclamation point.

EXAMPLES   Oh, my! How time flies!
             What hope a rainbow brings after a storm!

EXERCISE 25. Classify each of the following sentences according to its purpose. After numbering 1–10, write *declarative, imperative, interrogative,* or *exclamatory* after the corresponding number on your paper.

1. Wasn't that an exciting ending to our ball game?
2. The bases were loaded, and Roberta was next at bat.
3. What a tense moment!

4. Would she strike out, or would she make a miraculous hit?
5. After rubbing her hands in the sand, Roberta took a firm grip on the bat.
6. I'll knock this one to the west side of Kalamazoo!
7. Stand back out of my way.
8. The ball was low, fast, tricky.
9. Crack! The ball whizzed past the fielders and then crashed into a window a half block away!
10. When an angry face appeared at the broken window, all the players quickly scampered out of sight — except Roberta, who took plenty of time to enjoy her walk to home plate before going over to make friends with the window's owner.

EXERCISE 26. Copy the last word of each of the following sentences, and then give the correct mark of punctuation. Classify each sentence as imperative, declarative, interrogative, or exclamatory.

EXAMPLE   1. James Wong Howe filmed the scene
             1. *scene. declarative*

1. Have you ever seen a pilot fish
2. What an unusual species it is
3. No, it's nothing like a sailfish
4. Where are pilot fish found
5. You can seldom find them at a market
6. A pilot fish is one of the most interesting fish in the sea
7. Name a few facts, and tell a few legends about this fish
8. To ancient tribes, the pilot fish was a sacred animal
9. What curious companions pilot fish and sharks are
10. How did the pilot fish get its name

Chapter 3

The Phrase

Prepositional and Verbal Phrases, Appositive Phrases

In Chapter 1 you learned that two or more words (for example, *will be playing, were laughing, has done*) may be used as a verb, a single part of speech. Such a word group is called a *verb phrase.*

A word group may also be used as an adjective, an adverb, or a noun. You have already learned something about *prepositional phrases.* In this chapter, you will study prepositional phrases in greater detail, and you will learn about other kinds of phrases.

3a. A *phrase* **is a group of related words that is used as a single part of speech and does not contain a verb and its subject.**

EXAMPLES   **has been sitting** [verb phrase; no subject] **about you and me** [prepositional phrase; no subject or verb]

If a group of words has a subject *and* a verb, then the group of words is not a phrase.

EXAMPLES   **We found** your pen. [a subject and a verb; *we* is the subject of *found*] if **she will go** [a subject and a verb; *she* is the subject of *will go*]

EXERCISE 1. Study the following groups of words

and decide whether or not each group is a phrase. After numbering from 1–10, write *p.* for *phrase* or *n.p.* for *not a phrase* after the appropriate number.

1. was hoping	6. because Joyce won
2. if she really knows	7. after they leave
3. with Alice and me	8. has been cleaned
4. will be writing	9. on Lotte's desk
5. inside the house	10. as the plane lands

PREPOSITIONAL PHRASES

3b. A *prepositional phrase* **is a group of words beginning with a preposition and ending with a noun or pronoun.**

In the following examples of prepositional phrases, the prepositions are bold-faced.

> **in front of** our apartment building
> **like** them
> **during** the night

Some prepositions are made up of more than one word, like *in front of* in the first example. Notice that an article or other modifier often appears in the prepositional phrase: the first example contains *our;* the third, *the.*

3c. The noun or pronoun that ends the prepositional phrase is the *object* **of the preposition that begins the phrase.**

The prepositional phrases in the following sentence are in boldfaced type.

> **In their fight against cancer,** scientists have discovered interferon.

Here *fight* is the object of the preposition *in.* How is *cancer* used? What preposition does it follow?

Like other sentence parts, objects of prepositions may be compound.

EXAMPLES Yoko sat **between Elaine and me.** [Both *Elaine* and *me* are objects of the preposition *between.*]

We drove **to Sterling Park and North Star Lake.** [Both *Sterling Park* and *North Star Lake* are objects of the preposition *to.*]

Marilyn jogs **in front of the school and the church.** [The preposition *in front of* has a compound object, *school* and *church.*]

Do not be misled by a modifier coming after the noun or pronoun in a prepositional phrase; the noun or pronoun is still the object.

EXAMPLE Mother and Kay strolled **through the park** yesterday. [The object of the preposition *through* is *park; yesterday* is an adverb telling *when* and modifying the verb *strolled.*]

Lists of commonly used prepositions will be found on pages 29 and 30.

EXERCISE 2. List in order the twenty prepositions in these sentences. After each preposition, write its object. Indicate the number of the sentence from which each preposition and its object are taken. You may wish to refer to the list of prepositions on pages 29–30.

EXAMPLE 1. Oracles were the sources of wise prophecies in ancient Greece.
      1. *of—prophecies*
         in—Greece

1. One of the most famous oracles in Greece was the Delphic oracle.

2. It was located in Apollo's temple which was at Delphi.
3. The temple, supposedly the center of the earth, was a religious shrine for all Greece.
4. The temple's priestess inhaled vapors which rose from a pit, and then she went into a trance.
5. During the trance she delivered messages from Apollo.
6. Often the prophecies by the oracle were easily misunderstood.
7. The king Croesus began a war against the Persians on the strength of the oracle's prediction.
8. The oracle had foretold that a great empire would be destroyed through a war.
9. After the fight with the Persians, Croesus realized that the oracle meant *his* kingdom would be destroyed, not the Persians'.
10. Because of predictions like this one, the term *Delphian* aptly describes a statement that can be interpreted in two different ways.

The Adjective Phrase

Prepositional phrases are used in sentences mainly as adjectives and adverbs. Prepositional phrases used as adjectives are called *adjective phrases*.

EXAMPLE   Students **in the freshman class** are planning a television program **about their science project.**

The prepositional phrase *in the freshman class* is used as an adjective modifying the noun *students*. *About their science project* is also used as an adjective because it modifies the noun *program*.

Study the following pairs of sentences. Notice that the nouns used as adjectives may easily be converted to objects of prepositions in adjective phrases.

NOUNS USED AS ADJECTIVES	ADJECTIVE PHRASES
The **car** door is open.	The door **of the car** is open.
The **Miami** and **Houston** teams won.	The teams **from Miami and Houston** won.
This is a **house** key.	This is a key **for the house.**

Unlike a one-word adjective, which usually precedes the word it modifies, an adjective phrase always follows the noun or pronoun it modifies.

More than one prepositional phrase may modify the same word.

EXAMPLE The picture **of me in the newspaper** was not flattering. [The prepositional phrases *of me* and *in the newspaper* both modify the noun *picture.*]

A prepositional phrase may also modify the object of another prepositional phrase.

EXAMPLE The books **on the shelf of my closet** were all birthday gifts. [The phrase *on the shelf* modifies the noun *books. Shelf* is the object of the preposition *on.* The phrase *of my closet* modifies *shelf.*]

EXERCISE 3. Revise the following sentences by using adjective phrases in place of the italicized nouns used as adjectives. Be sure you can tell which word each phrase modifies.

1. Amy Patchell has several *opera* tickets.
2. The paper prints *school* news only.
3. I have bought some *cat* food.
4. We admired his *rose* garden.
5. The *hall* lamp is broken.
6. I need a new *typewriter* ribbon.

7. It was a melancholy *November* day.
8. The jeweler showed us a lovely *platinum* and *pearl* necklace. (*one phrase*)
9. The rain helped the *Indiana* córn crop. (*two phrases*)
10. Visitors to Washington, D.C., should have a *subway* map. (*one phrase*)

The Adverb Phrase

When a prepositional phrase is used as an adverb to tell *when, where, how, how much,* or *how far,* it is called an *adverb phrase.*

EXAMPLES   I dived **into the water.** [The adverb phrase *into the water* tells *where* I dived.]

Her train arrived **at noon.** [The adverb phrase *at noon* tells *when* her train arrived.]

She accepted the invitation **with pleasure.** [The adverb phrase *with pleasure* tells *how* she accepted the invitation.]

Martin missed the target **by a meter.** [*By a meter* is an adverb phrase telling *how far* Martin missed the target.]

In the previous examples, the adverb phrases all modify verbs. An adverb phrase may also modify an adjective or an adverb.

EXAMPLES   Dad smilingly tells Mother he is unlucky **at cards** but lucky **in love.** [The adverb phrase *at cards* modifies the adjective *unlucky; in love,* another adverb phrase, modifies the adjective *lucky.*]

I will see her later **in the day.** [*In the day* is an adverb phrase modifying the adverb *later.*]

Unlike adjective phrases, which always follow the

words they modify, an adverb phrase may appear at various places in a sentence.

Like adjective phrases, more than one adverb phrase may modify the same word.

EXAMPLE **At noon** my sister goes **to work.** [The adverb phrases *at noon* and *to work* both modify the verb *goes*. The first phrase tells *when* my sister goes; the second phrase tells *where* she goes. Notice that the first phrase precedes the word it modifies; the second phrase follows it.]

EXERCISE 4. Number 1–10 on your paper. List the prepositional phrases used as adverbs in each sentence. There may be more than one in a sentence. After each adverb phrase, write the word it modifies.

1. Yesterday, many residents of Chicago suffered from the heat.
2. In the morning, my friends and I drove to Lincoln Park.
3. At noon, we ate our big picnic lunch with gusto.
4. Later in the day, we walked around the park.
5. An unusual monument stands near the picnic grounds.
6. This monument shows humanity as it marches through time.
7. In Rockefeller Center I once saw another artist's concept of time.
8. Three figures are painted on the ceiling; they represent Past, Present, and Future.
9. Wherever you stand in the room, Past's eyes are turned away from you; Future's eyes look outward and upward.
10. The eyes of Present, however, look straight at you.

Diagraming Prepositional Phrases

The preposition is placed on a slanting line leading down from the word that the phrase modifies. Its object is placed on a horizontal line connected to the slanting line.

EXAMPLES **By chance,** a peasant uncovered a wall **of ancient Pompeii.** [adverb phrase modifying the verb; adjective phrase modifying the direct object]

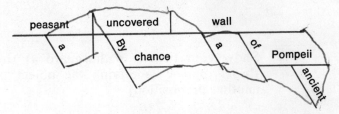

We will leave early **in the morning.** [adverb phrase modifying an adverb]

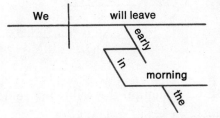

We strolled **down the hill** and **across the bridge.** [two phrases modifying the same word]

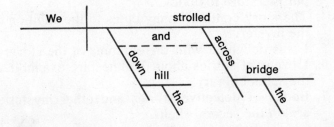

Father bought tickets **for Mother, my brothers, and me.** [compound object of preposition]

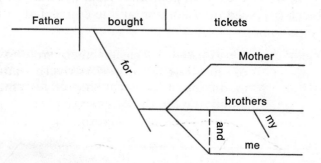

Show your tickets to the guard **at the door.** [phrase modifying the object of another preposition]

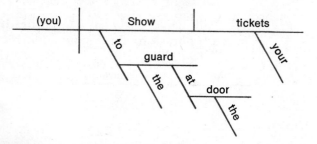

EXERCISE 5. Diagram the following sentences.

1. I have read many books by Arthur Conan Doyle about Sherlock Holmes.
2. Dr. Watson is the friend of the famous detective.
3. One story about Holmes and Watson appears in our literature textbook.
4. The story contains many clues to the solution of the mystery.
5. I was delighted with the outcome of the story.
6. Dozens of stories about Holmes are available in the school library.
7. Books of detective stories and other mysteries are on the second shelf.

8. Early in the afternoon, I went to the library.
9. The librarian took from his desk a new edition of one of Doyle's books.
10. He placed it in the display case in front of the window.

REVIEW EXERCISE A. There are twenty-five prepositional phrases in the following sentences. Number 1–10 on your paper. List the prepositional phrases in each sentence; and after each, write how the phrase is used—as an adjective or an adverb.

EXAMPLE   1. Theories about the universe have changed over the years.
1. *about the universe — adj.*
over the years — adv.

1. For over a thousand years people believed that the earth was at the center of the universe.
2. Astronomers thought the sun, the planets, and all the stars revolved around the earth.
3. During the early sixteenth century, however, Nicolaus Copernicus revised this popular theory about the earth's stationary position in the universe.
4. Copernicus studied the movements of the planets and the stars and published his radical view that the earth actually orbits around the sun.
5. He also explained the alternation of day and night by the earth's rotation on its axis.
6. His theory created a conflict between religion and science and challenged the belief that human beings were at the core of creation.
7. For the next four hundred years scientists believed that the universe was bounded by the edges of the earth's galaxy, the Milky Way.
8. About a half century ago at California's Mount Wilson Observatory, Edwin Hubble discovered that many other galaxies existed outside the Milky Way.

9. Now we know that there are perhaps a million galaxies inside the bowl of the Big Dipper alone.
10. Our galaxy is only one among billions throughout the universe!

VERBALS AND VERBAL PHRASES

Verbals are forms of verbs that are used as other parts of speech. These words are really two parts of speech in one. Verbals are formed from verbs and function very much like verbs; they may be modified by adverbs and may have complements. They are, however, used as other parts of speech.

There are three kinds of verbals: *participles, gerunds,* and *infinitives.*

The Participle

3d. A *participle* **is a verb form used as an adjective.**

The participle is part verb and part adjective. It might be called a "verbal adjective."

EXAMPLES **Leaping** the fence, the great cat surprised me.
Defeated teams should congratulate the winners.
Moving quickly, I intercepted the pass.

Leaping is part verb because it carries the action of the verb *leap.* It is also part adjective because it modifies the noun *cat—leaping cat. Defeated,* formed from the verb *defeat,* modifies the noun *teams. Moving,* formed from the verb *move,* modifies the pronoun *I.* Verb forms used as adjectives, *leaping, defeated,* and *moving* are *participles.*

There are two kinds of participles: *present participles* and *past participles.*

(1) *Present participles* **consist of the plain form of the verb plus** *–ing.*[1]

EXAMPLES   The **crying** baby hid under the table.
Pointing at me, the teacher asked a question.

In the first example, *crying* (formed by adding *–ing* to the verb *cry*) is a present participle modifying the noun *baby.* In the second, the present participle *pointing* (consisting of the plain form of the verb *point* plus *-ing*) modifies the noun *teacher — pointing teacher.* Verb forms used as adjectives, *crying* and *pointing* are participles.

Although participles are formed from verbs, they are not used to stand alone as verbs. A participle may, however, be used with a helping verb to form a verb phrase:

The baby **was crying.**
The teacher **had been pointing** at me.

When a participle is used in a verb phrase, it is considered as part of the verb, not as an adjective.

(2) *Past participles* **usually consist of the plain form of the verb plus** *–d* **or** *–ed.* **Others are irregularly formed.**[2]

EXAMPLES   A **peeled** and **sliced** cucumber can be added to a garden salad. [The past participles *peeled* and *sliced* modify the noun *cucumber.*]
The speaker, **known** for her eloquent speeches, drew applause from the audience. [The past participle *known* modifies the noun *speaker — known speaker.*]

Like a present participle, a past participle can also be

---

[1] The plain form of the verb is the infinitive form. See pages 153–54.
[2] See the discussion of irregular verbs on pages 155–56.

part of a verb phrase. Just as in the case of the present participle, a past participle used in a verb phrase is considered as part of the verb, not as an adjective.

EXAMPLES   She **had finished** the assignment by that time.
She **was warned** that the movie was extremely dull.

EXERCISE 6. Number 1–10 on your paper. List the participles used as adjectives in the following sentences, and after each participle write the noun or pronoun modified.

1. The prancing horses were loudly applauded by the delighted audience.
2. The colorful flags, waving in the breeze, brightened the gloomy day.
3. Swaggering and boasting, he made us extremely angry.
4. The game scheduled for tonight has been postponed because of rain.
5. Leaving the field, the happy player rushed to her parents sitting in the bleachers.
6. Rain pattering on the roof made an eerie sound.
7. We thought the banging shutter upstairs was someone walking in the attic.
8. Painfully sunburned, I vowed never to be so careless again.
9. Terrified by our big dog, the burglar turned and fled.
10. The platoon of soldiers, marching in step, crossed the field to the stirring music of the military band.

EXERCISE 7. Use any five of the following participles in sentences of your own. Be careful not to use a participle in a verb phrase.

EXAMPLE 1. latched
1. *The latched gate will keep trespassers away.*

1. running   6. missing
2. accepting   7. scorched
3. leaping   8. hitting
4. hidden   9. written
5. challenged   10. devised

EXERCISE 8. Number your paper 1–10. Next to each number write a participle that fits the meaning of the sentence.

EXAMPLE 1. The —— tide washed over the beach.
1. *rising*

1. Jan Evers, —— in a recent magazine, describes a tragic forest fire.
2. —— from the point of view of a firefighter, the story is full of accurate detail.
3. A mountain lion, —— by the sweeping flames, is dramatically rescued by the firefighters.
4. —— by the traffic police, the motorist tried to offer an excuse.
5. The tourists —— in the hotel were given a free meal.
6. —— as an excellent place to camp, the park lived up to its reputation.
7. —— by a bee, Candace hurried to the infirmary.
8. The poem describes a spider —— on a thread.
9. We stumbled off the race course, ——.
10. ——, I quickly phoned the hospital.

The Participial Phrase

A participle may be modified by an adverb or by a prepositional phrase, and it may have a complement. These related words combine with the participle in a *participial phrase.*

3e. A *participial phrase* consists of a participle and its related words, such as modifiers and complements, all of which act together as an adjective.

The participial phrase in each of the following sentences is in bold-faced type. An arrow points to the noun or pronoun that the phrase modifies.

EXAMPLES **Outwitting the hounds,** the raccoon easily escaped. [participle with object *hounds*]

I saw her **fishing contentedly.** [participle with adverb modifier *contentedly*]

Tackled on the one-foot line, he fumbled the ball. [participle with prepositional phrase modifier *on the one-foot line*]

Wildly cheering for the team, we celebrated the victory. [Notice that *wildly,* which precedes the participle and modifies it, is included in the phrase.]

A participial phrase should be placed very close to the word it modifies. Otherwise the phrase may appear to modify another word, and the sentence may not make sense.[1]

MISPLACED The clerk handed the gift box to the customer tied with red ribbon. [The placement of the modifier calls up a silly picture. The gift box, not the customer, is tied with ribbon.]

IMPROVED The clerk handed the customer the gift box tied with red ribbon.

---

[1] The punctuation of participial phrases is discussed on pages 495–96 and 500. The participle as a dangling modifier is discussed on pages 210–12. Combining sentences using participles is discussed on pages 262–63.

EXERCISE 9. Use the following participial phrases in sentences of your own. Be sure to place each phrase very close to the noun or pronoun it modifies, and to punctuate the phrases correctly.

EXAMPLE 1. swirling the beaker of liquid
1. *Swirling the beaker of liquid, Angie watched the solution slowly change color.*

1. stating her objections
2. excusing me from the test
3. decorated with streamers of crepe paper
4. laughing at my silly joke
5. charging like an angry bull
6. kept in a sunny spot
7. speaking as quickly as possible
8. confused by the wording of the question
9. destined to achieve fame
10. standing with one foot in the rowboat

The Gerund

3f. A *gerund* **is a verb form ending in** *–ing* **that is used as a noun.**

A participle is part verb and part adjective. A *gerund* is part verb and part noun. It is formed by adding *–ing* to the plain form of the verb. Like nouns, gerunds are used as subjects, predicate nominatives, direct objects, or objects of prepositions.

EXAMPLES **Walking** is good exercise. [subject]
My hobby is **sewing.** [predicate nominative]
Lauren enjoys **reading.** [direct object]
That is used for **drilling.** [object of preposition]

Like nouns, gerunds may be modified by adjectives and adjective phrases.

EXAMPLES   We listened to the **beautiful** singing **of**
the glee club. [The adjective *beautiful*
and the adjective phrase *of the glee club*
modify the gerund *singing. Singing* is
used as the object of the preposition *to*.]

The **gentle** ringing **of the church bells**
wakes me every morning. [Both the adjective *gentle* and the adjective phrase *of
the church bells* modify the gerund *ringing*, which is the subject of the sentence.]

Like verbs, gerunds may also be modified by adverbs
and adverb phrases.

EXAMPLES   Basking **quietly in the sun** is my favorite summer pastime. [The gerund *bask-
ing*, used as the subject of the sentence,
is modified by the adverb *quietly* and also
by the adverb phrase *in the sun*, which
tells *where*.]

Brandywine enjoys galloping **briskly on**
a cold morning. [The gerund *galloping*,
which is a direct object of the sentence,
is modified by the adverb *briskly* and also
by the adverb phrase *on a cold morning*,
which tells *when*.]

Gerunds, like present participles, end in *-ing*. To
be a gerund, a verbal must be used as a noun. In the
following sentence, there are three words ending in
–ing, but only one of them is a gerund.

EXAMPLE   **Heeding** the ranger's advice, she was not
planning to go on with her **hunting.**

Heeding is a present participle modifying she, and

planning is part of the verb phrase *was planning.* Only *hunting,* used as object of the preposition *with,* is a gerund.

EXERCISE 10. After you have listed each gerund in the sentences below, write how each is used: subject, predicate nominative, direct object, or object of preposition.

1. Her whistling attracted my attention.
2. By studying, you can raise your grades.
3. One requirement is thinking.
4. Yelling violates basic rules of courtesy.
5. Frowning, Dad discouraged our quarreling.
6. Carmen's favorite sport is fishing.
7. Before eating, we sat on the lawn and watched the frolicking puppies.
8. Yesterday, Mrs. Jacobs was discussing flying.
9. One of Steve's bad habits is boasting.
10. Without knocking, the hurrying child opened the door.

The Gerund Phrase

3g. A *gerund phrase* consists of a gerund together with its complements and modifiers, all of which act together as a noun.

EXAMPLES   **The loud knocking by the visitor** awakened the beagle. [The gerund phrase is used as the subject of the sentence. The gerund *knocking* is modified by the article *the,* the adjective *loud,* and the prepositional phrase *by the visitor.* Notice that modifiers preceding the gerund are included in the gerund phrase.]

I dislike **talking loudly in the corridor.**

[The gerund phrase is used as the object of the verb *dislike*. The gerund *talking* is modified by the adverb *loudly* and by the prepositional phrase *in the corridor*.]

His favorite pastime is **telling us his troubles.** [The gerund phrase is used as predicate nominative. The gerund *telling* has a direct object, *troubles,* and an indirect object, *us.*]

Mary Lou Williams gained widespread fame by **singing gospel music.** [The gerund phrase is the object of the preposition *by.* The gerund *singing* has a direct object, *music.*]

► NOTE Whenever a noun or pronoun comes before a gerund, the possessive form should be used.

EXAMPLES We were entertained by **Jorge's** clever joking.

I dislike **your** teasing the little girl.

EXERCISE 11. Write five sentences, following the directions given. Underline the gerund phrase in each of your sentences.

EXAMPLE 1. Use *writing* as the subject of the sentence. Include an adjective modifying the gerund.

1. <u>*Effective writing*</u> *is a major part of our English course.*

1. Use *shouting* as the subject. Include an adjective phrase modifying the gerund.
2. Use *playing* as the direct object of the sentence. Include a direct object of the gerund.
3. Use *telling* as the object of a preposition. Include in the gerund phrase a direct object and an indirect object of *telling.*

4. Use *arguing* as the predicate nominative. Include an adverb and an adverb phrase modifying the gerund.
5. Use *speaking* as a gerund in any way you choose. Include in the gerund phrase a possessive pronoun modifying the gerund.

The Infinitive

3h. An *infinitive* **is a verb form, usually preceded by** *to,* **that is used as a** *noun, adjective,* **or** *adverb.*

An infinitive consists of the plain form of the verb, usually preceded by *to.* It can be used as a noun, an adjective, or an adverb. Carefully study the following examples.

Infinitives used as nouns: **To forget** is **to forgive.** [*To forget* is the subject of the sentence; *to forgive* is the predicate nominative.]

Libby offered **to help** in any way except **to wash** dishes. [*To help* is the object of the verb *offered; to wash* is the object of the preposition *except.*]

Infinitives used as adjectives: The player **to watch** is the quarterback. [*To watch* modifies *player.*]

That was a day **to remember.** [*To remember* modifies *day.*]

Infinitives used as adverbs: Mrs. Chisolm rose **to speak.** [*To speak* modifies the verb *rose.*]

Eager **to please,** my dog obeyed my command. [*To please* modifies the adjective *eager.*]

► **NOTE** *To* plus a noun or pronoun (*to town, to him, to the store*) is a prepositional phrase, not an infinitive. An infinitive is always the first principal part of the verb.

The Infinitive Phrase

3i. An *infinitive phrase* consists of an infinitive together with its complements and modifiers.[1]

Infinitive phrases, like infinitives alone, can be used as adjectives, adverbs, or nouns.

EXAMPLES   **To interrupt a speaker abruptly** is impolite. [The infinitive phrase is used as a noun, as the subject of the sentence. The infinitive has an object, *speaker,* and is modified by the adverb *abruptly.*]

We had hoped **to leave at noon.** [The infinitive phrase is used as a noun—the object of *had hoped.* The infinitive is modified by the phrase *at noon.*]

She is the person **to see about the job.** [The infinitive phrase is used as an adjective modifying the predicate nominative *person.* The infinitive is modified by the adverbial prepositional phrase *about the job.*]

They were glad **to hear an answer.** [The infinitive phrase is used as an adverb modifying the predicate adjective *glad.* The infinitive has a direct object, *answer.*]

The Infinitive with "to" Omitted

Sometimes the *to* of the infinitive will be omitted in a sentence. This frequently occurs after such verbs as *see, hear, feel, watch, help, know, dare, need, make, let,* and *please.*

---

[1] An infinitive may have a subject: I wanted him to help me with my algebra. [*Him* is the subject of the infinitive *to help.* The infinitive, together with its subject, complements, and modifiers, is sometimes called an *infinitive clause.*]

EXAMPLES   Did you hear the band **play** yesterday?
Cathy did not dare **tell** us the bad news.
We have done everything except **make**
the beds.

EXERCISE 12. Make a list of the infinitives or infinitive phrases in the following sentences. After each one, give its use: *noun, adjective,* or *adverb.*

1. To give advice is easy.
2. We had hoped to solve the problem.
3. Judy plans to go.
4. I went to the gymnasium to find him.
5. One way to keep a secret is to forget it.
6. They dared discuss her mother's nomination.
7. We expect to leave immediately after school.
8. The best way to have a friend is to be one.
9. Pam and Carlos helped move the couch.
10. The door is not easy to open.

EXERCISE 13. Write five sentences, following the directions given below. Underline each infinitive phrase on your paper.

1. Use *to play* as a direct object.
2. Use *to ask* as an adjective, with a phrase modifier.
3. Use *to show* as an adverb modifying an adjective.
4. Use *to write* as the subject of a sentence. Include a direct object of the infinitive.
5. Use *to think* in any way you choose. Then write how you used it: *noun — direct object, adverb modifying the verb,* etc.

Diagraming Verbals and Verbal Phrases

Participial phrases are diagramed as follows:

EXAMPLE **Carrying a large package,** the messenger stumbled through the door.

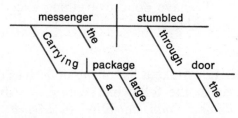

Gerunds and gerund phrases are diagramed this way:

EXAMPLE **Being unaware of the traffic regulations** is no excuse for **breaking the law at any time.** [Gerund phrases used as subject and as object of preposition. The first gerund has a subject complement (*unaware*); the second one has a direct object (*law*) and an adverb prepositional phrase modifier (*at any time*).]

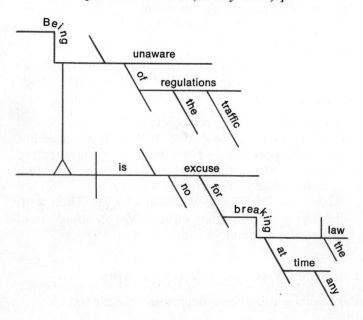

Infinitives and infinitive phrases used as modifiers are diagramed like prepositional phrases.

EXAMPLE   We are going **to see the parade.** [Infinitive phrase used as adverb. The infinitive has an object, *parade*.]

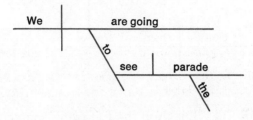

Infinitives used as nouns are diagramed as follows:

EXAMPLE   **To enlist in the Peace Corps** is his present plan.

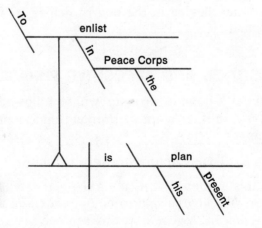

Notice how the subject of an infinitive is diagramed and how the infinitive is diagramed when *to* is omitted:

EXAMPLE My father helped me **wash** the car.

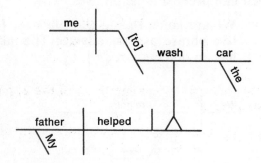

EXERCISE 14. Diagram the following sentences.

1. Playing the radio at night may disturb our neighbors.
2. Hearing our footsteps, the dog ran to greet us.
3. To reach the fifth floor, take the other stairs.
4. After hearing her assembly speech, I decided to become an architect.
5. The man digging in the quarry helped us find our baseball.

APPOSITIVES AND APPOSITIVE PHRASES

Sometimes a noun or pronoun will be followed immediately by another noun or pronoun that identifies or explains it.

EXAMPLE   The sculptor **Noguchi** is famous.

In this sentence, the noun *Noguchi* tells *which* sculptor. *Noguchi* is said to be *in apposition with* the word *sculptor*. *Noguchi* in this sentence is called an *appositive*.

3j. An *appositive* **is a noun or pronoun that follows another noun or pronoun to identify or explain it.**

EXAMPLE   Jimmy, a star athlete, will surely go to college.

Like any noun or pronoun, an appositive may have adjective and adjective phrase modifiers. If it does, it is called an *appositive phrase.*

3k. An *appositive phrase* **is made up of the appositive and its modifiers.**

In the following sentences the appositives and appositive phrases are in bold-faced type.

EXAMPLES   Our mathematics teacher, **Ms. Franklin,** also coaches our tennis team, **this year's conference champions.**

Joan Simpson, **the captain of the team,** received an award, **an engraved bronze trophy.**

► **NOTE**   Occasionally the appositive phrase precedes the noun or pronoun explained.

EXAMPLES   **A man of integrity,** Mr. Aldrich never cheats anyone.

The adviser for our school paper, Mrs. Frank is always there after school.

Appositives and appositive phrases are usually set off by commas, unless the appositive is a single word closely related to the preceding word. The comma is always used when the word to which the appositive refers is a proper noun.

EXAMPLES   Dr. Reed, **the woman sitting in the front row,** is my dentist.

Her son **Clint** is my classmate.

Judith, **her daughter,** is a senior in college.

In diagraming, place the appositive in parentheses after the word with which it is in apposition.

EXAMPLE   Our honored guest, **the author of the book,** is a friend of Mr. Sutherland, **our mayor.**

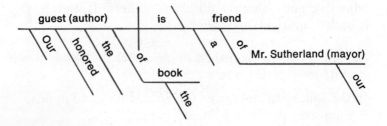

EXERCISE 15. List on your paper the appositive phrases in each of the following sentences. Underline the appositive in each phrase, and be sure that you know the word to which each appositive refers.

1. Our school has a dramatic club, the Masquers.
2. Ms. Harlow, my English teacher, is adviser for the Masquers.
3. Members of the club, mostly freshmen, planned an assembly program.
4. The program was presented on Friday, the day of our monthly meeting.
5. Duncan Bradley, the program coordinator, introduced Mr. Wilson, director of the summer theater in Burnsville.
6. From Rebecca Bryant, president of the Masquers, Mr. Wilson received our Achievement Award, a scroll signed by all club members.
7. After the program, Mr. Wilson was interviewed by Lucille Grant, editor of *Insights,* our school newspaper.

REVIEW EXERCISE B. After numbering 1–10, list the verbals and appositives in each sentence. After each, write in parentheses what the word is.

EXAMPLE 1. Lucky, a performing seal, was able to attract the audience's attention by slapping the surface of the water.

    1. *performing* (*participle*)
      seal (*appositive*)
      attract (*infinitive*)
      slapping (*gerund*)

1. Jumbo, the largest bush elephant ever held in captivity, was bought by the London Zoological Gardens in 1865.
2. Children enjoyed riding on a seat strapped to its back.
3. Sold to P. T. Barnum in 1882, Jumbo was sent to the United States.
4. Performing in Barnum's circus made the elephant rich and famous.
5. A star circus attraction until its death, Jumbo was tragically killed in a railroad accident in 1885.
6. Bobbie, a sheep dog from Oregon, accompanied its master on a trip to Indiana.
7. Its master stopped at a garage to make repairs one day.
8. As a result of fighting with a big bull terrier, Bobbie was chased away from the garage.
9. Having lost its way back to the garage, the dog headed back to Oregon.
10. Crossing rivers, deserts, and mountains, the dog managed to complete the long journey in only six months.

Chapter 4

The Clause

Independent and Subordinate Clauses

Like a phrase, a clause is a word group used as a part of a sentence. The difference is that a clause contains a verb and its subject, while a phrase does not.

4a. A *clause* **is a group of words that contains a verb and its subject and is used as part of a sentence.**

Although every clause has a subject and verb, not all clauses express a complete thought. Those that do are called *independent clauses*. Such clauses could be written as separate sentences. We think of them as clauses when they are joined with one or more additional clauses in a single larger sentence. Clauses that do not make complete sense by themselves are called *subordinate clauses*. Subordinate clauses do the job of nouns, adjectives, or adverbs just as phrases do. In this chapter you will become better acquainted with both kinds of clauses.

KINDS OF CLAUSES

4b. An *independent* **(or** *main***)** *clause* **expresses a complete thought and can stand by itself.**

We said that an independent clause could be written as a separate sentence. To see how this works out, consider the following example, in which the independent clauses are underlined:

EXAMPLE   <u>Ms. Torres cut pieces of stained glass with a diamond wheel</u>, and <u>her partner put the pieces together with wax and lead.</u>

Each clause has its own subject and verb and expresses a complete thought. In this example, the clauses are joined by a comma and the coordinating conjunction *and*. They could also be written with a semicolon between them:

> Ms. Torres cut pieces of stained glass with a diamond wheel; her partner put the pieces together with wax and lead.

or as separate sentences:

> Ms. Torres cut pieces of stained glass with a diamond wheel. Her partner put the pieces together with wax and lead.

4c. A *subordinate* (or *dependent*) *clause* **does not express a complete thought and cannot stand alone.**

Subordinate means "lesser in rank or importance." Subordinate clauses (also called *dependent* clauses) are so described because they need an independent clause to complete their meaning.

SUBORDINATE CLAUSES   before you know it
                       because I told him
                       after the show is over

These clauses sound incomplete to our ears because we know the subordinate part they play in sentences. Notice that the reason they sound incomplete is not that something is missing in the clause. Just the reverse is true, for by omitting the first word we can make each of these subordinate clauses into a complete sentence: *before you know it* becomes

You know it. Most subordinate clauses are introduced by a word like *when, if, until,* or *because* that makes them subordinate. When we hear a clause that starts with one of these words, we know that there has to be at least one more clause in the sentence, and that at least one of the other clauses must be an independent clause.

EXERCISE 1. Number your paper 1–10. Identify each clause in italics by writing either *independent* or *subordinate* after the corresponding number.

1. *When my family went to New York last summer,* we visited the Theodore Roosevelt museum.
2. *The museum has been established in the house* where Roosevelt was born.
3. It is located on the basement floor of Roosevelt's birthplace, *which is on East Twentieth Street.*
4. *The museum contains books, letters, and documents* that pertain to Roosevelt's public life.
5. There are mounted heads of animals, a stuffed lion, and zebra skins from the days *when Roosevelt was big-game hunting in Africa.*
6. *Because Roosevelt was once a cowboy,* there are also branding irons and chaps.
7. Before Theodore Roosevelt became President, *he gained fame in the Spanish-American War.*
8. During that war he led the Rough Riders, *who made the famous charge up San Juan Hill.*
9. Trophies *that Roosevelt received during his life* are on exhibit in the museum.
10. *The Roosevelt Memorial Association,* which established the museum, *charges a nominal admission fee to visitors.*

THE USES OF SUBORDINATE CLAUSES

Subordinate clauses, like phrases, function in sentences as single parts of speech. A subordinate clause can be used as an adjective, an adverb, or a noun, thus enabling us to express ideas that are difficult or impossible to state with single-word nouns and modifiers alone.

The Adjective Clause

4d. An *adjective clause* **is a subordinate clause used as an adjective to modify a noun or pronoun.**

In the following sentences the arrow points to the noun or pronoun that each adjective clause modifies.

EXAMPLES   In the case at school is the trophy **that Patsy won.**

Smog, **which is fog and smoke,** filled the sky.

The adjective clause follows the word it modifies, and it is sometimes set off by commas and sometimes not. Commas should be used unless the clause answers the question "Which one?" in which case no commas are used. In the first example, the clause *that Patsy won* tells *which* trophy; no comma is used. In the second example, the clause *which is fog and smoke* does not tell *which* smog. It merely describes smog. The clause is therefore set off by commas. (See page 495, rule 20i.)

Relative Pronouns

Adjective clauses are generally introduced by *relative pronouns.* The relative pronouns are *who, whom, whose, which,* and *that.* They are called *relative* because they *relate* the adjective clause to the word that the clause modifies. In Chapter 1, you learned that the noun to which a pronoun refers is the *antecedent* of the pronoun. The noun or pronoun modified by the adjective clause, then, is the antecedent of the relative pronoun that introduces the clause.

Besides introducing the adjective clause, the relative pronoun has a function in the clause.

EXAMPLES   Yvonne, **who lives in Iowa,** quickly learned Southern customs. [The relative pronoun *who* relates the adjective clause to *Yvonne. Who* is used as the subject of the adjective clause.]

Mrs. Daly recommended the book **that I am reading.** [*Book,* the word that the clause modifies, is the antecedent of the relative pronoun *that.* The pronoun is used as the direct object in the adjective clause.]

Here is the letter **for which I have been searching.** [The relative pronoun *which* is the object of the preposition *for* and relates the adjective clause to the pronoun's antecedent, *letter.*]

The reporter visited the family **whose house had been shown in the movie.** [The relative pronoun *whose* shows the relationship of the clause to *family. Family* is the antecedent of *whose.*]

Frequently the relative pronoun in the clause will be omitted. The pronoun is understood and will still have a function in the clause.

EXAMPLE   This is the dress **I want.** [The relative pronoun *that* is understood. This is the dress *that* I want. The pronoun relates the adjective clause to *dress* and is used as the direct object in the adjective clause.]

Occasionally an adjective clause will be introduced by the words *where* or *when.*

EXAMPLES   Across the street is the house **where I was born.**
Midnight is the hour **when ghosts walk abroad.**

EXERCISE 2. After the proper number on your paper, list the adjective clause from the corresponding sentence, underlining the relative pronoun that introduces the clause. Then list the antecedent of the relative pronoun after the clause.

EXAMPLE   1. People who want to learn languages must discipline themselves to study every day.
1. _who_ want to learn languages — People

1. Doctors who study the nervous system are called *neurologists.*
2. Some of the dinosaurs that existed 120 million years ago weighed over five tons.
3. Mercury, who served as the messenger for the gods, wore a pair of winged sandals.
4. The author whom we have been studying wrote under a pen name.
5. Can any country whose resources are limited afford the luxury of being wasteful?

EXERCISE 3. Number your paper 1–5. Follow the directions for Exercise 2.

1. Galileo is usually remembered as the scientist who invented the telescope.
2. The telescope helped to prove the theory of Copernicus, who believed the sun, not the earth, to be the center of the solar system.
3. With the telescope Galileo studied the Milky Way and discovered a fact that startled many people: the Milky Way is made up of millions of stars.
4. Galileo's discovery threatened the thinking of those

people who believed the earth to be the center of the universe.

5. After his discovery was made known, many of those whom Galileo had considered his friends avoided him.

EXERCISE 4. Write ten sentences using subordinate clauses as adjectives. Draw an arrow from each adjective clause to the noun or pronoun it modifies.

EXERCISE 5. Rewrite each of the following sentences by substituting an adjective clause for each italicized adjective. Underline the adjective clause in your sentence. Try to write clauses which add interest to each sentence.

EXAMPLES   1. The *angry* citizens gathered in front of City Hall.
           1. *The citizens, who were furious over the recent tax increase, gathered in front of City Hall.*
           2. The *old* history books lay on the shelf.
           2. *The history books, which were yellow and tattered from many years of use, lay on the shelf.*

1. The *colorful* painting caught our attention at the gallery.
2. The *patient* photographer sat on a small ledge all day.
3. The two parties argued all week over the *important* contract.
4. We decided on a camping expedition to the top of the *high* peak.
5. During class this morning, Lenora made a *surprising* remark.
6. Edgar and his friends cautiously entered the *dark* cave.

7. *Trustworthy* Mrs. Jackson easily won her first political campaign.
8. The trainer used a tight leash for the *disobedient* dog.
9. Dodging to his left, Manuel scored the *winning* goal.
10. Near the stable, Pamela walked sadly with her *lame* horse.

The Adverb Clause

4e. An *adverb clause* is a subordinate clause that modifies a verb, an adjective, or an adverb.

An adverb clause tells *how, when, where, why, how much, to what extent,* or *under what condition* the action of the main verb takes place.

EXAMPLES   **Before the game started,** Bryan and I ate lunch in the stadium. [The adverb clause *Before the game started* tells when Bryan and I ate lunch.]

Because she felt dizzy, Paula sat down for a while. [*Because she felt dizzy* tells why Paula sat down.]

I will attend the wedding **if it takes place on Saturday.** [*If it takes place on Saturday* tells under what condition I will attend the wedding.]

The adverb clauses in the examples above modify verbs. Adverb clauses may also modify adjectives or adverbs.

EXAMPLES   His pitching arm is stronger today **than it ever was.** [The adverb clause modifies the adjective *stronger,* telling to what *extent* his arm is stronger.]

> My sister awoke earlier **than I did.** [The adverb clause modifies the adverb *earlier*, telling how much earlier my sister awoke.]

Subordinating Conjunctions

Adverb clauses are introduced by *subordinating conjunctions*. Become familiar with these words.

Subordinating Conjunctions

after	before	unless
although	if	until
as	in order that	when
as if	since	whenever
as long as	so that	where
as soon as	than	wherever
because	though	while

► **NOTE** Remember that *after, before, since, until,* and *as* may also be used as prepositions.

EXERCISE 6. After numbering 1–10, write the subordinating conjunction and the last word of each adverb clause in the following sentences; then write what the clause tells: *when, where, how, why, how much, under what condition?* A sentence may have more than one adverb clause. (Notice that introductory adverb clauses are usually set off by commas.)

EXAMPLES
1. If you will take my advice, you can be the death of a party.
1. *If — advice   under what condition*
2. You can easily follow my instructions because they are clear and simple.
2. *because — simple   why*

1. If you wish to be the death of a party, do these things.

2. When other people are speaking, interrupt them.
3. As soon as they start telling jokes, you can steal their thunder by giving away the punch lines.
4. You can then act as if the jokes weren't funny.
5. Later you can change the subject so that you can brag about yourself.
6. While you are talking about your heroic deeds or keen intelligence, emphasize many uninteresting details.
7. Before you describe saving a child's life, make yourself out to be nobler than anyone else is.
8. Whenever the occasion arises, you should complain to your host and criticize the guests.
9. Unless you monopolize every conversation, you won't be a professional "party pooper."
10. Enjoy yourself as you crowd others off the floor, because you will probably never be invited again.

EXERCISE 7. Write ten sentences of your own, using the following subordinate clauses as adverbs.

EXAMPLE   1. as the strangers talked
              1. *As the strangers talked, the icy distance between them gradually melted.*

1. although I am one of Barbara Walters' fans
2. while he was honking the horn impatiently
3. as soon as we had finished eating
4. although she hit two home runs
5. unless my aunt changes her mind
6. so that it will be a complete surprise
7. if the concrete has too much water in it
8. as if he had just seen a monster from Mars
9. after you add the eggs to the mixture
10. when she was leaving the theater

The Noun Clause

4f. A *noun clause* is a subordinate clause used as a noun.

A noun clause may be used as a subject, a complement (predicate nominative, direct object, indirect object), or the object of a preposition.

Study the structure of the following sentences.

NOUNS	NOUN CLAUSES
Subject Her **words** surprised me.	**What she said** surprised me.
Predicate nominative The champion will be the best **fighter**.	The champion will be **whoever fights best.**
Direct object She knows our **secret.**	She knows **what our secret is.**
Indirect object They give each **arrival** a name tag.	They give **whoever comes** a name tag.
Object of preposition He often sends flowers to sick **people.**	He often sends flowers to **whoever is sick.**

Noun clauses are usually introduced by *that, what, whatever, who, whoever, whom,* and *whomever.*

EXAMPLES   We could not tell **who she was.** [The introductory word *who* is the predicate nominative in the noun clause — *she was who.*]

Tell us **whom you saw.** [The introductory word is the direct object of the noun clause — *you saw whom.*]

She thought **that** I knew. [The introductory word *that* has no other function in the clause.]

EXERCISE 8.   List on your paper the first and the last word of each noun clause in these sentences. Then tell how the noun clause is used: *subject, predicate nominative, direct object, indirect object,* or *object of* *a preposition.* (You will not find noun clauses in every sentence.)

EXAMPLE 1. You can never accurately predict what will happen at a rodeo.
      1. *what — rodeo*   *direct object*

1. What I like at a rodeo is the excitement. ⌒
2. My cousin Maria often tells stories about what she has done at rodeos.
3. She will give whoever is interested an exciting account of her adventures.
4. In Arizona all the other riders knew that "Five Minutes till Midnight" was too dangerous a horse to ride.
5. That she had the courage to ride the wild horse was what Maria wanted to prove to everyone.
6. The tense crowd watched Maria as she jumped upon the back of the horse that no rider had ever ridden before.
7. She won the prize money for what she did; she stayed on the bucking horse until the whistle blew.
8. Upon hearing the whistle, Maria knew that she had won.
9. The second that Maria relaxed, however, the angry stallion tossed her high into the air.
10. Whoever saw Maria sail through space that day will never forget how she turned a flip in midair and then landed safely on her feet.

Diagraming Subordinate Clauses

In a diagram, an adjective clause is joined to the word it modifies by a broken line leading from the relative pronoun to the modified word — that is, to the antecedent of the relative pronoun.

EXAMPLES The movie **that we saw yesterday** won the Academy Award.

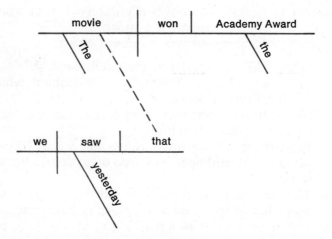

He is the man **from whom we bought the decorations.**

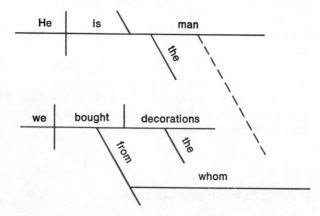

In diagraming an adverb clause, place the subordinating conjunction that introduces the clause on a broken line leading from the verb in the adverb clause to the word the clause modifies.

EXAMPLE **Before we leave the party,** we must thank the hosts.

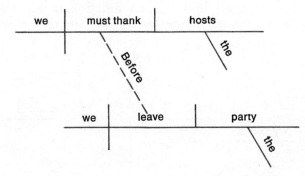

How a noun clause is diagramed depends upon its use in the sentence. It also depends on whether or not the introductory word has a specific function in the noun clause. Study the following examples.

EXAMPLES **What you believe** is important to me. [The noun clause is used as the subject of the independent clause. The introductory word *what* is the direct object in the noun clause.]

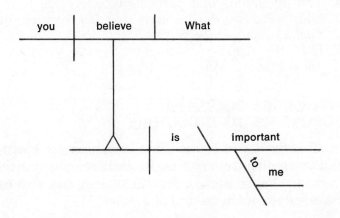

Columbus knew **that the world was round.** [The noun clause is the direct object of the independent clause. The word *that* has no function in the noun clause except as an introductory word.]

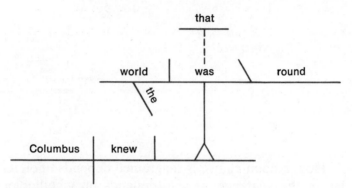

EXERCISE 9. Diagram the following sentences.

1. What Catherine saw at Monticello was extremely interesting to all of us.
2. Monticello, which was the home of Thomas Jefferson, is located near Charlottesville, Virginia.
3. If you visit Monticello, you will see many fascinating devices that Jefferson invented.
4. The inventions that particularly interested Catherine were two dumbwaiters that ran between the dining room and the cellar.
5. If I ever visit my cousin who lives in Virginia, I know that we will go to Monticello.

SENTENCES CLASSIFIED ACCORDING TO STRUCTURE

In Chapter 2 you learned that sentences are classified according to *type* as declarative, imperative, interrogative, or exclamatory. Sentences may also be classified according to *structure*.

4g. Classified according to structure, there are four kinds of sentences: *simple, compound, complex,* and *compound-complex.*

(1) A *simple sentence* has one independent clause and no subordinate clauses. It has only one subject and one verb, although both may be compound.

EXAMPLE   George Vancouver was exploring the Northwest.

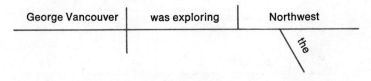

(2) A *compound sentence* has two or more independent clauses but no subordinate clauses.

In effect, a compound sentence consists of two or more simple sentences joined by a comma and a coordinating conjunction or by a semicolon.

EXAMPLE   In 1792 Vancouver discovered a channel, and he gave it an unusual name.

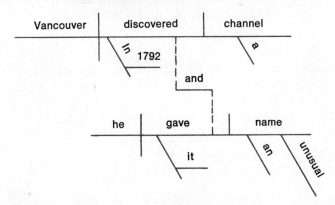

▶ **NOTE**   If the compound sentence has a semicolon and no conjunction, place a straight broken line between the two verbs.

(3) A *complex sentence* **has one independent clause and** *at least* **one subordinate clause.**

EXAMPLE   He originally thought that the channel was a harbor. [Here the subordinate clause is the direct object of the independent clause.]

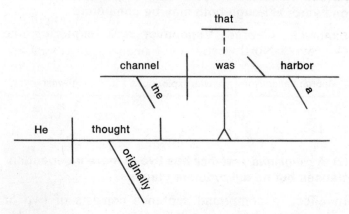

(4) A *compound-complex sentence* **contains two or more independent clauses and** *at least* **one subordinate clause.**

EXAMPLE   Since it was not a harbor, Vancouver had been deceived, and Deception Pass became its name.

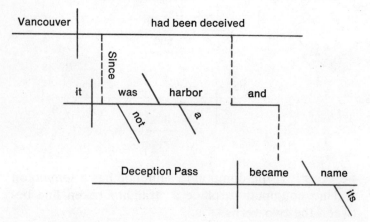

EXERCISE 10. Number your paper 1–10. Classify each of the following sentences according to its structure. Next to each number, write *simple, compound, complex,* or *compound-complex.* Be sure that you can identify all subordinate and independent clauses.

1. Since President Franklin Roosevelt appointed Frances Perkins as Secretary of Labor in 1933, several other women have been cabinet members.
2. Oveta Culp Hobby was the first head of the Women's Army Corps, and later she became Secretary of Health, Education, and Welfare.
3. When Carla Anderson Hills was appointed by President Ford to be Secretary of Housing and Urban Development, she became the third woman to hold a cabinet position.
4. In 1977 President Carter appointed Patricia Roberts Harris as Secretary of Housing and Urban Development, and thus the United States had its first black woman cabinet member.
5. The fifth woman to achieve cabinet rank was Juanita M. Kreps, President Carter's first Secretary of Commerce.
6. How many women have been appointed to cabinet positions in the 1980's?
7. In 1924 two women, Miriam Wallace Ferguson of Texas and Nellie Taylor of Wyoming, became state governors; each was elected following the death of her governor husband.
8. Ella Tambussi Grasso of Connecticut was the first woman in the nation's history to be elected a state governor who did not follow her husband into office.
9. Although she had never run for political office before, Dixie Lee Ray became the first woman governor of the state of Washington.
10. We know that women will continue to hold such high positions as cabinet member and governor, but when will a woman win the Presidency?

EXERCISE 11. Diagram the following sentences.

1. Tonight I am going to a concert with my parents, but I would prefer to play chess with you.
2. When she saw the accident, she looked for help and then telephoned the police.
3. Twenty seniors in the graduating class will be attending college, and twelve of them have received scholarships.
4. Leaving for school, I knew that it would rain today; yet I did not carry my umbrella.
5. When my sister practices her singing lessons, Muff curls up on the piano bench and purrs; but when I play my trumpet, that cat yowls and hides under the sofa.

REVIEW EXERCISE A. Number your paper 1–10. Decide whether each numbered and italicized clause below functions as an adjective, an adverb, or a noun, and write *adjective, adverb,* or *noun* after the proper number. Be prepared to explain your answers.

(1) *As we left the courtroom,* we did not feel very sorry for the men (2) *who had been on trial.* (3) *Although they had not committed a serious crime,* they had broken the law. The law says (4) *that removing sand from a beach is illegal.* They were caught (5) *because they could not move their truck,* (6) *which had become stuck in the sand.* (7) *After the judge read the law to them,* the men claimed (8) *that they had never heard of it.* The judge, (9) *who did not believe this,* fined each man twenty-five dollars. The men promised (10) *that they would not steal any more beach sand.*

REVIEW EXERCISE B. Number your paper 1–10. If the subordinate clause in each of the following sentences is used as an adjective or an adverb, write the word the clause modifies. If the clause is used as a noun, write *subj.* for subject, *d.o.* for direct object, *i.o.* for indirect object, *p.n.* for predicate nominative, or *o.p.* for object of a preposition.

EXAMPLE 1. When our science book described insect-eating plants, we were amazed.

        1. *were amazed*

1. Plants that eat flies and other insects usually live in swampy areas.
2. Because the soil in these regions lacks nitrogen, these plants do not get enough nitrogen through their roots.
3. The nitrogen that these plants need must come from the protein in insects.
4. How these plants catch their food makes them interesting.
5. A pitcher plant's sweet scent attracts whatever insect is nearby.
6. The insect thinks that it will find food inside the plant.
7. What happens instead is the insect's drowning in the plant's digestive juices.
8. The Venus' flytrap has what looks like small bear traps at the ends of its stalks.
9. When a trap is open, an insect can easily fit inside it.
10. An insect is digested by the plant in a slow process that takes several days.

REVIEW EXERCISE C. Write your own sentences according to the following guidelines.

1. A simple sentence with a compound verb
2. A complex sentence with an adjective clause
3. A compound-complex sentence
4. A compound sentence with two independent clauses joined by the conjunction *but*

5. A complex sentence with a noun clause used as a subject

REVIEW EXERCISE D. Diagram the following sentences.

1. Do you know who Alan Shepard is?
2. This astronaut wrote an exciting article that appears in our literature book.
3. He described the historic flight, which was the first trip into space by an American.
4. Because he had trained beforehand, the flight seemed familiar.
5. At one point the capsule in which Shepard was riding began to vibrate.
6. Shepard knew what caused the vibration.
7. It occurred when the capsule passed through the zone of maximum pressure.
8. The vibration was somewhat heavier than Shepard had expected.
9. Finally it stopped, and the flight continued on schedule.
10. Shepard said that he felt fine after the flight, and he praised the many hard-working people who had contributed to its outstanding success.

Usage

PART TWO

Chapter 5

Agreement

Subject and Verb, Pronoun and Antecedent

Certain words that are closely related in sentences have matching forms. Subjects and verbs have this kind of close relationship, as do pronouns and their antecedents. When such words are correctly matched, we say that they *agree* grammatically. Have you ever heard someone say, "He don't," or "One of the girls forgot their book"? Each of these errors shows lack of agreement, the first one between subject and verb and the second one between a pronoun and its antecedent.

One way in which two words can agree with each other grammatically is in *number.* Number indicates whether the word refers to one person or thing, or to more than one.

5a. When a word refers to one person or thing, it is *singular* **in number. When a word refers to more than one, it is** *plural* **in number.**

Nouns and pronouns have number. The following nouns and pronouns are singular because they name or refer to only one person or thing: *hunter, child, it, story.* The following are plural because they refer to more than one: *hunters, children, they, stories.*

EXERCISE 1. Number 1–20 in a column on your paper. After each number, write whether the word is *singular* or *plural*.

1. dentist	6. each	11. his	16. woman
2. dentists	7. both	12. our	17. months
3. someone	8. these	13. several	18. its
4. their	9. this	14. foot	19. cities
5. meter	10. hoof	15. motor	20. dollars

AGREEMENT OF SUBJECT AND VERB

Verbs have number, too. In order to speak and write standard English, you must make verbs agree with their subjects.

► **NOTE** To understand this chapter and the following chapters on usage, you should know the meaning of the terms "standard English" and "nonstandard English." The word *standard* suggests a model with which things can be compared. In this case, the model —standard English—is the set of usage conventions most widely accepted by English-speaking people. It is the English used, for instance, by radio and TV announcers and newscasters, and in most newspapers, magazines, and books. All other kinds of usage are referred to as *nonstandard* English. This is the term used in this book to describe variations in usage that are avoided in formal writing and speaking. Nonstandard English includes local speech dialects, slang, and various idiomatic usages. Study the following examples:

STANDARD	NONSTANDARD
Were you there?	Was you there?
It doesn't matter.	It don't matter.
They played well.	They played good.

| Can you teach me the rule? | Can you learn me the rule? |
| Lena and she went early. | Lena and her went early. |

5b. A verb agrees with its subject in number.

(1) Singular subjects take singular verbs.

EXAMPLES My **friend likes** algebra. [The singular verb *likes* agrees with the singular subject *friend*.]

A **girl** in my class **sings** in the city chorus. [The singular verb *sings* agrees with the singular subject *girl*.]

(2) Plural subjects take plural verbs.

EXAMPLES My **friends like** algebra.

Many **girls** in my class **sing** in the city chorus.

The plural subjects *friends* and *girls* take the plural verbs *like* and *sing*.

Generally, nouns ending in *s* are plural (*friends, girls*), but verbs ending in *s* are singular (*likes, sings*). Since the form of the verb used with the singular pronouns *I* and *you* is regularly the same as the plural form, agreement in number presents problems mainly in the third person forms.

	SINGULAR	PLURAL
First person	I work	We work
Second person	You work	You work
Third person	She works	They work

EXERCISE 2. Number your paper 1–10. Write the verb in parentheses that agrees with the subject.

1. several (has, have)
2. many (arrives, arrive)
3. everyone (tries, try)
4. you (was, were)

5. both (is, are)
6. no one (seems, seem)
7. few (does, do)

8. either (looks, look)
9. anyone (reads, read)
10. it (gives, give)

5c. The number of the subject is not changed by a phrase following the subject.

Remember that a verb agrees in number with its subject, not with the object of a preposition. *The subject is never part of a prepositional phrase.*

EXAMPLES   **One** of the kites **has** caught in a tree.
The **paintings** of Emilio Sanchez **were** hanging in the gallery.

Compound prepositions such as *together with, in addition to,* and *along with* following the subject do not affect the number of the subject.

EXAMPLES   **Mimi,** together with her sisters, **has** been taking voice lessons.
Charles, along with Maria and Dan, **was** elected to the Student Council.

EXERCISE 3. *Oral Drill.* Repeat each of the following sentences, stressing the italicized words.

1. Many *facts* in this textbook *are* important.
2. A *knowledge* of rules *helps* you use standard English.
3. Correct *usage* of verbs *is* especially important.
4. Correct *spelling,* in addition to usage of verbs, *is* essential to good writing.
5. *People* in the business world *look* carefully at letters of application.
6. *Letters* with nonstandard English *do* not make a good impression.
7. My *mother,* along with two other officials, *has* been interviewing high school students.
8. *One* of my friends *hopes* to work for Mother's company this summer.

9. Not *one* of the employers, however, *was* pleased with my friend's letter of application.
10. "Every *person* in my office *needs* to know standard English," commented my mother.

EXERCISE 4. Number your paper 1–10. Write after the corresponding number the subject of each sentence. After the subject, write the verb in parentheses that agrees with it.

EXAMPLE   1. Our units of measure often (causes, cause) confusion.
　　　　　1. *units — cause*

1. The confusion among many American consumers (is, are) understandable.
2. The traditional system of measuring quantities (makes, make) shopping rather difficult.
3. The quantity printed on packages of products like ice cream and yogurt (tells, tell) the number of ounces the package contains.
4. Shoppers who are concerned with value (doesn't, don't) know whether this indicates liquid or solid measure.
5. Different brands of fruit juice (shows, show) the same quantity in different ways.
6. One can with a label showing 24 ounces (equals, equal) another which shows 1 pint 8 ounces.
7. There (isn't, aren't), in the traditional system of weights and measures, a logical relationship between volume and weight.
8. The metric system, which is used throughout the European countries, (solves, solve) much of this confusion.
9. The units of weight and measure in this system (has, have) a relationship to each other.
10. For instance, each liter of water — a thousand cubic centimeters — (weighs, weigh) one kilogram — a thousand grams.

5d. The following pronouns are singular: *each, either, neither, one, everyone, everybody, no one, nobody, anyone, anybody, someone, somebody.*

Read the following sentences aloud, stressing the subjects and verbs in bold-faced type.

EXAMPLES   **Each** of these sounds **causes** drowsiness. [each one causes]
Neither of the girls **is** here. [neither one is]
Either of the dresses **is** appropriate. [either one is]
Everyone in the class **has** read the novel.
Someone in the choir **was** whistling softly.

Note that the first word in each of the example sentences is followed by a phrase. The object of the preposition in each of the first three sentences is plural: *sounds, girls, dresses.* There is a natural tendency to make the verb agree with these words rather than with its subject. However, since each of the five sentences has a singular pronoun as subject, each verb is also singular.

5e. The following pronouns are plural: *several, few, both, many.*

Study the use of subjects and verbs in these sentences. Read the sentences aloud.

EXAMPLES   **Few** of the students **have** failed the test.
Several of these plants **are** poisonous.
Many in the group often **ask** questions.
Were both of the problems difficult?

5f. The pronouns *some, all, most, any,* and *none* may be either singular or plural.

These pronouns are singular when they refer to a

singular word and plural when they refer to a plural word.

EXAMPLES   **Some** of the food **was** eaten. [*Some* refers to singular *food*.]

Some of the apples **were** eaten. [*Some* refers to plural *apples*.]

All of the furniture **looks** comfortable.

All of the chairs **look** comfortable.

Most of his writing **sounds** witty.

Most of his essays **sound** witty.

Was any of the jewelry stolen?

Were any of the jewels stolen?

None of this work **is** hard.

None of their jobs **are** hard.

The words *any* and *none* may be singular even when they refer to a plural word if the speaker is thinking of each item individually, and plural if the speaker is thinking of several things as a group.

EXAMPLES   **Any** of these students **is** qualified. [*Any one* is qualified.]
Any of these students **are** qualified. [*All* are qualified.]
None of the cartons **was** full. [*Not one* was full.]
None of the cartons **were** full. [*No cartons* were full.]

EXERCISE 5. This exercise covers rules 5d, 5e, and 5f. Number your paper 1–10. Write the subject of each sentence on your paper. Select the correct verb, and write it after the subject.

1. Many of us actually (likes, like) long books.
2. Some of the children (seems, seem) shy.
3. Somebody in the audience (was, were) snoring.
4. Each of us (tries, try) to outdo the other.
5. Both of my parents (has, have) red hair.
6. Few of the pies (was, were) left after the sale.
7. Sometimes everyone in the office (works, work) late.
8. Nobody in my family (is, are) able to remember telephone numbers and addresses.
9. (Has, have) all of the senators returned?
10. (Does, do) either of the students need money to buy decorations?

REVIEW EXERCISE A. Number your paper 1–10. Read each sentence aloud. If the verb agrees with the subject, write a plus (+) on your paper after the corresponding number. If the verb does not agree with the subject, write a zero (0).

1. One of the cabinets contain the club's banner, account books, and membership rolls.
2. Each of the flight attendants are by the plane.
3. Do the new uniforms for the band include hats?
4. Sometimes a leak in the gas pipes is hard to find.
5. The bridges on Highway 34 are extremely narrow.
6. The numbers on the license plate was covered with mud.
7. Yesterday you was asking me about camp.
8. Every one of the clerks have to punch the time clock.
9. One of her assistants answer the telephone.
10. Our assignment for the next two days cover events during the American Revolution.

REVIEW EXERCISE B. Follow the instructions for Review Exercise A.

1. Some of these pictures in the family album show how hair styles change.
2. A bag of baseballs, in addition to three tennis rackets, sit in the corner of her closet.
3. Most of us now agree to these plans.
4. Each of the farmers use heavy machinery for plowing.
5. Some of the salt in these shakers is damp.
6. A carton of fresh eggs was in the refrigerator.
7. Neither of the paintings look finished.
8. Each of the contestants has a chance to win.
9. Does both of the hedges need trimming?
10. Melba, together with other school newspaper editors, are attending a national convention.

The Compound Subject

5g. Subjects joined by *and* take a plural verb.

The following compound subjects joined by *and* name more than one person or thing and must take plural verbs:

> **Lucille Clifton** and **Leslie Silko are** writers. [Two persons are.]
> **Poetry** and **prose differ** in form. [Two things differ.]

If a compound subject names only one person or thing, then the verb must be singular:

> **The secretary and treasurer plans** to resign. [One person plans.]
> **Ham and eggs is** a good breakfast dish. [The one combination is.]

In the sentences above, the compound subjects are thought of as units (one person, one dish) and are therefore singular.

5h. Singular subjects joined by *or* or *nor* take a singular verb.

EXAMPLES   Every Saturday, **Gail** or **Ernie takes** the wash to the Laundromat. [Either Gail *or* Ernie takes the wash, not both.]
Neither the **customer** nor the **clerk is** always right. [Neither *one* is always right.]

EXERCISE 6. Number your paper 1–10. Then rewrite the sentences below according to these instructions. If the sentence has a compound subject joined by *and,* change the conjunction to *or,* and make the necessary change in the number of the verb. If the sentence has a compound subject joined by *or,* change the conjunction to *and,* and make the necessary change in the number of the verb.

EXAMPLES   1. A dog and a cat are tearing up the paper.
1. *A dog or a cat is tearing up the paper.*
2. My father or his friend has finished the plans for the house.
2. *My father and his friend have finished the plans for the house.*

1. Ned and Elena have gone to the science fair.
2. Your jacket and your coat are at the cleaners.
3. The girl and her mother are telling fortunes for the National Honor Society's booth at the school fair.
4. The house on the hill and the cottage in the valley are for sale.
5. *The Contender* or *The Good Earth* has been assigned.
6. Jane or Scott has prepared the punch.
7. Each week a poem and an essay appear in the school newspaper.
8. Rain or snow has been predicted for tomorrow.

9. Venus and Mars do not seem far away when one considers the distance from Earth to the nearest star.
10. The car in front of us and the car parked on the wrong side of the street are to blame for the accident.

5i. When a singular subject and a plural subject are joined by *or* or *nòr*, the verb agrees with the subject nearer the verb.

ACCEPTABLE Neither the singers nor the **accompanist has** memorized the music.

ACCEPTABLE Neither the accompanist nor the **singers have** memorized the music.

Because of awkwardness, these constructions should usually be avoided.

BETTER The music has not been memorized by either the singers or the accompanist.

REVIEW EXERCISE C. *Oral Drill.* Read each of the following sentences aloud several times.

1. The *plants* in the window box *need* watering.
2. A *can* of mixed nuts *is* on the coffee table.
3. *You were* asleep.
4. *Carmen* and *Alicia are* distantly related.
5. *Reading* a book or *writing* letters *is* an enjoyable way to spend the evening.
6. *Neither* of you *believes* us.
7. *Several* of these pests *annoy* the wild deer.
8. Every *one* of you *knows* Jack.
9. Either *Leah* or *Josie has* brought the records.
10. Neither *Charlene* nor *Myron likes* ghost stories.

REVIEW EXERCISE D. Rewrite each of the following sentences (1) following the directions in parentheses and (2) changing the number of the verb to agree with the subject if necessary.

EXAMPLE   1. The teachers have finished grading the tests. (Change *The teachers* to *Each of the teachers.*)
           1. *Each of the teachers has finished grading the tests.*

1. My sister is planning to work for the FBI. (Change *sister* to *sisters.*)
2. Have Camille and Roberta asked to go with us? (Change *and* to *or.*)
3. Nobody in our town intends to participate in the ceremony. (Change *Nobody* to *Many.*)
4. My grandmother, as well as my mother, hopes to see our play. (Change *grandmother* to *grandparents.*)
5. Most of the money was contributed by children in elementary school. (Change *money* to *quarters.*)
6. Neither the students nor the teacher has found the missing book. (Change *Neither the students nor the teacher* to *Neither the teacher nor the students.*)
7. The president and the vice-president have promised to address the meeting. (Change *president and the vice-president* to *secretary and treasurer.*)
8. Some of the employees spend too much time in the coffee shop. (Change *Some* to *One.*)
9. The children playing with the puppies do not want to go home. (Change *children* to *child.*)
10. Few of my questions were answered to my satisfaction. (Change *Few* to *Neither.*)

Other Problems in Agreement

5j. *Don't* and *doesn't* **must agree with their subjects.**

Don't and *doesn't* are contractions—two words combined into one by omitting one or more letters. *Don't* is the contraction for "do not," *doesn't* for "does not."

With the subjects *I* and *you* and with plural subjects, use *don't* (*do not*).

EXAMPLES   I **don't** cook.   They **don't** protest.
           You **don't** mean it. These **don't** fit.
           We **don't** help.   Adults **don't** understand me.

With other subjects, use the singular *doesn't* (*does not*.)

EXAMPLES   He **doesn't** cook.   One **doesn't** protest.
           She **doesn't** mean it. This **doesn't** fit.
           It **doesn't** help.   Sue **doesn't** understand me.

The errors in the use of *don't* and *doesn't* are usually made when *don't* is incorrectly used with *it, he,* or *she*. Remember always to use *doesn't* with these singular subjects.

EXERCISE 7.   *Oral Drill.* Read these sentences aloud.

1. It doesn't matter now.
2. This doesn't bother me.
3. Ella doesn't frighten easily.
4. One doesn't brag after a defeat.
5. He doesn't ever sleep late.
6. Doesn't she live here?
7. Doesn't that amuse you?

EXERCISE 8. After numbering your paper 1–10, write the correct form (*doesn't* or *don't*) for each sentence below.

1. This —— influence me.
2. —— she like sour pickles?

3. No, he ——.
4. These —— suit me.
5. It —— look much like rain.
6. One of them —— expect to win.
7. They —— intend to go.
8. —— Edmund have a birthday soon?
9. —— one of you want a piece of pie?
10. Valerie and Beth —— like to wear hats and gloves.

5k. Collective nouns may be either singular or plural.

Collective nouns are singular in form, but they name a *group* of persons or things.

group	committee	club	family
flock	herd	swarm	public
jury	army	audience	assembly
class	team	faculty	fleet

Collective nouns are used with plural verbs when the speaker or writer is referring to the individual parts or members of the group acting separately. They are used with singular verbs when the statement refers to the group acting together as a unit.

EXAMPLES   The jury **was** ready to announce its decision. [*Jury* is thought of as a unit.]
The jury **were** arguing among themselves. [*Jury* is thought of as individuals.]

► USAGE NOTE   Be sure that any pronoun referring to the collective noun has the same number as the noun (*its* in the first example above, *themselves* in the second).

EXERCISE 9. Select five collective nouns and write five pairs of sentences showing clearly how the nouns you choose may be either singular or plural.

EXAMPLE   1. *The class has elected its officers.*

The class have finished their projects.

5l. A verb agrees with its subject, not its predicate nominative.

When the subject and the predicate nominative are of different numbers, you should always remember that *the verb agrees with the subject.*

STANDARD Traffic **jams are** one problem of commuters.

STANDARD One **problem** of commuters **is** traffic jams.

5m. When the subject follows the verb as in sentences beginning with *there* and *here* and in questions, be careful to determine the subject and make sure that the verb agrees with it.

Each subject below agrees with its verb.

EXAMPLES Here **is** a **letter** for you.
Here **are** two **letters** for you.
There **is** my **friend** now.
There **are** my **friends** now.
Where **is Edith?** Where **is Donald?**
Where **are Edith** and **Donald?**

In conversations we frequently use contractions such as *here's, there's, where's, how's, what's, when's,* and the like. Since each of these includes the contracted form of *is,* do not use one of these contractions unless a singular subject follows it.

NONSTANDARD There's many old magazines in the attic.

STANDARD There **are** many old **magazines** in the attic.

STANDARD There**'s** an **attic** filled with old magazines.

5n. Words stating amount are usually singular.

A word or group of words stating an amount of money, time, weight, or measurement is usually considered as one item and takes a singular verb.

EXAMPLES   **Thirty dollars is** a high price for sneakers.
             Three days was all it took.
             Two thirds of the food **was** eaten.

Sometimes, however, the amount is thought of as individual pieces or parts. If so, a plural verb is used.

EXAMPLES   **Thirty** of the **dollars are** his.
             Three of the **days were** spent rehearsing.
             Two thirds of the **doughnuts were** eaten.

5o. The title of a work of art, literature, or music, even when plural in form, takes a singular verb.

In the following sentences, notice that each title takes a singular verb, since it is only one work of art.

EXAMPLES   *Great Expectations* **is** one of my favorite novels. [one book]

             Blue Lines **is** an early painting by Georgia O'Keeffe. [one work of art]

             The Gondoliers **was** presented by the Dramatic Club and the Glee Club. [one opera]

5p. *Every* or *many a* before a subject calls for a singular verb.

EXAMPLES   **Every** student and teacher in our school **has** contributed to the scholarship fund.
             Many a member complained about the high annual dues.

5q. A few nouns, although plural in form, take a singular verb.

Some nouns, although they end in *s,* are considered singular in meaning. The word *news* is a common example; the singular verb is used.

> The **news** of Louis Armstrong's death **was** indeed sad.

Names of certain diseases also end in *s* but are singular nouns: *measles, mumps, rickets.*

> **Mumps has** prevented my little sister's attendance at kindergarten.

Words ending in *–ics* are generally used with a singular verb: *athletics, mathematics, physics, civics, economics, politics, ethics.*

> **Physics is** my most difficult subject.

REVIEW EXERCISE E. *Oral Drill.* Repeat each of the following sentences, stressing the italicized words.

1. *Jo's Boys is* not as well known as Louisa May Alcott's other books, but I found it surprisingly delightful.
2. His chief *worry is* his increasing *debts.*
3. *Many a* man, woman, and child in India *does* not have enough food.
4. Do you feel that *athletics is* overemphasized in your school?
5. *Where are* my *clothes?*
6. My *family plans* to take *its* vacation in August.
7. My *family plan* to take *their* vacations in August.
8. *Are there* any *objections?*
9. *Romeo and Juliet is* a play, a ballet, and a movie.
10. *Two weeks is* enough time to complete the project.

REVIEW EXERCISE F. Number your paper 1–10. Choose the correct verb in parentheses, and write it after the appropriate number.

1. Diane, as well as Lee, (thinks, think) that women should participate more in professional sports.
2. "Snow White and the Seven Dwarfs" (is, are) a children's story which was made into a delightful movie by Walt Disney.
3. Fifteen pounds (is, are) a lot of weight to lose.
4. I simply cannot study when there (is, are) radios, record players, or television sets blaring.
5. Measles (is, are) common among children in the primary grades.
6. Taxes (is, are) a problem facing the governor.
7. Not one of the teachers (intends, intend) to help us with the decorations.
8. The basketball team (was, were) handicapped by injuries in its last game.
9. (Has, Have) either of them seen the sculptures by Isamu Noguchi?
10. In every detective story, there (is, are) usually a motive, suspects, clues, and discovery and punishment.

REVIEW EXERCISE G. Follow the instructions for Review Exercise F.

1. Ulysses S. Grant, along with Zachary Taylor, (was, were) probably better as a general than as a President.
2. Every student (is, are) taking the examination.
3. Her comic manner (adds, add) to the merriment.
4. The captain or a coach (lead, leads) the rally.
5. Paintings by Oscar Howe (have, has) Sioux motifs.
6. Nobody except spiteful people (rejoices, rejoice) at the misfortunes of others.
7. *Promises, Promises* (was, were) the first musical I saw.

8. When I am on the stage, neither my memory nor my voice (is, are) reliable.
9. Why (doesn't, don't) that clever girl join the club?
10. A few of us (has, have) a perfect attendance record.

AGREEMENT OF PRONOUN AND ANTECEDENT

You learned in Chapter 1 that the word to which a pronoun refers is called its *antecedent*. (For example, in the preceding sentence, *pronoun* is the antecedent of *its*.) There should always be agreement between the pronoun and its antecedent.

5r. A pronoun agrees with its antecedent in number and gender.

A few singular personal pronouns have forms that indicate the gender of the antecedent. *He, his,* and *him* are used if the antecedent is masculine. *She, her,* and *hers* are used if the antecedent is feminine. *It* and *its* are used if the antecedent is neither masculine nor feminine.

Study the following sentences, noticing how pronouns and antecedents agree in number and gender.

EXAMPLES   **Marguerite** showed **her** paintings yesterday.
Today **Clarence** will make **his** report.
My **term paper** has as **its** subject "Two Distinguished American Poets."

When the antecedent of a personal pronoun is another kind of pronoun, it is often necessary to look in a phrase following the antecedent to determine gender.

EXAMPLES One of the girls in our group has created
her own design.
Each of the men performed his duties
admirably.

Sometimes the antecedent may be either masculine or feminine; sometimes it may be both. Generally, in standard written English, the masculine form
of the personal pronoun is used to refer to such
antecedents.

EXAMPLES A person can choose his friends but
rarely his relatives.
Every one of the parents is interested in
his own child.

In conversation, you may find it more convenient
to use a plural personal pronoun when referring to
singular antecedents that can be either masculine or
feminine. This form is becoming increasingly popular
in writing as well and may someday become acceptable as standard written English.

EXAMPLES Every member of the class received
their instructions.
Each individual should follow their
own conscience in this matter.

(1) Use a singular pronoun to refer to *each, either,*
neither, one, everyone, everybody, no one, nobody, any-
one, anybody, someone, **or** *somebody.*

EXAMPLES Each of the actors forgot his lines.

One of the birds built its nest there.

Notice in the sentences above that a prepositional
phrase does not alter the number of the antecedent.
The antecedent is singular in each sentence, and a
singular pronoun (*he, she, him, her, it,* or *its*) must
be used for agreement.

EXCEPTION Sometimes the meaning of the antecedents *everyone* and *everybody* is clearly plural. In such cases the plural pronoun should be used.

ABSURD Everyone moaned when he saw the fumble.
BETTER **Everyone** moaned when **they** saw the fumble.

(2) Two or more singular antecedents joined by *or* or *nor* should be referred to by a singular pronoun.

EXAMPLES Neither **Eugene nor Roy** blamed **himself.**
Just then **Jill or Jana** cleared **her** throat.

▶ **USAGE NOTE** You will find that Rules (1) and (2) are often ignored in conversation; nevertheless, they should be followed in writing.

(3) Two or more antecedents joined by *and* should be referred to by a plural pronoun.

EXAMPLES **Nina and Theresa** acted quickly because **they** could see what was going to happen.
Edna and Peter have made up **their** own minds.

EXERCISE 10. Number your paper 1–10. First, copy the antecedents for each blank in the following sentences; then, for each blank, write a pronoun that will agree with its antecedent. Follow the rules for standard written English.

1. A person should not expect too much from —— friends.
2. The bookstore sent Jack and Ray the books that —— had ordered.
3. Norma or Gina will stay after school so that —— can help decorate the room.

4. Several of the convicts refused to eat —— food.
5. Each of the seals caught the fish that were thrown to ——.
6. Both of the boys forgot —— promises.
7. Everyone needs —— own fountain pen.
8. Neither apologized for —— blunder.
9. Each of the players looked unhappy because —— had failed the coach.
10. When Susan sees someone that she knows, she always stops and talks to ——.

EXERCISE 11. Most of the following sentences contain errors in agreement of pronoun and antecedent. Number your paper 1–10. If the sentence is correct, write *C* after the corresponding number. If there is an error in agreement, write the correct form of the pronoun so that it will agree with its antecedent. Follow the rules for standard written English.

1. One of my aunts takes a great deal of pride in her furniture.
2. Knowing this, nobody in our family puts their feet on chairs or sits on beds at Aunt Mary's house.
3. One of her brothers used to think they could be an exception to the rule.
4. Uncle Charlie would often come home late at night, undress in the darkness, and then dive into his bed, nearly knocking every slat out of their place.
5. Each of these plunges left their mark on the rickety bed.
6. At first, both Aunt Mary and my mother offered their advice to Uncle Charlie and asked him to take better care of the furniture.
7. Anybody else in my family would have mended their ways, but not Uncle Charlie; he needed discipline, not advice.
8. Late one night there was a loud crash, and every-

one ran out of their rooms to see what was wrong.
9. Not one of the family could believe their eyes! Lying in the middle of the floor was Uncle Charlie, groaning loudly.
10. If anybody ever asks you why Uncle Charlie suddenly reformed, tell them that one day Aunt Mary merely decided to rearrange her furniture.

REVIEW EXERCISE H. In the sentences below, if the verbs agree with their subjects and the pronouns with their antecedents, write *C* (for *correct*) after the appropriate number on your paper. If the verb does not agree with its subject, or if a pronoun does not agree with its antecedent, write the correct form of the verb or the pronoun after the proper number. Follow the rules for standard written English.

1. Nearly everybody in our crowd collect things. 2. Some of my friends collect stamps, and a few save old coins. 3. One of the girls keep locks of hair clipped from the heads of various friends. 4. Every lock in the collection are put in a small envelope and pasted in a book. 5. Ann Reeves and her two brothers have a collection of old baseball pictures, made as long ago as the 1920's. 6. It seems that almost all of my classmates are always adding to a collection of one kind or another. 7. Each of these friends is proud of his varied assortment.

8. Jack Thompson, however, don't collect anything. 9. One of his favorite pastimes is just watching things—like lizards or birds. 10. If someone goes with Jack on a Saturday walk through the woods, Jack doesn't say much to them. 11. He is too busy watching one of the birds build their nest.

12. Not one of my friends, however, like to read about things as much as I do. 13. Instead of collecting old bottles or watching robins, I learn about things in other lands. 14. Several of my

friends says I read too much *about* doing things without *doing* anything. 15. Each book, as well as every magazine, teaches me far more than some of my friends are willing to admit. 16. For me, the habits of elephants in Africa or of kangaroos in Australia makes interesting reading.
17. In Australia there's many kinds of birds.
18. One of the most interesting birds is the kookaburra. 19. Neither Tina nor Bill knows about the kookaburra, which doesn't live in America. 20. Every one of these birds laugh. 21. It don't chirp, sing, or call as other birds do. 22. Several of them often get together on a fence, and then one of them starts cackling. 23. Quickly the others on the fence add their voices to the chorus. 24. Each bird seems to be enjoying a joke all their own.
25. Any person passing by will notice the noise, and they will soon burst out laughing, too.

Chapter **6**

The Correct Use
of Verbs

**Principal Parts,
Regular and Irregular Verbs**

People frequently use verbs in a nonstandard way. You may hear someone say, "He has spoke," "She swum," "The glasses were broke," or "The book is laying on the table." Nonstandard English is very noticeable in a conversation or in a composition. Nonstandard English in formal speaking or writing may indicate to others a lack of knowledge of the standard usage of English.

THE PRINCIPAL PARTS OF VERBS

The four basic forms of a verb are called the *principal parts* of the verb.

6a. The four principal parts of a verb are the *infinitive*, the *present participle*, the *past*, and the *past participle*.

The four principal parts of the verb *do*, for example, are *do* (infinitive), *doing* (present participle), *did* (past), and *done* (past participle).

EXAMPLES   I **do** my homework after supper.
I am **doing** my homework now.
I **did** my homework this morning.
I have **done** my homework.

Notice that the forms of the present participle and past participle are used with helping verbs — *am, is, are, has, have, had,* etc.

Regular Verbs

6b. A verb that forms its past and past participle forms by adding –*d* or –*ed* to the first principal part (infinitive) is a *regular verb*.[1]

INFINITIVE	PRESENT PARTICIPLE	PAST	PAST PARTICIPLE
use	using	used	(have) used
suppose	supposing	supposed	(have) supposed
risk	risking	risked	(have) risked
ask	asking	asked	(have) asked
dust	dusting	dusted	(have) dusted

You will observe that the present participle of many regular verbs ending in –*e* drops the –*e* before adding –*ing.*

The first principal part (infinitive) of a regular verb presents no usage problems. Errors do occur, however, in the choice of the past and the past participle forms. Do not carelessly omit the –*d* or –*ed* of the past or past participle of regular verbs like those listed above.

NONSTANDARD	Later Elbert ask the teacher.
STANDARD	Later Elbert **asked** the teacher.
NONSTANDARD	She is suppose to be there early.
STANDARD	She is **supposed** to be there early.
NONSTANDARD	We use to ride our bicycles.
STANDARD	We **used** to ride our bicycles.

You can avoid other mistakes with regular verbs

---

[1] A few regular verbs have an alternate past form ending in –*t;* for example, the past form of *burn* may be *burned* or *burnt.*

by correcting faulty spelling and pronunciation of words like *attacked* and *drowned.*

NONSTANDARD Athens was attackted by Sparta.
STANDARD Athens was **attacked** by Sparta.
NONSTANDARD Fortunately nobody had drownded.
STANDARD Fortunately nobody had **drowned.**

EXERCISE 1. *Oral Drill.* Read each sentence aloud, stressing the correct pronunciation of the italicized verb.

1. Bertha *used* to be shy.
2. Jennifer *asked* a few questions.
3. Why has this *happened?*
4. Several were *drowned.*
5. The firefighters *risked* their lives.
6. Are we *supposed* to help?
7. Donald is *experienced.*
8. The product is well *advertised.*
9. The satire *attacked* tyranny.
10. They were *surprised* to see us.
11. He *dusted* the table.
12. They *basked* in the sun.

Irregular Verbs

6c. A verb that forms its past and past participle in some other way than a regular verb is an *irregular verb.*

Irregular verbs form their past and past participle in various ways: by changing the vowel, by changing consonants, by adding *–en,* or by making no change at all.

INFINITIVE	PAST	PAST PARTICIPLE
begin	began	(have) begun
bring	brought	(have) brought
put	put	(have) put

Irregular Verbs Frequently Misused

INFINITIVE	PRESENT PARTICIPLE	PAST	PAST PARTICIPLE
begin	beginning	began	(have) begun
blow	blowing	blew	(have) blown
break	breaking	broke	(have) broken
bring	bringing	brought	(have) brought
burst	bursting	burst	(have) burst
choose	choosing	chose	(have) chosen
come	coming	came	(have) come
do	doing	did	(have) done
drink	drinking	drank	(have) drunk
drive	driving	drove	(have) driven
eat	eating	ate	(have) eaten
fall	falling	fell	(have) fallen
freeze	freezing	froze	(have) frozen
give	giving	gave	(have) given
go	going	went	(have) gone
know	knowing	knew	(have) known
ride	riding	rode	(have) ridden
ring	ringing	rang	(have) rung
run	running	ran	(have) run
see	seeing	saw	(have) seen
shrink	shrinking	shrank	(have) shrunk
speak	speaking	spoke	(have) spoken
steal	stealing	stole	(have) stolen
swim	swimming	swam	(have) swum
take	taking	took	(have) taken
throw	throwing	threw	(have) thrown
write	writing	wrote	(have) written

Since so many English verbs are regular, we naturally tend to make some irregular verbs follow the same pattern. However, you should avoid such forms as *throwed, knowed, bursted,* or *blowed,* which are regarded as nonstandard. If you are in doubt about the parts of a verb, consult your dictionary, which lists the principal parts of irregular verbs.

Remember that the present participle and past participle forms, when used as main verbs (simple predicates) in sentences, always require helping verbs. The present participle is used with forms of the verb *be: am taking, was throwing.* The past participle is used with *have, has,* or *had: have broken, had chosen;* or with a form of *be: was chosen.* When you memorize the principal parts of a verb, you need not worry about the present participle, which always ends in *–ing,* but you will help yourself if you always include *have* with the past participle. As you repeat principal parts, say, for example: *do, did, have done* or *see, saw, have seen.*

NONSTANDARD	I already seen that movie.
STANDARD	I **have** already **seen** that movie.

EXERCISE 2. Your teacher may dictate to you the first principal part of the irregular verbs listed on page 156. Study the list so that you can write from memory the other principal parts of each verb. Place *have* before the past participle.

EXERCISE 3. Number your paper 1–20. If the first principal part is given, change it to the past form. If the past form is given, change it to the past participle. Write *have* before the past participle form.

EXAMPLES
1. give
1. *gave*
2. wrote
2. *have written*

1. do	6. know	11. choose	16. shrank
2. began	7. spoke	12. broke	17. ran
3. see	8. stole	13. drink	18. ring
4. rode	9. blew	14. drove	19. fell
5. went	10. bring	15. froze	20. swim

EXERCISE 4. Number 1–10. Choose the correct one of the two verbs in parentheses, and write it after the corresponding number on your paper. When your paper has been corrected, read each sentence aloud several times, stressing the correct verb.

1. Have you ever (saw, seen) the Grand Canyon?
2. Glowing in the darkness, the lantern fish had (came, come) to the surface.
3. I (drank, drunk) a cup of hot chocolate.
4. Has the nine o'clock bell already (rang, rung)?
5. The water pressure (bursted, burst) the pipes.
6. Thurgood Marshall (give, gave) the majority opinion of the Supreme Court.
7. The clanking under the hood (began, begun) to grow louder.
8. Kathleen (did, done) much to help me.
9. In a matter of seconds, the hot water had (froze, frozen).
10. No one has ever (rode, ridden) that colt before.

EXERCISE 5. Follow the instructions for Exercise 4.

1. I have never (drove, driven) a car in town before.
2. Yesterday I (swam, swum) across the lake.
3. The sweater had (shrunk, shrank) in the wash.
4. Has it (began, begun) to rain?
5. We (brung, brought) our lunches all last week.
6. Gwendolyn Brooks had (wrote, written) sonnets.
7. Have they all (went, gone) swimming already?
8. For fourteen years, I (drank, drunk) milk daily.
9. Suddenly the package (bursted, burst) open.
10. Has Ms. Crane actually (gave, given) us permission to go?

EXERCISE 6. Write two original sentences using correctly each verb you missed in Exercises 4 and 5. Use the form of the verb that you missed. After your sentences have been checked for accuracy, read the sentences aloud until you feel that you have mastered the troublesome verbs.

EXERCISE 7. *Oral Drill.* Read each of the following sentences *aloud* three times, stressing the correct verbs.

1. She *asked* us to go with her.
2. How long *have* you *known* her?
3. They *have broken* the lock.
4. One balloon *burst.*
5. My uncle *came* to see us yesterday.
6. I *had begun* to worry.
7. I *saw* him yesterday.
8. Then the bell *rang.*
9. She *has written* the invitations.
10. He *brought* his first-aid kit.

REVIEW EXERCISE A. Number your paper 1–25. Write the correct form (past or past participle) of the verb given at the beginning of each sentence.

1. *swim*   Avery had —— in deep water before.
2. *break*   The windshield was ——.
3. *run*   Everyone —— as fast as he could.
4. *attack*   Grasshoppers have —— the crops.
5. *eat*   Has Brenda —— breakfast?
6. *write*   Have you —— to your grandmother?
7. *bring*   Anna —— a raincoat yesterday.
8. *give*   After I explained, he —— me another chance.
9. *steal*   A thief had —— our car.
10. *burst*   The pile of brush —— into flames.
11. *drink*   Emma sat down and —— her tea.
12. *use*   When I was a child, I —— to dig tunnels.
13. *do*   She —— her best yesterday.
14. *give*   Sallie has —— us some suggestions.

15. *know*   We have —— about the test for some time.
16. *risk*   The police officer —— her life.
17. *ring*   The bell —— an hour ago.
18. *run*   Last year, Mrs. Evans —— for mayor.
19. *break*   The champion has —— the record.
20. *speak*   Has anyone —— to you about me?
21. *drive*   Have you —— one of the new cars?
22. *choose*   Have they —— a leader?
23. *fall*   You might have —— over the edge.
24. *go*   He has —— after groceries.
25. *speak*   The principal has —— to me about it.

REVIEW EXERCISE B. Follow the instructions for Review Exercise A.

1. *ride*   That actor has never —— a horse.
2. *begin*   It has —— to clear in the north.
3. *come*   I noticed that he —— in late today.
4. *ring*   Has the bell ——?
5. *happen*   Has this —— before?
6. *see*   Last night I —— her at the drugstore.
7. *take*   Since I had —— my camera along, we looked for wildlife as we hiked through the woods.
8. *fall*   A child has —— from the ledge.
9. *climb*   Has he —— the ladder of fame?
10. *go*   I was sure Suellen had —— riding.
11. *drink*   I had —— the milk too fast.
12. *throw*   I should have —— to second base.
13. *freeze*   Had the lake ever —— so early before?
14. *throw*   I —— his letters away when he left.
15. *write*   Janet will have —— me by then.
16. *see*   I have —— the President in person.
17. *ask*   She —— for a dog yesterday.
18. *swim*   Have you ever —— here before?
19. *swim*   I —— here last summer.
20. *shrink*   Had that material —— in the washing?

21. *choose* By the end of next week, we will have
—— our class officers.
22. *blow*   Yesterday the wind —— with gale force.
23. *take*   I haven't —— the test yet.
24. *write* She had —— down the new address.
25. *drown* The number of people who —— last
summer is alarmingly high.

REVIEW EXERCISE C. Number your paper 1–20.
Read each of the following sentences aloud. If a
sentence is correct, write *C* after the proper number.
If the form of a verb is wrong, write the correct verb
form after the appropriate number.

1. There is no single incident that begun the French
Revolution of 1789.
2. After surrendering to the Union forces, General
Robert E. Lee ask that his soldiers be allowed to
keep their horses.
3. On May 6, 1937, the German airship *Hindenburg*
burst into flames while approaching Lakehurst,
New Jersey.
4. In medieval days, a person might be drownded
as punishment for a capital offense.
5. By nightfall Anita had drove 500 miles.
6. The Greeks attackted the city of Troy, and the
siege lasted ten years.
7. Many people wept upon hearing that the Alamo
had fell.
8. Jesse Owens run the 100-meter dash to tie the
world record.
9. During the Revolutionary War, continental dollars shrank in value and became almost worthless.
10. When the ball cleared the left-field fence, millions
of television viewers knew that Hank Aaron had
broke Babe Ruth's home run record.
11. Carson McCullers, a twentieth-century novelist,
has wrote about her memories of the South.

12. Harpies were mythical winged creatures who were suppose to have the bodies of birds and the faces of women.
13. According to legend, many knights had risk their lives while they were searching for the Holy Grail, the cup which was used at the Last Supper.
14. After Satan in *Paradise Lost* had cautiously swum, crawled, and flown through Chaos, he reached the ladder extending from Heaven to Earth.
15. Beowulf drunk deeply from the mead cup after defeating Grendel.
16. After Alice had fell down the rabbit hole, she found a bottle with a curious label which had the instruction, "Drink me."
17. When the death bell rung for her lover, Barbara Allan knew that it was also ringing for her.
18. The Green Knight, who come dressed entirely in green, challenged one of King Arthur's men. "I dare you to cut off my head with an ax."
19. According to the ancients, Atlantis, an island supposedly west of the Pillars of Hercules, had sunk to the bottom of the ocean.
20. Romeo had chose to die rather than live without Juliet.

Tense

We speak of the time expressed by a verb as the *tense* of the verb. Every verb has six tenses: the *present tense,* the *past tense,* the *future tense,* the *present perfect tense,* the *past perfect tense,* and the *future perfect tense.* The tenses are formed from the principal parts.

Study the list of the six tense forms of *fly* on the next page. Giving all the forms of a verb in this way is called *conjugating* the verb; the list is called a *conjugation.*

Conjugation of Fly

Present Tense

Singular	Plural
I fly	we fly
you fly	you fly
he flies	they fly

Past Tense

Singular	Plural
I flew	we flew
you flew	you flew
he flew	they flew

Future Tense

Singular	Plural
I will (shall) fly	we will (shall) fly
you will fly	you will fly
he will fly	they will fly

Present Perfect Tense

Singular	Plural
I have flown	we have flown
you have flown	you have flown
he has flown	they have flown

Past Perfect Tense

Singular	Plural
I had flown	we had flown
you had flown	you had flown
he had flown	they had flown

Future Perfect Tense

Singular	Plural
I will (shall) have flown	we will (shall) have flown
you will have flown	you will have flown
he will have flown	they will have flown

Each of the six tenses has an additional form called the *progressive form,* which expresses continuing action. It consists of a form of the verb *be* plus the present participle of the verb. The progressive forms of *fly* follow.

Present Progressive	am, are, is flying
Past Progressive	was, were flying
Future Progressive	will (shall) be flying
Present Perfect Progressive	has, have been flying
Past Perfect Progressive	had been flying
Future Perfect Progressive	will (shall) have been flying

Remember: the progressive is not a separate tense but an additional form of each of the six tenses in the conjugation.

Consistency of Tense

6d. Do not change needlessly from one tense to another.

When writing about events in the past, choose verbs in the past tense. Do not suddenly shift, without reason, to the present. Similarly, if action takes place in the present, do not use verbs in the past tense unnecessarily.

NONSTANDARD Chris grabbed her coat and rushes out. [The verb *grabbed* is past tense; *rushes* is present tense.]

STANDARD Chris **grabbed** her coat and **rushed** out. [Both *grabbed* and *rushed* are in the past tense.]

NONSTANDARD When my brother cried, he wins the argument. [*Cried* is past tense, and *wins* is present.]

STANDARD When my brother **cries,** he **wins** the argument. [The verbs are both in the present tense.]

or When my brother **cried,** he **won** the argument. [Both verbs are in the past tense.]

The perfect tenses are mainly used in expressing action that has been completed, or finished. When one thing happened before something else, the perfect tense form shows the relation.

NONSTANDARD I immediately felt sorry that I spoke so harshly. [Since *felt* is past tense and the speaking preceded it, the verb should be *had spoken,* not *spoke.*]

STANDARD I immediately felt sorry that I **had spoken** so harshly.

EXERCISE 8. Rewrite the following paragraph, eliminating the needless changes of tense. First decide whether the paragraph should be told in the present or past tense. Then you will need to change the tense of many of the verbs to achieve consistency.

It all started as soon as I came home from school. I am in my room, and I have planned to study for two hours. It was about five o'clock. To my surprise, Nancy Chang decided to drop by. She dashes into the house, slams the door behind her, and yells for me. What she wanted is a fishing companion. She has been thinking about going fishing all week. Getting my gear together, I become excited and can almost see the fish fighting over which one is to be my first catch. On our way out to the lake, we see clouds begin to form, and we knew we are in for trouble. It rains all right, for the whole weekend. Once again the fish had been granted a week's reprieve.

ACTIVE AND PASSIVE VOICE

A verb is said to be in the *active* voice when it expresses an action performed *by* its subject. A verb is in the *passive* voice when the action it expresses is performed *upon* its subject.

ACTIVE VOICE   The manager hired us. [The subject performs the action.]

PASSIVE VOICE   We were hired by the manager. [The subject receives the action.]

Only transitive verbs — those that can take objects — can be used in the passive voice. Compare the subjects of the following related sentences:

ACTIVE   The $\overset{\text{S}}{\text{judge}}$ carefully instructed the $\overset{\text{O}}{\text{jury}}$.

PASSIVE   The $\overset{\text{S}}{\text{jury}}$ was carefully instructed by the judge.

Notice that the object of the active sentence has become the subject of the passive one. The subject of the active sentence is expressed in the passive sentence only in a prepositional phrase. In fact, it can be omitted from the passive sentence altogether.

PASSIVE   The jury was carefully instructed.

The verb in a passive sentence is always a verb phrase that includes a form of the verb *be* and the past participle of the main verb. If other helping verbs appear in the active sentence, they must also be included in the passive. Here are some more examples of related active and passive sentences:

ACTIVE   Willa $\overset{\text{S}}{\text{Cather}}$ **wrote** $\overset{\text{O}}{My\ Ántonia}$.

PASSIVE $My\ \overset{\text{S}}{Ántonia}$ **was written** by Willa Cather.

S   O
ACTIVE   Someone **has stolen** my watch.

S
PASSIVE   My watch **has been stolen.**

The passive voice puts the emphasis on the person or thing receiving the action rather than upon the one performing it. It is often used in situations in which the speaker does not know or does not wish to say who performed the action (as in the last example above). Although useful for these purposes, the passive construction can easily be overused. A succession of passive sentences has a weak and awkward sound and should be avoided.

EXERCISE 9. Number from 1–10. After the appropriate number, indicate whether each of the following sentences is active or passive.

1. The whole club elects the president.
2. A terrible accident has been prevented by Mario's quick thinking.
3. The leading role was played brilliantly by an understudy.
4. The book was unfavorably reviewed by the critics.
5. A fan recognized the popular movie star.
6. At first, the prophet's advice was ignored.
7. The mayor usually leads the discussion.
8. Children of many different countries play that game.
9. The contributions to jazz music by W. C. Handy are appreciated by all.
10. W. C. Handy composed the blues classic "St. Louis Woman."

EXERCISE 10. Change the active verbs in the sentences in Exercise 9 to passives, and the passive verbs to active ones.

EXAMPLE 1. Anne wrote the skit.
1. *The skit was written by Anne.*

SPECIAL PROBLEMS WITH VERBS

Lie and *Lay*

The verb *lie* means "to rest" or "to recline," "to remain in a lying position." Its principal parts are *lie, lying, lay, (have) lain.* The verb *lie* never takes an object.

The verb *lay* means "to put" or "to place (something)." Its principal parts are *lay, laying, laid, (have) laid.* These forms may have objects (receivers of the action).

INFINITIVE	PRESENT PARTICIPLE	PAST	PAST PARTICIPLE
lie (to rest)	lying	lay	(have) lain
lay (to put)	laying	laid	(have) laid

Study these examples of the use of the verb *lie,* meaning "to rest" or "to recline."

Occasionally I **lie** down.
The letter **is lying** on the desk.
Yesterday Bennett **lay** on the sand.
How long **have** you **lain** here?

Notice how the following examples of the use of the verb *lay* differ from those above. In the sentences below, each verb means "to put" or "to place (something)."

Lay the boards down.
I **was laying** the letter on the desk.
Yesterday Bennett **laid** these towels on the sand.
Have you **laid** your work aside?

If you do not habitually use these verbs correctly, you must begin your work on them slowly and thoughtfully. Only by taking time to think through each form you use can you eventually establish the habit of using the verbs correctly. When faced with a *lie–lay* problem, ask yourself two questions:

1. What is the meaning I intend? Is it "to be in a lying position," or is it "to put something down"?

2. What is the time expressed by the verb, and which principal part is required to express this time?

Remember that the verb *lie* may be used to describe the lying position of inanimate objects as well as people and animals. Regardless of its having once been put down, the object *lies* (not *lays*) there.

PROBLEM	After the alarm had awakened me, I (lay, laid) in bed too long.
Question 1	Meaning? The meaning here is "to remain in a lying position." The verb which means "to remain in a lying position" is *lie*.
Question 2	Principal part? The time is past and requires the past form, which is *lay*. [lie, *lay*, lain]
SOLUTION	After the alarm had awakened me, I **lay** in bed too long.
PROBLEM	Lamont (lay, laid) his coat on the table.
Question 1	Meaning? The meaning here is "to put." The verb which means "to put" is *lay*.
Question 2	Principal part? The time is past and therefore requires the past form, which is *laid*. [lay, *laid*, laid]
SOLUTION	Lamont **laid** his coat on the table.
PROBLEM	How long had it (lain, laid) there?
Question 1	Meaning? The meaning here is "to be in a lying position." The verb which means "to be in a lying position" is *lie*.
Question 2	Principal part? The time requires the

past participle with *had*. The past participle of *lie* is *lain*. [lie, lay, *lain*]

SOLUTION   How long **had** it **lain** there?

EXERCISE 11. *Oral Drill.* Read each of the following sentences aloud several times. In the light of the information just given, be able to explain why the verb is correct.

1. I foolishly *laid* the matches near the open fire.
2. Yesterday I *lay* too long in the hot sun.
3. A book *was lying* on the floor.
4. Nina *was laying* the books on the table.
5. Diane *laid* the cushion on the floor.
6. The cushion *lay* there while she dusted the chair.
7. The rake and hoe *have lain* in the yard for days.
8. The construction workers *have laid* the foundations.
9. His interests *lie* elsewhere.
10. Yesterday I *laid* the scissors on the machine, and they are probably *lying* there now.

EXERCISE 12. After numbering 1–10, write the correct form of the proper verb (*lie–lay*) for each of these sentences. Make a perfect score by referring to the forms on page 168 if necessary.

1. An old mine used to —— at the foot of the mountain.
2. He —— his glasses aside and frowned.
3. I shall —— down for a few minutes.
4. She had —— on the divan before.
5. The baby was still —— quietly in the cradle.
6. The father —— the baby in the cradle an hour ago.
7. Is the newspaper —— in the rain?
8. No, I have —— the paper near the fire to dry.
9. Last summer my dog often —— in his doghouse.
10. —— down, Snoopy.

EXERCISE 13. Complete the explanation of the correct usage of *lie* and *lay* by filling in the blanks below with the right form of each verb. Use a separate sheet of paper, and number your answers correctly.

The verb (1) ―― means "to put" or "to place (something)." The present participle of *lay* is (2) ――. The past and the past participle have the same form, which is (3) ――. The infinitive form is (4) ――.

The verb (5) ―― means "to rest" or "to recline." The present participle of *lie* is (6) ――. The past form of *lie* is (7) ――, and the past participle is (8) ――.

The verb (9) ――, with all of its forms, never has an object; however, the forms of (10) ―― may have objects.

Sit and Set

The verb *sit* means "to rest in an upright, sitting position." The principal parts of *sit* are *sit, sitting, sat, (have) sat.*

The verb *set* means "to put," "to place (something)." The principal parts of *set* are *set, setting, set, (have) set.*

INFINITIVE	PRESENT PARTICIPLE	PAST	PAST PARTICIPLE
sit (to rest)	sitting	sat	(have) sat
set (to put)	setting	set	(have) set

Study the following examples:

Sit down.	Vases **sit** on the shelf.
Set that down.	I **set** them on the shelf.

You will have little difficulty using these verbs correctly if you will remember two facts about them: (1) Like *lie,* the verb *sit* means "to be in a certain position." It almost never has an object. (2) Like *lay,* the verb *set* means "to put (something)." It may take an object. *Set* does not change to form the past or the past participle. Whenever you mean "to place" or "to put," use *set*.[1]

EXERCISE 14. *Oral Drill.* Read the sentences below aloud several times. Think of the *meaning* of the verbs, and do not go on to other exercises until you feel that you know the right uses of *sit* and *set.*

1. I usually *sit* close to the stove.
2. I *set* the chair close to the wall.
3. Faye *was sitting* beside Keith.
4. Faye *was setting* the canned goods on the shelf.
5. Don't just *sit* there; *set* the dishes in the sink.
6. The grapes *are sitting* on the coffee table.
7. Where *was* he *setting* it?
8. I *have* never *sat* in this rocker before.
9. I *have* never *set* aside enough money for a trip.
10. Estelle *sat* down and *set* the picture on the easel.

EXERCISE 15. Number 1–10 on your paper. Fill the blanks in the following sentences with a correct form of *sit* or *set,* whichever is required by the meaning.

1. Have you —— the flowers in the sunshine?
2. Will Mrs. Davis —— at the head of the table?
3. I was —— on the steps.
4. I was —— the lamp beside the sofa.
5. Father has been —— out some tomato plants.
6. Yesterday Katherine —— near James.
7. The excited children will not —— still.
8. The old car is still —— in the garage.
9. We had —— there an hour.
10. Has Vernon —— in the front row all year?

---

[1] There are several uses of the verb *set* which do not mean "to put" or "to place"; for example: "The sun *sets,*" "Hens *set* on eggs," "*set* one's watch," "*set* a speed record," "*set* out to do something."

Rise and Raise

The verb *rise* means "to go in an upward direction." Its principal parts are *rise, rising, rose, (have) risen.* Like *lie* the verb *rise* never has an object.

The verb *raise* means "to move something in an upward direction." Its principal parts are *raise, raising, raised, (have) raised.* Like *lay* and *set, raise* may take an object.

INFINITIVE	PRESENT PARTICIPLE	PAST	PAST PARTICIPLE
rise (to go up)	rising	rose	(have) risen
raise (to move something up)	raising	raised	(have) raised

> You **should rise** early.
> Who **will raise** the flag?
> Prices **rose.**
> Grocers **raised** prices.

EXERCISE 16. *Oral Drill.* Repeat each of the following sentences aloud three times, stressing the italicized verbs and thinking of the *meaning* of the sentence.

1. The sun *has* already *risen.*
2. I *raised* my hand.
3. The river *rises* in the spring.
4. My family *rises* early.
5. We *raise* our voices.
6. The woman *rose* from her chair.
7. The man *raised* his eyebrow.
8. By noon the fog had *risen.*
9. When should the flag be *raised?*

EXERCISE 17. Number 1–10, and write the correct form of *rise* or *raise* for each of the following blanks.

1. The prisoner will —— and face the jury.
2. Last week, the committee —— no objections.
3. When will the moon ——?
4. Has the legislature —— taxes?
5. The biscuits have ——.
6. The curtain will —— at 8:30.
7. Todd will —— the curtain.
8. The price of gasoline has —— steadily.
9. When the President entered the room, all the reporters ——.
10. Ms. Henly had —— to speak.

REVIEW EXERCISE D. Correctly use each of the following as verbs in a sentence.

1. rise   5. was lying   9. has been rising
2. raised   6. was laying   10. had lain
3. have sat   7. will sit
4. have set   8. has been setting

REVIEW EXERCISE E. *Oral Drill.* Answer the following questions in complete sentences by choosing correct verb forms.

1. Do you lie or lay down for a nap?
2. Does the temperature rise or raise?
3. Have the guests sat or set down?
4. Have they lain or laid the foundation for the building?
5. Had the team's morale risen or raised?
6. Has a picture been sitting or setting on the table?
7. Was the rug lying or laying near the fire?
8. Was Elena lying or laying the rug near the fire?

REVIEW EXERCISE F. Number your paper 1–20. Choose the correct verb in parentheses, and write it after the proper number.

1. (Lie, Lay) the magazine on the coffee table.

2. The magazine is (lying, laying) on the coffee table.
3. Scott (sat, set) the birdcage in the backyard.
4. The cage (sits, sets) in the backyard.
5. Kate (rose, raised) from her chair and went to the door.
6. The kite was swiftly (rising, raising) skyward.
7. He (lay, laid) on the bank and looked at the stars.
8. Has Mother (lain, laid) down yet?
9. The paper is (lying, laying) on the sidewalk.
10. The river is (rising, raising) steadily.
11. We were (sitting, setting) on a large rock.
12. A hand-painted vase (sits, sets) on the mantelpiece.
13. He had already (lain, laid) the cloth on the table.
14. (Sit, Set) down and talk for a while.
15. I (lay, laid) the keys there a few minutes ago.
16. The main pipes (lay, laid) under the floor.
17. A rope was (lying, laying) near the saddle.
18. The sun is (rising, raising) now.
19. Had you (sat, set) on her hat?
20. (Lying, Laying) in the top drawer was the necklace.

REVIEW EXERCISE G. Correctly use each of the following verbs in brief sentences. Supply appropriate helping verbs if needed.

1. set	6. drunk	11. chose	16. rode
2. laid	7. shrank	12. begun	17. rang
3. rose	8. raised	13. went	18. fell
4. give	9. lying	14. seen	19. lain
5. done	10. laying	15. wrote	20. burst

REVIEW EXERCISE H. Number your paper 1–25. After the number of the corresponding sentence, write the correct form of the verb given at the beginning of the sentence. In some instances you will have to add *have, has,* or *had.*

1. *rise, raise*   When the ship came within firing range, a pirate flag was ——.

2. *ask*   The telephone interviewer —— the people she called who their favorite comedian was.

3. *lie, lay*   The committee —— aside all personal feelings and tried to find a solution to their common problem.

4. *take*   The editor had —— all responsibility for the story in the newspaper.

5. *read*   I was halfway through the assignment before I realized that I —— it the day before.

6. *swim*   While we were lowering sail, a group of natives —— out to our boat.

7. *choose*   She —— her words carefully when she spoke to the professor.

8. *suppose*   The captured sailor —— that the captain of the pirates would make him walk the plank.

9. *lie, lay*   Very tired, she —— on the bank of the river and waited for her friends.

10. *see*   How could the thief be so sure that no one —— him?

11. *know*   My friend —— that she had been tricked after she had waited thirty minutes for the rest of the guests to arrive.

12. *begin*   Scientists have —— to explore the polar regions extensively.

13. *sit, set*   After the children had —— still for fifteen minutes, they began to squirm.

14. *choose*   The company has —— its employees carefully and has assigned them to appropriate jobs.

15. *burst*   The monkeys —— out of their cages and headed for the forest.

16. *take*   As the country began to look more and more unfamiliar, we began to

	sense that we —— a wrong turn miles before.
17. *use*	Until the medical supplies arrived, the survivors —— their shirts for bandages.
18. *rise, raise*	Some writers of ghost tales like to create people who have —— from the dead.
19. *break*	Records in track and field are —— every year.
20. *shrink*	Either I have grown a lot since last spring, or else this suit has ——.
21. *write*	Did you know that Carole King has often —— music for herself and others to sing?
22. *lie, lay*	For centuries minerals and other natural resources on the ocean floor have —— untouched by humans.
23. *come*	As usual, Jerry —— rushing up to me and slapped me hard on the back.
24. *sink*	The *Merrimack* had —— several ships before it was met by the *Monitor*, the Union's vessel.
25. *give*	The crazed and fiendish hunter —— the man whom he intended to capture a day's head start.

REVIEW EXERCISE I. Number 1–25 in a column on your paper. Read each of the following sentences aloud, and determine whether the verbs are correct or incorrect. If the sentence is correct, write a plus sign (+) after the corresponding number. If a verb in a sentence is misused, write a zero (0) after the proper number. Be prepared to give the correct verb form for each sentence that you label 0. Some sentences may have more than one incorrect verb.

1. I use to want a pet monkey all my own. 2. About a year ago, I set in a park for hours and watch the

antics of the caged monkeys. 3. Since I've took care of Corky, though, I haven't had the slightest desire to have a monkey.

4. Alexis, my friend who owns the monkey, ask me to keep Corky for six hours. 5. Since I was very pleased about keeping a real monkey all afternoon, Alexis brung Corky over early one Saturday. 6. About one o'clock, after Alexis had went on her way, I made friends with the monkey. 7. For a while we chose to play in the yard.

8. The trouble began when I went into the house to lie down for a nap. 9. As soon as Corky saw me laying on the bed, she started to think of mischief. 10. I seen that she was not ready to settle down. 11. Suddenly she jump upon a chair, raised her arms, grabbed the pictures on the wall, and began to throw them at me. 12. I sat up and warned Corky to behave. 13. After rising from my bed, I tied the scoundrel to the leg of the bed.

14. After I had lain down again, I bursted out laughing at her angry chattering. 15. No harm had been done; none of the picture frames were broken. 16. Soon, however, Corky thought of a new way to annoy me; her chain give her enough freedom to climb upon the high bedstead. 17. After sitting there quietly for an instant, she jump hard, right onto the middle of my stomach. 18. I howled, "You've went too far, Corky!" 19. Defiantly putting her hands over her ears, Corky begun to bounce up and down as though she were celebrating a major victory.

20. After she had attack me, I no longer wanted her around. 21. Picking her up, I set her outside on the back porch. 22. Then I gave her some peanuts and went back to lie down. 23. I had to bribe her because I knowed that I couldn't teach her any manners.

24. When Alexis finally came for Corky, I was never so happy to get rid of a guest. 25. After what she done, I won't ever invite that monkey—or any other monkey—to my house again.

Chapter 7

The Correct Use of Pronouns

Nominative and Objective Uses

Nouns and pronouns have *case*. The case of a noun or pronoun depends upon the word's use in the sentence. In English, there are three cases: *nominative, objective,* and *possessive.*

Choosing the correct case form for a noun is no problem, since the form remains the same in the nominative and objective cases.

EXAMPLE The **girl** [nominative] blamed another **girl** [objective].

Only in the possessive case does a noun change its form, usually by adding an apostrophe and an *s*.

EXAMPLE One **girl's** handbag matched another **girl's** shoes.

Personal pronouns, however, have various case forms. In the following sentence, for example, the pronouns in bold-faced type all refer to the same person. They have three different forms because of their different uses.

EXAMPLE **I** [nominative] do not think that **my** [possessive] big brother understands **me** [objective].

You can avoid using pronouns incorrectly by learning the case forms of pronouns and their use in sentences.

THE CASE FORMS OF PERSONAL PRONOUNS

Study the following list of personal pronouns, noticing the changes in form.

Personal Pronouns

NOMINATIVE CASE	OBJECTIVE CASE	POSSESSIVE CASE
	Singular	
I	me	my, mine
you	you	your, yours
he, she, it	him, her, it	his, her, hers, its
	Plural	
we	us	our, ours
you	you	your, yours
they	them	their, theirs

As you see, *you* and *it* have the same form in the nominative and the objective case. You may therefore ignore them in your study of correct pronoun usage. Only the following pronouns have different nominative and objective forms. Memorize both lists.

NOMINATIVE CASE	OBJECTIVE CASE
I	me
he	him
she	her
we	us
they	them

EXERCISE 1. Number your paper 1–10. If the pronoun is in the nominative case, write the corresponding objective case pronoun; if it is in the objective

case, write the corresponding nominative case pronoun.

1. they	6. he
2. him	7. I
3. me	8. them
4. we	9. us
5. she	10. her

THE NOMINATIVE CASE

7a. The subject of a verb is in the nominative case.

EXAMPLES   **He** and **I** joined a book club.
We students are planning a field trip.
She was glad that **they** were elected.

In the first sentence, *He* and *I* are subjects of the verb *joined*. In the second, *We* is the subject of *are planning*. In the third, *She* is the subject of *was; they* is the subject of *were elected,* the verb in the subordinate clause.

Most errors in the use of pronouns as subjects are made when the subject is compound, particularly when both parts of the compound subject are pronouns.

COMPOUND SUBJECT   **She** and **they** passed the test.

You can often avoid using the incorrect form by trying each pronoun separately with the verb. Of course you would never say *Him passed the test* or *Them passed the test.*

> **She** passed the test. **They** passed the test.
> **She** and **they** passed the test.

Sometimes a pronoun will have a noun appositive.[1]

> **We students** have volunteered to count ballots.

---

[1] For the definition of an appositive, see page 102.

You can arrive at the correct form for the pronoun in such sentences by reading the sentence without the noun appositive: *We have volunteered to count ballots.*

Sometimes the pronouns *we* and *they* sound awkward when used as parts of a compound subject. In such instances, it is often advisable to restate the sentence.

AWKWARD We and they hope to sit together at the game.

BETTER We hope to sit with them at the game.

EXERCISE 2. *Oral Drill.* Read each sentence aloud, stressing the correct italicized pronouns.

1. *We* girls built a pyramid of snowballs.
2. *She* and her sister have suggested three additional ways to conserve fuel.
3. Why do you and *she* quarrel?
4. May *he* and *I* be partners?
5. Can you or *she* do twenty-five push-ups?
6. Where are Willy and *they?*
7. My brother and *I* knew that he would crash the party.
8. *We* girls learned that Ben and *she* were blamed.
9. Both *he* and *she* understood that *we* students needed to rest.
10. It was decided that *he* and *I* had tied.

EXERCISE 3. Number 1–10 on your paper. List the pronouns that are used as subjects in the following sentences. Do not include *you.*

1. In yesterday's game, we halfbacks ran effective interference.
2. Neither she nor Al has promised anything.
3. I hope that you and I can go to camp this summer.
4. Why did you and she refuse our invitation?
5. We think that you and they will like this joke.

6. Either you or I must take Pat to the zoo tomorrow.
7. Do you know why she and I were late?
8. We two have been neighbors since childhood.
9. Both Denise Tanaka and he were prompt.
10. Both he and I enjoyed preparing the report.

EXERCISE 4. Use the following as subjects in sentences of your own.

1. he and I
2. Harvey and we
3. we amateurs
4. you and I
5. Jane and he

6. her parents and she
7. Mary, Pedro, and they
8. she and my best friend
9. they and their escorts
10. you girls and we boys

7b. A predicate nominative is in the nominative case.

A predicate nominative is a noun or pronoun that follows a linking verb and explains or identifies the subject of the sentence (see pages 66–67). A pronoun used as a predicate nominative always follows a form of the verb *be* or verb phrases ending in *be* or *been*.

EXAMPLES   This is **he.**
It may be **she.**
It should have been **they.**

► USAGE NOTE   Listening to conversations, you will often hear people say, "It's me." Although *I*, not *me*, is the nominative case pronoun, widespread usage has made *It's me* acceptable spoken English. Either *It's me* or *It's I* is acceptable. Similar expressions such as *That's him* or *Could it have been her?* (in which the rule calls for *he* and *she*) may be considered as acceptable in speaking, but you should avoid them in writing.

As you do the following exercises, follow the rule for written English: *A predicate nominative is in the nominative case.*

EXERCISE 5. Number 1–10 on your paper. Complete the following sentences by adding pronouns in the nominative case used as predicate nominatives. Write each pronoun after the corresponding number on your paper. Don't use *you* or *it;* use a variety of pronouns.

1. This is ——.
2. Are you ——?
3. That was ——.
4. Those are ——.
5. Can it be ——?
6. It can't be ——.
7. It is ——.
8. It might be ——.
9. Was that ——?
10. I knew it was ——.

THE OBJECTIVE CASE

The following pronouns are in the objective case:

me	us
him, her	them

These pronouns are used as objects: direct objects, indirect objects, objects of prepositions. (Review pages 67–70 and 79–80.)

7c. **The direct object of a verb is in the objective case.**

STANDARD   Clyde thanked **her.** [*Clyde* is the subject of the verb *thanked.* Clyde thanked *whom?* The answer is *her,* which is the direct object of *thanked.*]

NONSTANDARD   Dad's story surprised Miles and I. [*I* is a nominative case pronoun and should not be used as direct object of the verb.]

STANDARD   Dad's story surprised Miles and **me.**

When the object is compound, try each pronoun object separately as you learned to do with compound subjects. "Dad's story surprised I" is obviously incorrect. Hence, "Dad's story surprised Miles and I" is also incorrect.

NONSTANDARD	He helped we students with our homework.
STANDARD	He helped **us** students with our homework.

EXERCISE 6. *Oral Drill.* Recite each of the following sentences aloud, stressing the correct italicized pronouns. After you become familiar with the right sound of pronouns, your ear will tell you which pronoun is correct.

1. The letter carrier disappointed Nilda and *me*.
2. The Solomons did not invite *us* boys.
3. The magician's tricks amazed their teacher and *them*.
4. Vanessa often imitates Caroline and *her*.
5. Won't you believe *us* girls?
6. Have you seen *her* or *him* lately?
7. A lost child was following *her* and *me*.
8. Did Mr. Cass take Willis and *them* to the banquet?
9. Julia said that she recognized *her* and *me* at once.
10. Did you call *them* or *us?*

EXERCISE 7. Number 1–10 on your paper. Supply appropriate pronouns for the blanks in these sentences. Use a variety of pronouns. (Do not use *you* or *it.*) After you have checked the exercise, read each sentence aloud.

1. The doorbell startled Allen and ——.
2. Will you oppose —— or ——?
3. Johnny Estrada loves both —— and ——.
4. Can't you trust Aline and ——?
5. Aline and —— you cannot trust!
6. I found Nancy and —— hard at work.
7. We watched Clay and ——.
8. Sue Tam took Janet and —— to the game.
9. Now he needs you and —— more than ever.
10. Those jeans fit both Hilda and ——.

7d. The indirect object of the verb is in the objective case.

As you have already learned, an indirect object tells *to whom* or *for whom* something is done. (See pages 69–70.) Pronouns used as indirect objects are in the objective case: *me, him, her, us, them.*

EXAMPLES The teacher paid **her** a compliment.
Polly sent **me** some photographs.

EXERCISE 8. *Oral Drill.* Recite each of the following sentences aloud, stressing the correct italicized pronouns.

1. Nora made Roy and *me* a carrot cake.
2. Show Ruth and *her* your ring.
3. They will bring you and *him* some pamphlets.
4. Will you please fix Alba and *me* some lunch?
5. Mrs. Carter handed *him* and *her* questionnaires.
6. Our teacher gave *us* students a test.
7. The principal told *her* and *me* the news.
8. Did Howard buy *him* and *her* what I suggested?
9. Send Bob and *me* a postcard from Florida.
10. Tell Jack and *me* what you told your parents and *them.*

REVIEW EXERCISE A. Number 1–25. Write after the proper number the correct pronoun in parentheses. Be prepared to give the use of each pronoun in the sentence.

1. Where have you and (she, her) been?
2. (He, Him) and (I, me) have been to the fair.
3. (We, Us) boys spent hours looking at the displays.
4. One of the guides showed (we, us) boys a new computer model.
5. She told Angus and (I, me) about the computer's capability.

6. Another guide and (she, her) turned on the computer.
7. After (they, them) had pushed a few buttons, the cathode-ray tube lit up, and words appeared on the screen.
8. One of the guides asked Angus and (I, me) if (we, us) wanted to operate the controls.
9. (He, Him) and I quickly agreed and asked for instructions.
10. In under an hour, we surprised (they, them) with our ability to use the computer.
11. Angus and (I, me) then found another display at the fair.
12. A girl named Sarah showed Angus and (I, me) all kinds of pottery.
13. (She, Her) and her sister were selling the handmade pottery at discount prices.
14. We bought two bowls and a vase from Sarah and (she, her).
15. They gave (us, we) boys an extra bowl as a gift.
16. (They, Them) and the other people at the fair seemed to enjoy their work.
17. Have you and (she, her) ever seen their "House of Chills"?
18. (Him, He) and (I, me) were horrified by the appearance of Dracula.
19. Of course, (they, them) and (we, us) knew that it was a wax statue.
20. As we have told you and (she, her), we later visited the "House of Magic."
21. A clown and his partner singled out (we, us) boys to tease.
22. Seeing my white sweater, the clown and (he, him) scooted over to me.
23. (He, Him) and his partner kept waving very big fountain pens in the air.
24. When they squirted black ink all over my white sweater, you can imagine how worried he and (I, me) were.

25. In a matter of seconds, however, (we, us) boys
watched the magic ink disappear before our eyes.

7e. The object of a preposition is in the objective case.

A prepositional phrase begins with a preposition (see
the list on pages 29–30) and ends with a noun or pronoun. The final word in a prepositional phrase is the
object of the preposition that begins the phrase. When
the object of a preposition is a pronoun, you must be
careful to use the objective case. The words in bold-
faced type below are objects of prepositions.

to **me**	before **her**	for **them**
by **him**	beyond **us**	

Errors in usage often occur when the object of a
preposition is compound. Again, you can usually tell
the correct pronouns by trying each one separately
in the prepositional phrase.

toward Rachel and **her**	with **you** and **them**
except Suzanne and **us**	about Joe and **him**

EXERCISE 9. *Oral Drill.* Read each of the following
sentences aloud, stressing the italicized words.

1. *Beside* Jess and *me* sat Mrs. Bigay.
2. I wrote notes *to* my sister and *her.*
3. The boldness *of* Mark and *them* startled Lee.
4. *Between* you and *me,* she is worried *about him.*
5. Dr. Williams rode in her car *in front of us* students.
6. She was very rude *to them* and *me.*
7. The man was walking *toward* Dale and *her.*
8. With the help *of* Tamara and *him,* we can soon
finish.
9. Discuss your plans *with her* and *them.*
10. Did you sit *near him* and *her* in assembly?

EXERCISE 10. Number 1–10 on your paper. If the

sentence is correct, write *C.* If there are pronoun errors, write the prepositional phrase, correcting the pronoun forms.

EXAMPLES   1. Did you go with Flora and them?
           1. *C*
          2. I sent copies of the report to both Mac and she.
          2. *to both Mac and her*

1. Nobody but Julie and me volunteered.
2. Everyone slept except Barry and I.
3. Like he and us, she has the flu.
4. I have received no word from Jack or she.
5. Mr. Welch pointed toward we students.
6. In front of Antonia and him stood Ella.
7. Shall we visit later with Karen and them?
8. Karana, like you and I, dislikes tea.
9. In addition to her and me, Oscar will serve on the committee.
10. Between you and I, no one here wants to participate in that project.

▶ **USAGE NOTE** Pronouns used in apposition are in the same case as the word to which they refer.

EXAMPLES   The committee members, **he, she,** and **I,** made our report. [Since *members* is the subject of the sentence, the pronouns in apposition with it (*he, she, I*) must be in the nominative case.]

Every player except two, **him** and **her,** was eliminated from the tournament. [Since *two* is the object of the preposition *except,* the appositives must be in the objective case.]

The master of ceremonies introduced the cocaptains, Linda and **me.** [Since *cocaptains* is the direct object of *introduced,* the pronoun *me,* which is in apposition to *cocaptains,* must be in the objective case.]

REVIEW EXERCISE B. Number your paper 1–18. Choose the correct pronoun in parentheses, and write it after the proper number. Two sentences have two sets of parentheses.

1. What do you and (he, him) know about it?
2. I don't think it was (they, them).
3. Was it Ellen or (she, her) that won the game?
4. No one told Fred and (I, me) about the test.
5. You must have been talking to Bob and (he, him).
6. Viola Herrera hired (we, us) boys for the job.
7. I planned to go to the game with Cindy and (she, her).
8. (He, Him) and (I, me) did our homework together.
9. When are you expecting your family and (they, them)?
10. Ms. Kay said that (we, us) students were not polite.
11. Dick and (I, me) were asked to prepare a report.
12. The winner was probably Harriet or (he, him).
13. Is the gift for Jean or (she, her)?
14. I don't know Julia and (he, him) very well.
15. If you and (she, her) are on time, we'll be surprised.
16. He would not believe either the teacher or (we, us) students.
17. You asked (he, him) and (I, me) for our opinion.
18. This argument is strictly between Sue and (I, me).

SPECIAL PRONOUN PROBLEMS

There are two kinds of problems you will frequently run across. One is the choice between *who* and *whom;* the other is which pronoun to use in an incomplete construction.

Who and Whom

The pronoun *who* also has different forms in the nominative and the objective cases. *Who* is the nominative form; the objective form is *whom*. Similarly, *whoever* is nominative; *whomever* is objective.

► **USAGE NOTE** In spoken English, the use of *whom* is becoming less common. In fact, when you are speaking, you may correctly begin any question with *who* regardless of the grammar of the sentence.

In written English, however, you should distinguish between *who* and *whom*. *Who* is used as subject or predicate nominative, and *whom* is used as an object.

Often *who* or *whom* will appear in subordinate clauses — in adjective clauses or noun clauses.

7f. **The use of *who* or *whom* in a subordinate clause is determined by the pronoun's function in the clause.**

When you are deciding whether to use *who* or *whom* in a subordinate clause, follow these steps:

1. Pick out the subordinate clause.
2. Decide how the pronoun is used in the clause — as subject, predicate nominative, object of the verb, or object of a preposition.
3. Determine the case of the pronoun according to the usual rules.
4. Select the correct form of the pronoun.

PROBLEM   Dorothea Lange was the woman (who, whom) photographed migrant laborers.

Step 1   The subordinate clause is *(who, whom) photographed migrant laborers.*

Step 2   In this clause, the pronoun is the subject of the verb *photographed.*

Step 3   Since it is the subject of the verb, the pronoun is in the nominative case.

Step 4   The nominative form is *who.*

SOLUTION   Dorothea Lange was the woman *who* photographed migrant laborers.

PROBLEM   Do you know (who, whom) she is?

Step 1   The subordinate clause is (*who, whom*) *she is.*

Step 2   In this clause, the subject is *she,* the verb is *is,* and the pronoun is the predicate nominative: *she is* (*who, whom*).

Step 3   As predicate nominative, the pronoun is in the nominative case.

Step 4   The nominative form is *who.*

SOLUTION   Do you know *who* she is?

PROBLEM   I voted for Margaret O'Rourke, (who, whom) my friends recommended.

Step 1   The subordinate clause is (*who, whom*) *my friends recommended.*

Step 2   In this clause, the subject is *friends;* the verb is *recommended.* The pronoun is the object of the verb: *my friends recommended* (*who, whom*).

Step 3   The object of a verb is in the objective case.

Step 4   The objective form is *whom.*

SOLUTION   I voted for Margaret O'Rourke, *whom* my friends recommended.

PROBLEM   Herb Matthews, (who, whom) I sat next to, fell asleep during the last act of the play.

Step 1   The subordinate clause is (*who, whom*) *I sat next to.*

Step 2   In this clause, the subject is *I;* the verb is *sat.* The pronoun is the object of the preposition *next to: I sat next to* (*who, whom*).

Step 3   The object of a preposition is in the objective case.

Step 4   The objective form is *whom.*

SOLUTION   Herb Matthews, *whom* I sat next to, fell asleep during the last act of the play.

The sentence, of course, would also be correct with the preposition before the pronoun: *Herb Matthews, next to whom I sat, fell asleep during the last act of the play.*

Remember that no words outside the clause affect the case of the pronoun. In the second problem, the entire clause was used as a direct object of the verb *do know,* but the pronoun was used as a predicate nominative (nominative case).

EXAMPLE   Do you know who she is?

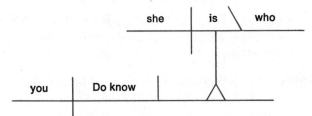

► USAGE NOTE   Frequently, *whom* in subordinate clauses is omitted (understood).

EXAMPLES   The man (whom) I just met is Mr. Nevins.
The man (whom) I just waved at is Mr. Nevins.

EXERCISE 11.   Copy on your paper each subordinate clause in the sentences that follow. Then tell how the pronoun (*who* or *whom*) is used in its own clause—as subject, predicate nominative, object of the verb, or object of a preposition.

EXAMPLE 1. Give the job to Stuart, whom you can trust.

  1. *whom you can trust, object of verb*

 1. Mr. Doyle is a man who likes young people.
 2. Mr. Doyle is a man whom young people like.
 3. The woman who was speaking to me is conducting a market survey.
 4. The woman to whom I was speaking is conducting a market survey.
 5. Can you tell me who that player is?
 6. She is a casual friend whom I seldom see.
 7. Students who attend the meetings will be excused from class.
 8. I wondered who it could be at the door.
 9. Whom Della finally appointed I do not know.
10. There is no one who really understands me.

EXERCISE 12. Number your paper 1–10. After the proper number, give the use of the pronoun in parentheses. Then write the correct pronoun.

EXAMPLE 1. I wondered (who, whom) it was.

  1. *predicate nominative, who*

 1. Women (who, whom) lived during the fifteenth century painted their teeth instead of their nails.
 2. Her older sister, to (who, whom) she sent the article, has moved to Santa Fe.
 3. It was Napoleon (who, whom) invaded Spain in 1808.
 4. Maureen finally guessed (who, whom) it was.
 5. I visited with Mr. Windlow, (who, whom) was trimming his rosebushes.
 6. Mrs. Harvey, (who, whom) I work for on Saturdays, owns two poultry farms.
 7. Is there anyone (who, whom) plans to leave early?
 8. She is the only member of the city council (who, whom) I respect.

9. The actor (who, whom) you were asking about will be on television tonight.
10. Dong Kingman, (who, whom) I admire, often works in watercolor.

REVIEW EXERCISE C. Number your paper 1–20. As you read the following sentences, notice carefully the case form of each pronoun. If all of the pronouns in a sentence are correct, write a *C* after the corresponding number on your paper. If a pronoun has been used incorrectly, write the correct case form of the pronoun.

1. Claire and me are the editors of the literary magazine that our school publishes. 2. Students who wish to submit manuscripts for publication give their material to either Claire or I. 3. After us two have gone over all the material submitted, a general staff meeting is called. 4. Then we students who make up the staff read the manuscripts together.

5. When the material for the month's publication has been selected by we staff members, it is sent to the printer. 6. Both Claire and I go periodically to the printing house to make sure that the people there know what we want done. 7. Sometimes they question Claire and I about the make-up of a page.

8. Meanwhile, Lance and Dolores, who the art teacher recommended, are working on the illustrations and cover design for the magazine. 9. Claire checks the work done by them because she knows more about art than I do.

10. All of us who have worked hard on the magazine are relieved when it is finally ready for distribution.

11. Last month a prize was offered by we members of the staff to whomever should write the best short story. 12. The students who submitted stories selected pen names for themselves, so that even those

of us on the staff did not know whom had written a particular story. 13. We did have an alphabetical list of all the students who had submitted stories, and we entertained ourselves by trying to match each story with an author on our list.

14. "Could 'The Last Journey' have been written by Carl or she?" Claire asked, pointing to names on the list.

15. "Neither he nor she wrote it," Dolores replied.
16. "This," Dolores continued, pointing to another name on the list, "is obviously the work of Jim or he."

17. "But the author could be she," Lance argued, "since this looks like the kind of story that only she could write."

18. And so the arguments went for each story that we read because all of us were sure that we could analyze the story and determine whom the writer was.

19. "The Last Journey" was chosen by the judges as the winner of the contest, and we staff members were surprised when the author was identified.

20. "It was not *he* or *she,* but *them!*" Claire exclaimed. Two students had collaborated on the mystery story.

The Pronoun in an Incomplete Construction

Notice the difference in meaning that the choice of pronouns can make in sentences with incomplete constructions.

EXAMPLES You like Rita better than **I.**
You like Rita better than **me.**

In the first sentence, the choice of the pronoun *I* indicates that it is the subject of an understood verb: *You like Rita better than I like Rita.* In the second sentence, since the pronoun *me* is in the objective case, the meaning is: *You like Rita better than you like me.*

The case of the pronoun depends upon how the omitted part of the sentence would be completed.

7g. After *than* and *as* introducing an incomplete construction, use the form of the pronoun that you would use if the construction were completed.

The following sentences are correct because they clearly express the meaning intended by the writer. The words in the brackets show how each could be completed.

EXAMPLES   I lent you more money than **he** [lent you].
I lent you more money than [I lent] **him**.
Did he tell Alma as much as **I** [told Alma]?
Did he tell Alma as much as [he told] **me?**

EXERCISE 13. Beginning with the *than* or *as,* complete each sentence, using the correct form of the pronoun. After the sentence, write the use of the pronoun in its clause, telling whether it is a subject or an object.

EXAMPLE   1. Fran was as delighted as (I, me).
    1. *as I was — subject*

1. Lester can varnish floors better than (I, me).
2. The letter was odd; it baffled Sam as well as (we, us).
3. Is Eleanor younger or older than (he, him)?
4. Have they practiced as much as (we, us)?
5. We have known Lucy longer than (she, her).
6. Perhaps you are more idealistic than (he, him).
7. Did you enjoy the movie as much as (I, me)?
8. The long trip exhausted them more than (we, us).
9. Were you as thoroughly uncomfortable as (she, her)?
10. Their children were even less fortunate than (they, them).

REVIEW EXERCISE D. Number your paper 1–25. After each number, write the correct form of the pronoun in parentheses. Be able to give reasons for your answers.

1. Can you or (he, him) describe Mary Cassatt's style of painting?
2. (We, Us) students gave reports on baseball.
3. Each of (we, us) mentioned Roberto Clemente.
4. In Egypt the nobles (who, whom) ruled were rich.
5. The laborers, (who, whom) the nobles ruled, were extremely poor.
6. Between you and (I, me), I think that Bob is deceiving himself.
7. Did the gift surprise Beth as much as (she, her)?
8. Is it really (they, them)?
9. Please give those pictures to Wanda and (I, me).
10. He can't swim as fast as (I, me).
11. Behind us stood Irene and (he, him).
12. My mom taught Clarence and (I, me) how to drive.
13. Do you need someone (who, whom) is dependable?
14. The winners, Carl and (I, me), got a free trip to New York.
15. Father told Cliff and (I, me) the answer.
16. Some of (we, us) girls preferred to skate.
17. Everyone except (she, her) has joined the club.
18. Surely you can do as well as (he, him).
19. Her sister and (she, her) will help us.
20. Mary Ann, (who, whom) you have met, will be at the party.
21. At the end of the story, who married (who, whom)?
22. Please tell (we, us) boys what you know.
23. Tashina and (we, us) went fishing at dawn.
24. The man stopped Steve and (we, us) at the gate.
25. Are you and (they, them) going to the dinner?

REVIEW EXERCISE E. Number your paper 1–10. If a sentence has no errors in usage of pronouns, write a *C* after the corresponding number on your paper. If a pronoun is incorrect, give the correct form.

1. Last year Helen and me put on a Halloween show for the youngsters staying in a nearby hospital.
2. The show was so successful that this year her and I decided to put on a show for the neighborhood children as well.
3. After school and on weekends, us students made decorations and other preparations for the show in our house.
4. As the show opened, we played the record "Night on Bald Mountain," a very eerie piece of music; and as the music grew louder I, whom was standing near the door, turned off the lights.
5. The room was extremely dark, yet the children could see smoke, which poured from the dry ice Helen and me had bought and hidden behind a screen.
6. I focused a flashlight on Helen, who was sitting in a chair and dressed in a terrifying, ghostly costume.
7. When she rose from the chair, she opened her mouth slowly and, in a very scary voice, said, "I am her whom you fear – the Great Zombie."
8. In the front row, a little boy and his sister sat so still that I could almost hear him and she breathing.
9. Finally, after Helen and I were satisfied that us two had frightened the audience enough, we turned on the lights and handed out baskets of popcorn and glasses of cider.
10. The children enjoyed the treats and soon left to tell their friends about the Halloween show which they had seen.

REVIEW EXERCISE F. Number your paper 1–10. If a sentence is correct, write *C* after the number. If a pronoun is used incorrectly, write the correct form of the pronoun after the number.

1. The politician spoke to us members of the Debate Society.
2. During the Olympic trials, every diver except she received a low score from the judges.
3. The children who Inez brought home from the fair were sleeping in the car.
4. My instructor, who had been stunned by my quick recovery after a fall from the high bar, gave me an excellent score.
5. I wrote a beautiful poem about my grandfather and he.
6. I hope that you and them can manage the fruit stand this afternoon.
7. Sometimes it was difficult to tell who was having a better time, them or us.
8. Many people in the audience wanted to know whom the winners were.
9. It is unlikely that Betty and me can make enough money this summer to pay for a trip to the Canadian Rockies.
10. The Steins and us watched the trapeze artist swinging in the air.

REVIEW EXERCISE G. Number your paper 1–15. If a sentence is correct, write *C* after the proper number. If a pronoun has been used incorrectly, write the correct form of the pronoun after the appropriate number.

1. Keep this a secret between you and I.
2. Us weight lifters will carry the baggage.
3. At camp Sam and me were tentmates.
4. If it is she who is supposed to be in charge, let me know.

5. Were you calling Jerry or me?
6. If you and her can't go to the concert, I'll go.
7. He kept Howard and I after school.
8. Please don't tell anyone but Mrs. Carter or her about our plan.
9. He thought it was us.
10. Please wait for Ramona and him.
11. Are you and him related?
12. Gladys and he are absent.
13. We girls were pretty angry.
14. Have you seen Helen or she?
15. It couldn't have been them.

REVIEW EXERCISE H. Write twenty sentences correctly using the following:

1. who
2. whom
3. we students
4. us students
5. you and I
6. you and me
7. her son and she
8. her son and her
9. Mr. Jordan and we
10. Mr. Jordan and us
11. as much as he
12. as well as him
13. Wesley and she
14. Wesley and her
15. he or she
16. him or her
17. my mother and they
18. my mother and them
19. more than I
20. more than me

Chapter 8

The Correct Use of Modifiers

Comparison and Placement

A modifier describes or limits the meaning of another word. There are two kinds of modifiers, adjectives and adverbs. Besides one-word modifiers, you have studied several other kinds of modifiers—prepositional phrases, verbal phrases, and subordinate clauses, all of which may be used as adjectives or adverbs.

COMPARISON OF MODIFIERS

Adjectives state qualities of nouns or pronouns:

rough road, **happy** children, **friendly** dog

You can show the degree or extent to which one noun has a quality by comparing it with another noun which has the same quality. For instance:

This road is **rougher** than that road.

Similarly, you can show degree or extent by using adverbs to make comparisons:

Although I did my chores **quickly,** Gwen did her work **more quickly.**

8a. The forms of modifiers change as they are used in comparison.

There are three degrees of comparison: *positive, comparative,* and *superlative.* Notice below how the forms of modifiers change to show comparison.

POSITIVE	COMPARATIVE	SUPERLATIVE
big	bigger	biggest
old	older	oldest
fearful	more fearful	most fearful
promptly	more promptly	most promptly
bad	worse	worst
good	better	best

Regular Comparison

(1) A modifier of one syllable regularly forms its comparative and superlative by adding *-er* and *-est.*

POSITIVE	COMPARATIVE	SUPERLATIVE
low	lower	lowest
soon	sooner	soonest
kind	kinder	kindest

(2) Some modifiers of two syllables form their comparative and superlative degrees by adding *-er* and *-est;* other modifiers of two syllables form their comparative and superlative degrees by means of *more* and *most.*

In general, the *-er, -est* forms are used with two-syllable modifiers unless they make the word sound awkward. The *more, most* forms are used with adverbs ending in *-ly.*

POSITIVE	COMPARATIVE	SUPERLATIVE
simple	simpler	simplest
pretty	prettier	prettiest
foolish	more foolish	most foolish

gracious   more gracious   most gracious
slowly   more slowly   most slowly

▶ **USAGE NOTE** Some two-syllable modifiers may take either *-er, -est* or *more, most: handsome, handsomer, handsomest* or *handsome, more handsome, most handsome.*

When in doubt about which way a two-syllable modifier is compared, consult an unabridged dictionary.

EXERCISE 1. Write the forms for the comparative and superlative degrees of these words:

1. loose
2. often
3. lazy
4. harmful
5. gentle
6. funny
7. wise
8. safely
9. eager
10. lovely

(3) Modifiers having more than two syllables form their comparative and superlative degrees by means of *more* and *most*.

POSITIVE	COMPARATIVE	SUPERLATIVE
intelligent	more intelligent	most intelligent
favorably	more favorably	most favorably

EXERCISE 2. *Oral Drill.* Give comparative and superlative degrees of (1) *original,* (2) *reasonably,* (3) *significant,* (4) *appropriately,* and (5) *pessimistic.*

(4) Comparison to indicate less or least of a quality is accomplished by using the words *less* and *least* before the modifier.

POSITIVE	COMPARATIVE	SUPERLATIVE
useful	less useful	least useful
often	less often	least often

EXERCISE 3. *Oral Drill.* Give comparison to indicate less and least of the five words listed in Exercise 2.

Irregular Comparison

Adjectives and adverbs that do not follow the regular methods of forming their comparative and superlative degrees are said to be compared irregularly.

POSITIVE	COMPARATIVE	SUPERLATIVE
bad	worse	worst
good ⎱ well ⎰	better	best
many ⎱ much ⎰	more	most

Caution: Do not add the *–er, –est* or *more, most* forms to irregularly compared forms: *worse,* not *worser* or *more worse.*

EXERCISE 4. Be prepared to give the correct forms of the comparative and superlative degrees when your teacher dictates the positive forms of the five adjectives and adverbs listed in the previous table.

REVIEW EXERCISE A. Write the comparative and superlative forms of the following modifiers. If you are in doubt about the forms of two-syllable modifiers, look up the positive forms in an unabridged dictionary.

1. bad	6. witty	11. quiet	16. firmly
2. good	7. tough	12. widely	17. practical
3. neat	8. lonely	13. little	18. absorbent
4. late	9. weak	14. comic	19. precisely
5. many	10. well	15. trivial	20. desolate

REVIEW EXERCISE B. Use the comparative or superative forms of items 1–5 in Review Exercise A in sentences of your own.

Use of Comparative and Superlative Forms

8b. Use the comparative degree when comparing two things; use the superlative degree when comparing more than two.

The comparative form of a modifier is used for comparing two things, as these examples indicate.

EXAMPLES   Mount McKinley is **higher** than Pikes Peak.

Skywriting is **more spectacular** than billboard advertising.

The superlative form of a modifier is used for comparing three or more items.

EXAMPLES   Mount McKinley is the **highest** peak in North America.

Skywriting is the **most spectacular** way to advertise.

► **USAGE NOTE**   In everyday conversation, it is acceptable in some cases to use the superlative degree in comparing two things: *Put your best foot forward.*

EXERCISE 5.   Using the correct forms of adjectives or adverbs, write five sentences comparing two things and five comparing more than two.

8c. Do not omit the words *other* or *else* when comparing one thing with a group of which it is a part.

It is illogical to say "Mary Lou is more imaginative than any student in her class." Obviously, Mary Lou is a member of her class, and she cannot be more imaginative than herself. The word *other* should be supplied: "Mary Lou is more imaginative than any *other* student in her class."

ILLOGICAL   My cat Grumpy is smarter than any cat.

CORRECTED   My cat Grumpy is smarter than any **other** cat.

Similarly, "The left tackle weighs more than anyone on the football team" is incorrect, since the left tackle is a member of the team. Here *else* should be added: "The left tackle weighs more than anyone *else* on the team."

ILLOGICAL   Naomi jumped higher than anyone.

CORRECTED   Naomi jumped higher than anyone **else.**

EXERCISE 6. *Oral Drill.* The comparisons in this exercise are illogical because of the omission of the words *other* or *else.* Supply the needed word as you read the sentences, so that the sentences will be logical.

1. Dora Yardley is wiser than any person I know.
2. My sister receives more mail than anyone in my family.
3. Your suggestion may be more sensible than any suggestion that has been made so far.
4. Russ can run faster than anybody on the team.
5. The picture he gave me is more valuable to me than anything I own.

8d. Avoid double comparisons.

A double comparison is one in which the degree is formed incorrectly by both adding *–er* or *–est* and using *more* or *most.*

NONSTANDARD   Kay is more friendlier than Morris.

STANDARD   Kay is **friendlier** than Morris.

NONSTANDARD   This coin is the most unusualest item in my collection.

STANDARD   This coin is the **most unusual** item in my collection.

EXERCISE 7. Number your paper 1–10. Copy each incorrect modifier, crossing out the unnecessary part in order to eliminate the double comparison.

EXAMPLE   1. I am determined to study more harder this term than I did last.
   1. *~~more~~ harder*
   2. That is the most elegantest tablecloth I have ever seen.
   2. *most elegant~~est~~*

1. Today is more colder than yesterday.
2. Mother is the most patientest person in our family.
3. Is Nita now working even more faster than before?
4. A jaguar runs even more faster than a horse.
5. He is the most stubbornest child in the family.
6. About nine o'clock, the noise became more louder.
7. This is the most loveliest day!
8. Rosemary Casals had a more harder serve than her tennis partner.
9. The patient is more quieter than he was last night.
10. Then I made the most stupidest remark.

8e. Be sure your comparisons are clear.

Your sentences should state clearly what things are being compared; for example, in the sentence "The population of New York is greater than Chicago," the comparison is not clear. *The population of New York* is not being compared to *Chicago,* but rather to *the population* of Chicago. The sentence should read: *The population of New York is greater than the population* (or *that*) *of Chicago.*

UNCLEAR   Statistics prove that traveling in airplanes is safer than automobiles.

BETTER   Statistics prove that traveling in airplanes is safer than traveling in automobiles.

Often an incomplete construction will be used in a comparison: *I am happier than she.* Both parts of the comparison should be stated if there is danger of misunderstanding.

UNCLEAR   I like her better than Isabel.

BETTER   I like her better than I like Isabel.

or   I like her better than Isabel likes her.

REVIEW EXERCISE C. Number your paper 1–20. If all the modifiers in a sentence are correct, write a *C* after the corresponding number on your paper. If a modifier is incorrect, rewrite the sentence, making whatever correction is needed.

1. When the tortoise and the hare raced, the hare proved to be faster, but the tortoise won the race because it was more persistent.
2. Of all the animals at the zoo, the monkeys were the noisier creatures.
3. She is the most happiest child I know.
4. My friend, who later became a star on Broadway, had more talent than any actor in his class.
5. Sarah has read many detective stories, and this is the best one that she has found.
6. Our guide explained that the next place we were to visit would be farther from town.
7. Earth is more nearer the sun than Mars is.
8. She skied better than anyone in her group.
9. After the stranger had examined the two paths, he took the one that looked easiest to follow.
10. Tantalus was more cruelly punished than any legendary figure.

11. My aunt, who is a born pessimist, felt much more securer after she had inspected the plane.
12. Of the two pieces of cake, he politely chose the smallest one.
13. Which city is largest—Chicago or Los Angeles?
14. Sherlock Holmes is more famous than any detective in literature.
15. Donna thought that the masks worn in the ancient Greek plays were the most grotesque ones that she had ever seen.
16. After examining all three costumes, the director decided that this one was the most appropriate for her play.
17. Today, Kevin worked longer on the parallel bars than anyone on the gymnastic squad.
18. Which country is farthest from the United States —France or Japan?
19. Many people think that the panther is the most fiercest animal in the world.
20. We were more interested in studying the history of the Egyptians than any other ancient people.

DANGLING MODIFIERS

8f. A modifying phrase or clause that does not clearly and sensibly modify a word in the sentence is a *dangling modifier.*

When a modifying phrase containing a verbal comes at the beginning of a sentence, the phrase is followed by a comma. Immediately after that comma should come the word that the word group modifies. Notice in the following two examples how the introductory expressions clearly and sensibly modify the words which follow the commas.

Recovering from an illness, I was marked absent. [*I* was recovering.]

Nailed to the gate, a no-trespassing sign attracted Patty's attention. [The *sign* was nailed to the gate.]

Each of the following sentences contains a dangling modifier — that is, a modifier which either appears to modify a word other than the one it is meant to modify or doesn't modify any word at all.

Recovering from an illness, the teacher marked me absent. [The sentence implies that the teacher was recovering.]

Nailed to the gate, Patty noticed a no-trespassing sign. [Obviously, Patty was not nailed to the gate.]

Walking down the street, his eyes showed constant surprise. [Did his eyes walk down the street?]

EXERCISE 8. Write complete sentences using the following introductory modifiers. Follow each modifier by a word it can *clearly* and *sensibly* modify.

EXAMPLE   1. Dodging his opponents,
          1. *Dodging his opponents, Jim Plunkett passed the ball.*

1. Exploding unexpectedly,
2. Shocked by Gerald's rudeness,
3. Leaping from branch to branch,
4. Waddling along the beach,
5. Scratching her head,
6. Not expecting the interruption,
7. Planning a birthday party for her,
8. Paying close attention in class,
9. To avoid being caught in the rain,
10. Trying to keep from laughing,

Correcting Dangling Modifiers

To correct a dangling modifier, you should either rearrange the words in the sentence or add words to make the meaning logical and clear.

DANGLING   To win and hold friends, petty quarrels and criticism should be avoided.

CORRECTED   To win and hold friends, you should avoid petty quarrels and criticism.

or   If you wish to win and hold friends, you should avoid petty quarrels and criticism.

DANGLING   While lighting the birthday candles, the cake started to crumble.

CORRECTED   While I was lighting the birthday candles, the cake started to crumble.

or   While lighting the birthday candles, I noticed the cake starting to crumble.

EXERCISE 9. Eliminate the dangling modifiers in the following sentences by rewriting each sentence so that each modifier clearly and sensibly modifies a word in the sentence. You will have to supply words.

1. Jogging along the path, the fresh air made me feel truly alive.
2. While putting the roast in the oven, the doorbell suddenly rang.
3. To finish my term paper on time, all my holidays and weekends were spent in the library.
4. Warped all around the edge, I promptly returned the record album for a refund.
5. After looking at hundreds of new coats, a beautiful parka suddenly caught my eye.
6. Having turned on the video cassette player, the opening credits of a movie appeared on the screen.
7. While landing at Dulles Airport, Arlington National Cemetery came into view.
8. Feeling very tired, the overstuffed chair looked inviting to me.

9. To get a driver's license, a written test is required first.
10. Having just bought a new aquarium, two guppies became its first occupants.

EXERCISE 10. Many sentences below contain dangling modifiers; some do not. Number your paper 1–20. If a sentence is correct, write a *C* after the corresponding number. If it is incorrect, rewrite the sentence to eliminate the dangling modifier.

1. After saying grace, dinner was served.
2. To appreciate good music, you should learn to play an instrument. *C*
3. While trimming the rosebushes this morning, a spider bit me.
4. Made of durable plastic, a child cannot easily break these toy trucks.
5. Glittering in the soft, silent moonlight, the water looked beautiful and seemed inviting to us.
6. Filled with high school students, the visitors could not find an empty seat in the auditorium.
7. While listening to the radio, I soon fell asleep.
8. While reading my assignment by the river, the wind kept blowing dust into my eyes.
9. Although ringing loudly, no one seemed to hear the bell.
10. Running across the meadow, my ankle was sprained.
11. To become a great athlete, physical endurance is necessary.
12. To become well informed, you should make a habit of reading newspapers and magazines.
13. To earn spending money, Mrs. Lewis gave me a job as cashier in her store.
14. After mopping the kitchen, the baby woke up and began to cry.
15. After being in school all day, a long hike is refreshing.

16. Sitting up on its hind legs, the squirrel munched an acorn.
17. When learning to swim, everything that one tries seems ridiculous at first.
18. While walking alone in the woods, it is good to hear the birds singing.
19. Before going to bed on a cold night, the thermostat setting should be lowered.
20. When trying to understand the meaning of a sentence, look at the little words, the prepositions and conjunctions.

MISPLACED MODIFIERS

A dangling modifier, as the preceding exercises have shown, makes the meaning of a sentence absurd because the modifier either seems to modify a word which it cannot sensibly modify or is left without any word to modify at all. Just as damaging to the clear expression of ideas are misplaced modifiers.

8g. Modifying phrases and clauses should be placed as near as possible to the words they modify.

Misplaced Phrase Modifiers

The following examples of misplaced phrases show the importance of placing phrase modifiers as near as possible to the words they modify.

MISPLACED   Skipper enjoyed the chunks of steak slipped to him by the guests under the table. [Here *under the table* seems to indicate where the guests were.]

CORRECTED   Skipper enjoyed the chunks of steak slipped under the table to him by the guests.

MISPLACED	At the age of four, my mother taught me a lesson.
CORRECTED	At the age of four, I learned a lesson from my mother.
or	My mother taught me a lesson when I was four years old.
MISPLACED	A lovely rose garden was planned by the President's committee behind the White House.
CORRECTED	A lovely rose garden behind the White House was planned by the President's committee.

EXERCISE 11. Rewrite the following sentences so that they make sense. Either place phrase modifiers as near as possible to the words they modify or turn a phrase into a clause. Be sure that you do not misplace another modifier in rewriting.

1. At five years of age, my grandmother bought me a pony.
2. On the bottom shelf of the refrigerator, I could not find the fruit juice.
3. There should be a letter written by Aunt Lizzy in your post office box.
4. I ate two peaches and a plate of strawberries with relish.
5. The police officer told the frightened children what they were doing wrong with a smile.
6. Homesick, Norma yearned to see the Rocky Mountains in Europe.
7. The job was selling boxes of candy to children with prizes in them.
8. In a tiny cage at the dog pound, we felt very sorry for the little bulldog.
9. I read about the kidnappers who were captured in this morning's paper.

10. The names of the players were called out by the announcer in the starting lineup.
11. I saw her make a thrilling slalom run on my cousin's television set.
12. He told us about roping steers in the school cafeteria.
13. The principal congratulated three students for their community work during the school assembly.
14. The governor agreed to punish every driver who endangers the lives of others without delay.
15. The play by Lorraine Hansberry will be performed for the benefit of the local hospital in the school auditorium.
16. On the way to the grocery store, the streets seemed slippery.
17. The fans jeered at the referee in the stands.
18. The thief was arrested soon after her grocery store had been robbed by the police.
19. Inside the oven I noticed that the turkey was burning.
20. We waved at the workers repairing the highway from our car.

Misplaced Clause Modifiers

Place an adjective or adverb clause as near as possible to the word it modifies. Notice how the meaning of the sentence below is distorted by a misplaced clause modifier.

MISPLACED   The car belongs to our neighbor that has long, sweeping tail fins.

Since the modifying clause *that has long, sweeping tail fins* seems to modify *neighbor,* the sentence is ridiculous. The clause should be close to the word it modifies, as follows:

CORRECTED   The car that has long, sweeping tail fins belongs to our neighbor.

To correct misplaced clauses, place the modifying clause as close as possible to the word it modifies.

MISPLACED   The book is still in my locker that I should have returned weeks ago.

CORRECTED   The book that I should have returned weeks ago is still in my locker.

MISPLACED   There was a flag on the stage which had only forty-eight stars.

CORRECTED   On the stage there was a flag which had only forty-eight stars.

EXERCISE 12. Read each of the following sentences. Decide what word the misplaced clause should modify, and rewrite the sentence, placing the clause near this word.

1. A trunk stood on the step which was covered with labels.
2. A dog ran onto the football field that looked a lot like our club mascot.
3. We waved to the girl as we left the town that had given us directions.
4. There are several books on our shelves which were written by Jessamyn West.
5. The battered car now sits in the garage that went out of control on the expressway yesterday.
6. There was a rosebush behind the pile of trash which was very beautiful.
7. Birds were kept away by scarecrows, which like to eat seeds.
8. We crossed the Mississippi River on a long bridge which was almost a mile wide.
9. A large dog was trotting behind the little boy that was growling as if he were getting ready to attack me.
10. We played in two old shacks between the post office and the bank which weren't being lived in at the time.

REVIEW EXERCISE D. The sentences below contain dangling modifiers, misplaced modifiers, and errors in comparison. Rewrite the sentences so that the meaning is clear.

1. She plays both tennis and golf, but she likes tennis best.

2. He served sandwiches to Elmer and me, packed with pickles, garlic, tomatoes, and cheese.

3. Everyone was waiting for the teacher in English class.

4. Jill is certainly more taller than you.

5. We didn't see the tornado approaching in the storm cellar.

6. After boiling for exactly three minutes, Emma poured cold water over the eggs.

7. The dead snake was brought into camp by a cub scout six feet long.

8. Trying to remember my lines, my heart pounded against my ribs.

9. While taking her final exam, Yvonne's pen ran out of ink.

10. The height of these new buildings is not so great as the old buildings.

11. The hotel was pointed out to us by a tourist that had hot and cold running water, television, and a swimming pool.

12. To avoid the hot sun, our plans were to travel at night.

13. Flying at half-mast, my heart grew sad when I saw the flag.

14. After completing my homework, the doorbell rang.

15. Before leaving school, my homework was all done.

16. We waited for you until the movie started at the theater entrance.

17. Stepping out into the blinding snowstorm, my teeth chattered, and my hands grew numb.

18. To find jack rabbits, my neighbor's oat field is a good place.
19. After knocking out the heavyweight champion, the referee announced the winner.
20. We found an old jack in the trunk which wouldn't work.

REVIEW EXERCISE E. All of the following sentences contain errors in the use of modifiers or appositives: mistakes in comparisons or dangling or misplaced modifiers. After the proper number, rewrite each sentence so that it is clear and correct.

1. When traveling through the highlands in Scotland, I discovered that stories about monsters were more popular than any kind of story.
2. Having received a great deal of publicity, I already knew about the so-called Loch Ness monster.
3. The first person to sight the monster, a veterinary student from Edinburgh, was Arthur Grant.
4. One day, Grant came upon a strange creature cycling on a road near the shore of Loch Ness.
5. On cycling closer, the monster took two great leaps and plunged into the lake.
6. As you might expect, numerous theories were presented about the identity of the monster in the local newspaper.
7. Some people thought the monster must be a freshwater species of sea serpent, and others believed the whole story was a hoax; of these two theories, the first is obviously the most fascinating.
8. Having found a huge, dead creature on the shore of the lake in 1942, the mystery of the monster was believed finally to be solved.
9. The scientists called it a large shark who examined the specimen.
10. Though having supposedly gone from the lake, many new sightings of the monster have been reported.

Chapter 9

Glossary of Usage

This chapter contains a short glossary of English usage, supplementing the material in Chapters 5–8. The words and expressions in this glossary are listed for your reference. You may, if you wish, work straight through the chapter, studying the problems and using the exercises to test your knowledge of the various items. However, the glossary is included in the book mainly for you to refer to when you are uncertain about a question of usage.

Several kinds of usage problems are treated in this glossary. Some require the writer or speaker to choose between two words, according to the meaning intended. Others involve a choice between two words, in which one word is less acceptable than the other. A few of the words and expressions discussed here should be avoided altogether. (Spelling problems arising from the confusion of similar words are treated in Chapter 28.)

accept, except *Accept* is a verb; it means "to receive." *Except* may be either a verb or a preposition. As a verb, it means "to leave out" or "to omit"; it is usually used in the passive voice. (See pages 166–67.) As a preposition, *except* means "excluding."

EXAMPLES I **accept** your invitation.

Honor roll students will be **excepted** from this requirement.

I have done all my homework **except** my history assignment.

affect, effect *Affect* is a verb meaning "to influence." *Effect* used as a verb means "to accomplish." Used as a noun, *effect* means "the result of some action."

EXAMPLES The crisis may **affect** the outcome of the election.

The government is working to **effect** a solution to the crisis.

The **effect** of the crisis is being felt in government circles.

ain't Avoid this word in speaking or writing; it is nonstandard English.

all the farther, all the faster Used in some parts of the country to mean "as far as" or "as fast as."

DIALECT This is all the farther we can go.
STANDARD This is **as far as** we can go.

among See **between, among.**

and etc. *Etc.* is an abbreviation of the Latin phrase *et cetera,* meaning "and other things." Thus, *and etc.* means "and and other things." Do not use *and* with *etc.*

EXAMPLE The school store sells pencils, paper, notebooks, ink, **etc.** [not *and etc.*]

anywheres, everywheres, nowheres, somewheres Use these words without the final *s.*

EXAMPLE My family didn't go **anywhere** [not *anywheres*] on the Fourth of July.

as See like, as.

as if See like, as if.

at Do not use *at* after *where.*

NONSTANDARD   Where does she live at?
STANDARD   Where does she live?

beside, besides *Beside* means "by the side of" someone or something; it is always a preposition. *Besides* as a preposition means "in addition to." As an adverb, *besides* means "moreover."

EXAMPLES   Come and sit **beside** me.

Besides cold cuts and sandwiches, we will have lemonade and fresh fruit.

I cannot stay any longer. **Besides**, I am already late for my appointment.

between, among Use *between* when you are thinking of two things at a time, even though they may be part of a group consisting of more than two.

EXAMPLES   In math, Carol sits **between** Geraldine and me.

The team has a short rest period **between** quarters. [Although there are more than two quarters, a rest period occurs only *between* any two of them.]

We are studying the War **Between** the States. [Although thirty-five states were involved, the war was *between* two sides.]

I could not decide which of the four candidates to vote for, as there was not much difference **between** them. [Although there are more than two candidates, each one is being thought

of and compared with the others separately.]

Use *among* when you are thinking of a group
rather than of separate individuals.

EXAMPLES   There was considerable disagreement
among the hunters as to the direction
of the camp. [The hunters are thought
of as a group.]
We had only four dollars **among** the
six of us.

bring, take   *Bring* means "to come carrying something." *Take* means "to go carrying something."
Think of *bring* as related to *come, take* as related
to *go*.

EXAMPLES   **Bring** the book here.
Now **take** it over there.

bust, busted   Avoid using these words as verbs.
Use a form of either *burst* or *break*.

EXAMPLES   The beach ball **burst** [not *busted*]
when Judy Ikeda kicked it.
The bat **broke** [not *busted*] when
Don Swenson hit the ball.

EXERCISE 1. This exercise covers the usage problems discussed on pages 220–23. Number your paper
1–20. After each number, write the correct word from
the parentheses in the corresponding sentence.

1. Is page 216 (all the farther, as far as) you have
read?
2. (Beside, Besides) the players themselves, their
families and friends attended the dinner.
3. Will she (accept, except) the explanation for my
absence?

4. She divided the work (between, among) the club members.
5. May I (bring, take) this book down to the library for you?
6. I (busted, broke) my leg skiing.
7. I could not find the answer to that question (anywhere, anywheres).
8. I saw no one I knew at the dance (beside, besides) Jane.
9. The audience seemed greatly (affected, effected) by her moving speech.
10. One of Nathan's bicycle tires (busted, burst) while he was racing down the hill.
11. I have to (bring, take) these books to the library before it closes.
12. The topic I chose for my term paper was (accepted, excepted) by my teacher.
13. The dry farmlands clearly showed the (affect, effect) of the drought.
14. I'm not eager to see that film. (Beside, Besides), I have spent all my allowance.
15. (Bring, Take) the report downstairs to the principal's office.
16. Prize money is distributed equally (between, among) the six team members.
17. Experiments with the new laser showed surprising (affects, effects).
18. Basketball, volleyball, fencing, tennis, (etc., and etc.) are taught by the physical education staff.
19. He divided the toys (between, among) the three children.
20. I (brought, took) some flowers to my aunt, who is in the hospital in Jacksonville.

can't hardly, can't scarcely See **The Double Negative** (page 235).

could of *Could have* sounds like *could of* when spoken. Do not erroneously write *of* with the helping verb *could*. Write *could have*. Also avoid *ought to of, should of, would of, might of,* and *must of.*

> EXAMPLE Diane could **have** [not *of*] telephoned us.

discover, invent *Discover* means "to be the first to find, see, or learn about something that already exists." *Invent* means "to be the first to do or make something."

> EXAMPLES Marie Curie **discovered** the element radium.
>
> Edison **invented** the phonograph.

don't *Don't* is the contraction of *do not; doesn't* is the contraction of *does not.* Use *doesn't*, not *don't*, with *he, she, it, this,* and singular nouns.

> EXAMPLES It **doesn't** [not *don't*] matter.
>
> This **doesn't** [not *don't*] make sense.

effect See **affect, effect.**

everywheres See **anywheres**, etc.

fewer, less *Fewer* is used with plural words, *less* with singular words; *fewer* tells "how many," *less* "how much."

> EXAMPLES **Fewer** guests were expected.
>
> **Less** punch was needed.

good, well *Good* is always an adjective. Never use *good* to modify a verb; use *well,* which is an adverb.

> NONSTANDARD Pancho Gonzales played good.
>
> STANDARD Pancho Gonzales played **well.**

Although it is usually an adverb, *well* is used as an adjective to mean "healthy."

EXAMPLE She does not feel **well.** [predicate adjective meaning "healthy"]

► USAGE NOTE *Feel good* and *feel well* mean different things. *Feel good* means "to feel happy or pleased." *Feel well* simply means "to feel healthy."

EXAMPLES After a victory, he feels **good.**
The warm sun made me feel **good.**
She went to the nurse because she didn't feel **well.**

The use of *good* as an adverb is increasing in conversational English, but it should not be so used in writing.

EXERCISE 2. This exercise covers the usage problems discussed on pages 224–26. Number your paper 1–10. After each number, write the correct word in parentheses in the corresponding sentences.

1. He could (of, have) been seriously injured.
2. Who (discovered, invented) the automobile that runs on solar energy?
3. (Don't, Doesn't) Stanley know that Labor Day is a holiday?
4. I don't sing too (good, well) when my throat gets dry.
5. Next time you bake a cake, use (fewer, less) eggs.
6. He (don't, doesn't) seem to know the meaning of work.
7. If you had called, I might (of, have) gone with you.
8. We have (fewer, less) school holidays this term.
9. The coach (don't, doesn't) want the players to stay up late.
10. Whoever it was that first (discovered, invented) the wheel was a great scientist.

REVIEW EXERCISE A. This exercise covers the most important usage problems discussed in the glossary so far. If a sentence is correct, write *C* on your paper beside the number of the sentence. If a sentence contains an error in usage, write the correct form.

1. Beside you and Marie, no one else has heard anything yet about the summer job program.
2. The soap bubble floated upward and burst.
3. Are you planning to bring a house gift to your aunt and uncle when you go to Chicago?
4. Why does February have less days than any other month?
5. I wish I had excepted your assistance.
6. My feeling drowsy is effecting my ability to concentrate.
7. Little Susie came home from the zoo, talking excitedly about lions, tigers, elephants, seals, and etc.
8. The accident could of been prevented.
9. Don't anyone know who invented the steam engine?
10. I thought the rehearsal went rather well.
11. Is that all the faster you can type?
12. We can't decide between the red flowers and the blue ones.
13. Everywheres we looked there were people.
14. I was surprised that no one would except my suggestion.
15. Did Thomas Edison discover the phonograph?
16. What affect did the operation have on his speech?
17. We sat beside the pool and watched the girls' diving exhibition.
18. Between the five of us we managed to raise a dollar.
19. The girl wearing the pearls don't look familiar.
20. Should I of consulted Mr. Madison before writing my essay?

had of See **of.**

had ought, hadn't ought Unlike other verbs, *ought* is not used with *had.*

NONSTANDARD Guy had ought to study harder; he hadn't ought to have gone to the movies last night.

STANDARD Guy **ought** to study harder; he **ought not** to have gone to the movies last night.

or Guy **should** study harder; he **shouldn't** have gone to the movies last night.

haven't but, haven't only See **The Double Negative** (page 235).

he, she, they In writing do not use an unnecessary pronoun after a noun. This error is called the *double subject.*

NONSTANDARD Mrs. Page she is my algebra teacher.

STANDARD Mrs. Page is my algebra teacher.

kind, sort, type In writing, the demonstrative words *this, that, these,* and *those* must agree in number with the words *kind, sort, type: this type, these types.*

EXAMPLE I like **this kind** of story better than any of **those** other **kinds.**

learn, teach *Learn* means "to acquire knowledge." *Teach* means "to instruct" or "to show how."

EXAMPLE Directors often **teach** classes in acting, and a young drama student can **learn** many valuable things from them.

leave, let *Leave* means "to go away" or "to depart from." *Let* means "to allow" or "to permit."

NONSTANDARD Leave her do what she wants to do.
STANDARD Let [allow] her do what she wants to do.
STANDARD Leave the house at nine.

less See **fewer, less.**

lie, lay See page 168.

like, as *Like* is a preposition, introducing a prepositional phrase. In informal English, *like* is often used as a conjunction meaning "as"; but in formal English, *as* is always preferable.

EXAMPLES She looks **like** her mother. [*Like* introduces the phrase *like her mother.*] We should do as your parents suggest. [*Your parents suggest* is a clause and needs the conjunction *as* (not the preposition *like*) to introduce it.]

like, as if In formal written English, *like* should not be used for the compound conjunctions *as if* or *as though.*

EXAMPLE Scottie looks **as though** [not *like*] he has been in a fight.

might of, must of See **could of.**

no, none, nothing See **The Double Negative** (page 235).

nowheres See **anywheres,** etc.

of Do not use *of* with prepositions such as *inside, off, outside,* etc.

EXAMPLE   He jumped **off** [not *off of*] the diving board into the pool **outside** [not *outside of*] the hotel.

What was resting **inside** [not *inside of*] Pandora's box?

Of is also unnecessary with *had*.

EXAMPLE   If I **had** [not *had of*] seen you, I would have told you about it.

ought to of   See **could of.**

EXERCISE 3. This exercise covers the most important usage problems discussed on pages 228–30 of this glossary. Number your paper 1–20. Beside each number, write the correct word in parentheses in the corresponding sentence.

1. You (hadn't ought, ought not) to have missed class yesterday.
2. Mr. James (learned, taught) us the background of *Romeo and Juliet.*
3. (Shakespeare, Shakespeare he) wrote the play when he was a young man.
4. (Leave, Let) me tell you about the story.
5. I particularly like (these kind, these kinds) of plots.
6. The (Montagues they, Montagues) were rivals of the Capulets.
7. Perhaps Romeo, a Montague, (hadn't ought, ought not) to have gone to the Capulets' party.
8. However, if he (hadn't, hadn't of), he would not have met Juliet.
9. After the party, Romeo stood in the garden (outside, outside of) Juliet's room.
10. He (left, let) Juliet declare her love for him before he spoke to her.
11. Shakespeare writes (these kind, these kinds) of scenes very well.

12. Do you think Friar Laurence (ought, had ought) to have performed the marriage ceremony?
13. Perhaps the young couple (hadn't ought, ought not) to have been married at all.
14. Certainly Romeo (shouldn't have, shouldn't of) become involved in a fight so soon after his wedding.
15. Mr. James (learned, taught) us that in the fight Romeo killed Juliet's cousin Tybalt; because of this, Romeo was banished from Verona.
16. Juliet could hardly bear to (leave, let) Romeo go.
17. If Lord and Lady Capulet (had, had of) been more understanding, the tragedy might never have happened.
18. Nevertheless, Juliet (hadn't ought to, shouldn't) have taken the sleeping potion.
19. Believing Juliet dead, Romeo returned to Verona and killed Paris (outside of, outside) Juliet's tomb. Then he killed himself.
20. When (the Montagues and the Capulets, the Montagues and the Capulets they) learned of the death of Romeo and Juliet, they ended their feud.

rise, raise   See page 173.

said, same, such   Avoid artificial uses like these:

> AVOID   I entered P.S. 41 in the first grade and attended said school three years.
>
> The police officer chased the bandit and finally caught same.
>
> Mrs. Nunez wanted an eight-room house with a yard, but such was not available in her town.

shall, will   Some people prefer to use *shall* with first person pronouns and *will* with second and third person in the future and future perfect tenses. Nowadays, most Americans do not make this distinction. *Will* is acceptable in the first person as well as in the other two.

sit, set See pages 171–72.

so This word is usually overworked. Avoid using it in writing as a conjunction meaning *therefore.*

NOT GOOD The baseball game lasted for twelve innings, so we did not interview the coach afterward.

BETTER Because the baseball game lasted for twelve innings, we did not interview the coach afterward.

or The baseball game lasted for twelve innings; therefore, we did not interview the coach afterward.

some, somewhat In writing do not use *some* for *somewhat* as an adverb.

NONSTANDARD My spelling has improved some.
STANDARD My spelling has improved **somewhat.**

than, then Do not confuse these words. *Than* is a conjunction; *then* is an adverb.

EXAMPLES This pitcher of lemonade is sweeter **than** the first one was.
We finished drying the dishes. **Then** we watched television.

them *Them* should not be used as an adjective. Use *these* or *those.*

EXAMPLE Where did you find **those** [not *them*] pencils?

this here, that there The *here* and the *there* are unnecessary.

EXAMPLE   I like **this** [not *this here*] dress better than **that** [not *that there*] one.

this kind, sort, type   See **kind,** etc.

way, ways   Use *way,* not *ways,* in referring to a distance.

EXAMPLE   We have a long **way** [not *ways*] to go.

when, where   Do not use *when* or *where* incorrectly in writing a definition.

NONSTANDARD   A "bomb" in football is when a quarterback throws a long pass.
STANDARD   A "bomb" in football is a long pass thrown by the quarterback.

where   Do not use *where* for *that.*

EXAMPLE   I read in yesterday's paper **that** [not *where*] your sister won the race.

which, that, who   Remember that the relative pronoun *who* refers to people only; *which* refers to things only; *that* refers to either people or things.

EXAMPLES   There is the man **who** telephoned us. [person]
Here is the car **which** she bought from my mother. [thing]
It is the kind of car **that** I like. [thing]
She is a person **that** can be trusted. [person]

who, whom   See pages 190–94.

without, unless   Do not use the preposition *without* in place of the conjunction *unless.*

EXAMPLE   I will not be able to go **unless** [not *without*] I finish my homework.

would of See **could of.**

EXERCISE 4. The sentences in this exercise cover the most important usage problems presented on pages 231–33 of the glossary. Number your paper 1–20. Beside each number, write the correct one of the two expressions in parentheses in the corresponding sentence.

1. The doctor said that Aunt Edna is starting to get her strength back (some, somewhat).
2. Do not make any more noise (than, then) you have to.
3. On the newscast I heard (that, where) the strike had been averted.
4. What did you do with (them, those) tennis balls?
5. (This, This here) watch belonged to my great-grandfather.
6. People came a long (way, ways) to attend the celebration.
7. (Them, Those) records should be stored upright in a cool place.
8. (Without, Unless) it stops raining, we shall have to cancel our picnic.
9. My parents hope to buy (that, that there) car.
10. Athena was one of the goddesses (who, which) lived on Olympus.
11. Please hand me (them, those) nails and (that, that there) hammer.
12. It is only a short (way, ways) to town.
13. The question was less complicated (than, then) it seemed at first.
14. At school today we learned (where, that) we will have a half-holiday on Friday.
15. Elizabeth Bishop is the American poet (who, which) interests me most.
16. Janet relaxed (some, somewhat) after she began to speak.

17. He would not have made that statement (without, unless) he had first checked his facts.
18. Please set (those, them) chairs around the table.
19. Is she the one (who, which) was elected captain of the hockey team?
20. (This, This here) tie and (that there, that) jacket need to be cleaned.

REVIEW EXERCISE B. This exercise covers the most important usage problems on pages 220–33. Rewrite each of the following sentences, correcting the errors in usage.

1. Smog is when auto exhaust and other types of air pollution mix with fog.
2. Marion she is a more accomplished violinist than Rodney is.
3. Take this here cake and them jars of jam to Mr. Mackintosh like I requested.
4. If I had of studied last night, I might of improved some my performance on the test.
5. I saw in the paper where people may not vote without they have registered.
6. The apple fell off of the tree and rolled a long ways down the hill.
7. Kira Crowell promised to learn us about these kind of chemicals.
8. The man which saw the accident hadn't ought to have left.
9. My little brother he refused to leave me read in peace.
10. Them seniors could of helped us.

THE DOUBLE NEGATIVE

A *double negative* is a construction in which two negative words are used when one is sufficient. Before the eighteenth century, the double negative — or triple negative or quadruple negative—was both useful and popular. The more negatives used in a sentence, the more emphatically the writer or speaker meant "No!" For example, look at the following sentence:

Barney does not never do no work.

This piling up of negatives is no longer good English usage. We now express the same idea with only one negative in the sentence:

EXAMPLE Barney does **not** ever do any work.
  or Barney **never** does any work.
  or Barney does **no** work.

Keep your usage up-to-date by avoiding such double negatives as those listed below.

can't hardly, can't scarcely The words *hardly* and *scarcely* convey a negative meaning. They should never be used with another negative word.

EXAMPLES I **can** [not *can't*] **hardly** lift this suitcase.
We **had** [not *hadn't*] **scarcely** enough refreshments for everyone.

haven't but, haven't only In certain uses, *but* and *only* convey a negative meaning and should not be used with *not*.

EXAMPLE We **have** [not *haven't*] **but** five dollars to spend.

no, nothing, none These words are, of course, negative. Do not use them with another negative word.

NONSTANDARD It doesn't make no difference to me.
STANDARD It **makes no** difference to me.

STANDARD	It **doesn't make any** difference to me.
NONSTANDARD	The searchers haven't found nothing.
STANDARD	The searchers **haven't found anything.**
STANDARD	The searchers **have found nothing.**
NONSTANDARD	We looked for gold, but there wasn't none.
STANDARD	We looked for gold, but there **wasn't any.**
STANDARD	We looked for gold, but there **was none.**

EXERCISE 5. Rewrite each of the following sentences, correcting the usage errors.

1. Paula hasn't done nothing to make him angry.
2. There isn't no ice cream left in the freezer.
3. I must go shopping, for I haven't only a few winter clothes.
4. Terry couldn't hardly move her arm yesterday.
5. This paragraph doesn't make no sense to me.
6. I went back to get another helping of potato salad, but there wasn't none.
7. We haven't but two more weeks of school before vacation.
8. Didn't you ever do nothing about that?
9. Nothing seems to make no difference to him any more.
10. I haven't ever seen no flamingos.

REVIEW EXERCISE C. This exercise, which contains fifty usage errors, covers most of the problems discussed in this glossary. If a sentence is correct, write the number of the sentence and then write *C* after the number. If a sentence contains usage errors, write the number of the sentence and then rewrite the sentence, correcting the errors.

1. I heard where the committee must now choose between three different proposals.
2. I hadn't ought to go to the movies, for I haven't but two dollars to spend this week.
3. Unless the person which borrowed my book takes it back to me, I won't be able to do no more work on my essay.
4. Surely you could of done this here assignment sooner then you did.
5. Mr. Newlan learned us about Samuel Morse, the man who discovered the telegraph.
6. My having slept less hours then usual last night may effect my performance on today's test.
7. The reward was divided equally among the three contestants.
8. That there debating team they spoke extremely good and must of done a great deal of research.
9. This semester I have accepted fewer invitations to parties and dances than I did last term.
10. Patricia doesn't never enjoy discussing those kind of subjects with people she don't trust.
11. I wish I had of told them children not to play inside of that old hut besides the quarry.
12. I can't hardly understand how you could of busted them dishes.
13. Sally don't plan to bring her tennis racket to camp next summer without she can find someone to learn her how to play.
14. Among my classmates, three students besides Mona and me have decided to learn more about that kind of architecture.
15. Leave me read you this here list of persons which have excepted our invitation.
16. I read where unemployment is having a serious

affect everywheres on sales of food, clothing, automobiles, and etc.

17. We don't plan to go anywheres during our vacation accept to visit my grandmother, who lives in Princeton.
18. An improper fraction is where the numerator is bigger then the denominator.
19. Eli Whitney had ought to be remembered because he was the man which discovered the cotton gin, the machine that affected great changes in the economy of the South.
20. Shira she hiked a good bit farther than anyone else.

Sentence
Structure

PART THREE

Chapter **10**

Writing Complete Sentences

Sentence Fragments and Run-on Sentences

In writing, the best way to communicate your ideas is to use effective, forceful sentences. To ensure that your meaning will be clearly understood, you should make certain that your sentences are punctuated correctly. Most important, you should know where they begin and where they end. In other words, you must develop *sentence sense* in writing.

You already have sentence sense regarding spoken language. When you are speaking, your voice rises and falls naturally to indicate the beginning and the end of a sentence.

You can develop sentence sense in writing by "listening" to the sentences you write. If you practice "listening" to the exercise sentences in this chapter, you will learn to avoid the two common errors of writing discussed here: the *fragment* and the *run-on sentence*.

THE SENTENCE FRAGMENT

10a. A *fragment* is a separated sentence part that does not express a complete thought.

A fragment is usually an additional idea that has been incorrectly cut off from the sentence in which it belongs.

EXAMPLES Scratching noises on the cabin porch indicated that I had a visitor. *Probably a raccoon or a wildcat.*

As we ran toward the bus, it drove off. *Leaving Nan and me standing helplessly on the corner.*

In the first example above, *Probably a raccoon or a wildcat* is a fragment cut off from the preceding sentence. It does not make sense by itself. In the second example, *Leaving Nan and me standing helplessly on the corner* is also a fragment; without a subject and verb, it does not express a complete thought. These fragments should be joined to the sentences preceding them.

EXAMPLES Scratching noises on the cabin porch indicated that I had a visitor, **probably a raccoon or a wildcat.**

As we ran toward the bus, it drove off, **leaving Nan and me standing helplessly on the corner.**

Sometimes a fragment should be corrected by being placed at the beginning or within the sentence from which it was separated.

FRAGMENT Hubert works slowly and deliberately on the mound. *Taking plenty of time between pitches.*

CORRECTED **Taking plenty of time between pitches,** Hubert works slowly and deliberately on the mound.

FRAGMENT We talked with Mrs. Jackson in her office. *The principal of the school.*

CORRECTED   We talked with Mrs. Jackson, **the principal of the school,** in her office.

EXERCISE 1. How good is your "sentence sense"? Find out by deciding whether or not each group of words is a sentence. Number 1–10 on your paper. After the proper number, write *F* for fragment or *S* for sentence.

1. Thumbing through the first few pages of *The Way to Rainy Mountain* by N. Scott Momaday.
2. To warn motorists of the ice forming on bridges.
3. On the other side of the mountain is a beautiful valley.
4. Can you prove it?
5. After rehearsal we got together and memorized our lines.
6. Leroy, playing defensive end for the Lions.
7. Singing is Martina Arroyo's profession.
8. An old two-story house with spacious rooms, designed to accommodate a large family of a dozen or more.
9. In the spring, when the warm sun shines upon the fresh green beauty of the earth and when red tulips wave in the March winds.
10. Even though she had to support her mother and three younger brothers and sisters with her earning as a stockbroker.

EXERCISE 2. Number on your paper from 1–10. If a numbered item contains a fragment, write *F* after its number. If it contains only sentences, write *S* for sentences.

1. A few Eskimos live on the Barren Grounds. A remote area of northern Canada.
2. The flycatcher has a forked tail almost a foot long. In flight this bird looks like something from outer space.

F 3. Four of us were standing on the corner. Waiting for the five o'clock bus to Riverside Skating Arena in the downtown mall.

S 4. The editor of the school paper interviewed Mrs. Franklin. She is the new history teacher and coach of the debating team.

F 5. I wrote to an office in Tallahassee, Florida. To get some information for my report on environmental protection laws.

S 6. I cast my plug about twenty yards from where I was standing. I waited for a long silver bass to strike the bait.

F 7. We tried to do an especially good job on our first day at work. Hoping to earn a generous tip from customers.

F 8. In Wyoming we traveled through Cody, a city named for W. F. Cody. Who is better known as "Buffalo Bill" Cody.

S 9. P. T. Barnum was a legendary American figure. He was a showman who is best known for his circus, *The Greatest Show on Earth.*

F 10. Yesterday at the ice-cream parlor I ordered a shipwreck. A banana split without the banana.

Common Types of Sentence Fragments

10b. A subordinate clause must not be written as a sentence.

A subordinate clause always depends on an independent clause to complete its meaning. Notice that the subordinate clause fragment below does not express a complete thought.

Although Bertha receives a large allowance

The clause has a verb, *receives,* and a subject, *Bertha.* Because of the word *although,* however, the thought is not complete. Like all fragments, this one may be corrected by being placed in a sentence — that is, by being attached to an independent clause.

> Although Bertha receives a large allowance, she often seems miserly.
> Bertha often seems miserly although she receives a large allowance.

Remember that relative pronouns (*which, that, who, whom, whose*) and subordinating conjunctions (see the list on page 114) introduce subordinate clauses. These little words are very important; they can change a complete thought to a fragment.

SENTENCE	Claude told the truth.
FRAGMENTS	**Unless** Claude told the truth
	That Claude told the truth
	Claude, **who** told the truth

EXERCISE 3. Most of the following items contain subordinate clauses which are punctuated as sentences. Correct these fragments by making them a part of the sentence in the item. You may have to leave out or add words. When you are rewriting, be particularly careful to avoid misplaced modifiers. If an item is correct, write a *C* after the appropriate number.

1. Next week we are going to Williamsburg. Which is a historic city in Virginia.
2. Although it was nothing more than a small village in the seventeenth century. Williamsburg was the scene of several important events in the eighteenth century.
3. Though many of the buildings in Williamsburg today are not the original ones, they are exact likenesses. The town's only major industry is restoration.
4. What I want most to see is the Public Gaol.

Which once housed fifteen of Blackbeard's pirates, thirteen of whom were hanged.
5. Completed in 1720, the Governor's Palace was later the official residence of the first two governors of the state. Who were Patrick Henry and Thomas Jefferson.
6. The Raleigh Tavern, which was the center of many heated political discussions. It was the inn in which both George Washington and Thomas Jefferson frequently dined.
7. The tools which were used for trade in the eighteenth century. These have been re-created in various craft shops.
8. In Virginia, we will see my sister. She is a student at the College of William and Mary.
9. William and Mary is the second oldest college in the United States. Which is located in Williamsburg.
10. Because we want to see the White House. We may stop in Washington, D. C., on the way home.

10c. A verbal phrase must not be written as a sentence.

As you learned in Chapter 3, present participles and gerunds are verbals ending in –*ing* (*coming, working, being*). Past participles usually end in –*d*, –*ed*, –*t*, –*n*, or –*en* (*looked, slept, broken*). Infinitives usually consist of *to* plus the verb (*to go, to play*).

A verbal phrase is a phrase containing a verbal. It is often mistaken for a sentence because the verbal is often mistaken for a main verb. However, a phrase does not have both a subject and a verb; it cannot express a complete thought. By itself, a verbal phrase is a fragment.

FRAGMENTS   Spilling juice all over the floor
Poised on her toes
Saying goodbye
To approve his son's marriage

Like subordinate clauses, verbals depend upon independent clauses to make their meaning complete.

SENTENCES   Spilling juice all over the floor, I dashed back to the television.

A ballet dancer, poised on her toes, waited for the cue.

Carl and Shirley parted quickly without even saying goodbye.

Mr. Yen was happy to approve his son's marriage.

EXERCISE 4. Revise the ten fragments in the following paragraph by attaching them logically to independent clauses. Copy the paragraph, changing the punctuation so that there will be no verbal phrases standing by themselves.

Many stories and songs have been written about Lorelei. The name of a huge rock which juts from the Rhine River in Germany. According to one song the rock is inhabited by a woman. Blessed with supernatural powers. Glittering in the sunlight. Her gold jewelry catches the attention of a sailor. Passing in a sailboat. By singing a magical song. She casts a spell on the sailor. Forcing him to stare up at her. As a result he never sees the dangerous obstacles in the water. The jagged rocks which can tear into a ship's hull. Deprived of his senses. The sailor runs his boat upon the rocks. Then, still caught within the woman's spell. He follows his boat to a watery death. Many ships have sunk near Lorelei. Destroyed by the power of this magical woman.

EXERCISE 5. Below are ten verbal phrases incorrectly written as sentences. Use each in a complete sentence.

1. Pushing her way forward.
2. Disturbed by a fidgety conscience.

3. To mutter to himself and to the typewriter.
4. After sharpening four red pencils.
5. Before getting a new pair of boots.
6. Encouraged by my teacher's praise.
7. Patiently accepting the stern advice.
8. Somewhat amused by Gilda's cartoon.
9. To be not only wealthy but also healthy.
10. Convinced by her persuasiveness and logic.

REVIEW EXERCISE A. Some of the following groups of words are sentences; others are subordinate clauses or verbal phrases incorrectly written as sentences. Number your paper 1–20. Place *S* after the corresponding number of each complete sentence. Write *F* after the corresponding number of each fragment. Be prepared to tell how you would correct each fragment by making it a part of a related sentence.

1. In 1628 William Harvey published his new theory.
2. Which explained the circulation of the blood by the motion of the heart.
3. Stated twelve years earlier.
4. This theory set forth the idea that the heart is a kind of pump.
5. To force the blood through the veins.
6. As scientists began studying the circulation of the blood.
7. They learned that the blood gives life to cells in the body.
8. Blood also helps to clean the cells.
9. By carrying away waste products.
10. In the bloodstream are red blood cells.
11. Which are carriers of oxygen.
12. Provided by the lungs.
13. Every day new red blood cells are born.
14. As old ones wear out.
15. There are also white cells in the bloodstream.
16. These white cells destroy harmful germs.
17. Some cells die as they fight the germs.

18. Too many white cells in the bloodstream may indicate a serious infection.
19. When they are needed to fight hordes of germs.
20. The body manufactures a great number of white cells.

10d. An appositive phrase must not be written as a sentence.

An appositive is a word which means the same thing as the noun or pronoun it follows. (See Chapter 3.) An appositive phrase is made up of the appositive and its modifiers. Like other phrases, it does not contain the basic parts of a sentence. It is set off within a sentence by commas but cannot stand by itself as a complete thought. By itself it is a fragment.

FRAGMENT   The reaper was invented by Cyrus McCormick. *A famous farmer of Virginia.*

SENTENCE   The reaper was invented by Cyrus McCormick, **a famous farmer of Virginia.**

Occasionally an appositive fragment may be separated by other words from the noun or pronoun it refers to.

FRAGMENT   Cyrus McCormick invented the reaper. *A famous farmer of Virginia.*

SENTENCE   Cyrus McCormick, **a famous farmer of Virginia,** invented the reaper.

REVIEW EXERCISE B. Number your paper 1–10. Each item in this exercise has two parts. If both parts are sentences, write after the corresponding number the last word in the first sentence, and follow it with a period. Then write the first word in the second sentence, using a capital letter. If one of the parts is a fragment requiring a comma, write the word preceding the comma, add the comma, and write the word that should follow the comma. Be sure you put the fragment in its proper place in the sentence. If no punctuation is required, write *C* for *correct*.

EXAMPLES   1. In English class we are studying types of humor   my teacher is Ms. Blevins.
1. *humor. My*
2. Ms. Blevins defined two literary terms indirect satire and irony.
2. *terms, indirect*

1. Ms. Blevins gave us an interesting assignment   a composition dealing with an ironical situation.
2. In his paper Roy Welch described what recently happened to Mrs. Myer   Roy's next-door neighbor.
3. A detective with wide experience   Mrs. Myer gave a lecture to the Civic Club.
4. She is an interesting speaker   the stories she tells are fascinating.
5. In her lecture, she gave advice on one topic   methods of outwitting pickpockets.
6. The audience listened intently   because they had heard stories about citizens who had had their pockets picked.
7. An ironic thing happened the very next Saturday   the day of the big game.
8. Mrs. Myer went to the game   expecting to meet at the ticket booth several invited friends.
9. In her wallet Mrs. Myer had a great deal of money approximately seventy dollars.
10. When she reached for her wallet to pay for her tickets   she discovered that her purse had been picked by somebody in the crowd.

10e. Avoid other sentence fragments.

On page 253 is a list of other common types of fragments. Although you do not need to learn the names of these, you should be able to recognize them as incomplete ideas so that you can avoid writing them as sentence fragments in your compositions.

1. *Prepositional phrases:* The annual athletic awards were presented. After the last game of the season.
2. *Compound of parts of a sentence:* On July 4 Donna packed everything for our picnic. But forgot paper plates.
3. *Parts of a comparison:* The dinner tempts me. As much as a cage tempts a sparrow.
4. *Items in a series:* All her essays are written in the same fine style. Clear, concise, and interesting.

Each fragment should be attached to a complete sentence. Sentence 1, for example, may be rewritten as follows:

After the last game of the season, the annual athletic awards were presented.

The annual athletic awards were presented **after the last game of the season.**

REVIEW EXERCISE C. Rewrite each item below so that the fragment is eliminated.

1. The woman skipped briskly down the sidewalk in front of me. Like a child playing hopscotch on a summer afternoon.
2. When the parakeet hid under the chair, Sue gently broomed it out. And eventually returned it to its cage.
3. The people of Grand Rapids, Michigan, manufacture many products. Such as chemicals, furniture, and tools.
4. Acorns are eaten not only by squirrels. But also by pigs.
5. Before going to sleep, I like to eat something. Especially ham sandwiches and cold chicken.

6. This all-purpose cleanser brightens pots and pans. Including copper-bottomed skillets.
7. I don't know how to cook vegetables. To keep them from tasting flat.
8. On Saturdays I not only help around the house. But also work in the yard.
9. Louise bought herself a ruling pen. After deciding to learn mechanical drawing.
10. I learned many things at camp. Such as how to put up a tent.

THE RUN-ON SENTENCE

Sentence fragments are usually the result of ending a sentence too soon — before a final idea has been included.

Sometimes writers don't recognize where a sentence ends, and they keep on going into the next sentence. They use a comma or no mark of punctuation at all instead of a period after a sentence. They permit the sentence to "run on" into the next.

10f. A *run-on sentence* consists of two or more sentences separated only by a comma or by no mark of punctuation.

Every sentence should begin with a capital letter and should be followed by an end mark: period, question mark, or exclamation point. Sentences should never be run together without punctuation.

RUN-ON   Where are Riff and Raff those cats won't come when I call them.

CORRECTED   Where are Riff and Raff? Those cats won't come when I call them.

The comma should never take the place of an end mark.

RUN-ON   Last year we spent our vacation in Pennsylvania, this summer we plan to drive through the Southwest.

CORRECTED   Last year we spent our vacation in Pennsylvania. This summer we plan to drive through the Southwest.

Correcting Run-on Sentences

In the previous example, the run-on sentence was corrected by making two separate sentences. Notice, however, that the sentences are closely related. (Writers usually do not run unrelated sentences together.)

Instead of punctuating it as two sentences, you may prefer to correct a run-on sentence by making a compound sentence. If you do, use either a comma and a coordinating conjunction (*and, but, or*) or a semicolon and no conjunction between the two independent clauses.

EXAMPLES   Last year we spent our vacation in Pennsylvania, **but** this summer we plan to drive through the Southwest.

Last year we spent our vacation in Pennsylvania; this summer we plan to drive through the Southwest.

Occasionally a run-on sentence may be corrected by expressing one of the parts in a subordinate clause.

EXAMPLE   Although we spent our vacation in Pennsylvania last year, this summer we plan to drive through the Southwest.

EXERCISE 6. You will find the following passages hard to read because run-on sentences always interfere with the clear expression of ideas. Exercise your sentence sense to decide where each sentence should end. Then write the last word of each sentence on your paper after the corresponding number. Place the proper mark of punctuation after the word, and then write the first word of the next sentence, beginning it with a capital letter.

If you make the run-on sentence into a compound sentence, write the last word of the first clause, follow it with a comma and a coordinating conjunction or with a semicolon, and write the first word of the second clause.

If you decide to subordinate an element, write the first word of the clause or phrase, a dash, and the last word.

EXAMPLE   1. We were eating breakfast, Dad made a dramatic gesture and knocked over the sugar bowl, I choked a bit on my milk my grandmother chuckled so hard that the table quivered.

         1. *While — breakfast, Dad bowl. I milk, and my*

1. The inventor of the typewriter probably thought that he was doing the world a favor, it's too bad that he didn't consider the effect of his invention on me, in fact, typewriting lessons are making a nervous wreck out of me.
2. Why must all the letters of the alphabet be in such confusion on the keyboard why must typewriters in school have black tabs covering the jumbled letters why must my typewriter play hopscotch when I rest my thumb on the long bar?
3. It is fun to grow ornamental peppers, if you have one plant, you can start a forest of them because each pod has scores of seeds, each seed is a potential plant in the spring tiny white and purple blossoms appear.

4. These blossoms slowly transform themselves into green pods later the green turns to purple then it changes to yellow and orange finally it becomes a bright red, since each pod is at a different stage of growth, the plant looks like a Christmas tree.

5. After graduating from college, my mother took graduate courses in environmental studies at night, worked part-time as a reporter during the day, and helped fight fires as a volunteer on Saturdays, since she was very concerned with the condition of the environment she enjoyed all her activities.

6. She had two boyfriends—Frank, my father, and Percival, a neighbor neither one could convince Mother to marry for several years Percival tried in vain.

7. Finally Father succeeded though she took fewer night classes, Mother continued to do research on ecology, eventually she organized an ecology study center for our town.

8. Have you ever asked an experienced cook for a recipe, the cook probably told you that the dish is extremely easy to prepare, "just fill the bowl and add a dash of this and a bit of that."

9. You decide to put the ingredients on the kitchen table, then you watch how to mix everything together, however, this procedure fails to teach you the recipe because the cooking is done the same way as the directing, pouring flour from the sack and scooping sugar out by the handful.

10. You should take my advice be content to eat these tasty meals be patient until fifty years from now then you can confuse others with the same kind of "dash of this, bit of that" directions.

REVIEW EXERCISE D. Rewrite the following paragraphs, removing all fragments and run-ons.

I enjoyed history class this morning. Although I

sometimes think that dates and historical events are dull. Today I learned many interesting facts about the history of medicine. Especially about the work of Harvey, Jenner, Pasteur, and Nightingale.

For many centuries scientists knew very little about the blood, in the early seventeenth century William Harvey's theory of blood circulation started a kind of revolution in medicine. One hundred and fifty years later Edward Jenner found out that a person who had had cowpox was immune to smallpox, this discovery helped Jenner find a good way to fight smallpox, by vaccination. Thus preventing the disease rather than attempting to treat it. In the nineteenth century Louis Pasteur proved that germs cause disease, he also discovered several methods of killing germs. Including pasteurization, a process named after him. Though Florence Nightingale was not a scientist, she was dedicated to the nursing profession, after studying the latest nursing techniques, she traveled to the Crimea, there she helped wounded soldiers. Often working nineteen hours a day. Modern medicine is greatly indebted to these pioneers.

Chapter 11

Sentence Combining and Revising

Achieving Sentence Variety

You can add interest to your compositions by varying the way you construct sentences. As you study this chapter, remember that *how* you express your ideas will affect your reader's reaction to *what* you are saying. The way in which you express your ideas will help determine the amount of attention and interest given you by your reader. If too many of your sentences are short and choppy or long and stringy, your style becomes monotonous and makes the most interesting topic seem dull. Avoid monotony of style by learning to combine sentences and to vary sentences effectively.

SENTENCE COMBINING

Short sentences are often effective in a composition, but a long series of short sentences is a sign of an immature style. Notice how the short, choppy sentences in the following paragraph sound childish and make the paragraph difficult to read.

In my hands money doesn't last long. My aunt sent me ten dollars. It was a birthday present. I held onto the money for about ten minutes. My

brother demanded repayment. I had borrowed two
dollars from him a week before. Marcia and Jennie
are my best friends. They had treated me to lunch
a long time ago. They suddenly suggested that I return the favor. My mother's birthday is next week.
I am almost broke. Maybe I can make something
for her, like a cake. It won't cost me any money.

The next paragraph shows how these short, choppy
sentences can be combined into longer sentences.

> In my hands money doesn't last long. When my
> aunt sent me ten dollars as a birthday present, I
> held onto the money for about ten minutes. My
> brother demanded repayment of the two dollars
> I had borrowed from him a week before. Marcia
> and Jennie, my best friends, who had treated me to
> lunch a long time ago, suddenly suggested that I re-
> turn the favor. My mother's birthday is next week.
> Since I am almost broke, maybe I can make some-
> thing for her that won't cost me any money, like
> a cake.

The rewritten paragraph still contains two short
sentences. However, they contribute to effective sentence variety. Used with the longer sentences, they
do not create a choppy effect.

Combining short, related sentences into longer sentences is valuable practice for improving your writing
style. The following rules offer several ways to combine sentences. When you have completed the sentence-combining practice in this book, remember the
rules as you revise and improve your own sentences.

**11a. Combine short, related sentences by inserting
adjectives, adverbs, or prepositional phrases.**

TWO SENTENCES   Billie Jean King is a tennis champion.
She is courageous.

ONE SENTENCE	Billie Jean King is a courageous tennis champion. [The adjective *courageous* in the second sentence is inserted into the first sentence.]
TWO SENTENCES	She answered my questions during an interview. She was patient.
ONE SENTENCE	She patiently answered my questions during an interview. [The adjective *patient* in the second sentence has been changed into the adverb *patiently* and inserted into the first sentence.]
TWO SENTENCES	Billie Jean King paced the base line. She paced before the start of the game.
ONE SENTENCE	Before the start of the game, Billie Jean King paced the base line. [The second sentence, *She paced before the start of the game,* has been changed into two prepositional phrases, *before the start of the game,* and inserted into the first sentence.]

Notice in the last example that the sentences could have been combined in another way: *Billie Jean King paced the base line before the start of the game.* You, the writer, should decide which sentence sounds best.

EXERCISE 1. Combine each group of short, related sentences into one sentence by inserting adjectives, adverbs, or prepositional phrases. There may be more than one way to combine the sentences.

EXAMPLE   1. Billie Jean King waited for the next serve.

Her muscles were tensed.
She was eager.
1. *With her muscles tensed, Billie Jean King waited eagerly for the next serve.*

1. Doctors huddle over the patient.
   They are in the emergency room.
   The patient is badly injured.
2. One doctor checks for a heartbeat.
   He checks immediately.
   He checks with his stethoscope.
3. Another doctor peers into the patient's eyes.
   The eyes look glassy.
   The doctor uses a special light.
4. The eyes act as windows.
   They are windows into the body.
   They are windows for doctors.
5. Doctors detect clues to disorders.
   They look through the eyes.
   The disorders are medical.
6. Problems show up in the eyes.
   They are problems of the blood system.
   They usually show up.
7. Therefore doctors check the eyes.
   The check is routine.
   They check in any emergency.
8. After the examination, the patient is moved.
   The examination is brief.
   The patient is moved to another room.
9. When surgery begins, the patient is given blood.
   The surgery is an emergency.
   It begins in less than an hour.
   The blood is given in large amounts.
10. The patient recovers from surgery.
    The recovery is quick.
    The recovery is fortunate.

11b. Combine closely related sentences by using participial phrases.

A participial phrase (see page 92) is a group of related words that contains a participle and that acts as an adjective, modifying a noun or a pronoun. In the following sentences, all the words in heavy type are part of a participial phrase.

EXAMPLES **Beginning a stamp collection,** I found ten valuable stamps in less than a week.
Begun by concerned citizens, the ecology patrol was a neighborhood success.

Two closely related sentences can be combined by making one sentence a participial phrase.

TWO SENTENCES   The batter was hit by the pitch.
He stood too close to the plate.

ONE SENTENCE   Standing too close to the plate, the batter was hit by the pitch.

A participial phrase must be placed close to the noun or pronoun it modifies. Otherwise the phrase might confuse the reader.

MISPLACED   The batter went to first hit by the pitch.
IMPROVED   Hit by the pitch, the batter went to first.

► NOTE   Use a comma after a participial phrase that begins a sentence.

EXAMPLE   Leaning perilously over the guardrail, Janet shouted her name and waited for the echo.

EXERCISE 2. Combine each of the following groups of sentences into one sentence by using a participial phrase. There may be more than one correct way to combine the sentences. Add commas where they are necessary.

EXAMPLE   1. Lisa bought a bicycle.
We saw her.
1. *We saw Lisa buying a bicycle.*

1. Ursula Le Guin spoke about science fiction.
   We listened to her.
2. Rita was pleased by the invitation.
   She accepted it immediately.
3. I applauded wildly at the end of the play.
   I rose from my seat.
4. The raccoon escaped from its cage.
   It chewed through metal bars.
5. We were encouraged by Ida's success.
   We decided to try trout fishing.
6. She read the news over the radio this morning.
   She spoke with an excited voice.
7. Mozart wrote musical compositions at the age of five.
   He astounded his family.
8. I spilled ink onto my best pair of jeans.
   I had leaned over my desk.
9. The moped weaved between parked cars.
   It barely missed a small child.
10. A team of scientists entered the pyramid's secret chamber.
    They sought pottery and other relics.

11c. Combine short, related sentences by using appositive phrases.

Appositive phrases (see page 103) are useful for explaining or identifying nouns or pronouns. The following sentence contains an appositive phrase in boldface type.

EXAMPLE   Inez Mexia, **a famous botanist,** explored the jungles of Brazil.

Two related sentences can be combined by using an appositive phrase.

TWO SENTENCES   Dr. Stone is my teacher at medical school.
She is the author of several books.

ONE SENTENCE   Dr. Stone, the author of several books, is my teacher at medical school.

EXERCISE 3. Combine each group of sentences by using an appositive phrase. Place the phrase next to the noun or pronoun it explains or modifies. Put commas at the beginning and end of each appositive phrase to set it off from the rest of the sentence.

EXAMPLE   1. Maggie L. Walker is honored at the Mary McLeod Bethune Museum.
            She was one of the first woman bank presidents in our country.
           1. *Maggie L. Walker, one of the first woman bank presidents in our country, is honored at the Mary McLeod Bethune Museum.*

1. Brenda Washington gave her report on Tuesday.
   Tuesday was the last day of classes.
2. The race car belonging to Janet Guthrie was in the parking lot.
   Janet Guthrie was a driver at the Indianapolis 500.
3. Soccer is gaining fans in the United States.
   It is the most popular sport in the world.
4. As an explorer, Roald Amundsen was bold and courageous.
   He became the first person to reach the South Pole by land.
5. *Roots* is the story of seven generations of one man's family.
   The book is an important contribution to American studies.
6. The Mayan kingdom covered most of Central America.
   The Mayan kingdom was a loose federation of cities.

7. Mystery Hill poses a riddle for archaeologists.
   It is a group of large stone buildings in New
   Hampshire.
8. Witchcraft is often associated with the site's past.
   Witchcraft is another name for sorcery.
9. Ellen Goodman's newspaper column won the
   Pulitzer Prize.
   It is the highest award given to journalists.
10. My cousin broke his ankle during a ski-jumping
    competition.
    He is an inexperienced skier.

Another method of combining short, related sentences is to join the subjects to make a compound
subject or to join the verbs to make a compound verb.

**11d. Combine short, related sentences by using com-
pound subjects and verbs.**

The subjects in a compound subject, like the verbs in
a compound verb, are joined by conjunctions such as
and, but, or *or* and by correlative conjunctions such
as *neither — nor, either — or,* and *both — and* (see pages
51–54).

EXAMPLES   **Both** Nancy Lopez **and** Tracy Austin
began their sports careers at a young age.
The soldiers **neither** ate **nor** rested during the long march.

To combine short sentences by using a compound
subject, look for sentences with the same verb but
different subjects.

TWO SENTENCES   Maria wrote a long story about
family life.
Leonard wrote one, too.
ONE SENTENCE   Maria and Leonard wrote long
stories about family life.

To combine sentences by using a compound verb, look
for sentences with the same subject but different verbs.

TWO SENTENCES   The yellow blossoms appear in late
                 April.
                 They last until the middle of May.
ONE SENTENCE   The yellow blossoms appear in late
                 April and last until the middle of
                 May.

A combined sentence may have both a compound subject and a compound verb.

THREE SENTENCES   The secretary typed the letter.
                   The treasurer also typed letters.
                   They both addressed envelopes.
ONE SENTENCE   The secretary and the treasurer
                   typed letters and addressed en-
                   velopes.

EXERCISE 4. Combine the following groups of sentences into one sentence by using compound subjects
and verbs. There may be more than one correct way
to combine the sentences. In the combined sentences,
be sure the subjects and verbs agree in number.

EXAMPLE   1. A slight rise in temperature will not be
              noticed.
              A slight drop in temperature will not be
              noticed either.
           1. *Neither a slight rise nor a slight drop
              in temperature will be noticed.*

1. The lifeguard was not able to see the stranded
   swimmer.
   The sunbathers on the beach also could not see
   the swimmer.
2. What Jeremy said was important.
   How he said it was also important.
3. The guard had turned away.
   He did not notice the general approaching.
4. Diana Nyad maintained her lead in the grueling
   marathon.
   She eventually won the race.

5. While I was there, I did not glimpse any of the birds.
I did not hear any of the birds either.

11e. Combine short, related sentences by writing a compound sentence.

A compound sentence (see page 121) is really two or more simple sentences joined together by one of the conjunctions *and, but, or, for, nor,* or *yet.*

EXAMPLE   The sandbags were piled high along the river, yet the flood waters crashed through the fortifications with ease.

When writing a compound sentence, be sure the ideas you connect are related and equal in importance.

UNRELATED IDEAS   The helicopter safely rescued the mountain climbers.
The mountain was in California.
RELATED IDEAS   The helicopter safely rescued the mountain climbers.
Their perilous adventure was over.
UNEQUAL IDEAS   The national census is taken every ten years.
I was interviewed by a census taker.
EQUAL IDEAS   The national census is taken every ten years.
The results are tabulated by computer.

► NOTE   Use a comma before *and, but, or, nor, for,* and *yet* when they join independent clauses.

EXERCISE 5. Most of the following items consist of two or more closely related ideas. Combine these ideas into a single compound sentence, using *and, but, or, for, nor,* or *yet.* A few items contain unrelated or unequal ideas. In such cases, write *U* after the appropriate number on your paper.

1. Rainfall is scarce in desert regions.
   Some plants and wildlife can thrive in this arid climate.
2. A desert may receive no rain for several years.
   Then torrents of rain may fall in a few hours.
3. Desert plants cannot store this sudden flood of water.
   The desert soil cannot absorb it.
4. The rainfall quickly erodes the desert landscape.
   Deserts have highly varied landscapes.
5. After a rainfall, colorful flowers bloom in the desert.
   These plants live only a short time.
6. During dry periods, desert plants are widely scattered.
   Many of them store large amounts of water in their leaves, roots, or stems.
7. The stem of the barrel cactus bulges with water after a rainfall.
   The plant depends on this private water supply for its life.
8. Desert animals include many kinds of insects, spiders, reptiles, birds, and mammals.
   The camel is one example of a desert animal.
9. Desert conditions have not changed for thousands of years.
   The size of deserts has grown considerably in recent centuries.
10. Trees have been planted to prevent desert expansion.
    Destructive high winds still cover fertile land with desert soil.

When combining equal ideas, you use a compound sentence. When combining unequal ideas, however, you should use a complex sentence.

11f. Combine short, choppy sentences into a complex sentence. Put one idea into a subordinate clause.

A complex sentence (see page 122) has an independent clause and at least one subordinate clause.

(1) Use an adjective clause to combine sentences.

An adjective clause (see pages 109–11) is a subordinate clause which, like an adjective, modifies a noun or a pronoun. In the following example, the adjective clause is in heavy type.

EXAMPLE   Eight of the planets **that orbit the sun** are named after Roman gods.

Adjective clauses begin with one of the relative pronouns — *who, whom, whose, which,* or *that.* When two sentences are closely related, they may be combined by using an adjective clause.

TWO SENTENCES   The belladonna plant is also called deadly nightshade.
Brad brought this plant into the house.

ONE SENTENCE   The belladonna plant that Brad brought into the house is also called deadly nightshade.

EXERCISE 6. Combine each of the following groups of sentences into one sentence by putting one of the ideas into an adjective clause. In the combined sentence the adjective clause should be placed as close as possible to the word it modifies.

EXAMPLES   1. He does not have "a right to his own opinion."
He knows nothing about the topic.
1. *He who knows nothing about the topic does not have "a right to his own opinion."*

2. The test covered yesterday's assignment.
I did well on it.

2. *I did well on the test that covered yesterday's assignment.*

1. The student enjoys practical jokes.
She put pepper on my popcorn.
2. The player stole second base.
He was covered with dust.
3. The horse once belonged to my grandmother.
It has a broken leg.
4. The dress is too large for me.
It may fit Marian.
5. Manuel drove the new red station wagon.
The car led the parade.
6. I fell madly in love with the artist.
She lives next door.
7. I stumbled over the shovel.
It was lying on the sidewalk.
8. My parents paid over a hundred dollars for a chair.
It was once owned by the first governor of the state.
9. At the zoo a monkey lost its temper.
It began throwing rocks at us.
10. The tall man coaches our football team.
I introduced him to you at the picnic.

Another type of subordinate clause is an adverb clause.

(2) Use an adverb clause to combine sentences.

An adverb clause (see pages 113–14) is a subordinate clause which, like an adverb, modifies a verb, adjective, or adverb.

EXAMPLE   **After she had seen the terrible effects of slavery,** Harriet Beecher Stowe wrote *Uncle Tom's Cabin.*

Adverb clauses, like adverbs, may tell *when, how, where, to what extent,* or *under what condition* an action is done. An adverb clause begins with a subordinating conjunction. Study the following list:

Common Subordinating Conjunctions

after	before	than	whenever
although	if	unless	where
as	since	until	wherever
because	so that	when	while

When you combine two short sentences by turning one of them into an adverb clause, be careful to choose the correct subordinating conjunction. Because a subordinating conjunction shows the relationship between clauses, a poorly chosen conjunction will show a false or meaningless relationship. For example, a number of subordinating conjunctions could be used to join the two sentences in the following example, but not all of them would show a relationship that makes sense.

TWO SENTENCES   The alarm rings.
I leap out of bed.

FALSE RELATIONSHIP   Until the alarm rings, I leap out of bed.

CLEAR   When the alarm rings, I leap out of bed.

▶ **NOTE** A comma sets off an introductory adverb clause.

EXERCISE 7. Combine each of the following groups of sentences into a single complex sentence by changing the sentence in italics into an adverb clause. Refer to the list of subordinating conjunctions on this page. Add commas where they are necessary.

EXAMPLE   1. *I can begin my sketch.*
I must sharpen all my pencils.

1. *Before I can begin my sketch, I must sharpen all my pencils.*

1. *I visit the city.*
   I like to see a play.
2. I found my glasses.
   I had looked for them all morning.
3. Michael hasn't spoken with Jeannie.
   She made the soccer team.
4. *We were at the movies.*
   Someone ran into our parked car.
5. *Rachel filled out the job application carefully.*
   She was interviewed immediately.
6. *Carlos canceled his subscription.*
   He still receives the magazine by mail.
7. Vicky collects shells.
   She can find them.
8. *The weather turned cold.*
   The pond froze.
9. You must register.
   You will be able to vote.
10. I learn something new.
    I open this dictionary.

REVIEW EXERCISE A. Combine each of the following groups of sentences into one sentence by using various sentence-combining techniques. Add commas where they are necessary.

EXAMPLE 1. Cora climbed up the hillside.
   She edged forward quietly and stealthily.
   She moved toward the spot.
   She had seen the gorilla there.
   1. *Climbing up the hillside, Cora quietly and stealthily edged toward the spot where she had seen the gorilla.*

1. The door swung open.
   We wheeled around.

We saw Mr. Cates.
He lumbered into the room.
2. We saw Hilda.
She was taking photographs.
She was by the lake.
She had her camera focused on a flock of geese.
3. My dog grew impatient.
He yowled at me.
He wanted to go for a walk.
It was not yet time.
4. Doctors use a stethoscope.
With it they listen to the heart.
They also listen to the lungs.
5. Hilary looked calmly over at the jury.
She picked up the letter.
She said the letter could prove her client's innocence.

A noun clause is a subordinate clause used as a noun.

(3) Use a noun clause to combine sentences.

Noun clauses (see pages 115–16) are usually introduced by *that, what, whatever, who, whoever, whom,* or *whomever.*

EXAMPLE   The scientists agreed **that the sun offered a huge supply of energy.**

Two sentences can combine with a noun clause.

TWO SENTENCES   Something puzzles me.
I don't know how the burglar broke the lock.
ONE SENTENCE   How the burglar broke the lock puzzles me.

EXERCISE 8.   Combine each of the following groups of sentences by turning the italicized sentence into a noun clause.

1. *The road to Palo Alto was closed for repairs.*
   Pedro did not know this fact.
2. *He told us.*
   It was not what we expected to hear.
3. *The boat somehow capsized on calm water.*
   The mystery remains.
4. *There was a time to keep quiet.*
   The soldier knew.
5. *Someone wore my coat.*
   Someone will pay the dry-cleaning bill.

REVIEW EXERCISE B. Combine each of the following groups of sentences into one smooth, clear sentence by using the sentence-combining techniques you have learned. Do not change the meaning of the sentences you combine. Add commas where they are necessary.

1. My hobby is photography.
   I took an unusual picture.
   It is a picture of the stars.
   In this picture, the stars are long white streaks.
2. I worked hours to get this effect.
   I propped the camera in my backyard.
   Then I set the time exposure.
   Hours later, I closed the shutter.
3. My sister graduated from high school last year.
   She has started college.
   She is taking science courses.
   She wants to enter medical school.
4. The bicycling road trip was scheduled for September.
   It has been postponed.
   The newspaper reported the postponement.
   The trip will be rescheduled soon.
5. Wendy was running in the marathon this afternoon.
   She passed two people wearing roller skates.
   They were also entered in the race.
   They were probably disqualified.

REVIEW EXERCISE C. The following paragraph contains choppy sentences. Revise and rewrite the paragraph by combining sentences to create clear, varied sentences. Use the sentence-combining methods you have learned, and be careful not to change the meaning of the original paragraph. Add commas where they are necessary.

The North Pole is one of the most remote areas on the earth. The South Pole is too. They are different from one another. The difference is dramatic. The North Pole is covered by an ocean. The South Pole is within a frozen land. The polar region in the North is inhabited. It has been the home of Eskimo peoples for millennia. The Antarctic is still largely uninhabited. It was an unknown region until two centuries ago. The climate of Antarctica is harsh. It is many degrees colder than the Arctic.

REVIEW EXERCISE D. Revise and rewrite the following paragraph to eliminate choppy sentences. Use the sentence-combining methods you have learned, and be careful not to change the meaning of the original paragraph. Add commas where they are necessary.

American voters do not vote directly for the President. This is according to the Constitution. They vote for people called electors. These people cast the official vote for the President. Electors' names may appear on ballots. Then again, they may not appear on the ballots. The ballots are presented to voters on Election Day. Election Day is in November. Electors gather in each state capital. They gather early in December. Their votes are sent to the U.S. Senate. They are sent immediately. The votes are counted. This is official. One of the candidates is declared President. It is the candidate who receives a majority of electoral votes.

AVOIDING STRINGY SENTENCES

When you strive to eliminate short, choppy sentences by combining sentences, you may make the mistake of writing long, stringy sentences. An occasional long sentence is good; it characterizes a mature style, and it adds both smoothness and variety to your compositions. Stringy sentences, however, in which main clauses are monotonously strung together with *and, but, for, or, nor,* should be avoided. To correct the stringy sentences in your compositions, use subordinating conjunctions (see page 114), compound verbs, and verbals.

STRINGY   Cleveland caught the pass, and he ran twenty-two yards, and so he made a first down.

BETTER   **After** he had caught the pass, Cleveland ran twenty-two yards, **making** a first down.

STRINGY   Marc went to the board, and he drew a map, but his directions were still not clear to the class.

BETTER   **Although** Marc went to the board and drew a map, his directions were still not clear to the class.

Sometimes it is better to break a long, stringy sentence into two or more sentences.

STRINGY   I read the assignment, and then I began making notes on cards, for I wanted to memorize the main points in the lesson, but the bell rang, and I was not through, and so I had to carry my heavy book home.

BETTER   **After reading the assignment,** I began making notes on cards **so that** I could memorize the main points in the lesson. **Since I was not through when the bell rang,** I had to carry my heavy book home.

EXERCISE 9. Revise the following stringy sentences by using subordinating conjunctions, compound verbs, and verbals. Some of the very long sentences should be made into two or more sentences.

1. An accident occurred at the busy intersection, and several persons were injured, and then the police decided to put up a traffic light.
2. Small children may swallow a dozen aspirins, or they may wander out into the street, for they are not old enough to think for themselves, and adults must make decisions for them.
3. Fever is usually the first sign of measles, and the eyes soon grow red, or the eyelids swell, and later the sneezing and coughing make a person think that it's merely a cold.
4. The trouble with New Year's resolutions is that they are always broken, for people make too many of them, or they hope for impossible reform, and they often try to become perfect all at once.
5. We are all creatures of habit, and bad habits are hard to break, but a person can make one resolution a year, and can concentrate on that one aim, and then is able to keep it.

VARYING SENTENCE BEGINNINGS

Although sentences which have the subject first may be grammatically correct, too many of them in one paragraph are monotonous. Therefore, to avoid a common cause of dullness in writing, you should learn to vary the beginnings of your sentences.

11g. Vary the beginnings of your sentences.

Read the following paragraph, an example of monotonous writing in which every sentence begins with the subject.

I have now found a solution to my crying problems when I peel strong onions. I was at the dentist's office yesterday, and I read a magazine article entitled "Onions Without Tears." Seven persons, according to this article, once tested ways to peel onions without weeping. These guinea pigs, after making various experiments, discarded two popular but useless theories. Chewing buttered bread did not stop tears. Keeping an ice cube inside one's closed mouth did not help, either. The testers found three ways of helping to avoid watery eyes. The first one was keeping a bread slice between the teeth. The second one was biting on a sulfur-tipped match. The third way was using an electric fan to blow away onion fumes. All experimenters, however, agreed that there are only two really effective ways to peel an onion without crying. You can shut your nose with the same kind of clip that swimmers sometimes use. You can talk or sing to keep your mouth open. I may try these ways, but not until I have tried my own method. I will get a songbook and a swimmer's noseclip and give them to a friend. I will then ask my friend to peel the onions for me.

As you see, too many subject-first sentences in the paragraph lessen the effectiveness of the ideas presented. Notice the varied beginnings of sentences in a revision of the same paragraph.

Now I have found a solution to my crying problems when I peel strong onions. *At the dentist's office yesterday,* I read a magazine article entitled "Onions Without Tears." *According to this article,* seven persons once tested ways to slice onions without weeping. *After making various experiments,* these guinea pigs discarded two popular but useless theories. *Neither* chewing buttered bread *nor* keeping an ice cube inside one's closed mouth helped to stop tears. The testers found these three ways of helping to avoid watery eyes: by keeping a bread slice between the teeth, by biting on a sulfur-tipped match, or by using an electric fan to blow away onion fumes. *Finally,* however, all the experimenters agreed that there are only two really effective ways to peel an onion without crying. *First,* to shut your nose, you can use a swimmer's noseclip. *Second,* to keep your mouth open, you can talk or sing. *Although I may try these ways,* I will first try my own method. I will get a friend a songbook and a swimmer's noseclip and ask my friend to peel the onions for me.

As this paragraph shows, there are many ways to begin sentences. Instead of putting the subject first in every sentence, you can vary your style by starting with a modifying word, phrase, or clause.

(1) You may begin sentences with single-word modifiers.

Learn to use adjectives, adverbs, and participles at the beginnings of sentences.

ADJECTIVES **Angry,** the umpire turned his back.

Dark and **empty,** the house looked very different from the way I remembered it.

Informal and **friendly,** she put everyone at ease.

ADVERBS **Soon** her cold glances reached the freezing point.

Unfortunately, Aunt Eloise did not preheat the oven.

PARTICIPLES **Sighing,** Adam shoved the spinach aside.

Delighted, the squirrel grabbed the nut and bounded away to bury it.

EXERCISE 10. The following sentences, all of which begin with the subject, contain a modifier that can be placed at the beginning of the sentence. Rewrite each sentence, placing the modifier at the beginning of the sentence.

1. Theresa sings occasionally.
2. The ball, spinning, whirled past.
3. Monty and Earl, exhausted, pitched camp.
4. Camille often reads herself to sleep.
5. We approached the icy bridge cautiously.
6. The league leaders, unbeaten and untied, expected little trouble from our team.
7. My dog, wet and dirty, jumped onto the couch.
8. Mrs. Bermudez' fingers impatiently drummed on the desk.
9. The ghost appeared to Hamlet again.
10. Wilbur, stumbling, bumped into a passer-by.

EXERCISE 11. Use the following modifiers to begin sentences of your own.

1. often
2. hurriedly
3. whispering
4. bewildered
5. hungry and cold
6. surely
7. courageously
8. suddenly
9. daydreaming
10. alone and afraid

(2) You may begin sentences with phrases.

Another good way to achieve sentence variety is to place prepositional, participial, or infinitive phrases at the beginning of sentences.

PREPOSITIONAL PHRASES   **On the other side of the island,** there is a fine natural harbor.

Behind Helga and me stood Mr. Soames, the night guard.

PARTICIPIAL PHRASES   **Hanging in the spring breeze,** the laundry was a mixture of bright colors.

Turned to stone by Zeus, Niobe continued to shed tears.

INFINITIVE PHRASES   **To be polite,** I chuckled at all of her jokes.

To determine the age of the mummy, the scientists tried various chemical tests.

EXERCISE 12. The following sentences, all of which begin with the subject, contain phrase modifiers that can be placed at the beginning of the sentence. Rewrite each sentence, placing the modifying phrase at the beginning. (Remember that a modifying phrase used as an adjective should be placed as close as possible to the word it modifies.)

1. We should eat a well-balanced variety of foods, for the sake of our health.
2. The kitten, frightened by the thunder, cowered under the sofa.
3. The exterminators bored holes through the cement and poured poison beneath the porch to kill the termites.
4. The whole episode, to tell the truth, was a hoax.
5. The wispy fog along the highway looks like gray ghosts prowling in the darkness, in the Smoky Mountains about midnight.
6. Flood waters no longer cause severe soil erosion in the Tennessee River basin.
7. The hides of bears, stitched with the hair turned inward, provide warmth for Eskimos.
8. Our dog, having bitten the carpenter, spent ten unhappy days in a veterinarian's cage.

9. We never thought of looking there, to be truthful.
10. The animals outnumber the people in our house.

EXERCISE 13. Use the following phrases to begin sentences of your own. After each sentence, name the kind of phrase with which it begins.

1. After fourteen rainy days
2. Dripping from head to toe
3. To annoy me
4. Sounding like a moose
5. In the middle of the garden
6. Hidden behind the curtain
7. To begin the lesson
8. To surprise everyone at the concert
9. Trained to retrieve anything
10. Beside the dying soldier

(3) You may begin sentences with subordinate clauses.

EXAMPLES **After we had explored the dark cave for two hours,** we longed for the return to sunlight.

While the clerk waited patiently, Sheila and Lynn carefully read the list of ingredients on the cereal package.

If the cloud cover remains, temperatures over the state will be higher than predicted.

EXERCISE 14. The ten simple sentences in this exercise begin with the subject. Using the examples above as a guide, add an introductory subordinate clause that is related to the main idea. Place a comma after each one of your introductory clauses. (You may find the list of subordinating conjunctions on page 272 helpful.)

1. Milton always tried to do the right thing.
2. She could see the finish line ahead of her.
3. He obviously did not remember my name.
4. We could not answer the riddle.
5. The motor ran out of fuel.
6. The mouse raced into the living room.
7. I saw that the bed had not been slept in.
8. They decided to cancel the game.
9. They were determined to attract more attention.
10. We tried a different way to avoid eating snacks.

REVIEW EXERCISE E. Rewrite each of the following sentences, changing the beginning as directed.

Begin these sentences with single-word modifiers:

1. We finally reached the Tennessee River basin.
2. As we drove along the Tennessee River, we often saw dams and large reservoirs.
3. There is less soil erosion in this region nowadays.
4. The Tennessee Valley Authority has certainly made many improvements.
5. Our family, vacationing, saw many other points of interest in the South.

Begin these sentences with modifying phrases:

6. Some Eskimos live in igloos during the winter.
7. They hunt wild game to provide food for themselves.
8. Eskimos need warm clothing for the cold climate.
9. Eskimos use the hide of a walrus for making shoes.
10. The people in the Sahara, unlike the Eskimos, have no difficulty keeping warm.
11. The Arabs wear flowing garments to protect themselves from the hot wind and sun.
12. The Arabian nomads move about from place to place, seeking water and grass for their sheep and camels.
13. They use light, movable tents for shelter.

Begin each of the following sentences with a subordinate clause:

14. There are many coffee plantations in Brazil, because the mild climate is ideal for growing coffee.
15. The coffee thrives when heavy rains fall during the winter months.
16. Harvesting begins when the golden berries fall from the trees in May.
17. The harvest will be a good one if heavy rains have not damaged the blossoms in September.
18. A long process of washing and drying is necessary before the coffee beans are ready to sell.
19. Trains haul tons of coffee to market after the workers have dried the beans for two months.
20. These crops bring prosperity to Brazil because coffee is sold in countries around the world.

REVIEW EXERCISE F. In the following paragraphs, every sentence begins with the subject. Numbering your sentences, rewrite them to demonstrate what you have learned about varying the beginnings of sentences. Use single-word modifiers, phrases, and clauses.

1

(1) I laugh when I think about the first time I was really scared. (2) I overheard my parents one night when I was about six years old as they talked about a prowler in our neighborhood. (3) They, as usual, thought I was asleep in the next room. (4) I was awakened later by the crunch of footsteps on the gravel driveway outside my window. (5) I sat up in bed with my heart pounding and looked out. (6) Someone was standing in the driveway and looking at our house. (7) My voice failed me completely for a few seconds. (8) My scream, when it finally came, could have been heard a mile away. (9) Mother listened intently while I sobbed out my story. (10) The person

outside, probably startled by my scream, had disappeared. (11) The front door suddenly slammed, and my father dashed into the room. (12) He had remembered, just before going to bed, an important letter that he had forgotten to mail. (13) He had gone out to the mailbox down the block to mail it. (14) My prowler had obviously been my father.

2

(1) Isaac and I celebrate the Fourth of July together every year. (2) We usually either go to the lake for a swim or go on a picnic. (3) We decided this year, however, to take a boat ride up the river. (4) An outboard motor was out of the question because we didn't have much money. (5) We rented for a small sum a light boat with two battered oars. (6) We started upstream, attacking the swift water like a couple of woodchoppers clearing out underbrush. (7) The river, growing narrow, suddenly became shallow and made rowing a problem. (8) Isaac decided, after much thinking, that he would jump onto the bank in order to pull me with a rope. (9) He missed his footing when he tried to leap from the boat. (10) The expression on his face, as he sat in the river, showed that only his feelings were hurt. (11) He gradually fretted his way toward dry land, mumbling under his breath. (12) He informed me, "Next year we go to the lake."

VARYING SENTENCE STRUCTURE

Another common cause of sentence dullness is lack of variety in the kinds of sentences in a paragraph. Too many simple or compound sentences can make your style just as monotonous as too many subject-first sentences.

11h. Vary the kinds of sentences you write.

Study the following pairs of sentences. The first sentence in each pair is compound. The second sentence is complex. (See pages 120–22.) Notice that in the second sentence the relationship between ideas is clearer than in the first sentence. (The subordinate clauses are in boldfaced type.)

We visited the Old North Church in Boston, and we went to see the Bunker Hill Monument.

After we had visited the Old North Church in Boston, we went to see the Bunker Hill Monument. [The introductory subordinate clause tells *when* the visit to Bunker Hill was made.]

Rita apologized to Wilt; her conscience had been troubling her.

Rita apologized to Wilt **because her conscience had been troubling her.** [The subordinate clause tells *why* she apologized.]

I saw a woman running across the field, and she later proved to be an Olympic track star.

The woman **whom I saw running across the field** later proved to be an Olympic track star. [The subordinate clause tells *which* woman.]

EXERCISE 15. Change each compound sentence below to a complex sentence. Relate the ideas in each part of the sentence by using the subordinating conjunction or relative pronoun given in parentheses.

EXAMPLE 1. The frightened best man had unexpectedly run out of the church; an altar boy was asked to take his place. (after)

    1. *After the frightened best man had unexpectedly run out of the church, an altar boy was asked to take his place.*

1. Louise plays the piano beautifully, and so we will ask her to entertain at our party. (who)
2. The school bus suddenly slowed down, and we saw the roadblock. (when)

3. My cut hand was not healing properly, and so I finally saw a doctor. (because)
4. Charlene had studied the spelling list for thirty minutes, but she continued to examine the words. (although)
5. We harbor ill will, and it usually grows and becomes a troublesome grudge. (if)
6. The neighborhood children play soccer at my house, but they are careful about the lawn and the flowers. (who)
7. We put antifreeze into the radiator of our car, and the first cold wave struck. (before)
8. In the library, Kathryn was reliving joyous events of the summer; she sat with her elbows propped on her open history book. (as)
9. We saw the teacher approaching; we stopped talking and started studying. (as soon as)
10. I enjoy having a room of my own, and I try hard to take care of it. (since)

EXERCISE 16. Rewrite the following paragraph, which consists wholly of simple and compound sentences. To vary the style, change or combine some of the sentences into complex sentences using both adjective and adverb clauses. Do not, however, make all of the sentences complex, since your purpose is to achieve variety.

The music and thump of the drums grew louder, and the people lined up along the streets. In another minute, the high school band would come around the corner. Finally, with a blast of brass, the band emerged from behind the buildings. The drum major raised her feet high and proudly as she marched. She was followed by the musicians. Each of them was wearing a red jacket. The band led the parade of colorful floats. Cheers and applause came from the crowd. Every child stood watching with shining eyes. Each one dreamed of being in the high school band someday.

REVIEW EXERCISE G. Write a paragraph of about 100 words, describing a habit or attitude of yours or of a friend or relative. You may wish to write on one of these topics:

The ability to keep secrets
The knack of saying or doing the right thing at the right time
A tendency to neatness
The ability to make others feel at ease or important
A talent for seeing beauty in ordinary objects
A habit of asking timely questions or giving helpful advice

As you write, avoid monotony of style by varying the kinds of sentences you use.

REVIEW EXERCISE H. Write a composition of about 200 words, sharing a funny story, true or imaginary, with your classmates. You may want to include two or three of your favorite short anecdotes. As you write, pay close attention to your style. Underline all beginning phrases and clauses and all subordinate clauses.

Composition

PART FOUR

Chapter **12**

Writing Paragraphs

Structure and Development of Paragraphs

The paragraph as a part of a longer composition functions in two ways. First, it is a division that the reader can see. As the eye travels down the page, each paragraph, set off by spacing or indention, appears as a distinct part of the whole, like a brick in a wall. Second, and more important, a paragraph is a stage in the writer's thinking. Compositions are built with ideas, and each idea is developed or explained in a separate paragraph. The paragraph may be long or short, depending upon the idea it develops; but it must make a single point that the reader can grasp. It must stick to that point.

When you are learning to write, you can learn a great many skills by writing one-paragraph compositions. This chapter will show you the characteristics of a good paragraph, and the composition assignments will provide practice in writing one-paragraph themes.

THE STRUCTURE OF A PARAGRAPH

12a. A *paragraph* **is a series of sentences developing one topic.**

As a unit of thought, a paragraph contains a group of related sentences developing one central idea. This topic is usually stated in a *topic sentence* somewhere in the paragraph.

As you read the following model paragraph, notice that every detail the author gives is closely related to the main idea, which is stated in the first sentence. This paragraph succeeds because it focuses on only one main idea.

> Air pollution, a health hazard in many American cities, occurs every time something burns. Gasoline burned in automobiles accounts for half the pollution in the air. Oil burned in furnaces to heat factories and homes is another major pollution source. Burning garbage in incinerators and city dumps is a third cause of filthy air. The industrial world could not live without fire, yet its polluting effects continually endanger lives.

The Topic Sentence

12b. The topic sentence states the one topic of a paragraph.

In the preceding paragraph the topic sentence is the first sentence. This sentence contains the controlling idea of the whole paragraph; it tells the reader what the paragraph is about. The other sentences develop the idea expressed by the topic sentence.

As in this paragraph, the topic sentence ordinarily comes at the beginning. It may appear elsewhere in the paragraph—in the middle or at the end. Until you have had more experience in writing paragraphs, however, you should begin a paragraph with a topic sentence.

EXERCISE 1. Find the topic sentence in each of the paragraphs below. Be ready to explain how the other sentences develop the topic sentence.

1

Warts are wonderful structures. They can appear overnight on any part of the skin, like mushrooms on a damp lawn, full grown and splendid in the complexity of their architecture. Viewed in stained sections under a microscope, they are the most specialized of cellular arrangements, constructed as though for a purpose. They sit there like turreted mounds of dense, impenetrable horn, impregnable, designed for defense against the world outside.[1]

2

Wiping the sweat from his brow, it seemed to Kunta that his people were always enduring one hardship or another—something uncomfortable or difficult, or frightening, or threatening to life itself. He thought about the burning, hot days and the cold nights that followed them. And he thought about the rains that would come next, turning the village into a mudhole and finally submerging the walking paths until the people had to travel in their canoes from place to place where usually they walked. They needed the rain as much as they needed the sun, but there always seemed to be too much or too little.[2]

[1] From "On Warts" in *The Medusa and the Snail* by Lewis Thomas, Copyright © 1974, 1975, 1976, 1977, 1978, 1979 by Lewis Thomas. Reprinted by permission of Viking Penguin, Inc.
[2] From *Roots* by Alex Haley. Copyright © 1976 by Alex Haley. Reprinted by permission of Doubleday & Company, Inc. and Hutchinson Publishing Group Ltd.

12c. Every sentence in a paragraph should be closely related to the topic.

A paragraph is a unit. Any sentence in a paragraph which does not relate to the topic of that paragraph spoils the unity and should be taken out.

The paragraph which follows contains a sentence that is not related to the topic sentence. As you read the paragraph, notice how this sentence, printed in boldfaced type, distracts the reader from the problem of awkward hands.

> I never know what to do with my hands when I am in an awkward situation. For instance, when I am making an oral report in history class, I have trouble with my hands. Sometimes I self-consciously clasp them behind me so that they won't show. At other times, I hide them in my pockets and start jingling coins noisily. **A good speaker does not have distracting mannerisms — such as saying "uh" at every pause, pacing back and forth, or looking out the window instead of at the audience.** I can understand why Napoleon, the emperor of France, always kept one of his hands safely buried beneath his coat.

The topic of the following paragraph is the beauty of a perfect day. Every detail should relate to this central idea. Which sentence in the paragraph is not related to the topic?

> All of the elements of nature worked together to produce a perfect day. It was a day that made everything seem wonderful and anything possible. The sun didn't shine down — it drew one up to it. Every blade of grass was saturated with light. The wind whipped the leaves in the trees and then parted the wildflowers as it ran through them. In the wintertime I have to stay indoors so much

that I like to be outdoors in the spring and summer. It was a day when every living cell seemed to vibrate with the joy of life as the sun and wind had a glorious frolic with the earth.

EXERCISE 2. In each of the following paragraphs, there is one sentence that is not closely related to the topic. Find this sentence, and copy it on your paper.

1

Many people worry about the effects of television on the young. According to studies, some children spend more time watching television than they spend in school. Because of this extensive viewing, children may not develop the habit of reading and the ability of entertaining themselves. No one worries much about the radio programs young people listen to, although radios can be very noisy. People also wonder about the effects of television commercials. In one year an average child will see 25,000 television commercials, all planned and written by adults to make a child want things that, according to the pictures in the commercial, other children already have.

2

There is hardly a more exciting way to travel than by ship. Perhaps it is the complete isolation from land or the feeling of living in another world inhabited only by the passengers on board which makes one so ready for adventure. Of course, sometimes I get bored because every day is alike; it is as monotonous as riding a train across barren wastelands. What a thrill it is to wake early in the morning and go up on deck to see nothing but water sparkling in the morning air! How comforting it is to sight an occasional gray mound of land away in the distance. All day the ship breaks through the water with a burst of foam. Although the journey seems endless, there are no tracks in front or behind. At night the ocean around becomes a dark world with a moonlit path over its surface.

3

Diet books promise good health, but the promise is not always kept. I tried one "revolutionary" diet book by a noted doctor and gained three pounds in two days. I opened another glossy paperback "guaranteeing" healthful results and saw numerous illustrations of healthy-looking, smiling people but hardly a word about nutrition or the daily requirements of a diet. Nearly every best-selling book, I noticed, promised to reshape, revive, or reduce our bodies. For those who want to control body weight, the solution is simple. Exercise every day, eat three balanced meals, and never trust your diet to a slickly packaged, useless diet book.

4

Even though they know that speeding is a waste of fuel and a major cause of traffic accidents, many Americans persist in racing down the highway. Rather than be late for a movie or a visit with friends, drivers speed around sharp curves, pass other cars on steep hills, and squeeze in and out of a line of cars. Frequently other, law-abiding drivers must swerve to the shoulder of the road or crash headlong into a telephone pole to avoid speeders. Newspapers are filled with stories about the rising costs of fuel. Speeders are gas-guzzling daredevils who gamble that they will not become part of the annual highway death toll. These menaces to society must "make good time," even though they squander precious fuel, risk their lives, and endanger the lives of others.

THE DEVELOPMENT OF A PARAGRAPH

To write a paragraph, you usually supply specific information to make clear the meaning of the topic sentence. As you read the following paragraph, notice that the second and third sentences help explain the idea in the first sentence, which is the topic sentence.

> Because of his humanlike qualities, [the chimpanzee] is of inestimable value to many branches of scientific research. His ability to solve simple problems has helped psychologists to understand the learning process. As a part of the United States space program, doctors have used chimpanzees in test flights and in ground studies to determine the effects of space travel on astronauts.[1]

The first step in developing a one-paragraph composition is to choose a topic which can be treated adequately.

12d. Search your mind for subjects to write about.

When you are ready to write paragraphs of your own, you may encounter one hitch — what to write about. Deciding on a topic is not too hard if you first consider your own interests and experiences. Chances are that you know enough about many subjects to write 100 to 150 words on any of them.

Search your mind for subjects you know from your own interests and experiences. Make a list of subjects, or topics, as they occur to you. Write down a topic and then search for another. The first few topics will probably occur to you almost at once. The rest may

---

[1] From the special publication *My Friends the Wild Chimpanzees*. Copyright © 1967; courtesy National Geographic Society.

take more time, but with patience you can make a very respectable list.

For example, you might think of the activities you do regularly: a sport, a hobby, a school activity such as the newspaper, a club, or a game you and your friends enjoy. You might choose to tell about places you have visited, people you know, animals you have owned, or your opinions on current events. Even if you are not sure about a particular topic, write it down anyway, for you may find on further thought that you know more about it than you realized.

12e. Write a topic sentence.

Once you have selected a subject that you think can be developed in a single paragraph, you will face the task of writing a topic sentence. In most instances the topic sentence will be the first sentence in the paragraph. It will be a general statement designed to make clear what the passage is about.

EXERCISE 3. The following passages are paragraphs without topic sentences. Study each passage and then write a topic sentence that will be a clear introduction to the paragraph.

1

Today Little League is worldwide. It provides a well-planned and supervised sports activity for two and a half to three million boys and girls and thousands of adult volunteers. Throughout its history, it has observed rules of discipline, fair play, and safety. Many safety features developed by Little League have reached other areas of sports, including major league baseball. The list of those who moved through Little League to successful sports careers is very impressive. Congress recognized the value of Little League by granting it a federal charter—the only such sports program to be so honored.

2

Americans are now using six times as much electricity as they were using thirty years ago. To produce this vast amount of electricity, Americans are consuming four times as much coal, twelve times as much fuel oil, and ten times as much natural gas. These fossil fuels—coal, oil, gas—are also being consumed in great amounts by our automobiles and planes and locomotives and in the manufacture of insecticides, plastics, and other synthetic materials.

12f. Make a working plan for developing the topic sentence into a paragraph.

As you have now learned, a paragraph is a unit containing a series of closely related sentences developing one central idea. To organize a paragraph, it is important to plan ahead. Before you begin to write, you should learn to make a working plan for the paragraph.

In the paragraph about air pollution on page 294, the author's working plan was something like the following:

Topic sentence Air pollution, a health hazard in many American cities, occurs every time something burns.

Specific information
gasoline in automobiles
oil in factories and homes
garbage in city dumps and incinerators

As you write your plan of a paragraph, keep your topic sentence firmly in mind so that every bit of additional information will be closely related to your central idea.

Suppose, for example, that you are to write a paragraph with this topic sentence: "Everyone in my family likes to read different kinds of books." You should give the names of the members of your family and should tell exactly what each one likes to read. By holding strictly to the topic sentence, you are not likely to include any discussion of the reading taste of a friend or a teacher or someone else, nor will you ramble off to favorite radio or television programs. Notice how the additional information below sticks closely to the topic sentence.

Topic sentence   Everyone in my family likes to read different kinds of books.
Specific information
Brother — poetry
Sister — novels
Mother — magazines
Father — mystery books
I like science fiction.

EXERCISE 4. Choose two of the following topic sentences, and for each write a plan for a paragraph. First, copy the topic sentence, and then list four points to support it. Save your plans for use later in Review Exercise B.

1. There are several reasons why I like Friday evenings.
2. Small children are always pretending.
3. Bicycles need special care.
4. It's fun to take a walk in the snow.
5. Some television programs are really funny.

6. When riding in a jet, I never become bored.
7. Some remedies are worse than the disease.
8. I enjoy different kinds of music.
9. Basketball skills take practice.
10. Some promises are easy to make but hard to keep.

EXERCISE 5. Before going on with this chapter, try your hand at writing an interesting, well-structured paragraph. Choose a topic from your own list of possible subjects for paragraphs. First, write a topic sentence to introduce your paragraph. Second, make a working plan, or outline. Third, write the paragraph. As you write, keep your controlling idea—your topic sentence—in mind, and make sure that every sentence in your paragraph is closely related to it.

Ways of Developing a Paragraph

12g. A paragraph may be developed by giving details or examples.

The topic sentence can be supported by specific details and examples. Note how the opening general statement in the following paragraph is supported by a number of specific details. The details are facts about Babe Didrikson Zaharias.

Babe Didrikson Zaharias, who lived from 1914 to 1956, deserves the title of all-time champion woman athlete. During a twenty-three-year period, she won more medals and set more records in more sports than any other athlete, male or female. As a teen-ager, she won prizes in basketball, track and field, lifesaving, and figure skating. In the 1932 Olympics, she took three gold medals, setting world records in the javelin throw, 80-meter hurdles, and high jump. In the 1940's, she won every available golf title, including the

World Open and the National Open. Only eight male golfers could drive a ball farther than Babe. She could throw a baseball over 300 feet. She was even an expert diver and lacrosse player.

Compare the following two paragraphs, which begin with the same topic sentence. The first paragraph adds few details to its topic sentence. The second paragraph adds numerous details, so that the topic sentence is easier to understand.

GENERAL (skimpy development)

It is little wonder that wind-driven waves have been a powerful factor in carving the shore lines. These waves have an influence upon the various and sundry shapes of rocks on or near the shore. They are also the cause of caves and other types of holes in the ground.

SPECIFIC DETAILS (well developed)

It is little wonder that wind-driven waves have been a powerful factor in carving the shore lines. They can attack and remove even solid rock cliffs, often creating curious shapes such as rock pinnacles standing a little from shore or joined to it by a natural bridge. Similarly, waves can hollow out caves in the rock. Then, having eroded a cave, they may pound upward until they break through the roof. One sometimes sees spray shooting up out of apparently solid ground behind the main shore line.[1]

Sometimes you may wish merely to list details to explain or emphasize an important word in the topic sentence. By listing the items on the breakfast menu, Thomas Wolfe used this method of development in the following paragraph.

[1] From *Frontiers of the Sea: The Story of Oceanographic Research,* by Robert C. Cowen. Copyright © 1960 by Robert C. Cowen. Reprinted by permission of Doubleday & Company, Inc. and Victor Gollancz Ltd.

We could see the circus performers eating tremendous breakfasts, with all the savage relish of their power and strength. They ate big fried steaks, pork chops, rashers of bacon, a half-dozen eggs, great slabs of fried ham and great stacks of wheat cakes which a cook kept flipping in the air with the skill of a juggler, and which a husky-looking waitress kept rushing to their tables on loaded trays held high and balanced marvelously on the fingers of a brawny hand. And above all the maddening odors of the wholesome and succulent food, there brooded forever the sultry and delicious fragrance — that somehow seemed to add a zest and sharpness to all the powerful and thrilling life of morning — of strong boiling coffee, which we could see sending off clouds of steam from an enormous polished urn, and which the circus performers gulped down, cup after cup.[1]

Some topic sentences, like the one in the following paragraph, clearly call on the writer to provide supporting examples.

Whenever you buy a gift, you should always consider the interests of the receiver. For example, if you are buying a birthday present for a friend who likes to read detective stories, you might select *The Adventures of Sherlock Holmes* or *The Case of the Red Rooster.* If, on the other hand, you are choosing a gift for your little cousin who likes to play board games, you might select *Monopoly* or *Scrabble.* Similarly, if you must choose a gift for your mother on Mother's Day, you should carefully consider her interests. Perhaps you can please her with a book, a tennis racquet, or a plant.

---

[1] From "Circus at Dawn" by Thomas Wolfe, from *From Death to Morning* by Thomas Wolfe. Reprinted by permission of Charles Scribner's Sons and William Heinemann Ltd., London.

EXERCISE 6. Choose one of the following topic sentences and develop it into a paragraph. By answering the questions in brackets, you can make your paragraph interesting with specific details. Use the topic sentence provided as the first sentence of your paragraph.

1. I took a good, long look into the mirror. [What exactly did you see there? What was the condition of your hair? The expression of your eyes? What movements did you make?]

2. Almost everyone is a teacher. [Can you list several persons you know and point out specifically what they teach and to whom?]

3. Walking down the hall today, I heard many interesting sounds. [When did you notice the sounds — between classes, during the noon hour? Can you give specific details about each sound? How do these noises reflect the personalities and activities of the teachers and pupils?]

4. Ninety-five percent of the things we worry about never happen. [Can you apply this common saying to your own experiences? Are you a chronic worrier? Can you point out two or three things that once caused you needless anxiety? Can you convince your reader, by your specific details, that worry is senseless?]

5. Money cannot buy the best things in life. [What exactly are the "best things" in life? Who can possess or enjoy these things? How?]

6. When I criticize others, I usually complain loudest about those weaknesses that I dislike about myself. [Can you make a list of traits that you wish you didn't have, the very traits that you dislike and criticize most in others?]

7. Without actually saying so, they seemed glad that we had dropped by. [How did they greet you? Exactly what did they do? How did their actions indicate their pleasure?]

EXERCISE 7. Choose one of the following topic sentences and develop it into a paragraph by using specific examples. If you prefer, you may write on a topic of your own choosing.

1. The customer isn't always right.
2. When called upon to speak, people should consider the interests of their audience.
3. My friends have a strange assortment of pets.
4. Helen Keller rightly compares literature to utopia.
5. As Lincoln said, "Truth is generally the best vindication against slander."

12h. A paragraph may be developed by telling a story or relating an incident.

Another way to develop a paragraph is to select a story or incident from your own experience that will support and explain your topic sentence. The incident described in the paragraph below shows the modesty of the famous physicist Albert Einstein.

> Typical of Einstein is the story of the popular lecture he was finally prevailed upon to give, for it shows his incapability of behavior that was not genuine. He had been asked many times to speak to a certain audience, but had always begged off on the basis that he had nothing to say. Finally, however, the pressure became so great that he was forced to accede. Came the evening of the lecture, and amidst applause Dr. Einstein was led to the front of the stage and introduced. For a few moments he looked out at the audience, tongue-tied and silent. Finally he could stand it no longer and, smiling sheepishly, said, "I find that I have nothing to say," and returned to his seat.[1]

[1] From "Albert Einstein: Appraisal of an Intellect" by George R. Harrison from the June, 1955 issue of *The Atlantic Monthly*. Reprinted by permission of The Atlantic Monthly.

EXERCISE 8. Develop a paragraph by using a story or incidents from your experience to support your topic sentence. You may select one story to illustrate the truth or untruth of a well-known saying such as "Love is blind" or "Ignorance is bliss." Or you may first state in a topic sentence a lesson that you have learned—for example, "I have learned what responsibility means" or "Now I know the value of silence" —and then develop your topic by giving one incident from your experience.

12i. A paragraph may be developed by giving reasons.

When dealing with a debatable topic, you can develop a paragraph effectively by giving reasons for your opinion. In the following paragraph, which argues for the use of returnable glass bottles, the writer gives two reasons for the view stated in the first sentence.

> The use of returnable and reusable glass bottles makes more sense than the use of throwaway bottles and aluminum cans for two reasons. First, throwaways of any kind are wasteful. It is estimated that the average American produces about eight pounds of solid wastes a day. Removal of mountains of wastes costs billions of dollars annually. Reusing glass containers would reduce the waste. Second, while it is true that aluminum cans can be recycled to produce more aluminum, the recycling requires more energy than does the cleaning and refilling of glass containers.

12j. A paragraph may be developed by making comparisons or contrasts.

When developing a paragraph by making comparisons, you emphasize similarities; by making contrasts, you emphasize differences. The first of the following paragraphs is developed by comparison; it stresses the similarities of the Pacific Ocean and a highway. The second paragraph employs contrast; it points out the differences between a tornado and a dust devil.

1

There is only one sensible way to think of the Pacific Ocean today. It is the highway between Asia and America, and whether we wish it or not, from now on there will be immense traffic along that highway. If we know what we want, if we have patience and determination, if above all we have understanding, we may insure that the traffic will be peaceful, consisting of tractors and students and medical missionaries and bolts of cloth. But if we are not intelligent, or if we cannot cultivate understanding in Asia, then the traffic will be armed planes, battleships, submarines, and death. In either alternative we may be absolutely certain that from now on the Pacific traffic will be a two-way affair.[1]

2

A tornado is not, as is often assumed, merely an overgrown dust devil. The dust devil begins at the earth's surface as a whirlpool of air and builds upward. A tornado, on the other hand, is a funnel of whirling air that descends toward the earth. It begins revolving below heavy storm clouds. The dust devil is a product of sunshine, convection currents and the heat of the day. Tornadoes occur at night as well as during the day. They are often accompanied by rain, by hail that may hurl down ice stones as large as baseballs, and sometimes by tremendous displays of lightning in which the flashes may be green, yellow, or blue. Dust devils range from less than 10 to about 100

[1] From *Return to Paradise*, by James Michener. Copyright 1951 by James A. Michener. Reprinted by permission of Random House, Inc.

feet in diameter, while the funnel of the average tornado measures about 250 yards across. The direction of rotation of a dust devil is accidental. Some spin clockwise, others counterclockwise. But every tornado in the Northern Hemisphere whirls in the same way—counterclockwise.[1]

EXERCISE 9. The following topics can be developed by drawing a comparison or making a contrast. Select one of the topics; write a topic sentence stating the point of your paragraph; then develop the topic sentence into a paragraph of about 100 words by making a comparison or contrast. If you prefer, write on a topic of your own choosing.

1. Dogs and cats as pets
2. Football and soccer (or baseball)
3. My aunt and my uncle
4. Elementary school and junior high (or high school)
5. English and mathematics
6. This community and the one I formerly lived in
7. Two movies I have seen
8. Two jobs I have held
9. Hair styles
10. Two TV programs

REVIEW EXERCISE A. Choose any one of the following words (or any other word that your teacher may suggest) and use it as a key word in a topic sentence that clearly expresses an idea or opinion. Then develop the topic sentence by giving additional information—specific details, examples, a story, incidents, reasons, comparisons, or contrasts. As you go over your paragraph, be sure to remove any sentence that is not closely related to the topic sentence.

[1] "The Tornado" from *Journey into Summer* by Edwin Way Teale (New York: Dodd, Mead & Company, 1960). Reprinted by permission of Dodd, Mead & Company.

1. noses	5. spectacular	9. water
2. brave	6. surprise	10. bargains
3. watching	7. glamour	
4. nightmare	8. pigheaded	

REVIEW EXERCISE B. Using one of the plans that you prepared for Exercise 4, write a paragraph developed by one of the means listed in rules 12g–j.

COHERENCE

The sentences in a paragraph should all be closely related to the main point. In addition, they should flow smoothly and naturally from one to another. Such a paragraph is said to have *coherence.*

Arrangement of Ideas

One of the best ways to achieve coherence in a paragraph or a composition is to present a clear arrangement of ideas.

12k. To achieve coherence in a paragraph, arrange details in a logical order: chronologically, spatially, or in order of importance.

(1) Details in a paragraph may be arranged *chronologically.*

The natural way of telling how to do or make something is to arrange the steps of the process in the order in which they must be carried out. The natural way of relating a story or incident is to give the events in the order in which they happened. This method of organizing information is called *chronological*—the order of time.

| Let us make the simplest kind of photograph—a shadow picture. | If you have ·dark shades, pull them down and put out the lights in the room. Now, even if it is daylight outside, it is dark enough inside the room to take a piece of photographic "contact" paper out of its package for a moment without spoiling it. . . . In the darkened room, put on a table top the piece of paper you are going to use, with the smooth, coated side up. Lay two or three keys on top of the paper. Be sure they are separate and lying flat. Make sure the rest of the paper in the package is covered. Turn on the room lights for a minute. When the paper is developed, you will find it bears a white shadow picture, or photographic image, of the keys.[1]

— topic sentence

steps in process
arranged chrono-
logically

(2) Details in a paragraph may be arranged *spatially*.

Just as it is natural to take up events in the order they happen and to describe steps in doing or making something in order, it is natural to describe objects by their position in relation to each other. This arrangement of sentences is *spatial*. In the following paragraph from Mark Twain's *Autobiography*, the various details are arranged spatially, or by position.

---

[1] From *Exploring the Sciences* by Paul Brandwein et al. Reprinted by permission of Harcourt Brace Jovanovich, Inc., publisher.

The [1]farmhouse stood <u>in the middle</u> of a very large [2]yard, and the yard was fenced on three sides with rails and on the <u>rear side</u> with high [3]palings. <u>Against these</u> stood the [4]smoke house; <u>beyond the palings</u> was the [5]orchard; <u>beyond the orchard</u> were the [6]tobacco fields. The front yard was entered over a stile made of sawed-off logs of graduated heights; I do not remember any gate. <u>In a corner</u> of the front yard were a dozen lofty hickory [7]trees and a dozen black walnuts, and in the nutting season riches were to be gathered there.[1]

objects 1–7 described in relation to each other (Underscored words indicate spatial arrangement.)

(3) Details in a paragraph may be arranged in order of importance.

In a paragraph that deals with ideas that do not involve time or position, details or examples may be organized in order of their importance. Such a paragraph may be developed by facts, some of which are more striking or important than others. If it is an argumentative paragraph developed by listing reasons, undoubtedly some reasons will be more convincing than others. The order may be from least to most important, or vice versa. Either method, if followed consistently, should result in understandable arrangement.

[1] From *The Autobiography of Mark Twain* by Charles Neider. Reprinted by permission of Harper & Row, Inc., publisher.

In the following paragraphs, ideas are arranged in order of importance. In the first, the order is from least to most important; in the second, the order is reversed, with the most important idea stated at the beginning.

The world is running very quickly out of oil, and once it is gone, there is no more. [1] In the United States we have already discovered and have already consumed more than half the producible oil that was created by nature over hundreds of millions of years. [2] We have done this in fifty years, a brief interval since this country was founded, and a mere blip of time in the recorded history of mankind. [3] In fifty years we have used over half of all there ever was, and at the rate we are going, we'll finish off the rest very quickly. [1]

— topic sentence

(1) first idea

(2) more important idea

(3) most important idea

During the postwar period the interest in traditional spectator sports rose markedly. [1] Baseball remained the most popular professional game, with an average yearly attendance of between 9 and 10 million at major-

— topic sentence

(1) baseball, most important (most popular) supporting details

---

[1] From *Last Chance Energy Book* by Owen Phillips. Copyright © 1979 by Owen Phillips. Reprinted by permission of The Johns Hopkins University Press, publisher.

league games. Babe Ruth replaced
Ty Cobb as the idol of fans and in
1927 astounded the baseball world
by hitting a record number of sixty
home runs. [2]College football drew
some 30,000,000 spectators in the
same year. Red Grange, a halfback
for the University of Illinois, became a national hero and won a
movie contract. [3]Prizefighting continued to enjoy tremendous popularity, and in 1927 ardent boxing fans
spent $2,658,660 to see the famous
Dempsey-Tunney match. [4]Profes-
sional golf and tennis matches also
increased their audiences during the
1920's.[1]

(2) football, next
in importance

(3) prizefighting

(4) golf and ten-
nis — least popular

EXERCISE 10. For each of the following topics, indicate the kind of order — chronological, spatial, or order of importance — you would use in writing a paragraph on the subject. Number your paper 1–20, and
write *C* (for *chronological*), *S* (for *spatial*), or *I* (for
importance) beside the corresponding number. Be
prepared to explain the reasons for your choice of
each.

1. The double play in baseball
2. My newly decorated room
3. Ways to make yourself unpopular
4. Drawing a map

[1] From *Rise of the American Nation*, Heritage Edition, Combined Volume
by Lewis Paul Todd and Merle Curti. Reprinted by permission of Harcourt Brace Jovanovich, Inc., publisher.

5. Why homework (should, should not) be abolished
6. My plans for the future
7. A good place for a campsite
8. Washing my dog
9. The duties of the class secretary
10. Locating a book in the library
11. Why I frequently visit the library
12. The reference room in the library
13. How to make bread
14. A thrilling movie
15. An experiment in the laboratory
16. The reasons for organizing a drama club
17. My favorite picture
18. A historical monument
19. Learning to skate
20. Why nutrition is important for athletes in training

EXERCISE 11. Choose ten of the topics from Exercise 10 and write a topic sentence for each. Choose at least three that you would treat chronologically, three that you would treat spatially, and three that should be treated in order of importance.

EXERCISE 12. Using three of the topic sentences that you prepared for Exercise 11, write one chronologically arranged paragraph, one that is spatially arranged, and one arranged in order of importance.

Connecting Sentences in the Paragraph

In writing paragraphs, you need to connect the sentences, to bridge the gaps between them so that your paragraphs will read smoothly. There are two different ways in which this may be done: by *transitional devices* and by *direct references*.

12I. To make a paragraph read smoothly, use *transitional devices* **and** *direct references.*

Transitional devices are connecting words or phrases that show the relationship between ideas, details, examples and, in the paragraph. The following are examples of transitional expressions:

accordingly	first (second,	next
after	third, etc.)	one
after that	for example	once . . . now
afterward	for instance	on the contrary
also	for this reason	on the other hand
and	furthermore	or
another	hence	other
as a result	however	otherwise
as soon as	in addition	similarly
at first	in spite of	soon
at last	instead	that is
at the same time	in the first (etc.)	then
before long	place	therefore
besides	in the meantime	to begin with
but	later	thus
consequently	likewise	when
even if	meanwhile	yet
even so	moreover	
finally	nevertheless	

Of course, a paragraph in which all the sentences were linked by means of transitional devices would be dull. A transitional device is not required in every sentence and should not be used if it is not needed. Sentences may also be linked by *direct references.*

(1) Use pronouns that refer to nouns in a preceding sentence or to the idea in a preceding sentence.

EXAMPLE   Eva spent Saturday cleaning out the garage. **This** did not seem to **her** to be a proper use of the holiday; but **it** had to be done. [*This* refers to "cleaning out the garage," as does *it*. *Her,* of course, refers to "Eva."]

(2) You may repeat a word from the preceding sentence.

EXAMPLE   My personal library includes several rather valuable books. These **books** were a gift from my grandmother.

(3) Use a word or phrase that means the same thing as a word or phrase in a preceding sentence.

EXAMPLE   The runaway engine sped down the inclined track. On and on the **mighty monster** raced, as we watched in horror, overcome by the unharnessed power of the **giant machine.** [Both refer to *engine.*]

As you read the following paragraph, refer to the marginal key. It shows you how the numbered words link ideas.

The American Wheelmen and other bicycle groups are attempting to promote the bicycle as one solution to the problem of too many automobiles and too little gasoline. [1]They have some interesting facts to back up [2]their idea. [3]For example, a recent national transportation study shows that 62.4 percent of all automobile trips average less than five miles. [4]This is a distance that under reasonably good conditions can be covered by bicycle in about twenty minutes.

— topic sentence

(1) pronoun reference to words in topic sentence
(2) reference to topic sentence
(3) transition

(4) pronoun reference to five miles

In the United States last year, [5]these short trips used up approximately thirteen billion gallons of gasoline. The bicycle, [6]unlike the car, doesn't pollute and doesn't cause traffic jams. [7]Furthermore, [8]it does provide, in addition to transportation, a healthful kind of physical exercise.

(5) reference to preceding mention of trips

(6) transition

(7) transition
(8) pronoun reference

EXERCISE 13. In the following paragraph, connecting words are in boldfaced type. Study these words and be prepared to explain what ideas each connects and how it connects them. The lines of the paragraph have been numbered for your convenience.

1. A solitary traveler who stumbles into quick-
2. sand is in an awkward situation, but even his case
3. is not desperate if he knows what to do. Attempts
4. to force a way to shore will prove worse than use-
5. less; standing still and yelling will be fatal unless
6. help arrives soon. The trapped man's **first** move
7. must be to drop his pole behind him, if he is fore-
8. sighted enough to have one, and fall back upon it,
9. meanwhile stretching his arms out at right angles
10. to his body. In **this position** he could float in
11. water, and he will certainly float on sand if he
12. gets rid of any heavy object he may be carrying.
13. He may **now** call out for help. If there is no pros-
14. pect of **help,** the victim may begin to rescue him-
15. self. The **first** step in this operation is to get the
16. pole at right angles to the body beneath the shoul-
17. ders and then work it down until it is supporting
18. the hips. **It** is difficult work, but once done the
19. individual is in a position to pull his legs out of
20. the mire one at a time. He should do **this** slowly

21. and with frequent rests. **Once** his feet are out, he
22. looks about and selects the shortest route to solid
23. ground. He **then** begins rolling toward his goal.
24. **Rolling** is the easiest — and indeed the only — way
25. of getting off the soft area. **It** can be done in short
26. stages, but rests must be taken on the back with
27. arms outstretched or he will begin to sink again.
28. The pole is pulled along and used for support.[1]

EXERCISE 14. Write a paragraph explaining how to do something. Give each step clearly, and use transitional devices and direct references for bridging gaps between ideas. You may write on a serious topic, such as how to play a game or how to make good soup or build a bird feeder. Or you may write on a humorous topic, such as how to make others think that you are a genius or how to eat popcorn in a theater. Underline each transitional device or direct reference that you have used.

REVIEW EXERCISE C. Write a paragraph beginning with one of the topic sentences on page 321. Put into practice what you have learned in this chapter. After you have written your paragraph, ask yourself these questions about it:

Does the topic sentence clearly state the central idea of the paragraph?

Have I given enough additional information to develop the topic fully?

Is this information interesting and specific?

Does every sentence in the paragraph relate closely to the topic sentence?

Do connecting words help to clarify the explanation as they bridge the gaps between ideas?

[1] From "Quicksand" by Gerard H. Matthes from *Scientific American,* June 1953. Copyright © 1953 by Scientific American, Inc. All rights reserved.

1. My friends have different ideas about what success is.
2. I do not believe everything that I read in newspapers.
3. The three most popular magazines in my home are ...
4. My bicycle and I are no longer friends.
5. Only a few snakes are poisonous.
6. A hurricane can do great damage.
7. Educational TV programs vary in quality.
8. Anyone can learn to play volleyball (or another sport).
9. I have trouble making decisions.
10. There are many ways to use leftovers.
11. If you know how, you can build a fire without using a match.
12. The way that a thermometer works is interesting.
13. I notice other people's eyes.
14. There is an art to taking good photographs.

REVIEW EXERCISE D. Study the following paragraphs so that you can discuss them in class. Be prepared to give the topic sentence or the central idea of each paragraph and to tell what method (or combination of methods) is used to develop it: many details, examples, a story, incidents, reasons, comparisons, or contrasts. Point out transitional expressions.

1

Her religious bent shows in unexpected ways. For instance, we were discussing her work in "Cabin in the Sky." She said, "When we started to rehearse the spirituals, some of those no-manners people started to swinging 'em, and get smart. I told 'em they better not play with God's music like that. I told 'em if I caught any of 'em at it, I'd knock 'em clean over into that orchestra pit." Her eyes flashed fire as she told me about it. Then she calmed down and laughed. "Of course, you know, Zora, God didn't want me to knock 'em over. That was an idea of mine."[1]

2

History has thrust upon our generation an indescribably important destiny—to complete a process of democratization which our nation has too long developed too slowly, but which is our most powerful weapon for world respect and emulation. How we deal with this crucial situation will determine our moral health as individuals, our cultural health as a region, our political health as a nation, and our prestige as a leader of the free world. The future of America is bound up with the solution of the present crisis. The shape of the world today does not permit us the luxury of a faltering democracy. The United States cannot hope to attain the respect of the vital and growing colored nations of the world unless it remedies its racial problems at home. If America is to remain a first-class nation it cannot have a second-class citizenship.[2]

3

Most people who live in the cities also do some form of physical training. During the early hours of the morning, in the parks in Chinese cities and along the Bund in Shanghai, thousands of people

[1] From p. 146 in *Dust Tracks on a Road* by Zora Neale Hurston (J. B. Lippincott Company). Copyright 1942 by Zora Neale Hurston, renewed 1970 by John C. Hurston. Reprinted by permission of Harper & Row, Publishers, Inc.

[2] From pp. 196–197 in *Stride Toward Freedom* by Martin Luther King, Jr. (Harper & Row, 1958). Copyright © 1958 by Martin Luther King, Jr. Reprinted by permission of Joan Daves and Harper & Row, Publishers, Inc.

keep their bodies firm and supple with *tai chi chuan* or shadow boxing. *Tai chi chuan* is an exercise that involves a series of slow, ballet-like movements. Many old men also do sword dancing, which is much like *tai chi chuan* and is done with a stick in each hand. These traditional exercises are actively supported by the government, which views physical exercise as a means of keeping the public healthy. Radio broadcasters lead listeners in physical-fitness exercises, and workers in factories and government officials gather together during their breaks to do calisthenics. Physical-fitness exercises have become almost a national routine.[1]

4

The Pueblo Indians of America's Southwest have an age-old tradition that unites individuals with their forebears. Pueblo villagers in a region of New Mexico can follow trails that lead from their separate communities to an ancient shrine high in the mountains. The travelers know that for centuries before them, their ancestors followed the same trail and performed the same ceremony. They know that someday their own descendants will make the same journey, maintaining spiritual unity from one generation to the next. Most of us cannot journey along mountain trails that lead to communion with our ancestors. But we can travel through time, rescuing our ancestors from oblivion and ourselves from isolation. Family history is a journey of discovery. What you discover is your own heritage and a part of the collective heritage shared by all human beings.[2]

[1] From *The Chinese Way* by Gil and Ann Dull Loescher. © 1974 by Gil and Ann Dull Loescher, published in the United Kingdom by Harcourt Brace Jovanovich Ltd. Reprinted by permission of the British publisher, and Harcourt Brace Jovanovich, Inc., publisher.

[2] From *Your Family History* by Allan J. Lichtman. Copyright © 1978 by Allan J. Lichtman. Reprinted by permission of Random House, Inc., publishers.

5

The weather that winter was cold and sunny. We had one five-inch snow that lingered on the ground in patches for about a week, but little rain or sleet. The schools were bitterly cold, and there were many absences among the children. Three boys in the class dropped out with tuberculosis. Milk that winter was available only from the drugstore and on a doctor's prescription, for sick babies, but I was able to get powdered milk for them. Transportation was hideous. Trains and streetcars were cold, dirty, and often windowless as well as jammed to the roof. People climbed in through the windows after the aisles and steps were filled. Cloth of all kinds was so scarce that even the worn green plush upholstery had been cut off by passengers and taken home to patch clothes. It was not unusual for people to have their ribs broken in the crush, and I myself saw a pencil that had been splintered in a man's breast pocket.[1]

6

The hurricane charged into Connecticut coast lands, gutting seaside resorts, fishing fleets, summer homes, and industrial areas. Flying limbs and chimney bricks were spat like machine-gun fire through the air. As far inland as twenty miles, salt spray destroyed vegetation, and salt traces were later discovered nearly fifty miles from the sea. Winds far over a hundred miles an hour raked the peaceful New England countryside, uprooting some 275 million trees, destroying or damaging thousands of buildings, and chopping up thousands of miles of telephone lines.[2]

[1] Excerpt from *Windows for the Crown Prince* by Elizabeth Gray Vining (J. B. Lippincott Company). Copyright 1952 by Elizabeth Gray Vining. Reprinted by permission of Harper & Row, Publishers, Inc. and Curtis Brown, Ltd.

[2] Excerpt from *Nature on the Rampage: A Natural History of the Elements* by Ann and Myron Sutton. Courtesy of J. B. Lippincott Company, Publishers.

REVIEW EXERCISE E. Using a paragraph in Review Exercise D as a model (the numbered items correspond to the paragraph numbers in Review Exercise D), choose one of the following topic sentences and develop it into a paragraph. Put into practice what you have learned in this chapter, using any method of development that you feel is suitable for the topic.

1. My best friend has some interesting, eccentric habits.
2. History has thrust upon us the important task of achieving peace.
3. Most people who live in the cities participate in community activities.
4. Competing in a race teaches runners some valuable lessons.
5. The weather this summer was hot and wet.
6. The arctic blast charged across our state.

TYPES OF PARAGRAPHS

Paragraphs, like longer compositions, can be divided into types: narrative, descriptive, expository. Each type of paragraph varies according to its purpose. The narrative paragraph tells a story. The descriptive paragraph provides accurate detail and appeals to the senses. The expository paragraph explains how to do something or informs the reader about something.

The Narrative Paragraph

The paragraph developed by telling a story or relating an incident on page 307 is an example of a narrative paragraph. It concisely answers the question *What happened?*

Short, paragraph-length narratives should begin with a topic statement to let the reader know what the story is about. Try, as you write narrative paragraphs, to make this topic statement an interesting one. Try to catch the attention of the person to whom you are writing.

Narrative paragraphs are most effective when they follow chronological order. Notice how the author of the following model has used chronological order to tell his story.

Model Narrative Paragraph

When we were testing underwater breathing devices, we found that accidents showed us where improvements were needed. We were working on defenses against broken pipes one day with Dumas seventy-five feet down, breathing from the pipe. I was in the boat, watching the pipe, when I saw it rupture. Dumas was trapped in pressure three times greater than the pressure at the surface. I grabbed the pipe before it sank and reeled it in frantically, ill with suspense. I could feel heavy tugs from below. Then Dumas appeared, red-faced and choking, his eyes bulging. But he was alive. He had closed his glottis in time and had then climbed the pipe hand over hand. We worked on the gear until it operated more reliably.[1]

A narrative paragraph can be told from two points of view: *first person* or *third person*. (See pages 409–10.) In the preceding model, the author writes in the third person.

Before beginning to write a narrative paragraph, decide whether you will use first person or third person point of view. Stick to this point of view throughout the paragraph.

---

[1] Adapted from pp. 18–19 in *The Silent World* by Captain J. Y. Cousteau with Frederic Dumas. Copyright 1953, by Harper & Row, Publishers, Inc. Reprinted by permission of the publisher.

EXERCISE 15. Write a narrative paragraph about something that happened to you or to someone you know. Begin your paragraph with a topic statement that will catch the reader's attention. If you wish, you may choose one of the following topics for your paragraph.

1. The last inning of a baseball game
2. A disaster in the kitchen
3. A decision that was hard to make
4. Exploring a cave or other place
5. Swimming (skating, skiing) lessons

The Descriptive Paragraph

The paragraph developed by details on page 305 is an example of a descriptive paragraph. It gives a picture in words that appeal directly to the senses (sight, sound, smell, touch, taste).

A descriptive paragraph is normally full of vivid verbs and precise adjectives. It depends on details, not action, to hold the reader's interest. In the following model the writer uses an abundance of accurate detail to describe the sights and sounds of a city.

Model Descriptive Paragraph

In their hotel room the men could hear roosters crowing every morning. At night jackals yelped right in the heart of the city. In this land of fiery curry, of a plain or fancy dosa[1] for breakfast, where the sweet lemon was sweeter than an orange, and oranges tended to be flavorless, the young Americans found they had a lot of readjusting to do. Pedestrians and cows as gentle as kittens strolled in and out of the rush of bikes, rickshaws, auto-rickshaws, trucks, autos, and chemical-burn-

---

[1] *Dosa* is a dish made of rice and lentils.

ing buses spewing their showers of burning coals behind them. In the heat of the day men dragged their bedlike charpoys out onto the sidewalks and stretched out to nap with the expectation that the breeze from passing vehicles would keep them a trifle cooler. Bears danced for the entertainment of the crowds, flute-playing fakirs[1] charmed cobras, and, incredibly, in the open place in front of the Red Fort, built long ago by the Mogul emperors, a holy man actually levitated in broad daylight.[2]

Often a descriptive paragraph requires not only accurate detail but also clear organization, especially when the object of description is a particular place or person. Notice, in the model on page 313, how Mark Twain organizes details about a farm. The best organization for description is spatial arrangement because it is the clearest for the reader.

EXERCISE 16. Write a descriptive paragraph about something or someone very familiar to you. Emphasize the details of what you describe, and, if necessary, organize these details spatially. You may wish to use one of the following topics.

1. A meeting place
2. A busy downtown intersection
3. The water's edge
4. A car's interior
5. Deep in the wilderness

The Expository Paragraph

Most of the paragraphs that you write in school are expository paragraphs. They give the reader information or explain something.

[1] *Fakirs* are beggars.
[2] From *Behind Japanese Lines* by Richard Dunlop. Copyright 1979 by Rand McNally. Reprinted by permission of Rand McNally.

The paragraph on pages 303–04 gives information about Babe Didrikson Zaharias; therefore, it is an expository paragraph. The paragraph on pages 309–10 explains the difference between a tornado and a dust devil; it too is an expository paragraph. You will find expository paragraphs in newspapers, in textbooks, and wherever you look for information and explanations. The first of the following two models gives information about bore tides. The second model explains why weeds are a fact of gardening life.

Model Expository Paragraph

Among unusual creations of the tide, perhaps the best known are the bores. The world possesses half a dozen or more famous ones. A bore is created when a great part of the flood tide enters a river as a single wave, or at most two or three waves, with a steep and high front. The conditions that produce bores are several: there must be a considerable range of tide, combined with sand bars or other obstructions in the mouth of the river, so that the tide is hindered and held back, until it finally gathers itself together and rushes through. The Amazon is remarkable for the distance its bore travels upstream—some 200 miles—with the result that the bores of as many as 5 flood tides may actually be moving up the river at one time.[1]

Model Expository Paragraph

Weed plants, whether they are misplaced pleasant things like violets, or strangling menaces like bindweed, are a fact of gardening life, and it is quite impossible to set up a quarantine station

[1] From *The Sea Around Us* by Rachel L. Carson. Copyright © 1950, 1951, 1961 by Rachel Carson; renewed 1979 by Roger Christie. Published in Great Britain by Granada Publishing Ltd. Reprinted by permission of Oxford University Press, Inc. and Laurence Pollinger Ltd. for the Estate of the late Rachel Carson.

to keep them out. Their seed is in the loam you buy, in the compost you make, and in the root ball of the plant brought home from the local garden center. Weed seed is blown into a garden by wind, deposited there by birds, carried in on the shoes of visitors or on the coats of animals. Not all weeds are even intruders. Often they were in fact the original inhabitants of the site from which the gardener is now struggling to eradicate them, and they only came to be considered weeds when garden plants were introduced. The New England fall aster, for example, which can be found in corners of the most meticulously kept gardens in the Northeast, is the ancestor of the magnificent hybrid versions of this same plant that we grow today. Like the Indians, the native variety was here first, and it is not prepared to be completely shouldered out of its homeland. We pull it out by handfuls every year, and each year, equally tenaciously, it reappears somewhere else.[1]

Each of the preceding models employs a topic sentence, which is the mark of a successful expository paragraph. The topic sentence makes the purpose of the paragraph clear, so that the reader will not be confused by facts and details.

Organization in an expository paragraph depends upon the topic of the paragraph. Explanations, however, especially explanations of how to make or do something, are usually best organized in chronological sequence. A step-by-step process gives the reader a clear path to follow.

EXERCISE 17. Write an expository paragraph on an item in the news or on something that currently holds

---

[1] From *Making Things Grow* by Thalassa Cruso. Copyright © 1971 by Thalassa Cruso. Reprinted by permission of Alfred A. Knopf, Inc., publishers.

your interest. Be sure to write a topic sentence for your paragraph. If you wish, you may choose one of the topics below.

1. The latest fashion at school
2. The outlook for this year's team
3. How to repair a flat tire
4. How to keep in shape
5. How to tell a joke

Chapter 13

Writing Compositions

Some of the writing you do is purely personal, intended for you alone. This kind of writing includes your diary, the notes you take on your reading and in your classes, and the things you may occasionally write—or perhaps only outline—to clarify your thinking.

Most of your writing, however, is done to communicate your ideas and your experiences. Writing has been called a kind of shared living. It is a way of saying, "I want someone to know what I know, to see what I have seen, to feel what I have felt, to discover what I have discovered, to think what I think."

You learn to write by writing, just as a baseball player learns the game by playing it. This is why it is important for you to do a great deal of writing when you are in school. The only way your teachers can be sure that you are getting enough writing practice is by assigning many compositions.

You will help yourself best if you look upon your composition assignments as chances to communicate your thoughts in the most effective way possible. Do not consider them as tasks you do just because you have to, just to carry out an assignment. This may result in compositions that are lifeless, dull, and worth very little. Empty writing is bad writing.

THE MATERIALS OF WRITING

13a. Choose a subject that you know something about.

Your Own Experiences

Taking a good look at yourself and your life is an excellent way to begin to find materials for writing. You are unique, special. You are special in the things that have happened to you, in the people you know best, in the way you see things. Begin to share your uniqueness by writing about your special experiences.

What it takes, first of all, is a new way of looking at your experiences. People who say, "I haven't had any experiences worth writing about," just mean that they haven't learned how to look at their experiences. Here are some general topics that are part of everyone's experience but which may seem unique and special if they are described effectively in writing.

1. *People you've known.* The odd and the eccentric or the wonderfully "average person" both have uniqueness. In the first, the uniqueness comes from the surface nature of the person; people who act, dress, or talk differently fascinate us. In the second, the uniqueness comes from the way we look at a person who *seems* average or ordinary. If we explore deeply enough, even the ordinary becomes exciting.

Look at your grandmother with a "new eye," as if you had never seen her before. What would you say about her so that on reading it over twenty years from now you will remember her vividly? How would you describe her to a classmate who has never seen her, so that your classmate would not only be able to picture her but also to understand what kind of person she is?

2. *Trips and vacations.* Don't write the usual account of "first we did this, then we did that." Try instead to remember someone special whom you met, some little incident that you remember, some ordinary place that somehow impressed you. Focus on one person, one town, one motel, one little part of the trip. Enlarge its interest or its importance by the manner in which you write about it and remember it.

3. *Hobbies and special skills.* There would be little that is unique in a composition by you on the history of stamp collecting. This information can be obtained from any good encyclopedia. But you perhaps can tell something special about what stamp collecting means to you, what you have learned from it, what you know about your own special collection, what suggestions you would give to a person about to start the hobby.

What special skill do you have? What can you do that most young people cannot do so well? Put together a stereo set? Knit a sweater? Rope a steer? Repair a car?

4. *Ideas and information.* The two go together. What do you believe, and what facts do you know to support your belief? What about the topic, "The United States should withdraw from the UN," for example? It sounds imposing. But what facts do you have that would convince your reader? Do you have enough knowledge of your topic to discuss it effectively?

"High school students don't need a curfew." That's different. You have some special knowledge — about your habits and reactions to rules, your experiences with curfews, and your friends' attempts to avoid them. Tell what you think about curfews, and support what you say with your special experiences and special knowledge.

5. *Something you have owned.* Do you particularly remember a certain pet, a hat, a book, a picture, a toy, or something seemingly useless? Why do you remember it? What was special about it? How can you convince someone else of its specialness?

Places, events, skills, ideas, people, things — these make up some important materials of writing. You take a look at your own experience; you see it with a fresh eye; you "zero in" on one aspect of it; you share your uniqueness.

EXERCISE 1. Titles don't tell everything, but sometimes a title can give a clue to what follows. On the basis of what you have read about the use of experience in finding material, decide whether each of the following titles suggests a good topic for a composition based on someone's personal experience. Number your paper 1–10, and copy the titles. After each, write either "probably good" or "probably not good."

1. An Exhausting Vacation
2. A Visit to the Stock Exchange
3. Fashions Through the Ages
4. The Records I Always Listen To
5. Suburban Housing
6. Apartment Living
7. Juvenile Delinquency
8. Will an Honor System Work at Our School?
9. Famous Coin Collections
10. Why I Collect Pennies

EXERCISE 2. "There's something I have to tell you." That's the basis of all writing. What is it that you have to tell? Find five things in your own experience that you think are important and unique. Write them down in complete sentences (for example, "I have developed the world's speediest method of washing a car") and submit them to your teacher. Then select one that your teacher likes and write a composition of 100–150 words based on it. Begin the composition with the sentence you wrote.

The Experience of Others

Most composition books, including this one, tell you, "Write about the things you know." This doesn't mean, however, that you always have to write about things you know from *firsthand* experience, or that writing is always based on the world you know now. A good writing assignment can enable you to enlarge your world, to dig up information, facts, discoveries.

How can you enlarge your world, expand your horizons?

1. *Talk to people.* Ask them questions, and solicit their views.

2. *Look around.* Investigate out-of-the-ordinary places in your school, in your community, in your home, in a nearby city. Take along a pencil, a notebook, a sharp eye, and an inquisitive mind.

3. *Read.* Not all great writers have been great scholars or great travelers. They have all been great readers, however. Expand your world through reading. Read with pencil in hand to note interesting expressions, points you disagree with, quotations you wish to remember.

EXERCISE 3. Do any one of the following activities that seems most interesting to you. Then share your experience with the class by writing about it.

1. Visit the oldest building in your town or neighborhood.
2. Talk with the oldest resident in your town or neighborhood.
3. Find out when and how your church or synagogue was organized.
4. Interview an artist or skilled worker — anyone who may be able to teach a craft.
5. Interview a war veteran. Ask for war stories and for impressions of the changes that have taken place since the war.
6. Visit a local florist. What is the rarest flower in the shop? your favorite? the local best seller?
7. What is the unemployment rate in your town? Is anybody taking steps to find jobs for the unemployed?
8. Which teacher has served longest in your school? What was the school like when that teacher began teaching there?
9. What compact car is rated by consumer testing organizations as the best buy? Why is it so rated?
10. How did your town get its name?
11. Which basketball team does your coach consider the best?
12. Review the voting record of your local ward or precinct for the last twelve years. What pattern does it show?
13. Talk with the local fire chief. What is the chief cause of fires in your community?
14. When was your town or city paper first issued? What was it like in its early days?
15. Read any five consecutive issues of a weekly news magazine published the year you were born. What picture do they give of American life in those days?

Two Looks at Dogdom: An Illustrative Example

Perhaps all that has been said here about the materials of writing can best be illustrated by two examples. The first is a student composition. The second is from a best-selling book by a skilled writer of humorous essays based on experience.

DOGS

Dogs were probably the first domestic animals. They are descended from the wolf. They date back at least to the Paleolithic period, and two breeds were known in early Egypt.

From earliest times dogs have been bred for special purposes. Sporting dogs include the griffon, pointer, retriever, dachshund, setter, spaniel, and hound, and many breeds of terrier. Working dogs include the collie, Eskimo, German shepherd, and St. Bernard. Nonsporting dogs include the bulldog, chow, Dalmatian, and poodle. Toy dogs are small dogs bred as pets; among them are the toy spaniel, Mexican hairless, Pekingese, pug, and toy poodle.

Mongrels are mixtures of several breeds. They may look a little like the breed of the father or mother. Mongrels may be very clever and make fine companions; they can be trained to perform in circuses and they make good watchdogs.

Purebred dogs can be registered with the American Kennel Club, which will give them numbers to show that they are listed with the pedigreed dogs of their own breed. The American Kennel Club is the official club that regulates all matters that have to do with the dog breeds in America. It also makes the rules for the big dog shows that are given all over the country.

DOGS THAT HAVE KNOWN ME

I never meant to say anything about this, but the fact is that I have never met a dog that didn't have it in for me. You take Kelly, for example. He's a wire-haired fox terrier and he's had us for three years now. I wouldn't say that he was terribly handsome, but he does have a very nice smile. What he doesn't have is any sense of fitness. All the other dogs in the neighborhood spend their afternoons yapping at each other's heels or chasing cats. Kelly spends his whole day, every day, chasing swans on the millpond. I don't actually worry because he will never catch one. For one thing he can't swim. Instead of settling for a simple dog paddle like everybody else, he has to show off and try some complicated overhand stroke, with the result that he always sinks and has to be fished out. Naturally, people talk and I never take him for a walk that somebody doesn't point him out and say, "There's that crazy dog that chases swans."

Another thing about the dog is that he absolutely refuses to put himself in the other person's position. We have a pencil sharpener in the kitchen and Kelly used to enjoy having an occasional munch on the plastic cover. As long as it was just a nip now and then, I didn't mind. But one day he simply lost his head and ate the whole thing. Then I had to buy a new one and, of course, I put it high out of Kelly's reach. Well, the scenes we were treated to—and the sulking! In fact, ever since, he has been eating things that I know he doesn't like just to get even. I don't mean things like socks and mittens and paper napkins, which of course are delicious. Lately he's been eating plastic airplanes, suede brushes, and light bulbs. Well, if he wants to sit under the piano and make low and loving growls over a suede brush just to show me, OK. But frankly I think he's lowering himself.[1]

---

[1] From "Dogs That Have Known Me," by Jean Kerr. Copyright © 1957 by Conde Nast Publications, Inc. From the book *Please Don't Eat the Daisies* by Jean Kerr. Reprinted by permission of Doubleday & Co., Inc. and A. M. Heath & Company Ltd.

The second example is infinitely better for many reasons. Two of the most important are the uniqueness of the material and the sharpness of the focus. The student composition gives generalizations available from any encyclopedia. There is nothing special here, nothing known only to the writer. Nothing has been accomplished by writing this composition except the mechanical fulfilling of an assignment.

This is not to say that writing should not give information. Much good writing is done mainly for this purpose. However, it is not worthwhile simply to serve up information that someone else has already collected and organized. The difference between writing and copying is the addition of the writer's own information.

Sharpness of focus counts, too. Let us examine this important aspect of good writing.

BRINGING MATERIAL INTO FOCUS

Good writing has sharpness, vividness, clarity. It also has substance, body, "muscle." All these qualities come about when you write about a manageable subject, focus upon it, and portray its concrete details — when you look closely at something special. There are several ways of looking closely, of focusing material for writing.

13b. Limit your subject.

You could write a full-length book about a single dog, or you could write one paragraph about dogs in general. Ordinarily, neither attempt would be successful. In general, the scope of the subject determines the length of the treatment. The bigger the subject, the longer the writing.

In practical terms, this means that your shorter

compositions will be successful only if they deal with very limited subjects. How do you limit a subject? Here are some possibilities and examples of each:

a. *Deal with a limited time period.* (The Most Popular Breeds of Dogs Today)
b. *Deal with a limited place.* (Popular Breeds of Dogs in America)
c. *Deal with a limited type.* (Cocker Spaniels)
d. *Deal with a limited use.* (Dogs in Hunting)

Each topic will, of course, suggest its own limitations. The important thing is to carry on the limiting process until you have a subject to which you can add your own special point of view or knowledge within the length of your paper. The following examples may show the relationship between subject and length.

SUBJECT	LENGTH
1. Dogs	Book
2. History of Dogs	Encyclopedia article
3. Cocker Spaniel in America	Long magazine article
4. How to Judge a Cocker Spaniel	750-word article
5. Training My Cocker Spaniel	500-word article
6. One Trick My Dog Can Do	100-word paragraph

EXERCISE 4. On a separate sheet of paper, list for each of the following five subjects a topic which would be appropriate for these lengths: a book, a long article, 750 words, and a 100-word paragraph. In writing your topics, use the form shown in the following example.

EXAMPLE 1. Cars
           1. *Cars*
           Book: Cars
           Long article: American-made Cars
           750 words: The Compact
           100-word paragraph: The Advantages
           of Front-wheel Drive

1. Politics   4. Horses
2. Cooking   5. Inventions
3. Football

13c. Adapt your subject to your readers.

Even if you have a manageable topic, in terms of length, about which you are fully informed, you still need to make another adjustment. You must adjust the topic and the content to the audience for which you write. For example, suppose you were writing an article on "Training My Cocker Spaniel" for a magazine read by dog fanciers who know quite a bit about basic obedience training. The article would certainly have a focus and content different from an essay on the same subject written for students who know little about training dogs. The topic for the magazine article might be better stated, "Some Special Techniques I Have Learned in Training My Spaniel." The essay topic might be, "Basic Procedures for the Beginner in Training the Spaniel."

Just as important as knowing your subject, then, is knowing your audience: their interests, reading level, prior knowledge, and attitudes. This knowledge of your audience influences more than just your focusing of the topic and the content of your essay. It should affect also the way you begin, the number of examples you use, and the words you select.

EXERCISE 5. Choose two of the following topics and

write a brief composition on each. Choose one *a* and one *b*.

1. How We Elect Our Class Officers
   a. for a friend in a nearby school
   b. for a student in Germany
2. How to Find My House
   a. for a friend in a neighboring community
   b. for a visitor from a distant state
3. What It's Like to Be a High School Student Now
   a. for a fifth-grade pupil
   b. for an elderly person who graduated fifty years ago
4. How to Watch a Football Game
   a. for a person who has seen many games but knows little about the rules
   b. for a foreign visitor who has never seen a game
5. Why the Right to Vote Is Important
   a. for a classmate
   b. for a student living under a dictatorship

13d. Determine the purpose of your composition.

Assuming that you have a workable topic and a good idea of your audience, there is still one more basic decision you must make about the special direction or focus of your paper: the *effect* you wish to have on your audience. Do you want your paper to amuse them, inform them, anger them, persuade them, establish a certain mood, or make them visualize a scene or person?

Suppose that you have chosen the topic "Buying a Cocker Spaniel," and you intend it for an audience of high school students who know little or nothing about the subject. Do you wish to inform them so that they can make better choices? Do you wish to persuade them that they should buy a dog? Or do you wish to amuse them by describing humorously some of the difficulties involved in buying a dog? Your decision about purpose will have an important effect on your composition.

A good topic then is not selected by accident. You should decide upon it only after you have settled three important matters:

1. the way in which the subject will be limited;
2. the audience for whom it is intended; and
3. the effect you desire to produce.

EXERCISE 6. Below is a list of limited topics. Number your paper 1–10. After the appropriate number, write what your purpose would be in writing about each topic: (1) to amuse, (2) to inform, (3) to persuade, (4) to establish a mood, or (5) to make the reader visualize someone or something.

1. Why I Am a Conformist (or Nonconformist)
2. Three Routines in Our Home
3. Unusual Events Inside a Classroom
4. Characteristics of an Ideal Friend
5. Types of Car Dealers
6. Whose Side Is the Law On?
7. Facts About the Attitudes of Teen-agers
8. Traffic Laws Should Be More Strictly Enforced
9. Three Gifts I Like to Receive
10. How to Get Along with Your Neighbors

PLANNING YOUR COMPOSITION

13e. Plan your composition before writing it.

Some people like to take aimless trips, making no plans at all but rambling over the countryside, exploring side roads, stopping when they wish, and not much caring when or where they arrive. When people want to reach a definite destination at a specific time, however, they generally make detailed plans of their route and schedule their time.

Writing is much the same. Some writing—letters to friends, for example—is unplanned. It rambles on aimlessly and spontaneously, making digressions and having no fixed objective. For most formal writing, however, you need a plan which shows you where you are headed and how you expect to get there.

(1) List your specific ideas.

As soon as you have chosen and limited your subject and have decided upon your purpose, make a list of your ideas. Write them down rapidly as they come to you, without worrying too much at this time about their value or where you would include them in your composition. Later, when you are organizing, you can omit those that you decide not to use. The important thing is to see what material you have to work with. In a composition on "Things I Dislike," for example, the first list of ideas might look something like this:

FIRST LIST OF IDEAS

Title of Composition: Things I Dislike
Purpose: To define and give examples of things I dislike

long assignments, especially on Friday	arguing about TV channels
hats	riding with a back-seat driver
homework in general	interruptions when I am talking
hate to play cards	a showoff at a party
any dull game	boring talks in assembly
also games like charades	preparing oral reports
my brother's "I told you so"	stage fright
having to go to bed early	

(2) Group related ideas under headings.

After you have made a list of your ideas, you are
ready to group them so that your plan will gradually
develop into a few larger divisions. How you group
them will depend upon the subject. Some topics,
especially those dealing with a process, are easily
arranged in chronological (time) order. Other topics
also fall into a chronological pattern; for example,
morning, noon, night, or *childhood, youth, maturity,
old age.* For all subjects, however, you should group
your ideas according to the phase of the subject they
deal with.

IDEAS FOR THE COMPOSITION ON "THINGS I DISLIKE"
GROUPED UNDER HEADINGS

I. At home
arguing about TV channels
hearing "I told you so"
having to go to bed early

II. At school
homework
assignments on Friday
preparing oral reports
boring assembly programs

III. At parties
dull games
cards
charades
a showoff

Notice that four of the items on the first list have
already been omitted. "Hats," "riding with a back-
seat driver," "interruptions when I am talking," and
"stage fright" do not specifically fall under any of the
three main headings, *home, school,* and *parties.* With
the choice of these main headings and the omission
of some of the ideas on the first list, the topic has
been further limited.

(3) Arrange your ideas in order.

Your next job is to arrange the ideas in the order in which you will discuss them in your composition. Some subjects will require a certain order. For example, if your composition gives instructions on how to assemble the parts of a model airplane, you will need to follow a chronological order. If, on the other hand, you are writing about your reasons for joining the Scouts, you may arrange your ideas with the most important coming last.

Sometimes the material under one heading is necessary for understanding the material under one of the other headings. For instance, if you are explaining how to process a roll of film, you will first need to point out the differences between panchromatic and orthochromatic film (one heading) because the kind of film determines whether or not a person should develop the negatives in complete darkness (another heading). You would have to put the first heading before the one which depends upon it.

If the ideas themselves do not determine the order in which they should come, you must decide yourself upon the clearest and most interesting arrangement.

EXERCISE 7. Without listing minor points of development, list the main headings you would use in planning a composition on the following topics. List at least three headings for each topic.

1. How to find a book in the library
2. Music groups
3. A good club
4. The honor system in our school should be (abolished, retained)
5. Characteristics of a good teacher
6. My advice to next year's class
7. Television shows

8. The drawbacks of adolescence
9. Planning a career
10. The value of sports

Making an Outline

Your next step is to write down your plan in orderly fashion. This will enable you — and your teacher — to see exactly how your composition should grow. The easiest and best way to do this is by means of an outline.

The first step in making an outline is to arrange your ideas in a definite order. Besides indicating the order of ideas, an outline often shows the relative importance of the ideas.

The outline consists of main headings with subheadings under them. For most of the compositions you write, a *topic* outline is satisfactory. A topic outline is one in which the various items are topics, not complete sentences.

Remember that an outline is a working plan, the first step in writing the composition. Do not try to be literary or to crowd in too many details here. The language of the outline should be simple and clear. Use as few words as possible for each topic to make your meaning clear and to show the organization of your ideas.

On page 346 ideas for a composition on "Things I Dislike" were arranged under main headings. Here is a topic outline resulting from that arrangement of ideas. Refer to this outline as you study the rules that follow.

Topic Outline

THINGS I DISLIKE   title

Purpose: To define and give examples   purpose
  of things I dislike

I. At home   main topic
  A. Hearing "I told you so"
  B. Arguing about TV channels   subtopics
  C. Going to bed early

II. At school
  A. Boring assembly programs
  B. Homework
    1. Assignments on Friday   further subdivi-
    2. Preparation of oral reports   sions of subtopics

III. At parties
  A. Dull games
    1. Cards   note use of words or phrases,
    2. Charades   not sentences, throughout out-
  B. A showoff   line

Outline Form

13f. Observe rules for form in making an outline.

As you study these rules, refer to the example given above. Be sure to note the arrangement of the material. It will help you to remember the purpose and form of a topic outline.

(1) Place the title (and the purpose) above the outline. It is not one of the numbered or lettered parts of the outline.

(2) Use Roman numerals for the main topics. Subtopics are given capital letters, then Arabic numerals, then small letters, then Arabic numerals in parentheses, and then small letters in parentheses. Study this outline form:

Correct Outline Form

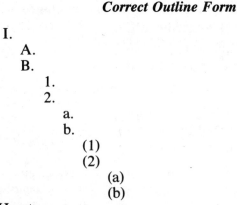

I.
  A.
  B.
    1.
    2.
      a.
      b.
        (1)
        (2)
          (a)
          (b)
II. etc.

(3) For each number or letter in an outline, there must be a topic.

Each number or letter must stand on a line by itself. Never, in an outline, write IA or A1.

(4) There must always be, under any topic, more than one subtopic.

Subtopics are divisions of the topic above them, and you cannot divide anything into fewer than two parts. If you find yourself wanting to use a single subtopic, rewrite the topic above it so that this "subidea" is included in the main topic.

IMPROPER A. Assembly programs
              1. Those that are boring
CORRECTED A. Boring assembly programs

(5) A subtopic must belong under the main topic beneath which it is placed. It must be closely related to the topic above it.

UNRELATED A. Dull games
           1. Cards
           2. Not enough refreshments [not related to topic]

(6) Indent subtopics. Indentions should be made so that all letters or numbers of the same kind will come directly under one another in a vertical line.

(7) Begin each topic with a capital letter.

Since a topic is not a sentence, you need not place a period after it.

(8) The terms *Introduction, Body,* **and** *Conclusion* **should not be included in the outline.**

Of course, you should have an introduction and a conclusion in your composition, but the terms are not topics that you intend to discuss. Therefore, they should not be listed as topics in the outline.

EXERCISE 8. The items in the unsorted list of ideas below can be grouped under the four main headings given before the list. On your paper, write these main headings, leaving several blank lines beneath each; then under each, list the topics which properly belong there. Number, letter, and arrange them in a correct outline.

TITLE   What I Like About My Hometown
MAIN HEADINGS   location
   school
   entertainment facilities
   people

UNSORTED LIST

friendly	well-trained teachers
near a large city	in the mountains
charitable	modern classrooms
superior library	recreation center
parks	well-balanced curriculum
on a river	theaters

EXERCISE 9. Decide on answers to the questions in one of the following numbered items. Then write a

topic outline based upon your answers. Group your subtopics properly under the main headings, and follow the correct form of an outline.

1. Do "good fences make good neighbors"? Why or why not?
2. What is the best book you have ever read? What are three reasons for its excellence? What specific references to the book will support your opinion?
3. Do you find cooking fun? What are three or four joys of cooking?
4. What exactly are the advantages or disadvantages of being the youngest (oldest) in the family?
5. Before joining a club, what three or four things should a person consider? Why?
6. Do high school athletics encourage sportsmanship, school spirit, and teamwork? How?
7. What are the main characteristics of a good speaker? Of what importance are preparation, voice, and delivery?
8. What are the necessary steps in getting ready for school, for church, or for a camping trip?
9. In your opinion, what are the most interesting attractions of a state or county fair—the midway, acrobats, motorcycle or automobile races, exhibits? Why?
10. How have your friends influenced your thinking? Which three or four friends have influenced you most? In what ways?

EXERCISE 10. Write a topic outline for any one of the subjects listed in Exercise 6, page 344.

EXERCISE 11. Write a composition of about 300 words based upon the outline you wrote for Exercise 10.

WRITING THE COMPOSITION

13g. Every composition has an introduction, a body, and a conclusion.

When you begin to write a composition, you should remember that you will need a good beginning (introduction), a main discussion of the topics in your outline (body), and an effective ending (conclusion).

(1) The introduction should arouse the reader's interest and state the main idea of the composition.

The beginning of every composition must do two things:

    a. It must catch the reader's interest.
    b. It must inform the reader about the main point of the composition.

How much space you devote to each will depend on your audience and on the length of the composition. If your readers already have a strong interest in your subject, you won't have to worry too much about arousing interest at the beginning. If they are likely to be uninformed, however, you must begin by arousing their interest and stimulating their curiosity.

In a very short composition, the introduction may be only the first one or two sentences of the first paragraph. In a composition of medium length, the introduction will probably be a 50–75 word paragraph. In a long composition, the introduction may run to 100–150 words. Generally one paragraph is sufficient for the introduction. A good practice for you to follow is to state the subject of the composition at the end of the first paragraph.

There are several specific ways of arousing audience interest and stating your subject.

1. *Begin with an interesting anecdote or example.* This is a useful device when you are writing for an uninformed audience. It should probably not be used in a very short composition, since the anecdote will take up too much of the total length.

For example, in a longer composition on "The Joys of Trimming the Hedge," you might begin:

> Standing behind a hedge trimmer was a teenaged girl with a blissful smile on her face. To passing friends who taunted her about her chore, she called out the same answer, "Best fun I ever had!" Far from being a lunatic or an idiot, this young girl was another member of the growing group of people who have discovered the joys of trimming the hedge.

2. *Begin with a question.* The question again stimulates interest because it seems to push the reader on to find an answer. For example:

> What is there about trimming the hedge that compels otherwise lazy individuals to do this weekly chore? My own experience as a practiced hedge trimmer indicates that it's the physical exercise, the routine nature of the job, and the sense of accomplishment involved that keep us hedge trimmers moving.

Be careful not to overuse this device; it may seem quite artificial if used too often.

3. *Begin with a direct statement of the topic.* In a short composition, and especially in one where reader interest is already strong, you may begin with a simple statement of your main idea. This device must be well handled, however; otherwise such beginnings can seem too abrupt and rather childish. Contrast these two examples:

INFERIOR   I would like to write about the joys of hedge trimming. It can be fun if you have the right hedge, the right tools, and the right attitude.

SATISFACTORY   Hedge trimming can be fun if you have the right hedge, the right tools, and the right attitude.

4. *Begin with a negative statement of your topic, followed by a positive or direct statement.* This technique is useful when you are taking a position that contradicts prevailing opinion. It catches the reader off guard by stating a widely held notion and then refuting it.

Most people think of hedge trimming as an arduous chore to be done only under threat of bodily injury. They couldn't be further from the truth. Given the right hedge, the right tools, and the right attitude, hedge trimming can actually be a joy.

5. *Begin by providing general background information.* Although this method can make for a very slow start, it can be useful when dealing with a topic about which the reader knows very little.

In recent years, hedge trimming has become big business. Each spring and summer, millions of dollars are spent by Americans on gadgets and devices designed to make the task easier and the results more attractive. All the gadgetry and all the advertising ballyhoo about hedge trimmers, however, tend to obscure the fact that trimming the hedge remains one of the simple joys of life.

EXERCISE 12. Rewrite the introduction to the composition that you wrote for Exercise 3 (page 336) in any *two* of the five ways you have just studied.

(2) The body should state and develop the main points in the outline.

In stating and developing your main points, you should pay special attention to the paragraphs comprising the body of your composition — the *developmental paragraphs*. In Chapter 12, you learned how to write a paragraph and how to develop paragraph ideas. As part of a longer composition, the paragraph still needs to be fully developed, unified, and coherent. Also it should still have a topic sentence. In addition, it must now fit into and become a natural part of the longer composition. Your task at this stage, then, is to move from the outline to a rough draft of the whole composition.

Decide on the number of paragraphs for each main topic of your outline. For the most part, your outline can be a guide to paragraphing. Ordinarily you will devote one paragraph to each of your main topics. However, there may be a topic which is so important that you will want to devote two or more paragraphs to it. The important thing to remember is that each paragraph must be the full development of a single idea.

You might find it useful at this stage to go back over your outline and indicate the number of paragraphs you intend to devote to each main heading.

(3) The conclusion should clinch the main points made in the body of the composition.

The conclusion of a composition may be an entire paragraph, or it may be only a sentence or two. No matter what its length, it has two important functions: to provide a graceful ending for your composition and to provide a final chance to stress the main points. There are no rules for ending a composition; however, some specific types of conclusions do seem to fit certain types of compositions.

1. Very short compositions should conclude with merely a restatement of the most important main topic.

EXAMPLE   I maintain, then, that hedge trimming, rather than being a tiresome chore, is actually fun.

2. Explanations of how to do, or make, something should conclude with a statement of the final product.

EXAMPLE   If you have followed my suggestions carefully, you should have a hedge that is attractive, easily cared for, and hardy under all conditions.

3. A persuasive composition should end with a final call to action or a warning of the consequences if no action is taken.

EXAMPLE   The challenge is clear. Grab that trimmer, whistle a happy tune, and make your hedge a work of art.

4. Longer compositions may end with a summary, a restatement of the main idea — but not a mere listing of the main points.

EXAMPLE   With a bad hedge, inferior tools, and a negative attitude, hedge trimming can be depressing, tedious work. Given the right conditions, however, it can be sheer pleasure.

5. Descriptive compositions should end with a general impression of the object, person, or place.

EXAMPLE   The whole hedge seems to be one large green velvet wall. The separate bushes are indistinct. One is aware only of where the hedge begins and where it ends.

6. Compositions of criticism or evaluation should end with a general judgment of the work you are writing about. You will find this technique extremely useful when you are writing book reports. For example, you might end a report on a relatively uninteresting book as follows:

All things considered, this book is merely a routine adventure story, with no glaring weaknesses but no special claims to our attention.

EXERCISE 13. In a magazine that you may cut up, find an effective introduction and a strong conclusion to an article. Paste these onto a sheet of paper, and in two or three sentences, tell why the introduction and conclusion are interesting or effective and how each is related to the body of the article.

REVIEW EXERCISE A. Choose a topic from the list of suggestions at the end of this chapter (pages 367–70), or select one of your own. Prepare a topic outline, and then write a composition based on it. Applying what you have learned in this chapter, make sure that you write an effective introduction, a well-developed body, and a smooth conclusion.

Connecting Paragraphs

13h. Use linking expressions to bridge the gaps between paragraphs.

You have already learned that bridging the gaps between ideas within a paragraph is essential for good writing (see pages 317–19). The very same words that connect ideas within a paragraph can help you bridge the gaps between paragraphs.

Become familiar with the following list of linking words so that you can use them to make your thoughts flow along smoothly. If you will make it a habit to use one of them in the first sentence of a new paragraph, you can clearly show your readers the relationship between the paragraph they are starting and the one that they have just read.

Linking Expressions

To indicate another point

finally	in addition	to begin with
at last	another	at the outset
then	after that	to sum up
too	first	in conclusion
moreover	second, etc.	also
besides	in the next place	furthermore

To indicate another time

next	not long after	meanwhile	later
soon	at length	then	finally

To indicate results

therefore   thus   consequently   as a result   hence

To show contrast

nevertheless	on the contrary	instead
however	on the other hand	in spite of this

To show relationships

accordingly   similarly   likewise   such

To introduce examples

for instance   an example of this   for example

When you write an explanatory composition in which ideas are often arranged in chronological (time) order, you will find transitional expressions such as *first* (*second, third,* etc.), *next, meanwhile, soon, later, then, finally* especially useful. (Avoid the overuse of *then.*)

As you read the following paragraphs, notice how the author uses linking words that express time in order to bridge the gap between the ideas of one paragraph and those in the next.

Eight years ago, when Enid Larson came to Carmel High, biology was virtually a dead subject. Only one year of it was offered, and only 30 out of 300 students took that. The "laboratory" boasted a single display: a pretty arrangement of sea shells purchased from a gift shop.

At first the students didn't know what to make of their new teacher. They kept asking, "When do we study animals?" She kept replying, "When you bring them in." Months passed without the class's studying a single animal.

Finally a boy brought in a strange, hard object shaped like a cocoon. He found from the reference shelves that it was a pellet regurgitated by a barn owl to dispose of indigestible wastes. Opening it before his awed classmates, the boy sorted out a collection of tiny bones that started the whole class doing detective work. It took them two weeks to identify the skull of a gopher and the bones of meadow mice and shrews.

The boy **later** went back to the reference shelves to prepare a painstaking paper on the food of predatory birds. His report on the great extent to which the barn owl aids man in checking our destructive rodent population was the first lesson Miss Larson's students ever had on the balance of nature. They were fascinated, and they reacted by swamping the laboratory with specimens of plant and animal life, whose behavior and interrelationships they proceeded to study.

Within two years more and more students were electing the course, and a second year had to be offered. Word got around: "She's fabulous." Students finally petitioned the Board of Trustees for a third year, and until recently Carmel High School was offering the state's only three-year sequence in biology. Miss Larson **now** teaches six crowded classes a day.[1]

EXERCISE 14. In a magazine that you may cut up, find three paragraphs that contain linking expressions which help to bridge the gap between paragraphs. Paste these paragraphs neatly on a sheet of paper. Underline the linking expressions.

13i. In the first sentence of a new paragraph, you may refer to the thought in the preceding paragraph.

You can bridge the gap between paragraphs by using words such as *this, that, those, these, such, other, another*. Suppose, for example, you are writing a composition about the traits of a woman you admire. You have just finished a paragraph about her consideration for other people, and now you are ready to begin a discussion of her ability to hold her temper. You may bridge the gap between these ideas by starting the second paragraph with: "*Another* praiseworthy characteristic is her ability to hold her temper."

A second method of making the change to another idea in a new paragraph is to refer directly to the preceding paragraph by mentioning again the principal idea in the preceding paragraph. For instance: "Rae is not only considerate of other people but also even-tempered in dealing with her associates." Another

[1] From "The Teacher Who Won't Answer Questions," by Frances V. Rummell, *The Reader's Digest,* April 1957. Copyright 1957 by The Reader's Digest Assn., Inc. Reprinted by permission of Reader's Digest.

way to do this is: "Just as important as her consideration for others is her ability to hold her temper."

Every time that you go from one paragraph to a
new one, you should use either a linking expression
or a linking reference in order to make a skillful and
clear connection between the ideas of the paragraphs.

EXERCISE 15. Assume that the first sentence in each
pair below is the last sentence of one paragraph and
that the second is the first sentence of the next paragraph. Your job is to rewrite the first sentence of the
second paragraph so that it will include a linking
expression or some other device to bridge the gap
between the ideas.

EXAMPLES 1. a. I found that visiting the Grand
Canyon was an unforgettable experience.
   b. The Yellowstone National Park is
filled with nature's wonders.
  1. *Although the Grand Canyon impressed me with its beauties, the
Yellowstone National Park has an
even greater variety of the wonders
of nature.*

2. a. Clean hands and fingernails, then,
are essential to good grooming.
   b. People should pay attention to the
appearance of ,their clothes.
  2. *Well-groomed people also pay attention to the appearance of their clothes.*

1. a. Of course, this kind of stamp collecting can
be a very expensive hobby.
   b. Building model airplanes does not require
much money.
2. a. Certainly boats built for racing should be
made of sturdy material.

    b. The engines of the racing boat should be capable of seven thousand revolutions a minute.

3. a. Perhaps I shall someday realize this secret ambition by riding in the caboose of a freight train.

    b. I have always wanted to wear a pair of blue jeans to a formal party.

4. a. In other words, calf ropers must have proper equipment.

    b. They should use "horse sense" as they practice roping a calf.

5. a. As this incident illustrates, my parents usually understand my personal problems.

    b. My friends sometimes do not care about what troubles me.

6. a. People who can sew can also design their own clothes.

    b. They can make decorations for the home.

7. a. As these figures show, students can earn a great deal of spending money by delivering newspapers.

    b. They can make several dollars a week by baby-sitting.

8. a. The band finished its performance with the "wagon wheel" stunt.

    b. Two high school girls began to twirl flaming batons.

9. a. You can see that my mother has a wonderful sense of humor.

    b. My father takes pride in telling the truth at all times.

10. a. It was certainly a lot of fun playing these games outdoors.

    b. We enjoyed the entertainment indoors.

Achieving Emphasis in the Composition

All the parts of your composition will not be of equal importance. The introduction and the conclusion are less important to the development of your ideas than is the middle section of your composition. This middle section, the main body of the composition, should reflect the proper emphasis. Even within this main section, however, you should indicate to the reader which parts should receive the strongest emphasis.

Emphasis in a composition is ordinarily achieved in three ways:

1. *Direct statement.* Phrases like "the most important reason," "the major step in preparation," and "the most significant result" are ways of stating directly which ideas you think are most important and should receive the greatest emphasis.

2. *Emphasis by position.* Ordinarily the strongest positions in the body of your composition are the first and last parts. In argumentation or persuasion, it is usually wise to begin and end strongly, putting your weakest arguments in the middle. Another type of emphatic organization frequently used is the *order of climax,* which moves from weakest to strongest.

3. *Emphasis by proportion.* The most important kind of emphasis is this type, in which the amount of space you devote to a phase of your subject reflects its importance. In other words, the more important the topic, the more space it gets. If you tell your readers that a given topic is important, they will expect that topic to be given extensive treatment.

Remember, however, that the number of subtopics a topic has in the outline does not necessarily determine the amount of emphasis that the topic should receive in the final composition.

SUMMARY OF THE STEPS IN WRITING A COMPOSITION

1. Choose an interesting subject that you have experienced or investigated.

2. Focus your material by limiting the subject, determining its purpose, and adapting it to your readers.
3. Plan your composition through specific ideas.
4. Organize your ideas by making an outline.
5. Write your composition, keeping in mind the following:
   a. Create interest and state your main idea in the introduction.
   b. State and develop the main points in the body.
      (1) Decide on the number of paragraphs for each main topic and on the method of development you will use for each paragraph.
      (2) Achieve emphasis through position, statement, and proportion.
      (3) Connect your paragraphs with linking expressions or by referring to the thought in the preceding paragraph.
   c. Write a concluding sentence or paragraph that clinches the main points made in the body of the composition.

REVIEW EXERCISE B. Write a composition of about 300 words based upon the outline that you prepared for Exercise 9. Write a brief and interesting introduction that states your purpose; carefully develop each paragraph in the body of your composition; and write a short concluding paragraph. When you hand in your paper, be sure to include your outline.

REVIEW EXERCISE C. Write about 300 words on any one of the following subjects. Word your own title as you decide upon your purpose. After making an outline, write the composition, carefully developing each paragraph.

1. How we lost (or won) the game
2. My fight with a wasp's nest
3. TV commercials
4. How to fight air pollution
5. Why I always trust people

6. Human beings can be parasites
7. When I get the fidgets
8. A definition of sportsmanship
9. An athlete I admire
10. How not to pack a suitcase
11. I think of clever remarks too late
12. Memories of my first days in school
13. My artistic efforts
14. It pays to be courteous
15. The value of basketball (or any other sport)
16. Mother and Father as disciplinarians
17. How important to success is good luck?
18. Tricks of memory
19. The promises of advertisers
20. The language of dogs (cats, flowers, birds)

REVIEW EXERCISE D. Following the "Summary of the Steps in Writing a Composition" on pages 364–65, write a composition about one of your discoveries, describing your search and leading up to your finding. You may wish to use one of these titles: "Finding a Loyal Friend," "Searching for a Notebook," "Solving a Mystery," or "Discovering a Treasure in My Own Backyard." If, however, you wish to describe an accidental discovery, you could use the title "Serendipity." *Serendipity* refers to the experience of happening onto a lucky discovery when you are not expecting it.

A CHECKLIST FOR WRITING COMPOSITIONS

The checklist below is for use **before** and **after** you write; use it to remind yourself of the techniques of good writing and to help you detect weaknesses in your writing.

1. Does my outline clearly and logically develop my subject?
2. Does every idea stick to the subject and carry out my purpose?

3. Is my composition properly divided into well-constructed paragraphs?
4. In developing each paragraph, have I been generous with interesting, specific details?
5. Are my paragraphs properly tied together with linking expressions?
6. Are all of my sentences clear, grammatically correct, and varied?
7. Are my punctuation and spelling accurate?
8. Can I improve the choice of words?

Suggested Topics for Compositions

Places

1. Exploring a Cave
2. Curiosities in a Museum
3. Western Movies
4. A Modern Turkey Farm
5. In the Corridor of a Hospital
6. Main Street at Disneyworld
7. My First Look into the Grand Canyon
8. Modern Wonders of the World
9. Legends About My State
10. Seeing New York City from a Plane
11. Sights Along the Seashore
12. Sailing down the Hudson River
13. A National Park
14. The Ideal Site for a School
15. Visiting a Zoo
16. My Favorite View
17. A Crowded Beach
18. A Day in the Mountains
19. The Comforts of a 747
20. The Lincoln Memorial at Night

School

1. Students Need a Code of Conduct
2. The Problem of Copying Homework
3. Stagehands Are Artists
4. Controlling Hall Traffic
5. A Teacher I Will Always Remember
6. Going Out for Track
7. What My History Book Doesn't Tell Me
8. In Study Hall

9. Getting on Good Terms with a Typewriter
10. I Like Foreign Languages
11. Student Types
12. Rummaging Through the Lost and Found Department
13. Subjects I'd Like to Study
14. Planning an Amateur Show
15. Our High School Orchestra
16. The Latest Fad at School
17. Presenting a One-Act Play
18. Learning About Nature's Laws
19. The Value of Mathematics
20. My School's Policies
21. An Important Class Meeting
22. Burning the Midnight Oil
23. Why We Learn Good Manners
24. Parents' Day
25. An Experiment in Shop
26. A Concert at School
27. We Put Out a School Paper
28. Raising Money for Group Projects
29. What I Admire About Teachers
30. What Sports Teach You

Personal

1. My Declaration of Independence
2. The Importance of Self-Discipline
3. My Reading Tastes
4. I Didn't Believe It!
5. I Had a Dollar to My Name
6. Idleness Is My Imagination's Workshop
7. A Fragment from My Diary
8. Teams I Have Known
9. Among My Souvenirs
10. Why I Gave Up Shortcuts
11. Adventures of a Would-be Hero
12. Why I Can't Save Money
13. Neighbors
14. A Struggle with My Conscience
15. Why I Like Folk Songs
16. My Impressions of the Ocean
17. Three of My Secret Ambitions

18. The Life and Death of a Daydream
19. My Luck Often Runs Out
20. Self-Examination
21. Am I Gullible!
22. Controlling My Temper
23. Three Things I Cherish
24. I Learned How to Say No
25. Traditions in My Family
26. My Good Intentions
27. I Always Do Things the Hard Way
28. If I Were a Newspaper Editor
29. Why I Hate Alarm Clocks
30. A Stroke of Luck

Occasions

1. A Family Reunion
2. Exploring the Attic
3. I Found Out the Hard Way
4. When to Be Silent
5. Effects of TV Sports on Family Life
6. On Making a Tape Recording
7. An Hour in a Bargain Basement
8. Holidays at Our House
9. Prizefights

10. Parents' Parties
11. Sleeping Outdoors
12. An Unlucky Winner
13. My First Ride in an Airplane
14. An Addition to Our Family
15. A Birthday to Remember
16. The Day Unexpected Relatives Moved In
17. The Night the Lights Went Out
18. Celebrating the Fourth of July
19. A Decision That Changed My Life
20. It Finally Happened

People

1. Characteristics of a Popular Teacher
2. People Are Complicated
3. Two Heads Are Not Better than One
4. The Wisdom of Little Children
5. The People on Our Block
6. Bores I Have Known
7. Two's a Crowd
8. A Stranger I'll Never Forget
9. My Admirable Aunt
10. Memories of My Grandfather

11. Four of a Kind
12. My Curious Kid Sister
13. The Voices in My Family
14. A Practical Joker
15. A Person of Action

Hobbies
1. A Bird's-Eye View of My Scrapbook
2. Saving Coupons
3. How to Care for a Pet Alligator
4. Photography Is My Hobby
5. Making Home Movies
6. The Art of Sailing
7. Model Building
8. I'm a Bird Watcher
9. My Astrological Sign
10. How to Handle a Bow and Arrow
11. My Parents' Hobbies
12. Water-Skiing
13. I Work with Wood
14. I Learned to Play the Harmonica
15. Weather Watching

Chapter **14**

Manuscript Form

Standards for Written Work

A *manuscript* is any typewritten or handwritten composition, as distinguished from a printed document. In your schoolwork this year and the years ahead, you will be writing more and more manuscripts. You should learn now to follow correct form for your written work.

14a. Follow accepted standards in preparing manuscripts.

Your teacher will find it easier to read and evaluate your papers if they are properly prepared. There is no single correct way to prepare a paper, but the rules below are widely used and accepted. Follow them unless your teacher requests you to do otherwise.

1. Use lined composition paper or, if you type, white paper 8½ by 11 inches in size.

2. Write only on one side of a sheet of paper.

3. Write in blue, black, or blue-black ink, or typewrite. If you type, double-space the lines.

4. Leave a margin of about two inches at the top of a page and margins of about one inch at the sides

and bottom. The left-hand margin must be straight; the right-hand margin should be as straight as you can make it.

5. Indent the first line of each paragraph about one-half inch from the left margin.

6. Write your name, the class, and the date on the first page. Follow your teacher's instructions in the placement of these items. You may put them on three separate lines in the upper right-hand corner of the sheet, or write them in one line across the top of the page. Either way, they should begin about one inch down from the top of the page.

7. If your paper has a title, write it in the center of the first line. Skip a line between the title and the first line of your composition. (Double-space twice if you are typing.)

8. If the paper is more than one page in length, number the pages after the first, placing the number in the center of the line, about one-half inch down from the top.

9. Write legibly and neatly. If you are using un-lined paper, try to keep the lines straight. Form your letters carefully, so that *n*'s do not look like *u*'s, *a*'s like *o*'s, and so on. Dot the *i*'s and cross the *t*'s. If you are typing, do not strike over letters or cross out words. If you have to erase, do it neatly.

14b. **Learn the rules for using abbreviations.**

In most of your writing, you should spell out words rather than abbreviate them. A few abbreviations, however, are commonly used.

The following abbreviations are acceptable when they are used along with a name: *Mr., Mrs., Ms., Dr., Jr.,* and *Sr.* If they do not accompany a name, spell out the words instead of using the abbreviations.

EXAMPLES   Mr. Casey   Dr. Macmillan
            Mrs. Murphy   George C. White, Sr.
            I have an appointment with our family doctor.
            Sally Wu is organizing the picnic that the junior class is giving for the seniors.

The abbreviations A.M. (*ante meridiem* — "before noon"), P.M. (*post meridiem* — "after noon"), A.D. (*anno Domini* — "in the year of the Lord"), and B.C. (before Christ) are acceptable when they are used with numbers.

EXAMPLES   The party is scheduled to begin at 7:30 **P.M.**
            Octavian (63 **B.C.–A.D.** 14) is now known as Augustus Caesar. [Notice that the abbreviation A.D. precedes the number, and B.C. follows it.]

Abbreviations for organizations are acceptable if they are generally known.

EXAMPLES   My father gave up his weekly swim at the **YMCA** to attend the **PTA** meeting.
            I am reading a book about the **FBI;** Margaret plans a report on a booklet published by the **UN.** [Abbreviations for government agencies are usually written without periods.]

14c. Learn the rules for writing numbers.

Numbers of more than two words should be written in numerals, not words. If, however, you are writing several numbers, some of them one word and some more than one, write them all the same way. Always spell out a number that begins a sentence.

EXAMPLES   Agnes has sold **257** magazine subscrip-
tions.
Mother has canned **thirty-seven** quarts
of peaches.
I have only **five** days in which to write
seven reports.
There are **563** students in the freshman
class, **327** in the sophomore class, **143**
in the junior class, and **98** in the senior
class.
One thousand five hundred band members attended the annual State Contest
Festival.

Write out numbers like *seventh, fifty-third,* and so
on. If they are used with a month, however, it is customary to use numerals only.

EXAMPLES   My brother graduated **second** [not 2nd]
in his class at the Naval Academy.
School closes on **June 6** [or the sixth of
June; not June 6th].

**14d. Learn the rules for dividing words at the end of a
line.**

Sometimes you do not have room to write all of a
long word at the end of a line. It may look better to
start the word on the next line; however, if doing
that would leave a very uneven right-hand margin,
you should divide the word, using a hyphen after the
first part. Learn the rules for dividing words (see
pages 553–54). Remember that you should try to
avoid dividing words if possible. Usually a slightly
irregular margin looks better than a hyphenated word.

14e. Learn the standard correction symbols.

In correcting your papers, your teacher may use some

or all of the symbols given below. If you memorize these symbols, you will understand at once what is wrong in your paper. If you are not sure how to correct your error, use the index of this book to find the section that you need to review.

ms	error in manuscript form or neatness
cap	error in use of capital letter
p	error in punctuation
sp	error in spelling
frag	sentence fragment
rs	run-on sentence
ss	error in sentence structure
k	awkward sentence or passage
nc	not clear
ref	unclear reference of pronoun
gr	error in grammar
w	error in word choice
¶	Begin a new paragraph here.
t	error in tense
ʌ	You have omitted something.

Writing Summaries and Reports

Most of the compositions you write are based on your personal experiences and opinions. Two important kinds of compositions, however, are based on your reading. These are (1) the *summary* of an article and (2) the *report* giving information taken from several sources.

Since the exercises in this chapter will require you to use the library, you should study Chapter 25 before you study this chapter.

WRITING A SUMMARY

In almost any of your classes, you may be asked to read an article in a magazine, an encyclopedia, or a book, and write a summary of it. Your problem is to give, in a brief composition, the main points of the article. To do this, you must read carefully and write a summary in your own words, being careful not to omit important information or to add any ideas of your own.

In preparing a summary, you should proceed in four steps, some of which overlap.

15a. Read the article carefully.

It is wise to read the article at least twice. The first time, you may skim it quickly to note the overall organization and to identify the major ideas. Pay special attention to any subtitles, because they indicate the important points made in the article.

The second time, you should read the article more carefully. Read the introductory paragraph slowly and thoughtfully, since the whole idea of the article is usually expressed there in a general way. As you read the body of the article, noting subtitles, pay special attention to the first and last sentences in each paragraph; the topic sentences and "clincher" sentences are usually found in these positions. Also, watch for signaling words and phrases (like *another factor, a major reason*) that indicate key supporting points. Finally, read the last paragraph carefully; it often sums up the major points of the article.

15b. Take notes in your own words, using your own abbreviations.

At the top of the page or card on which you are taking notes, record the facts about the article as follows: author (last name first); title in quotation marks; name of magazine or encyclopedia, underlined; date of magazine (volume of encyclopedia); page numbers. If the article is anonymous, begin with the title.

Magazine   Begole, Christine, "How to Make Cassette Recordings for Holiday Parties," *Glamour,* Dec. 1979, p. 64.

Encyclopedia   Grey, Francis Temple, "Capital Punishment," *Encyclopædia Britannica,* vol. 4, p. 809.

Book   Hamilton, Edith, "The Quest of the Golden Fleece," *Mythology,* p. 117.

Having recorded the facts about the article, you proceed to read and take notes on its contents. You will find it to your advantage to force yourself to use your own words in taking notes. You should do very little copying. If you find phrases or lines that will be useful as a direct quotation in your summary, copy the exact words accurately and enclose them in quotation marks. *Remember, however, that the summary is to be in your own words, not a series of sentences copied from the article.*

You will find it useful to use abbreviations in your note-taking. Be sure, however, that the abbreviations you use are clear so that you will understand them later.

The notes you take should consist of only the main ideas or the most important pieces of information in the article. You should omit examples, anecdotes, minor details, and digressions. Stick to the essentials. You are not rewriting the article; you are summarizing it.

15c. Write the summary, making it one fourth to one third the length of the article.

Put aside the article, and use your notes in writing the summary. If you have jotted down the principal ideas in the order in which the article presented them, you need only write out these ideas in sentence form, following your notes. In writing the summary, pretend that you are the author of the article, summarizing what your article said. Don't begin with "This article is about. . . ." or "In this article, Mr. White says. . . ." Begin directly, "Capital punishment, which is the death penalty for crime, has existed as long as there have been laws and courts. . . ." It is very important that you do not leave out any important ideas and that you do not add any that are not in the article.

15d. Compare your summary with the article.

If the article is still available, skim it rapidly, comparing your summary with it. Is the summary complete and accurate? Is it written in your own words, not those of the original? Does it follow the order of the original? Finally, is your summary free of grammatical and mechanical errors?

You will find on pages 383–84 two summaries of the following article on meteors. Read the article and the summaries.

METEORS AND METEORITES

On September 1, 1962, above Covington, West Virginia, and then again on September 5, over Clarksburg, West Virginia, great fireballs struck down through the atmosphere. The sky was ablaze with their bursting fragments, and sonic booms rattled dishes, furniture, and windows. Newspaper advertisements asked for eyewitness accounts to help plot the paths of these fireballs so they might be traced to the spots where they fell.

An amazing number of meteors hit the earth — at which time they become meteorites — in a 24-hour period, yet no one has ever been killed by one as far as is known. Only one human injury has been definitely recorded when, on November 30, 1954, "stars fell on Alabama." A small, stony meteoritic fragment weighing about 9 pounds crashed through the roof of a house in Sylacauga, Alabama, where Mrs. E. H. Hodges was resting on a sofa after lunch. The fragment ricocheted off a radio and struck her on the upper thigh, causing a slight bruise.

Called meteoroids in space, meteors as they penetrate the earth's atmosphere, and meteorites if they strike, very few of these stony, stony-iron, or iron bodies are ever recovered. For the most part, they land in the oceans, at the poles, or in such sparsely inhabited regions as forests and deserts. The bright but transitory streaks they make in the sky, which give them the name shooting stars, are due to friction with the atmosphere. The streaks are usually described as white, and sometimes as greenish, reddish, or yellowish. Very large and brilliant meteors are called fireballs, and when, rarely, these fireballs explode, they may be known as bolides. The term meteoroid, or meteoric body, is reserved for any small object in space, smaller than an asteroid and considerably larger than an atom or molecule, before it enters the earth's atmosphere, which only a very small proportion of them ever do. Meteoroids in space are nonluminous and thus not detectable by optical telescopes, but eventually some may be picked up by radar telescopes. Because of the threat to space probes and ships, meteoroid-detection satellites with 50-foot wings are being launched to measure the probable extent of meteoroid penetration to which spacecraft on long flights may be exposed.

Here is the history of one meteorite that fell in Alberta, Canada, just a few years ago and was observed in some detail. It entered the earth's atmosphere at 1:06 A.M., Mountain Standard Time, on March 4, 1960. It was an evening meteor, entered the atmosphere at a velocity close to 8 miles a second (29,000 miles an hour), and detonated when about 20 miles above the surface. Fragments from the explosion were discovered across an ellipse-shaped area about 3.3 miles long by 2 miles wide, near Bruderheim, 30 miles northwest of Edmonton, Alberta. The flash of the detonation was visible for some 200 miles, and the noise audible over an area of 2,000 square miles (the equivalent of a square 45 miles on a side). Many fragments were subsequently recovered. Some were picked up on the snow over which they had bounded and rebounded, and farmers plowed up others that spring. The fragments had not had time to disintegrate, as many do. Some 188 sizable chunks were collected, weighing a total of 670 pounds. The Bruderheim meteorite was a chondrite, one type of stony meteorite, gray in color, with a low iron content . . . .

It has been estimated that about 24 million visible meteors pass through the atmosphere of the entire earth in 24 hours. Observations with telescopes up to the 10th visual magnitude indicate that 8 billion meteors must plunge into the earth's atmosphere a day. Added to this are the much more numerous micrometeorites, objects with a diameter of less than a millimeter, and the cosmic debris or dust . . . .

Among the over 1,500 meteorites actually recovered, the stony type predominates, with over 900; then come the irons with about 550; and, finally, the very scarce stony-irons, of which only 67 are known. Of the total number of meteorites recovered, 680 were picked up or located after actually being observed falling. A greater number, 860, were discovered and identified merely by their characteristics . . . .

Meteoroids are traveling at many miles a second when they dash into the earth's atmosphere, but meeting the resistance of the gases high in the atmosphere begins to slow them down. Their great energy of motion must be dissipated, and by the time they have reached a height of 75 to 50 miles they are glowing in the sky because of the heat that has been produced. They become white-hot and their surfaces molten, streaming back from the direction of their travel, with drops flaming off and sometimes exploding or fragmenting and forming a number of wakes or trains in the sky. They lose fluid and vapors to the atmosphere in the process known as ablation, by which heat is rapidly carried away. The same ablation effects have been used to advantage in the design of spacecraft or missile cones, which must re-enter the atmosphere with as little destruction as possible. The intense heat produced by the friction of their passage through the air must run off or be shucked off, as it were, with the molten nose-cone material.

As they pass through the atmosphere the larger meteors produce loud booms, the result of shock waves formed by their supersonic speed of entry. Few meteors are large enough to survive the atmosphere. Those that reach the earth's surface have been so slowed down that they have lost most of their surface heat, have formed what is called a fusion crust on their surfaces, and are barely warm, or may even be cold. They cannot possibly start fires, as one might assume. The Hoba iron meteorite of southwest Africa probably weighed 100 tons when it fell, and a number of others weighing from 10 to 30 tons are known. Meteorites of over 100 tons will probably never be found, since their impact would be so explosive that they would be entirely vaporized or fragmented. Meteor craters constitute the sole evidence that such massive bodies have fallen from the sky . . . .

The place of origin of meteorites, particularly the stones, and the paths and times taken to reach the earth, are up in the air, both literally and figuratively. The theories now current hold that the meteorites came from the breakup of an original planet-sized body, occupying the space between Mars and Jupiter, from a number of bodies the size of the moon, from comets, or perhaps from a variety of smaller asteroidal or planetesimal bodies.[1]

[1] From "Meteors and Meteorites" (pp. 75–83) in *Pictorial Guide to the Planets,* Revised and Expanded Edition by Joseph H. Jackson (Thomas Y. Crowell Company). Copyright © 1965, 1973 by Joseph H. Jackson. Reprinted by permission of Harper & Row, Publishers, Inc.

An Acceptable Summary

Meteors are pieces of stone and iron from space that enter the earth's atmosphere. Those that land on the earth are called meteorites. Although a great many meteors do strike the earth, they are only a small proportion of those that enter the atmosphere. As far as is known, no one has ever been killed by a meteor, and there is only one known instance of anyone's being struck by one.

About 24 million visible meteors go through the atmosphere every 24 hours. From telescope observations, however, astronomers estimate that 8 billion actually enter the atmosphere daily.

Stone meteorites are the most common kind; iron are about half as common as stone; meteorites that are a combination of stone and iron are very rare.

Entering the atmosphere at a speed of many miles a second, meteors are slowed down and, at a height of 75 to 50 miles, become white hot from the heat generated by friction with the atmosphere. Pieces of their molten surface fly off, carrying away heat and forming a tail. Those meteorites large enough to get through the atmosphere are so cooled by the time they reach the earth that there is no danger of their starting fires. The largest known meteorite probably weighed 100 tons; others are known that weighed from 10 to 30 tons. A meteorite larger than 100 tons would be so vaporized or fragmented on landing that nothing would be left of it.

No one really knows the origin of meteors. Astronomers think they come from the breakup of a planet or some smaller bodies in space.

A Poor Summary

This article says that an amazing number of meteors hit the earth — at which time they become meteorites—in a 24-hour period, yet no one has ever been killed by one as far as is known. An Alabama woman, Mrs. E. H. Hodges of Syla-cauga, was struck on the thigh by a 9-pound meteor that came through the roof of her house after lunch one day.

Called meteoroids in space, meteors as they penetrate the atmosphere, and meteorites if they strike, very few of these stony, stony-iron, or iron bodies are ever recovered. Because of their appearance, they are called shooting stars.

A meteorite exploded over Alberta, Canada, in 1960 about 20 miles above the ground. The flash was visible from 200 miles away. Some 188 sizable chunks of meteorite were collected, weighing 670 pounds.

While about 24 million visible meteors pass through the atmosphere in 24 hours, astronomers with telescopes estimate that 8 billion must plunge into the earth's atmosphere a day.

Meteors glow in the sky because they are white hot as a result of friction produced when they hit the earth's atmosphere. They travel eight miles a second. By the time a meteor reaches the earth, it is so cooled off it can't start a fire.

This paper violates much of what is essential to a good summary. It begins incorrectly with, "This article says . . . ." Half of the summary consists of sentences copied word-for-word. The writer was so much interested in the examples in the original article —Mrs. Hodges and the Alberta incident—that there was little space for the main ideas the article expresses. The summary omits mention of the size of meteors and ignores the probable origin of meteors.

EXERCISE 1. Read the following article, carefully

taking notes on the most important ideas. Then write a summary based upon your notes. After you have written it, check your work by answering the questions in the first paragraph under rule 15d.

A professor who's spent thirty years gathering tall tornado tales says tornadoes are "pretty much like people."

"They have their likes and dislikes, whims and ambitions, their impulses good and bad," says Dr. Howard C. Key, North Texas State University English professor.

From folklore he has gathered, Dr. Key made this analysis of tornadoes' personalities:

1. Tornadoes are partial to infants. Dr. Key has collected thirty-two stories about miraculous preservation of infants. One tornado in southeastern Kansas about fifty years ago gathered a six-week-old baby out of its cradle and deposited him unscathed but plastered with mud in a haystack a mile away.

2. They like flowers. Houses and furniture have been scattered over many acres, but a vase of roses will be left undisturbed on the living room table. Dr. Key has this story from Arkansas, Oklahoma, Texas, and Louisiana.

3. Twisters don't care for chickens. One storm picked thirty chickens absolutely clean and left them bolt upright, but dead, on their perches. Another popped a rooster into a jug, leaving only its head sticking out.

4. Tornadoes are musically inclined. Dr. Key gave this account of Colonel William Porter, who was carried away in an 1893 twister at Cisco.

"He found that instead of running toward the back room as he intended, he was waving his arms and legs somewhere in mid-air. Seconds later he slammed into some object that felt like a wire fence. Then he heard music and decided he was either dead or dying.

"It was their new player piano, the kind that had to be pumped with foot pedals. The suction of the storm had somehow started it going and it was appropriately playing 'Nearer My God to Thee.' Both Mr. Porter and the piano were lodged in a pecan tree 50 yards away. Neither was much damaged."

5. Tornadoes can be accommodating. One lady in a farm town had written her sister in Ponca City, Oklahoma, 35 miles away. The letter was lying stamped and addressed on the dining room table and disappeared when the storm struck. The letter fell uncanceled in Ponca City in the yard of a neighbor only a block away from its intended address.

6. Tornadoes like to show off. An east-bound Northern Pacific locomotive was uncoupled from its freight cars by a twister, which set it down full steam ahead on a parallel track headed west. Tornadoes in East Texas and Arkansas have turned cast-iron washpots inside out. One in Central Kansas forty years ago whipped together the branches of a 60-foot cottonwood tree and dropped a cast-iron wagon wheel over it the way you would put a ring on your finger.

"The worst mistake tornadoes have ever made was to venture into New England in 1954," Dr. Key said. "Up until that time tornadoes had been running wild all over the rest of the United States and people had been accepting them—like measles.

"But not New Englanders. They immediately set up a public howl and demanded that Congress do something. So now, through special appropriations to the U.S. Weather Bureau, the awful eye of science has been turned upon these murderous intruders. And justice is about to be done."

Dr. Key is apparently optimistic about the results. He doesn't own a storm cellar.[1]

A REPORT BASED ON SEVERAL SOURCES

The second type of reading-based writing is the *report,* which might also be called the *library paper,* since it requires the use of library sources. The report, or library paper, is likely to be 500 words or more in length, factual in nature, and based on information derived from three or more sources.

Writing a report can be a challenging assignment. As with the summary, however, the task will be easier if you follow certain definite steps.

Choosing Your Subject and Sources

15e. Choose and limit the subject.

Frequently, you will be assigned a specific topic to investigate and write on. If you are given a choice of topic, however, much depends on how you choose. The wrong topic can result in additional work for you and an inferior report. Two considerations are important in choosing a topic:

(1) Choose a subject for which sufficient material is readily available.

Don't make trouble for yourself by selecting a subject not discussed in the books and periodicals in your school library. Subjects on which you are likely to find little or no information in your library include the following:

[1] From "Tornado Record Shows Humanlike Ambitions" by Dr. Howard C. Key, from an April 13, 1957 Associated Press article. Reprinted by permission of The Associated Press Newsfeatures.

a. Subjects too recent in development (a new kind of camera invented just last month)
b. Subjects too limited in scope (automobile production during the past few months)
c. Subjects too technical in content (the use of iambic meter in the poetry of Robert Frost)

After you have made a tentative choice of subject, check the card catalogue (books) and the *Readers' Guide* (magazines) in your library to make sure that there are enough references at hand.

(2) Choose a subject sufficiently limited in scope.

Good writing of any sort gains depth from full detail. Shallow writing, which just skims the surface, lacks conviction and interest. A 50-word report will be effective only if it deals with a topic sufficiently limited to permit you to discuss it in detail. (See page 340 in Chapter 13.)

Suppose, for example, you have become interested in exploration, after reading a book of short biographies of explorers. Would "Explorers" be a good subject for a short report? Probably not, for you would have space for only a very short account of many explorers. You decide to limit the subject. Note the successive stages of this limitation:

Explorers
Antarctic Explorers
Twentieth-Century Antarctic Explorers
Roald Amundsen

You could, of course, write a 500-word report on the life of Roald Amundsen, the heroic explorer who won the race with Robert Scott to the South Pole. Again, however, such a report would necessarily be rather sketchy. You decide to focus on one of the major expeditions: "Amundsen's Defeat of Scott in the Race to the Pole."

Perhaps it would be wise to limit this still further: "The Last Day of Amundsen's Race to the Pole." Your decision, again, would depend on the library resources available and on the amount of detail you wish to include in your report. Probably you would choose the broader subject. However, the title is a little long. You decide to revise it to "Amundsen's Discovery of the South Pole."

EXERCISE 2. For each of the following broad subjects, write a limited subject that can be handled in a 500-word paper. Since you will want a limited topic for use in succeeding exercises, pick the one that interests you most. If you prefer, choose another broad subject and limit it, after you finish limiting the ten subjects below. At the bottom of your paper, write: I have chosen as the topic of my report ——.

1. Microcomputers
2. Venezuela
3. Carson McCullers
4. The United Nations
5. Professional Soccer
6. Young People's Fashions
7. Home Vegetable Gardens
8. The Common Cold
9. Cancer
10. Space Exploration

15f. Locate source materials.

Suppose that you have decided upon the topic "Amundsen's Discovery of the South Pole." You are ready to begin your own exploration — for information. Since encyclopedias give a general description or history of a subject broader than the one you have chosen, you will need to use other sources, though you may use encyclopedias at first to familiarize yourself with general information about your topic. You should try to locate magazine articles, reference books, and nonfiction works that will give you the kind of factual detail you need. If in your preliminary check you do not find at least three good references, it would be wise (with your teacher's permission) to change your topic. Even in a short paper you should not rely on a single source, no matter how good it may be. Using three or more sources will enable you to include more detail, obtain a balanced view of your subject, and do a better job in your final paper.

You should list these sources, called your *bibliography,* on a separate sheet of paper so that you have them available for future reference. Or you may enter each source on a separate note card (3 × 5 inches or 4 × 6 inches). Give the author's name (last name first) if this is given, the title of the article (in quotation marks), the name of the book or magazine (underlined), the date for a magazine or newspaper, and page numbers. For a book, record also the place of publication (New York, Chicago, etc.), the name of the publisher, the year of publication, and page numbers.

EXAMPLES   Huntford, Roland, *Scott and Amundsen,* New York, G. P. Putnam's Sons, 1980, pages 375–508.

Vaeth, J. Gordon, *To the Ends of the Earth: The Explorations of Roald Amundsen,* New York, Harper & Row, 1962, pages 114–34.

EXERCISE 3. For the limited topic which you chose in Exercise 2, locate at least three books or magazine articles that would be of use. List these on a page headed "Bibliography," or record them on separate note cards, one source to a card. Give all the required information.

Reading and Taking Notes for the Report

With a limited topic and a preliminary outline, you are ready to begin reading and taking notes. In general, you follow the same procedure described for making the summary notes. Since, however, you are using several articles and are going to rewrite your notes into one long paper, you should use note cards.

15g. Develop a preliminary outline.

In Chapter 13 (pages 348–51), you learned how to make an outline. You can do a better job of reading and taking notes for your report if you first develop a rough outline for it. At this stage, the outline does not have to be too detailed; its chief purpose is to guide you in your reading. Of course, you will revise your outline when you are ready to write the report so that the outline will reflect the research you have done.

In making your preliminary outline, you may find it helpful to read one of your sources first, especially if you know little about your topic. The outline below shows the form the preliminary outline should take:

AMUNDSEN'S DISCOVERY OF THE SOUTH POLE
  I. Significance and importance of the discovery
 II. The decision and the preparations
     A. The decision to try for the South Pole
     B. Setting up the base at Framheim
     C. Winter preparations
     D. The false start

III. The journey to the Pole
   A. The first stage
   B. The second stage
   C. The third stage
   D. The last miles
IV. The journey back

EXERCISE 4. Submit a preliminary outline on the topic you chose in Exercise 2 and used for your bibliography in Exercise 3. Check Chapter 13 (pages 349–51) for proper outline form.

15h. Use a separate card for each topic and for each source.

To make it easy to gather together information on the same topic from several different articles, all notes on a card should relate to a single topic and be from the same source. Thus, notes for a single magazine article covering several of your outline topics might use up several cards.

The numbers at the side indicate the various entries which will appear on your note cards:

1. Outline topic
2. Source (author's name and page number)
3. Outline subtopic
4. Direct quotation

In the upper left-hand corner of each card, you should write the topic from your preliminary outline with which the note card deals. Since you have made a bibliography sheet or bibliography cards, you may identify the sources on your note cards with just the author's name and the page number. A good place for this information is in the upper right-hand corner of the card.

Suppose that in preparing the report on Amundsen, you have found the following selection. It deals

1 —

| *Preparation* | *Kearns, pp. 83-84* | — 2 |

Food: canned pemmican, choc., dried milk powder, trail bisc. (oatmeal, sugar, dr. milk). Planned to eat dogs as they became surplus.

3 —

| *First Stage* | *Kearns, p. 84* | — 2 |

Oct. 20. 4 sleds, 52 dogs. Hanssen, Wisting, Bjaaland, Hassel, Amundsen.

"...according to Amundsen, a beautiful day of clear mild weather..." — 4

Made better than 24 m. per day, one day just under 30 m.

with some of the topics in your preliminary outline; therefore, you want to take notes on it. Read the article and study the sample note cards on the top of this page.

RACE FOR THE SOUTH POLE

For food the Norwegians had canned pemmican, chocolate, dried milk powders in meal-sized packages, plus trail biscuits made of oatmeal, sugar, and dried milk. This was all, but Amundsen also counted on eating dog meat. He calculated that there was about fifty pounds of edible meat in a husky, and included that in his planning for both dogs and men.

This was another reason Amundsen had selected dogs to pull his sled. He calculated the day-to-day weight requirements on the sledges from Framheim to the Pole and back. The daily loss of weight in food and equipment, either eaten or stored, would finally result in the surplus pulling power of one dog at a time. At that point, the extra dog would be converted from pulling power into food.

On September 8, 1911, Amundsen was ready to head for the Pole. His entire party was to make the trip — seven sledges, eight men, and ninety dogs. But two days out from Framheim, Amundsen gave the order to turn back. Severe cold, with temperatures as low as 108 degrees below zero, hit the dogs and the strain was too great. He would have to wait.

When seals and skua birds appeared near Framheim, Amundsen set out again. This time he took five men, four sledges, and fifty-two dogs, plus provisions for four months. The party was made up of Hanssen, Wisting, Bjaaland, Hassel, and Amundsen. The date was October 20 — and according to Amundsen, a beautiful day of clear, mild weather, with temperature just above freezing. Across the barrier, the men moved on skis and the dogs pulled heavily loaded sledges. Amundsen planned to hold the teams to a maximum of about twenty-four miles a day. But the fresh dogs made better than that on good territory. One exceptional day's run was just under thirty miles.[1]

---

[1] From *The Silent Continent* by William H. Kearns, Jr. and Beverly Britton. Copyright 1955 by Beverly L. Britton and Wm. H. Kearns, Jr. Reprinted by permission of Harold Ober Associates Incorporated.

Writing the Report

15i. Revise the preliminary outline.

As explained previously, it usually is wise to revise your preliminary outline after you have finished reading and taking notes. You now have a better grasp of your subject; you can be more careful about form. For example, you may have decided that you have so much material on Amundsen's actual journey that you should not deal with his decision to try for the Pole or with his setting up the base at Framheim. The final outline might look like this:

AMUNDSEN'S DISCOVERY OF THE SOUTH POLE
  I. Significance and importance of the discovery
 II. The preparations
     A. Supplies for the journey
        1. Transportation and housing
        2. Clothing and other small articles
        3. Food
           a. Prepared food
           b. Decision to eat dogs
     B. The false start
        1. Concern about Scott
        2. Severe weather
III. The journey to the Pole
     A. The first stage: the shelf ice
     B. The second stage: Axel Heiberg
     C. The third stage: the polar plateau
     D. The last miles: the South Pole
        1. Good weather
        2. Planting of the flag
        3. Defeat of Scott in race
 IV. The journey back

15j. Write the rough draft.

With your final outline at hand, go through your note

cards, discarding those that are no longer needed and rearranging the remaining ones so that they conform to your final outline. In other words, all cards dealing with the same outline topic, regardless of the article from which they come, should be placed together.

Referring to your cards only for facts and information, begin to write your rough draft. You will use all those skills you learned in Chapter 13. In addition, here are two special reminders:

(1) Use your own words.

Again, be sure not to use exact words from your sources without giving credit. If you do so, you are committing *plagiarism*. This not only is dishonest but also diminishes the value of your paper as an original work. If you take notes in your own words, you will not be likely to plagiarize.

(2) Acknowledge sources when you do quote.

If you decide to use a word-for-word quotation from one of your sources, enclose it in quotation marks as you did in the summary. Also, you must identify the source by giving at least the author, title, and page number of the quotation.

There are three places where this information can be given: (1) in parentheses right after the quotation, (2) in a footnote at the bottom of the page, or (3) in a list with all the other sources on a page at the end of your paper. Your teacher will tell you how much identifying information is required and where it should be given.

15k. Write the final draft.

Read your rough draft carefully with the following points in mind:

CHECKLIST

1. Is there an effective introductory paragraph which states the main idea of the paper?
2. Are transitions used to show how paragraphs are related?
3. Is there a good concluding paragraph which effectively draws the paper to a close?
4. Is the paper written in your own words, with proper acknowledgment given when you have quoted directly?
5. Does your paper follow the order of your final outline and avoid digressions?
6. Have you used three or more sources of information?
7. Is the paper free from errors in spelling, punctuation, sentence structure, and usage?
8. Have you used the proper heading and form required by your teacher?

With these points all checked, type or write in ink your final draft. Include a footnote page if your teacher specifies this. Also list on a separate page entitled "Bibliography" the sources you have used, arranged alphabetically by the author's last name. Give all the information which was suggested for a bibliography list and note cards.

Here is an example of a final report. Notice how the writer smoothly transforms the information into a coherent paper by the various means you have learned in this chapter as well as in Chapter 13.

AMUNDSEN'S RACE TO
THE SOUTH POLE

Some people blunder into success, achieving victory only through sheer luck. Even some great explorers of the past have made discoveries in this way. The discovery

— begins with a contrary, provocative statement

leads into topic of explorers

of the South Pole by the Norwegian explorer Roald Amundsen, however, was a masterpiece of <u>planning</u>, ingenuity and dogged persistence.

The crucial <u>planning</u> actually began in February and March of 1911 at Framheim, Amundsen's base at the Bay of Whales in the Ross Sea. Sledges were rebuilt and shaved to reduce their weight; trail tents were painted a dark color to absorb the sun's rays. No detail was left to chance: boots and underwear were redesigned; tent pegs, skis, and ski bindings were carefully checked; special dog whips were fashioned. Prepared food included canned pemmican, chocolate, dried milk powders, and trail biscuits made of oatmeal, sugar, and dried milk. Crucial weight was saved by Amundsen's ingenious plan to eat the huskies as they became surplus on the trip. Though <u>impatient</u> to get started, Amundsen did not slight the most minute detail.

Events proved, <u>however</u>, that he was too <u>impatient</u>. Worried about the progress made by the British Captain Robert F. Scott, who was also planning to set out for the Pole,

repetition to link paragraphs; beginning of time sequence

(Note that paper reflects revised outline.)

(Compare these sentences with note cards)

transitions

Amundsen began his push on September 8, 1911, in the dead of winter. Two days later, he realized that he had made a mistake. Temperatures as low as 76 degrees below zero drove him back to Framheim.

The next try was successful. Four sledges, five men, and fifty-two dogs set out on October 20, a day that Kearns and Britton tell us was described by Amundsen as "a beautiful day of clear, mild weather."[1] Before them — according to Shackleton, the explorer who had made a previous, unsuccessful attempt to reach the Pole — was a <u>trek</u> consisting of three <u>stages</u>, plus the final push to the Pole.

— source briefly identified in body; actual words quoted

The first <u>stage</u> of the <u>trek</u>, the trip across the shelf ice, was uneventful. On very good days, the dogs made almost thirty miles across the ice. The <u>second stage</u> involved a climb of ten thousand feet up a glacier called Axel Heiberg; at one point in this climb, the expedition was pinned down by blizzards for four days. The men were all anxious to reach the polar plateau, which

transitions

chronological sequence

---

[1] William H. Kearns, Jr., and Beverly Britton, *The Silent Continent*, p. 84.

— footnote identifies source more fully

Shackleton had called the third stage of the journey.

This third stage was marked by two climactic events. Halfway up the plateau, twenty-four of the dogs had to be killed, at a spot Amundsen called "The Butcher's Shop." Although the men were reluctant to kill the dogs, they knew they had no choice if they were to survive. Then, on December 6, they reached the farthest point south that Shackleton had reached before them. After this, everything was virgin territory!

The final push into this unexplored land covered only sixty miles. Amundsen reported that the weather was surprisingly good; as Huntford wrote, "It was as if the gods had decided that it was no use trying to fight these persistent men and their loyal dogs any longer . . . ."[1] On December 13, the men realized they were within a day's journey to the South Pole; there was little sleep that night. Finally, at three o'clock in the afternoon of December 14, 1911, all five members of the expedition together planted the Norwegian flag

chronological sequence

chronological sequence

source for quotation identified briefly in body

[1] Roland Huntford, *Scott and Amundsen*, p. 484.

source identified more fully in footnote

at the South Pole. They had beaten
Captain Scott—by more than a
month, as was proved later.

The return journey was begun
on December 17. Since favorable
weather continued and their luck
held, Amundsen and his men were
able to complete the return journey
without mishap in thirty-nine days,
arriving at Framheim on January 25.
Thus, there was a small element of
luck in that the expedition was
blessed with good weather. The
real triumph, however, came about
only because of the wisdom and
courage of Roald Amundsen and his
four teammates.

— final sentence
ties in with first
paragraph of
report

Bibliography

"Amundsen, Roald," *The World Book Encyclopedia,*
1979, Volume 1, page 418.

Fox, Lorene K., *Antarctic Icebreakers,* New York,
Doubleday, 1937, pages 126–36.

Huntford, Roland, *Scott and Amundsen,* New York,
G. P. Putnam's Sons, 1980, pages 375–508.

Kearns, William H., Jr., and Beverly Britton, *The
Silent Continent,* New York, Harper & Row, 1955,
pages 74–93.

Pennington, Piers, *The Great Explorers,* New York,
Facts on File, 1979, pages 308–11.

Vaeth, J. Gordon, *To the Ends of the Earth: The
Explorations of Roald Amundsen,* New York,
Harper & Row, 1962, pages 114–34.

EXERCISE 5. You should now be ready to write a good library paper based on three or more sources. Either take the topic for which you have submitted outlines and bibliography, or start from scratch, using one of the topics listed below.

1. Origin of blues music
2. Life on other planets
3. Types of clouds
4. Care of houseplants
5. Solar energy
6. Hurricanes
7. Recent medical discoveries
8. Soap sculpture
9. Optical illusions
10. Tarantulas
11. Ventriloquism
12. Psychic phenomena
13. Artificial respiration
14. The Alaska pipeline
15. Strip mining
16. The Equal Rights Amendment
17. The World Series
18. Trout fishing
19. Science fiction
20. Acupuncture
21. Uses of lasers
22. Language of dolphins
23. Emotional maturity
24. Heart transplants
25. Noise pollution
26. Food additives
27. Hypnotism
28. Indira Gandhi
29. Digital recording
30. Space stations
31. Ice hockey
32. Oil spills
33. Insecticides
34. History of English dictionaries
35. Soapbox derbies
36. Suez Canal
37. Waterspouts
38. Sleepwalking
39. Microcomputers in the home
40. Silk-screen printing

Chapter 16

Writing Stories

Essential Elements in Narratives

As soon as people developed language, they began to tell *narratives,* or stories. They told what happened to themselves or to others, what they dreamed had happened, or what they wished would happen. They told their stories, and people listened. Good storytellers always have an audience.

When spoken language developed into written language, the stories that had been told from generation to generation were written down. These stories compose the vast literature of folklore, mythology, and legend. As civilization developed and life became less simple, more and more happened; people's imaginations broadened. Thus more and more stories were told and written. Those that were factual accounts of happenings to large groups of people became history. Those that were personal happenings to individuals and were told with some truth and more imagination, as well as those that were completely imaginative, became literature.

Essentially, all narrative writing is concerned with *what happened.* In telling what happened, storytellers concern themselves — though perhaps they do not always think of it in this way — with setting, characterization, action, climax, and outcome. These are the essential elements in narrative writing, and you will become a better storyteller and story writer if you learn something about how to handle them.

The Setting

Every story happens *somewhere at some time.* The place and time of a story form the *setting* of the story. In newspaper writing and historical writing, the *when* and *where* are clearly stated, but this is not necessarily so in story writing. American writers of today, writing about their own time, often take their settings for granted; so do their readers. However, if authors are writing about the past — for example, about the 1930's — they will be more explicit.

If a story of today is good enough and is still read twenty-five years from now, readers will be able to figure out from certain details that the story takes place in the 1980's. Thus we know when we read the works of O. Henry that the setting of most of his stories is New York in the early 1900's — O. Henry's "own time."

The Characters

Every story usually has at least one leading character. This hero or heroine of the story is called the *protagonist.* Often there will be another character, called the *antagonist,* who opposes the plans or wishes of the hero or heroine. There may also be other characters, of major or minor importance.

In our story, let us assume that the protagonist is a high school girl. (The other characters will appear later.)

The Situation or Conflict

A writer can set a group of characters somewhere at

some time and still not have a story. Something has to happen; the story has to have a *plot*. Nothing usually happens in the course of the plot, however, unless the leading character has a *problem*. This character must be in *conflict* with someone or something and must be in a *situation* which needs resolving. The situation of our story might be this: the girl is doing poorly in her work; she wants to drop out of school.

The Action

Now *action* begins to take place; things begin to happen. The situation sets events in motion. This is where "the plot thickens." For example, the girl's parents object to her dropping out of school. (Now, along with this action, we have two antagonists, the parents.) The girl decides to run away. She draws her savings from the bank and takes a bus to New York.

The Climax

The action arising out of the situation continues until it reaches the point of highest interest. This high point is called the *climax*. For example, in our story, perhaps the girl gets to New York, wanders around the streets, becomes lost, is stopped by a police officer, and is taken into custody. The officer notifies the girl's parents. The parents drive to New York and enter the station house. The girl sees her parents again, hesitates, then rushes toward them. The parents smile and hold out their arms to their daughter.

The Outcome

After the climax has been reached, the situation or conflict is resolved. This *resolution* is the outcome of the story. It winds up the plot (which, as you now . know, consists of the situation, action, climax, and outcome). For example, the girl returns home with her parents. On the drive back, they have a long talk. The girl decides to go on with school; the parents agree to be more understanding and to spend more time with their daughter.

Setting, characters, plot (situation, action, climax, outcome): you will find these essential elements in anything that tells what happened—in short stories, novels, plays, television shows, movies. The story may be simple or complicated, light or serious, sad or comic, dramatic or undramatic; but the elements of narrative are always present.

PLANNING A SHORT STORY

A short story is usually limited to *one* event. It happens once, at one time, in one place, to one set of persons. One thing happens (though several incidents may be involved in the one particular event).

Because of these limitations, a short story must be carefully planned in order to be effective. By now you must have realized this. You can see that writers don't just sit down and write a story; they first plan it. You, who are not a professional writer, must certainly plan your stories.

At this point, you may feel like saying, "That's right; I'm not a professional writer! What have I got to write about?" The answer is—*yourself.* Things have been happening to you since the day you were born. Some of them you remember dimly, some not at all; but you've heard your parents talk about them. Some were important, some may have been trivial; but *many of them were and still are interesting.* Everybody has similar experiences, but everybody also goes through the same experiences in different ways.

Where do writers get their story material? They make it up, of course; but *from what* do they make it up? The answer is from their own experiences, the world they know. They can do that much better than make up a world they don't know.

Of course, writers do not have to stick to the facts as they are. They change names, places, characters; they may use only one little part of what happened; they may leave things out or add things. This is where their imagination comes in — not in creating something out of nothing, but in creating something imagined out of something else. Science-fiction writers are one extreme example of this. They use their imagination primarily, but they do start with basic facts, with some part of the world they know. For example, their characters talk or communicate with each other. They are living beings. They may look different or act differently, but basically they are like people the author knows, and their feelings may be similar to those of the author. They may have six arms, purple hair, and three heads, but, again, they are living beings — like their author.

Your own experience means more than just what has happened to you alone. It includes what you have seen and heard and felt and thought and believed. It includes what has happened to your family, friends, and neighbors. Your experience is you and your world — at home, in school, away from both. That is what you have to write about.

16a. Plan a story before you write it, basing your plan on the elements of narrative writing.

The easiest kind of story for you to write is one based on a personal experience, something that happened to you. You have been writing compositions of this kind for a long time. Your letters to friends contain narratives—accounts of experiences.

Now, however, for purposes of planning, you should think of an incident in your life. Forget, however, that it happened to you. Think of the incident in terms of material for a story.

You may write your story in first person—from your own point of view, using first-person pronouns (*I, me*) to refer to yourself—or in third person—as if you were someone else, using *he, she*—whichever you find easier. Writing in the third person has distinct advantages. You can be the hero or heroine, just by giving yourself a name. You can have curly hair or brown eyes, be taller or shorter, fatter or slimmer, better-looking or plainer. You can make yourself be popular, brilliant, lucky. You can make your dreams and daydreams come true. And when you finish, the incident you have related will no longer be a simple event in your life—it will be a story.

When you begin to think about your story material, you should make a story plan. Jot down the following:

1. *Setting*—when and where the events take place. You may note the time and place specifically. This does not mean, however, that when you write the story, you must begin by describing the setting.
2. *Characters*—the persons involved. Name the characters, and next to each name, write something of importance about the character's role in the story.
3. *Situation*—the problem. Write down the problem facing your main character, the situation the character faces when the story opens.
4. *Action*—what happens. Write a brief summary.

5. *Climax*—the culminating point. Indicate the point to which the action leads.
6. *Outcome,* or *resolution*—the ending. Indicate what this will be.

EXERCISE 1. Select a personal experience or incident which you wish to use as the basis for a story. Describe the incident in a brief essay. Do not attempt to write a story at this time; just give a straight description of what happened.

EXERCISE 2. For the incident you have chosen in Exercise 1, write a story plan. Include the steps given above, and also indicate under *Characters* whether you plan to tell the story yourself. (See point of view, rule 16b, below.)

WRITING THE STORY

Planning a story is relatively simple compared with writing it. There are certain ways of handling the elements of narrative that will help you bring your story to life and keep your reader interested. These include establishing and maintaining a point of view, arousing interest from the beginning, using dialogue to carry the action forward and to reveal character, using description to present characters and setting, and bringing the story to a satisfactory close.

16b. Decide upon the point of view from which you will tell your story.

A story can be told from two points of view: *first person* and *third person*. A story that begins "*I* think the most remarkable day of *my* life occurred the summer *I* was ten, when *I* was visiting *my* grandparents" is an example of first-person narration. The first-person point of view is sometimes called the "I" point of view because the first personal pronoun *I* is used so frequently. It is the point of view of a person called the narrator, who has been involved in the story and is telling it from a personal point of view. The narrator is usually a central character in the story, but may be merely an observer who has witnessed the important events and has decided to tell about them. In either case only things that have happened to the narrator directly or things that the narrator actually saw happening to others can be described.

A story that begins "The most remarkable day in *Brie Toven's* life occurred the summer *she* was ten, when *she* was visiting *her* grandparents" and then goes on to describe Brie's actions and thoughts as though the writer had some way of knowing everything important about them is an example of the third-person point of view, often called the "omniscient author."

One of the first decisions writers must make is which point of view they are going to use. You may find the first person easier, especially if the story is actually something that happened to you. On the other hand, third person gives you more freedom because it allows you to tell everything the characters do and think, things you could not know as a first-person writer.

EXERCISE 3. Describe the incident you chose in Exercise 1 as someone else who participated in it or heard about it might write it. In other words, tell the incident from a different point of view.

16c. Try to arouse the reader's interest from the very beginning of the story.

Some people won't read beyond the beginning of a

story if they don't find it interesting. In writing a story, you should try to capture the reader's interest immediately. This may mean starting somewhere in the middle of the plot and then working back, or opening with a startling statement, or beginning with dialogue even before the characters have been introduced.

Here are some examples of story openings that arouse interest. Notice how the authors use elements of surprise, curiosity, or suspense to persuade the reader to read on.

1

"But, my dear," said Mrs. Culverin, with a tiny gasp, "you can't actually mean—*a tail!*"

Mrs. Dingle nodded impressively. "Exactly. I've seen him. Twice. Paris, of course, and then, a command appearance at Rome—we were in the royal box. He conducted—my dear, you've never heard such effects from an orchestra—and, my dear," she hesitated slightly, "he conducted *with it.*"[1]

2

Wed. Apr. 12

I am sixteen of age and am a caddy at the Pleasant View Golf Club but only temporary as I expect to soon land a job some wheres as asst pro as my game is good enough now to be a pro but to young looking. My pal Joe Bean also says I have not got enough swell head to make a good pro but suppose that will come in time, Joe is a wise cracker.[2]

---

[1] From *Selected Works of Stephen Vincent Benét.* Holt, Rinehart and Winston, Inc. Copyright, 1937, by Stephen Vincent Benét. Reprinted by permission of Brandt & Brandt.

[2] From "A Caddy's Diary," by Ring Lardner, from *The Best Short Stories of Ring Lardner.* Reprinted by permission of Charles Scribner's Sons, Chatto and Windus Ltd., and the Author's Literary Estate.

3

When the front door had shut them out and the butler Baines had turned back into the dark heavy hall, Philip began to live. He stood in front of the nursery door, listening until he heard the engine of the taxi die out along the street. His parents were gone for a fortnight's holiday; he was "between nurses," one dismissed and the other not arrived; he was alone in the great Belgravia house with Baines and Mrs. Baines.[1]

Narratives may start with a description of a person, a place, a situation, or an event. Writers try to give the setting, or to introduce one or more of the characters, or to create a mood or atmosphere. But while achieving this, they must above all create enough interest so that the reader will keep on reading.

Planning your story will help you with the opening, because you know what is going to happen. If you have difficulty getting started, just start. Once you get going, you may have an idea for a better beginning. When you reread the story and revise it, you may get still another idea.

16d. Use dialogue to tell part of the story and to reveal character.

When people talk, they reveal a great deal about themselves: their education, their intelligence, their personality, their social group, where they come from, their experiences. To seem real, the characters that you write about in a narrative must talk also.

It is sometimes said of particular writers that they

---

[1] From "The Basement Room" by Graham Greene. Copyright 1947, copyright renewed 1975 by Graham Greene, from *21 Stories* by Graham Greene. Published in England by The Bodley Head and William Heinemann in a collection titled *Collected Stories*. Reprinted by permission of Viking Penguin, Inc., and Laurence Pollinger Limited.

have an "ear" for dialogue. That is, the speech of their characters is very true to life. If you are writing about high school students, for example, your characters will use colloquial language and slang, and perhaps even make grammatical errors. The conversation of a teacher or other educated adult, on the other hand, will be somewhat different. If your characters live in or come from a foreign country, they may from time to time use expressions, usually short phrases or interjections, in their native language.

Before you attempt to write natural dialogue, spend some time listening to people in real life as they carry on conversations. Notice how they say things and what they do while they are talking. Observe their expressions and habits of speech. As you start writing conversations, keep in mind the following requirements of natural dialogue that will make your characters "come alive" and reveal themselves.

(1) *The words should fit the character.* Let all characters sound like themselves. Should you quote your six-year-old brother, do not give him the vocabulary and the attitudes of a high school sophomore. If you are quoting police officers reporting on an investigation, let them use appropriate vocabulary and grammar.

(2) *Long speeches are unnatural.* Orations are for political conventions or for conversational bores. In real life, most persons make brief comments; they say what they have to say in a few sentences or pieces of sentences. Even then, they are often interrupted by an impatient listener. To write natural conversations, be as brief as you can.

If you attempt to report all of the conversation of a character, your story will lose its focus and become boring. Always remember to edit the conversation so that it will (1) advance the action of your story and (2) reveal the personality of the speaker. For instance, if you are writing about an athlete trying to become a good blocker, do not waste space by having him talk about his girlfriends or his desire to get a summer job. Instead, let him talk enthusiastically about football plays involving skillful blocking, the excitement of a big game, and so forth.

In their conversation, your characters can help you get your story going and keep it moving. The characters can reveal what happened before the story began. Sometimes they even foreshadow what will happen. More important, the characters can tell things about themselves or other characters. By what they say and how they say it, we get to know what kind of people they are.

EXERCISE 4. Listed below are groups of characters in specific situations. After choosing one out of the seven, write a conversation (about 150 words) that reveals the personality of each speaker. For this exercise, use dialogue only.

1. Two girls have been shopping. One describes a camera she has bought on sale; the other girl discovers that she has one just like it.
2. Two football fans talk about an exciting game.
3. A police officer has difficulty trying to tell a driver how to make turns in heavy traffic.
4. Two strangers discuss the weather. One is a Missourian and the other a Texan.
5. A boy argues with his girlfriend on the telephone.
6. Two teen-age girls talk about their opinions of certain careers.
7. A gas station owner fires an employee for being late to work.

16e. Use description to present characters and setting.

A story with no description at all would be flat and colorless. Although lengthy descriptive passages like those in nineteenth-century stories and novels are rarely found in contemporary writing, every good writer uses bits of description throughout a story. Vivid description helps the reader visualize the people and places in the story.

When you write narratives, use words which appeal to the senses; make comparisons; select descriptive words carefully; include sharp, interest-arousing details. Notice how the writer Joseph Conrad does all these things in the following passage from his story "Youth," as he describes the skipper of a sailing ship.

> He was sixty if a day; a little man, with a broad, not very straight back, with bowed shoulders and one leg more bandy than the other, he had that queer twisted-about appearance you see so often in men who work in the fields. He had a nutcracker face—chin and nose trying to come together over a sunken mouth—and it was framed in iron-gray fluffy hair, that looked like a chin-strap of cotton-wool sprinkled with coal-dust. And he had blue eyes in that old face of his, which were amazingly like a boy's, with that candid expression some quite common men preserve to the end of their days by a rare internal gift of simplicity of heart and rectitude of soul.[1]

Descriptions of setting should create an atmosphere or mood for the development of the action. You know that you feel different on a bright, sunny day from the way you feel on a cold, windy, rainy day. Weather

[1] From *Youth* by Joseph Conrad.

is often used in a story to prepare the reader for something to match the mood created by the weather.

In today's writing, description of the setting does not always begin the story. Often it is included as an integral part of the action. But wherever it occurs, enough must be told to provide a convincing background.

EXERCISE 5. Write a short, but complete, description of one of the characters in your story plan.

EXERCISE 6. Write a description of the setting of the story you have planned. It is best, remember, to have a setting with which you are familiar.

EXERCISE 7. The following story has many of the elements — characters, conflict, climax, and outcome — that have been discussed in this chapter. There is enough action to maintain interest, and dialogue is held to a minimum. The ending gives a bizarre twist to the story. Read the story and discuss with your classmates how the storyteller uses the elements of narrative to hold the reader's interest.

CEMETERY PATH

Ivan was a timid little man — so timid that the villagers called him "Pigeon" or mocked him with the title "Ivan the Terrible." Every night Ivan stopped in at the saloon which was on the edge of the village cemetery. Ivan never crossed the cemetery to get to his lonely shack on the other side. The path through the cemetery would save him many minutes, but he had never taken it — not even in the full light of the moon.

Late one winter's night, when bitter wind and snow beat against the saloon, the customers took up the familiar mockery.

Ivan's sickly protest only fed their taunts, and they jeered cruelly when the young Cossack[1] lieutenant flung his horrid challenge at him.

"You are a pigeon, Ivan. You'll walk all around the cemetery in this cold—but you dare not cross the cemetery."

Ivan murmured, "The cemetery is nothing to cross, Lieutenant. It is nothing but earth, like all the other earth."

The lieutenant cried, "A challenge, then! Cross the cemetery tonight, Ivan, and I'll give you five rubles[2]—five gold rubles!"

Perhaps it was the vodka. Perhaps it was the temptation of the five gold rubles. No one ever knew why Ivan, moistening his lips, said suddenly: "Yes, Lieutenant, I'll cross the cemetery!"

The saloon echoed with their disbelief. The lieutenant winked to the men and unbuckled his sword. "Here, Ivan. When you get to the center of the cemetery, in front of the biggest tomb, stick the sword into the ground. In the morning we shall go there. And if the sword is in the ground—five gold rubles to you!"

Ivan took the sword. The men drank a toast: "To Ivan the Terrible!" They roared with laughter.

The wind howled around Ivan as he closed the door of the saloon behind him. The cold was knife-sharp. He buttoned his long coat and crossed the dirt road. He could hear the lieutenant's voice, louder than the rest, yelling after him, "Five rubles, pigeon! If you live!"

Ivan pushed the cemetery gate open. He walked fast. "Earth, just earth . . . like any other earth." But the darkness was a massive dread. "Five gold rubles . . ." The wind was cruel, and the sword was like ice in his hands. Ivan shivered under the long, thick coat and broke into a limping run.

[1] Cossack: Russian cavalryman.
[2] ruble: the basic unit of money in Russia.

He recognized the large tomb. He must have sobbed—that was drowned in the wind. And he kneeled, cold and terrified, and drove the sword into the hard ground. With his fist, he beat it down to the hilt. It was done. The cemetery . . . the challenge . . . five gold rubles.

Ivan started to rise from his knees. But he could not move. Something held him. Something gripped him in an unyielding hold. Ivan tugged and lurched and pulled—gasping in his panic, shaken by a monstrous fear. But something held Ivan. He cried out in terror, then made senseless gurgling noises.

They found Ivan, next morning, on the ground in front of the tomb that was in the center of the cemetery. His face was not that of a frozen man's, but of a man killed by some nameless horror. And the lieutenant's sword was in the ground where Ivan had pounded it—through the dragging folds of his long coat.[1]

EXERCISE 8. Having planned your story and worked on certain parts of it, you are now ready to write it. You have already made a story plan. You have chosen the incident, have possibly written some dialogue for it, and have prepared descriptions of a character and the setting. Using all these (adapting them if necessary), and applying the rules for good writing that you have studied in this chapter, write your story.

---

[1] "Cemetery Path" by Leonard Q. Ross. Copyright © 1941 by Saturday Review. All rights reserved. Reprinted by permission of Saturday Review.

Chapter 17

Making Writing Interesting

Words and Their Use

Writers, who are constantly working and playing with words, develop a deep respect for them. They know that whether their writing is interesting or uninteresting, clear or unclear, depends largely on the words they choose.

Writers enjoy studying words. They become fascinated by the characteristics words possess. They know that words may be noisy or quiet, beautiful or ugly, hard or soft, fresh or tired, calm or emotional, kind or cruel, formal or informal, general or specific.

Writers are aware, too, of the interesting histories of words — their origins, their changing forms, and their shifting meanings. As a young person interested in improving your writing, you can hardly do better than to cultivate the same strong interest in words that the experienced writer has.

The purposes of this chapter are, first, to try to arouse your curiosity about words and, second, to show you how an understanding of words and their ways can help you to write more interestingly.

THE SOUNDS OF WORDS — ONOMATOPOEIA

Some words have sounds that reflect their meaning.

These are words that have the sound of what they refer to. For example, the word *bubbling* has the sound made by a boiling liquid. The formation of words that imitate natural sounds, as *bubbling* does, is called onomatopoeia (on′·ə·mat′·ə·pē′·ə). The following words are examples of onomatopoeia: *buzz, clang, creak, groan, hiss, jangle, rattle, scratch, splash, thud.*

In writing certain kinds of description, writers find onomatopoetic words very useful. The American poet Amy Lowell, in writing a prose description of the bombardment of a French town during World War I, chose words for the effect of their sounds. Read aloud the following passage from "The Bombardment," emphasizing the sound words. You will find at least five examples of onomatopoeia. Notice also the poet's use of rhyme in this prose passage.

Slowly, without force, the rain drops into the city. It stops a moment on the carved head of St. John, then slides on again, slipping and trickling over his stone cloak. It splashes from the lead conduit of a gargoyle, and falls from it in turmoil on the stones in the Cathedral square. Where are the people, and why does the fretted steeple sweep about in the sky? Boom! The sound swings against the rain. Boom again! After it, only water rushing in the gutters, and the turmoil from the spout of the gargoyle. Silence. Ripples and mutters. Boom![1]

EXERCISE 1. Prepare a list of at least ten onomatopoetic words not included in the list at the top of the page or in the Amy Lowell selection. Compare your

[1] From "The Bombardment" by Amy Lowell from *The Complete Poetical Works of Amy Lowell.* Reprinted by permission of Houghton Mifflin Company, publisher.

list with those lists made by your classmates.

SOUND AND MEANING

Even when they are not onomatopoetic, word sounds often seem to reflect a word's meaning. The sounds of the words *alone, lonely,* and *loneliness,* for example, seem to suggest the feelings they refer to. No one knows exactly how or why certain sounds or combinations of sounds came to acquire certain meanings, except, of course, for words of onomatopoetic origin. Still it is interesting to notice the way word sounds, like the sound of *lonely,* do seem to suggest certain feelings. Is it possible that a made-up word, a meaningless word, can just by its sound suggest a meaning?

EXERCISE 2. Following is a list of five made-up words. Copy the list and after each word write the feeling it suggests to you, such as sadness, weariness, happiness, fear, loneliness.

1. siskilally
2. lornsorge
3. lumbergast
4. limmitypippiny
5. mogandroapal

Probably no one would insist that a general idea, such as sadness, has a particular sound, or that sounds in themselves are happy or sad. As a result of our experiences with words, however, we do find it hard to imagine that a word of an entirely different sound from a familiar word can mean the same thing. Here is a sentence containing the word *solemn.* "Throughout the funeral everyone was depressingly solemn." Now substitute for *solemn* the nonsense word *mippy.*

"Throughout the funeral everyone was depressingly mippy." Does *mippy* convey the feeling of depression? Now try another nonsense word, *gorlornal.* "Throughout the funeral everyone was depressingly gorlornal." Do you think the sound of *gorlornal* fits the meaning of the sentence better than *mippy?*

EXERCISE 3. Make up five nonsense words whose sounds suggest specific feelings to you. Ask your classmates what feelings your "words" suggest to them. What conclusion are you able to draw concerning the relationship between the sound of a word and the feeling it inspires?

Skillful writers, especially poets, sometimes choose words for the effect of their sound as well as for their meaning. Edgar Allan Poe said that when he was searching for a sorrowful word to use over and over as a refrain in his poem "The Raven," he chose the word *nevermore* because both its meaning and its sound are sad.

In his melancholy poem *Ulalume,* Poe showed clearly his remarkable ability to select just the right word for the effect he wanted. He wished to create an effect of mystery and sorrow with overtones of death, which brings the greatest sorrow we know. Read the following stanza aloud, noting the skillful use of sorrowful sounds.

> The skies they were ashen and sober;
> The leaves they were crispèd and sere —
> The leaves they were withering and sere:
> It was night, in the lonesome October
> Of my most immemorial year;
> It was hard by the dim lake of Auber,
> In the misty mid region of Weir —
> It was down by the dank tarn of Auber,
> In the ghoul-haunted woodland of Weir.

BEAUTY IN WORDS

The following paragraph expresses the pleasure one writer finds in words.

I like fat, buttery words, such as ooze, turpitude, glutinous, toady. I like solemn, angular, creaky words, such as strait-laced, cantankerous, pecuniary, valedictory. I like spurious, gold-plated, black-is-white words, such as gentlefolk, mortician, freelancer, mistress. I like crunchy, brittle, crackly words, such as splinter, grapple, jostle, crusty. I like suave *v* words, such as Svengali, svelte, bravura, verve. I like sullen, crabbed, scowling words, such as skulk, glower, scabby, churl. I like words such as trickery, tucker, genteel, and horrid. I like pretty-pretty, flowered, endimanche[1] words, such as elegant, halcyon, Elysium, artiste. I like wormy, squirmy, mealy words, such as crawl, blubber, squeal, drip. I like sniggly, chuckling words, such as cowlick, gurgle, bubble, and burp. I like words.[2]

Is there such a thing as a beautiful word or an ugly word? Some writers think there is. When asked to list what he considered the ten most beautiful words in the language, Wilfred Funk, a famous lexicographer, listed the following: *dawn, hush, lullaby, murmuring, tranquil, mist, luminous, chimes, golden, melody.* Saying these words aloud, you may react to them as Mr. Funk did and find them beautiful. Are their sounds beautiful, regardless of their meaning? Note that five of them contain the letter *l,* whose sound Mr. Funk apparently thought beautiful.

Fannie Hurst, an American novelist, offered six words as her candidates for the most beautiful: *serenity, beauty, mercy, peace, vitality, madonna.*

---

[1] *Endimanche* is a French adjective meaning "dressed up in Sunday clothes."

[2] From "Word's Worth" by Robert Pírosh, from *The Wolf Magazine of Letters.* Reprinted by permission of The Wolf Envelope Co.

To what extent do you think Miss Hurst was affected by the sounds and to what extent was she affected by the meaning of these words? Note, incidentally, that there is only one *l* in the words she suggested. H. L. Mencken, linguist and essayist, once said he thought *cellar door* to be a most beautiful expression. Certainly he was judging entirely by sound!

EXERCISE 4. Select, from the words given above, the five you consider the most beautiful. Then add five words of your own choice to the list. Compare your choices with those of your classmates.

EXERCISE 5. List ten words you consider the ugliest words you know. You may wish to begin with *ugly* itself.

While the sounds of most words are unrelated to the meanings of the words, some words, as you have seen, do reveal a close relationship between sound and meaning. We become so accustomed to this relationship that the sound of a word actually seems to suggest the meaning. When we write, we may increase the power of our writing by choosing words whose sound and meaning both work for us.

WORD HISTORIES—DERIVATION

No aspect of word study is more fascinating to word lovers than word histories. Tracing the history of a word to find out its origin and how it came to mean what it means today is an interesting study called *etymology*. Scholars engaged in this study are *etymologists*. Etymologists can trace a word back to what they call its origin. That is, they can tell us whether in the beginning it was a Greek or Latin or English

(Anglo-Saxon) word or a word from some other language. They can show us that many of our words are a combination of two or more ancient words. They can show us how a word's meaning has changed during its history. Etymologists can explain changes in the spelling and pronunciation of the word over the centuries, and they can give us the approximate times when the word took on additional meanings.

What etymologists cannot do, of course, is explain the great mystery of all word origins. This is the mystery of how or why certain sounds came to represent certain things or ideas. A word is merely a symbol representing the thing or the idea. The origins of some words like *bang* or *crack* are easy to explain because the sounds of these words are onomatopoetic. Other words, like our noun *bear,* can be traced back to the Anglo-Saxons, who gave the word *bera* to this animal; but this does not explain why the Anglo-Saxons chose to give this particular name to this particular beast. It is usually impossible for etymologists to explain why one symbol, one sound, was originally chosen to represent a particular idea or thing.

Sources of English Words

Words come into the language in many ways from many different sources. Some come from the names of persons. The sandwich acquired its name from John Montague, fourth Earl of Sandwich, who invented the sandwich in the eighteenth century. Some words are derived from myths. Our word *volcano* comes from Vulcan, Roman god of fire, whose fiery forge was said to be deep in a mountain. Words are derived from the names of places: *china* dishes; *damask* napkins, from Damascus. Some words are combinations of two or more words – *airplane, basketball, telecast* (television and broadcast). Etymologically, *television* derives from the Greek word *tele,* meaning "far," plus the Latin word *videre,* meaning "to see." *Broadcast* derives from the Anglo-Saxon word *brād,* meaning "wide or extended in breadth," plus the Old Norse word *kasta,* meaning "to throw."

The English language has been vastly enriched by words borrowed from other languages. Approximately 50 percent of English words are Latin in origin, including words that came from the Latin-based languages – French, Italian, and Spanish; 25 percent are Anglo-Saxon; 15 percent, Greek; 10 percent, all other languages. One can find English words that were borrowed from nearly every major language in the world. Here are a few familiar examples of words borrowed from other languages:

tepee	Dakota Indian
memoir	French
myth	Greek
piano	Italian
cigar	Spanish
kindergarten	German
yacht	Dutch
ski	Norwegian
alcohol	Arabic
pajama	Persian

EXERCISE 6. Using a dictionary that gives derivations, look up and record the language from which English borrowed each of the following words: *balcony, cargo, climax, cosmetic, slogan, succotash, wagon, waltz, kimono, tea.*

A great many English words are combinations of roots and prefixes from Latin and Greek. *Television,* mentioned earlier, is one example. You will find other examples on pages 631–34. On pages 635–36 you will find examples of words with interesting histories, and a list of common expressions that English borrowed from other languages.

EXERCISE 7. Select one of the following words, look up its origin – the interesting story behind it – and report to the class: *titanic, macadam, maverick, guillotine, utopian, braille, corduroy, limousine, pedagogue, quixotic, bonfire, curfew.*

NEW WORDS

A living language like English is constantly acquiring new words. Many words familiar to you were unknown when your parents were your age. New words, mostly nouns, come into the language as knowledge increases. The new words are formed in about the same way that words have always been formed. Sometimes they are coined from appropriate roots and prefixes from the Latin and Greek: *astronaut* – space traveler (*astro* – star + *naut* – sailor; literally, star sailor). Sometimes they are combinations: *bloodmobile.* Occasionally a new word is formed from the first letters of words in a descriptive phrase: *scuba* – *s*elf-*c*ontained *u*nderwater *b*reathing *a*pparatus.

The language changes and grows also when old words are used in new ways so that they acquire new meanings. You learned earlier that our word *bear* was originally the Anglo-Saxon word *bera,* the Anglo-Saxon name for this animal. The dictionary now lists these additional meanings for *bear:* (1) a gruff, ill-mannered, clumsy person; (2) a speculator, especially one in the stock exchange, who seeks to depress prices or who sells in the belief that a decline in prices is likely.

EXERCISE 8. Explain the method by which each of the following relatively new words was formed. Use your dictionary.

1. sit-in	6. stereophonic
2. skydiving	7. blitz
3. laser	8. cybernetics
4. Medicare	9. finalize
5. cosmonaut	10. antibiotic

You know that a word may be used as more than one part of speech. The word *cash,* for example, may be used as a noun: "She paid in cash"; as a verb: "Please cash this check"; and as an adjective: "He made a cash payment." A common kind of language change occurs when a word becomes accepted in use as a different part of speech. *Contact* was once used only as a noun. Today it is commonly used as a verb: "Contact me in the morning," and as an adjective: "contact lens" and "contact sport."

In these ways, then, a living language constantly grows and changes. As knowledge expands and life changes, so does language grow and change; new words come into the language, and old words take on new meanings.

THE DENOTATIVE AND CONNOTATIVE MEANINGS OF WORDS

As you know, a word may have many different meanings. The noun *ring,* for example, has such varied meanings as a band worn around a finger, a roped-off area for boxing, and a telephone call. These literal meanings of a word are its *denotative* meanings. In addition to their denotative meanings, many words have *connotative* meanings. The connotative meanings are meanings that may be associated with the word by a reader or listener. They are meanings that the word suggests beyond its denotative meanings.

The words *statesman* and *politician,* for example, may have the same denotative meaning—one who is skilled in the science of government or politics. In their connotative meanings, however, the words are different. When you refer to an elected government official as a statesman, you honor him. When you refer to him as a politician, you may be insulting him, for the word *politician* has unfavorable connotations for many people. It suggests an ambitious person who is more concerned with selfish interests than with the needs of the people represented.

Usually the connotations of a word stir our feelings, and we react to the word emotionally. The words *capitalist* and *capitalism,* although they have clear, technical, denotative meanings, might arouse strong antagonistic feelings in some countries whose industries are controlled by the state. Similarly, the words *dictator* or *dictatorship* might arouse antagonistic feelings in the United States, which has a democratic society. In using the words *communism* and *dictatorship,* a writer or public speaker may be using them more for their connotative meaning than for their denotative meaning. People often use words purely for their emotional effect. This is clearly a proper use of words, since connotations are often emotional, and are an important part—as in poetry—of language. In using words yourself, be aware of both their literal meaning and their emotional impact. The denotation and the connotation of a word are often different, and they are both important.

EXERCISE 9. The words in each group following are, to a degree, similar in their denotative meaning, but vastly different in their connotative meanings. List the words in each group in descending order according to the favorableness of their connotations; that is, put the word with the most favorable connotation first and the word with the most unfavorable connotation last. Opinions will differ.

1. thin, skinny, gawky, slender, lanky
2. defeat, edge-out, swamp, beat, overrun
3. conceited, vain, arrogant, cocky, self-confident
4. informer, stool pigeon, tattletale, spy, undercover agent
5. tight, thrifty, stingy, frugal, economical

As you may have discovered, words through their connotative meanings may affect people differently. Some words, like *motherhood, friendship, freedom, home, peace,* will have favorable connotations for almost everyone, but other words will cause widely varying reactions. People's reactions to various words are determined by their experience and knowledge. Your reaction to *Nazi* will be negative because of your knowledge of history. Your reaction to *Yankee* probably depends on whether you were born in the South or in New England.

EXERCISE 10. Read the following list of words and give your immediate reaction to each: negative, affirmative, or neutral. Be prepared to explain in class the reasons for your reactions. Ask your parents for their reactions to the words.

1. snake
2. dentist
3. chocolate
4. labor union
5. Republican
6. Frenchman
7. welfare
8. millionaire
9. teacher
10. breakfast

EXERCISE 11. Distinguish between the connotations of the words in each of the following pairs. The denotative meanings of the paired words are similar. Their connotative meanings may prove to be quite different.

1. dog, cur
2. idealist, dreamer
3. rare, half-cooked
4. determined, obstinate
5. fastidious, fussy
6. used, secondhand
7. graveyard, memorial park
8. job, chore
9. cook, chef
10. boat, yacht

LOADED WORDS

Closely related to the fact that words have important connotative meanings is the deliberate use by a writer of words that will prejudice the reader for or against something. Words that reveal the writer's opinion and tend to prejudice the reader for or against something are called loaded words.

EXERCISE 12. Both of the following descriptions of the same candidate contain loaded words. Read the two descriptions; the first is loaded against the candidate, and the second is in his favor. Make a list of the loaded words and expressions in the first selection; then beside each one write the corresponding loaded word from the second selection.

After suffering a major defeat in last week's presidential primary election, Senator Blank addressed a mere handful of people last night at the Civic Center. Looking drained and feverish, the senator threatened to continue his futile bid for the nomination. His voice rose hysterically as he ended his speech with these foolhardy words: "I intend to beat Governor Blab next week right here in his home state."

After suffering a temporary setback in last week's presidential primary election, Senator Blank addressed a small but spirited audience last night at the Civic Center. Looking tired but fiercely determined, the senator vowed to come from behind and win the nomination. His voice shook with emotion as he ended his speech with these courageous words: "I intend to beat Governor Blab next week right here in his home state."

FORMAL WORDS AND INFORMAL WORDS

You know the meanings of the word *formal* and its opposite *informal*. You know that a party may be formal or informal. You hear references to formal clothes and informal clothes. A class or a meeting may be conducted formally or informally. Reports and essays may be written in a formal style or in an informal style. Hence there is formal English and informal English. You use informal English far more than you use formal English, but as you grow older and continue on in school, you will find more use for formal English.

Although high school students seldom have occasion to speak or write the most formal English, they do have to learn that different situations call for different kinds of English. If you were speaking to a class of fourth-graders, you would naturally use different words from those you would use when speaking to a meeting of the Parent-Teachers Association, although you might be saying about the same thing to both groups. A report given in class or at a student council meeting or a talk delivered before the school assembly would require more formal English than would a conversation with friends or family. In fact, informal English is often called conversational English.

Most words may be used in both formal and informal situations, but some words are usually avoided in a formal piece of writing or a formal speech. For example, slang, because it is extremely informal, would not be used on a formal occasion, and would be used sparingly in class and in the writing done for school courses. In social conversation and in a friendly letter, you would probably use slang freely.

Slang

Slang consists of new words, or old words in new uses, that are adopted because they seem clever and colorful and show that the user is up-to-date, or, to use an informal phrase, "in the know." High school students are especially fond of slang and ingenious at inventing it. Sometimes a slang word becomes so completely acceptable that it is no longer slang but good informal English. Most slang words, however, live a short life. The popular slang of ten years ago would seem old-fashioned today. Only slang that lasts gets into the dictionary, where it is usually clearly labeled as slang. The following words, when used with the given meanings, are all marked *slang* in *Webster's New World Dictionary:*

bummer: a depressing experience
cool: having a dispassionate or detached attitude
cop out: to quit, abandon, renege
hassle: to annoy, harass
hang-up: an emotional problem
vibes: emotional reactions
weirdo: a bizarre or strange person

While slang is sometimes effective in informal talk, it is less effective in formal writing because it is too general. To write that a book you have just read is "cool" or "far-out" merely states your approval. It says nothing about the book that can help a reader understand its good points. When you write, you usually have time to choose words that are more specific and more informative than slang.

EXERCISE 13. Some slang words develop as part of a code shared by members of a group. Computer programmers, for example, use such expressions as "GIGO" or "glitch." The following slang words belong to the special language of CB-radio operators, especially truck drivers. Write a short definition for each word whose slang meaning is familiar to you.

1. bear
2. double nickel
3. hammer
4. ears
5. breaker

6. ten-four
7. handle
8. back door
9. camera
10. chicken coop

Slang, then, is a kind of language rarely used in essay writing because it is either too vague, too quickly out-of-date, or too private.

Degrees of Formality Among Synonyms

A synonym is a word that means almost the same thing as another word. *Huge* and *immense* are synonyms. But among some synonyms there are degrees of formality. The words in the following pairs of synonyms would be acceptable in any kind of writing, but notice the difference in the degree of their formality. Are there differences also in their connotative meanings?

necktie, cravat
stealthily, surreptitiously
write, inscribe
murder, homicide
commonplace, banal
kind, beneficent

nosy, inquisitive
unbelievable, incredible
small, diminutive
exclude, ostracize

Appropriate Words

When you write, choose words that are appropriate to the kind of writing the situation calls for. A young writer should not strain to use fancy words. Using a carefully high-toned vocabulary may annoy your reader, who will realize that you are putting on airs. On the other hand, you should not use language as informal as slang in serious compositions, where it is inappropriate.

EXERCISE 14. To understand how inappropriate words will affect the tone of a report, read the following one-paragraph book report. List the words and expressions that you consider too informal to be appropriate in a serious book report, and after each, write a more formal word or expression, one that will maintain the serious tone of the report. You should list at least five.

Maigret's Rival by Georges Simenon is a mystery story that takes place in France. A friend invites Maigret, a former police inspector, to a jerkwater town. There are some nasty rumors flying around town, and Maigret is supposed to keep a lid on them. Meanwhile one of Maigret's old buddies turns up, Cavre, who had been given the boot from the police force. Cavre gets the townspeople all worked up against Maigret, and they start to smell a rat regarding Maigret's visit. Naturally, since this is a murder mystery, it turns out that there is a stiff involved. I can't tell you any more without lousing up the story for you, so read it for yourselves. You'll get a big kick out of it.

TIRED WORDS

When writers refer to a word as "tired," they mean that the word has been used so much and so thoughtlessly that it has lost much of its meaning and its effectiveness. So-called tired words like *nice, swell, wonderful,* and *great* are common in conversation; they are, however, not exact enough to be effective in writing. When a friend asks you what kind of time you had at a party, you may use any one of those words to convey the idea that you enjoyed the party. However, if, again, you were writing a serious book report, you would be telling your reader little if you simply characterized the book as nice or swell or wonderful. These words have been so much used and so loosely used that they are almost without real meaning.

Another name for a tired word or a tired expression is *cliché* (klē·shā'). Clichés may be single words or they may be expressions containing more than one word. Among the most common clichés are comparisons — tired comparisons: busy as a bee, clear as crystal, quick as a flash, white as a sheet, fat as a pig, straight as an arrow, thin as a rail. Not all clichés are comparisons: few and far between, accidents will happen, gala occasion, last but not least.

Good writers avoid clichés in any form — tired words, tired comparisons, or other tired expressions.

EXERCISE 15. Prepare a list of five tired words, five tired comparisons, and five tired expressions that are not comparisons. Do not include in your list any of the words or expressions previously used as examples. Compare your list with those of your classmates. Combining lists, you should have a large collection of expressions to avoid whenever you write.

EXERCISE 16. The following is a series of four paragraphs written in an inappropriate style. The paragraphs contain slang, clichés, and trite expressions. Study the word choice in each paragraph and then rewrite the paragraph in a more formal style.

1. While gawking around in a pet store, did you ever feel real down when you saw all those cooped-up birds? Well I hate to bust your bubbles, but those pampered pets have it made. First and foremost, they're not being hassled by any predators. As far as Polly is concerned, that tooth-and-claw jungle scene is too hairy for words — in fact, it's for the birds.

2. Second, Polly gets all the eats it wants. I don't mean slim pickin's, either, but the cream of the crop — seeds, vegies, nuts, vitamins, the works. It's small wonder that caged birds have that laid-back look. They're living on easy street. And if they get daily exercise, their life is a bed of roses.

3. Last but not least, a caged bird is safe from all those weird tropical diseases it can get in the wild. There's never any need for Polly to get its feathers ruffled worrying about jungle rot or creeping crud or any of that jazz. If by a stroke of fate Polly does get its snoot stopped up with the sniffles, there are scads of vets who have hung out their shingles, all set to get Polly back into the pink of health.

4. To put it in a nutshell, a pet bird gets tender loving care and a free ride on the gravy train instead of a raw deal from Mother Nature. And when a pet bird returns its owner's affection, you know it's not feeling down-in-the-mouth. So before all you bleeding hearts get steamed up about birds' rights, just cool your jets. Remember, a well-treated pet bird is really flying high!

GENERAL WORDS AND SPECIFIC WORDS

Good writing is specific, not general or vague. It is specific in both its content and its language. If, for example, you begin a paragraph with the statement "Students are not helping to keep the school corridors neat and clean," you should devote the rest of the paragraph to giving specific evidence to support your beginning statement. You will give specific examples that show how cluttered and dirty the corridors are.

Language is specific when its words are clear and definite in meaning, not hazy and general. For example, in describing an encounter with a dog, you would not be content simply to say that a dog came across the street toward you. Such a statement, with its very general words *dog, came,* and *street,* does not give the reader a clear picture. If you tell the kind of dog and the manner in which it came, and give a more specific idea of the street, your description will be much clearer.

A huge Irish setter, its feathered tail swinging from side to side, bounded toward me through the heavy traffic on Branch Boulevard.

This picture has been made more vivid in two ways. First, the words *dog* and *came* have been changed to *Irish setter* and *bounded*. Second, specific details have been added — the tail swinging and the traffic. Naming the street will help anyone who is familiar with Branch Boulevard to picture the scene.

EXERCISE 17. Arrange the words in each of the following lists in descending order of general to specific; that is, put the most general word first, the most specific word last.

1. dog, animal, creature, golden retriever
2. foreigner, woman, person, Italian
3. building, edifice, office building, skyscraper
4. roast, main dish, food, meat
5. lineman, guard, football player, athlete

EXERCISE 18. Write the following words in a column and, after each, write three more specific synonyms:
1. enclosure 2. bird 3. cried 4. spoke 5. walked
6. church 7. athlete 8. vehicle 9. structure 10. field

EXERCISE 19. Rewrite each of the following sentences, substituting specific words and specific details for the general, vague words so that your reader will understand more clearly what you are trying to say.

1. A woman came into the room and spoke to the teacher.
2. His summer home on a beach faced the water.
3. She grew up in poverty in a city.
4. A defensive player stopped the play.
5. From a vantage point we were watching the game.

SUMMARY

You have learned that, when you write, you must make a great many decisions. You must decide which word out of the many available to you will best say what you want to say. In choosing a word, you should understand its connotative as well as its denotative meaning. You should choose words that are appropriate to the situation—formal or informal. You should avoid slang except in the most informal kind of writing. You should avoid tired words and expressions—clichés. You should choose the specific word, avoiding the general word. Above all, remember this: When you write, you have time to choose your words carefully. Take time! Do not just write down unthinkingly the first, or even the second word, that comes to you. The more time you spend on word choice the more effective your writing will be.

Composition Assignment—Specific Verbs

To demonstrate your ability to select from the many words available the one word that will be most specific and most effective, write a composition in which you describe a scene that is full of action. The verb is the key word in any description of action. Your verbs must convey clearly to your readers the action you want them to see. These verbs must be specific.

In preparation for your composition, work through the following exercises.

I

In each of the following sentences the verbs have been omitted. Select for each sentence a verb or verbs that will clearly show the picture you have in mind. Write the verbs in order, numbering them according to the sentence number. Exchange papers with your classmates. Discuss the relative effectiveness of the many verbs suggested.

a. Marta was ——ing her new bicycle down the driveway.
b. Late again, John —— through the classroom door, —— across the back of the room, and —— into a seat.

c. When the period bell ——, every door along the deserted corridor —— open, and the thundering herd —— forth.

d. Shielding her eyes from the sun, the right fielder —— forward, then —— abruptly, and with her bare hand outstretched, —— into the air, and —— the ball for the final out.

e. Balancing in the bow of the rocking skiff, Alicia and Julie —— each other, —— awkwardly, and —— overboard with a resounding splash.

II

The verb in each of the following sentences is vague and commonplace. It does not give as clear a picture as a more carefully selected specific verb can. After the proper sentence number, write a more specific verb that will make the picture clear as you see it. Compare your choices with those of your classmates.

1. She *hit* the ball over the fence.
2. He *ate* all the cake that was left.
3. She *called* for help.
4. The car *came* to a halt.
5. A trailer truck, its horn blaring, *went* past us down the hill.

III

In the following paragraph John Steinbeck tells what happened when, with his usually mild-mannered poodle Charley beside him in the car, he encountered a bear in Yellowstone Park. As you read, note how specific the verbs are.

> Less than a mile from the entrance I saw a bear beside the road, and it ambled out as though to flag me down. Instantly a change came over Charley. He shrieked with rage. His lips flared, showing wicked teeth that

have some trouble with a dog biscuit. He screeched insults at the bear, which hearing, the bear reared up and seemed to me to over-top the car. Frantically I rolled the windows shut and, swinging quickly to the left, grazed the animal, then scuttled on while Charley raved and ranted beside me, describing in detail what he would do to that bear if he could get at him. I was never so astonished in my life.[1]

IV

Visualize someone in action and write a one-sentence description similar to those in Part I on page 440 in which you make the picture vivid by using specific verbs.

V

Now you are ready to write a full-length description (about 150 words) of an action-filled scene with which you are familiar. Before you write, take plenty of time to visualize the scene in all its details. Decide what you are going to include. Decide from what viewpoint you are going to watch the scene. You will be judged in this composition by your success in selecting effective verbs.

If you need suggestions, the following may be helpful. Crowd scenes are good for an assignment of this kind because they provide many different actions to describe.

> The cafeteria at lunchtime
> The gym during an exciting basketball game
> The stadium at game time
> The school parking lot after school

[1] From *Travels with Charley* by John Steinbeck. Copyright © 1962 by John Steinbeck. Reprinted by permission of Viking Penguin, Inc., and McIntosh and Otis, Inc.

The beach or pool on a hot day
A busy intersection at rush hour
A riot or mob scene
A county fair
A public park on a weekend afternoon

You need not, however, use a crowd scene. You may prefer to describe an experience in which you performed or watched others perform many specific actions: a hike, a fishing exploit, a skiing or sailing experience, a storm, a time when you witnessed a frightening or exciting thing.

Chapter 18

The Business Letter

In school and out, almost everyone writes one kind of composition—the letter. Although the telephone satisfies many business needs, there are still occasions when a letter is the more effective means of communication. On the following pages you will find described some of the standard practices used in writing a business letter as well as some suggestions which can be applied to the writing of any letter. Learning the information given here and using it will help ensure a prompt and satisfactory response from the person to whom you are writing.

SOME TIPS ON WRITING LETTERS

1. *Use the proper form for your letter.* The forms for a friendly letter may vary considerably, depending on whom you are writing to and the purpose of the letter. In the business world, however, people expect the letters they receive to conform to certain standard forms so that they may more quickly and accurately respond to the writer. Therefore, be sure to examine carefully the section dealing with the standard forms for writing business letters.

2. *Make your letter clear.* Remember that when your letter is read, you will not be there to explain

what you mean. So that you do not leave out any important details, plan what you are going to say and how you are going to say it. If you think about what you are going to say *before* you write, you will avoid many careless errors that often interfere with clarity.

3. *Make your letter attractive.* A letter represents *you;* you can take pride in its appearance. Whether your letter is neat and clearly written or messy and illegible will affect your reader's opinion of you. Business people frequently receive letters from writers they have never met and may never meet. They must judge the writer entirely by the letter. If they receive a messy, illegible letter, they must assume that the writer either doesn't know any better or doesn't care enough to take the time to make the letter readable and attractive.

4. *Use correct grammar, punctuation, and spelling.* A letter filled with grammatical errors will not only make an unfavorable impression on the reader, but also mar the clear expression of your ideas. Be on the lookout for run-on sentences, sentence fragments, errors in usage, and misspelled words.

5. *Always reread your letters.* Check not only for clarity and grammatical errors, but also for the accuracy of the information given in the letter. This is very important in ordering merchandise. Mistakes in price, quantity ordered, or addressing can only cause delay and dissatisfaction later. Be sure you have supplied the reader with *all* the information needed to insure the response you want.

THE BUSINESS LETTER — STANDARD PRACTICES

The letters that you write to a place of business or to a person in a firm are business letters. Whether you are ordering merchandise, making a request, or applying for a job, you should make sure your letter is short and to the point, that your purpose in writing is clearly and courteously expressed, and that it conforms to the standard practices discussed below.

Stationery and Appearance

18a. Choose appropriate stationery for business letters.

For several reasons it is best to use white, unlined $8\frac{1}{2} \times 11$-inch paper for your letter. Many firms make photostatic copies of the letters they receive and white paper photographs best. Further, dark ink or typing on white paper is easiest to read.

18b. Make your business letters attractive and easy to read.

A neatly typed letter is more legible and therefore more quickly read than a handwritten one. When re-reading a typed letter, watch out for typographical errors. If you write the letter by hand use ink, preferably blue, blue-black, or black, rather than pencil. And always use your very best penmanship. Do not expect those who receive your letter to try to decipher or decode it — they haven't the time.

For the sake of appearance leave fairly wide margins on both sides, the top, and the bottom of the page. These margins should all be approximately equal in width. If you find that your letter will require a second sheet, be sure to carry over at least two sentences from your last paragraph onto the second sheet. It is standard practice never to write on the back of a page.

Letter Form

18c. Learn the proper form for the six parts of a business letter.

The parts of a business letter are the *heading, inside address, salutation, body, closing,* and *signature.* The parts labeled in the illustration below are discussed on the pages following.

The semiblock form is a popular type of business letter. As the model shows, the first line of each paragraph is indented; and the heading, closing, and signature are begun just to the right of the middle of the page. (The pure block form, which has no indentions of the first lines of paragraphs, is also acceptable for business letters.)

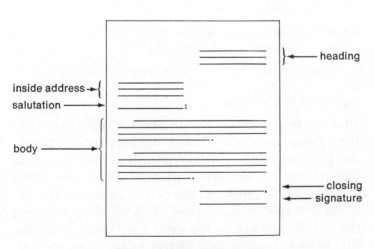

inside address
salutation
body
heading
closing
signature

Form of a Business Letter

Carefully notice the spacing between parts of the business letter above. The entire letter is centered on the page, with approximately the same margin at the top as at the bottom and with the same margin on each side of the page. If you type your business letters, double-space after the inside address, after the salutation, between paragraphs, and after the last line of the last paragraph.

1. The Heading

Beginning no less than one inch from the top of the page, put your *complete* address and the *full* date in the upper right-hand corner of the page. The heading usually consists of three lines, two for the address and one for the date. A comma is inserted between the city and the state, but do not insert one between the state and the zip code number. Insert a comma also between the day of the month and the year in the third line. It is better to write this heading without abbreviations.

EXAMPLE   685 Lawton Street
Dayton, Ohio 45411
October 9, 1981

2. The Inside Address

The inside address is placed several spaces (at least four if you are typing) below the heading, flush with the left-hand margin. It should include the full name and address of the company you are writing to. If you are writing to a person in the firm, use the full name and title of the person, with a comma between the two if they are on the same line. If the name and title are too long to look attractive on the same line, put the title on the next line.

EXAMPLES

Ajax Auto Supply
6890 Clifton Road
Dayton, Ohio 45412

Ms. Ann King, President
American Humane Society
P.O. Box 1266
Denver, Colorado 80201

Circulation Department
Field and Stream
1515 Broadway
New York, New York 10036

Dr. William N. Kirkpatrick
Assistant Director
Defense Research Laboratory
The University of Texas
Austin, Texas 78712

3. The Salutation

The salutation is your greeting to the reader. It is
placed two spaces below the last line of the inside
address and flush with the left-hand margin. If you
are writing to a group or a company, you may use an
impersonal salutation (*Customer Service, Editors*) or
the traditional salutation (*Gentlemen*) followed by a
colon. In using such salutations, it is understood that
the group you are writing to may be composed of both
men and women. When you are writing to an individual within the firm, the correct salutation is *Dear
Mr.* _____ (*Mrs., Ms.,* or *Miss*). If you are writing
to professional men or women, use their titles (*Dr.,
Professor,* etc.) instead of *Mr., Mrs.,* etc. A colon
always follows the salutation.

EXAMPLES
Gentlemen: Circulation Department:
Dear Sir: Dear Dr. Patrick:
Dear Madam: Dear Ms. King:

Note that the abbreviations of titles before a person's name are followed by a period.

If you know the name, use it in both the inside address and the salutation. If you don't, then use one of the general salutations mentioned previously.

4. The Body

The body is the actual message of the letter. The form of the body of a business letter is the same as that of any other letter. Be sure to divide your letter into fairly short paragraphs, making clear indentions of the first line of each paragraph if you are using the semiblock style. If your letter is very short (7 lines or less), you may double-space the entire body of the letter. When typing a longer letter, however, you normally single-space the paragraphs and double-space between them.

5. The Closing

The closing comes between the body of the letter and the signature. The closings that you use for friendly letters are *not* appropriate for business letters. In business letters, appropriate closings are limited.

Very truly yours, Yours truly, and *Yours very truly* are the ones most frequently used. *Sincerely yours* and *Yours sincerely* are also correct. The closing is placed just to the right of the center of the page, two spaces below the last line of the body of your letter. It is followed by a comma. Note that only the first word of each closing begins with a capital letter.

EXAMPLES Very truly yours,
Yours sincerely,

Do not end your letter with phrases such as "I beg to remain," "Hoping to hear from you soon, I am," or "Thanking you in advance, I am." End the body of your letter with a *period,* not a comma. Then begin your closing.

303 Clayton Street
Huntington, West Virginia 25703
February 10, 1982

Executive Secretary
Chamber of Commerce
Mystic, Connecticut   06355

Dear Sir:

    I am writing a report on whaling in old New England and would appreciate your sending me any pamphlets and pictures you have about Mystic Seaport.

    I would especially like pictures of the town itself, as well as information on early whaling ships and equipment. Any maps you have of Mystic Seaport and of early sailing routes would be useful, too.

                Very truly yours,

                Theodore Jonas

A Business Letter

6. The Signature

Sign your full name to your letter. Do *not* put *Miss, Ms.,* or *Mrs.* before your name. If a woman wishes to indicate her marital status, she may put *Miss* or *Mrs.* in parentheses before her signature. When a woman does not include a specific title in her signature, the receiver of the letter may feel free to use *Ms.* in the salutation of a letter of reply.

EXAMPLES

> (Miss) Mary Jane Fiske
> Sue Glucken

A signature should always be handwritten. If your letter is typewritten, type your name flush with the first letter of the closing and far enough (usually four spaces) below to allow room for your signature above it. Try not to let any part of the closing trail into the margin.

EXERCISE 1. After studying the proper form for the six parts of a business letter, close your book and write these parts in their proper places on a sheet of paper. Use your own address in the heading. Draw 12 lines to represent the body, dividing them into two paragraphs. Be careful about spacing and about correct punctuation of the heading, salutation, and closing. In the margins of your paper, label each part of the letter. You may use either block or semiblock style, but be consistent.

EXERCISE 2. On your paper, using the information given below, write a business letter. Be sure to use the proper form and include all necessary punctuation.

1. *Heading:* 2420 Nicholson Drive, Portland, Oregon 97221, November 12, 1981
2. *Inside Address:* Mr. James E. Clark, Business Manager, Allison's Greeting Card Company, P.O. Box 3452, Los Angeles, California 90035
3. *Salutation:* Dear Mr. Clark
4. *Body:* As the secretary of the ninth grade at my high school, I am writing to you to find

out more about the offer you are advertising in local newspapers. Since my class is working to raise money for the "Toys for Tots" campaign, we are interested in selling your Christmas cards. Will you please send me more information about the kinds of cards you have, the price range, and the percentage of profit made on each box sold.

5. *Closing:* Very truly yours
6. *Signature:* Charles Evans

Request Letters

18d. Make your letters of request simple and clear.

A letter of request asks for information from the company or business firm to whom you are writing. It is a good idea to state your request in your first sentence. The other sentences can give further details. The business letter on page 451 and the letter in Exercise 2 are examples of the request letter.

EXERCISE 3. Write to any place of business (a department store, a publishing firm, a motor company, an equipment-rental house, a sporting goods store, etc.) requesting information about a particular product. Ask for circulars describing the merchandise and listing the prices. (This is an exercise in letter-writing. Do not mail the letter unless you are seriously interested.)

EXERCISE 4. Thumb through one of your favorite magazines, noticing the advertisements. Choose a firm that interests you, and write a letter of request. A steel company, for example, may send you circulars about the uses of steel. A manufacturer of flour may give away a recipe book. A travel bureau may have interesting, free pamphlets available. Some companies may have information that will help you in making reports in your classes at school. (Don't mail the letter unless you really need the information and unless the information cannot be found in the library.)

Order Letters

18e. Write order letters that contain complete and accurate information.

Although printed order blanks and "clip-it-out-and-mail" coupons are growing in popularity, there are still times when you need to write a letter ordering merchandise.

When writing an order letter, you should list the items you wish, one below the other, with complete information (style, size, price, catalogue number, or trade name) about each item. The price should be put at the right-hand side (flush with the right-hand margin). Each price should be placed directly under the one above so that the column of figures will be easy to add. List the cost of shipping, if you know it, and include it in the total, unless you know that the firm pays for shipping. Also be sure to say how you are paying for the order—by check, money order, or C.O.D.

EXERCISE 5. Write an order letter to Academy Novelty Company, P.O. Box 3975, Los Angeles, California 90064, for the following merchandise: 2 green Wizard shirts, one size 14 and the other size $15\frac{1}{2}$, at $9.98 each; one OO–GA whistle, at $1.49; 6 yellow Bond pencils, with the name "Skippy" printed in gold, at $.25 each; and 1 set of six Canton steak

R.F.D. 2
Cedar Falls, Iowa 50613
April 30, 1982

Ajax Auto Supply
6890 Clifton Road
Dayton, Ohio 45410

Gentlemen:

    Will you please send me the following merchandise
as advertised in your spring catalogue:

1 pr. swimming fins, Cat. No. S20, adjustable
    straps, heavy-duty $19.00

2 skull caps, Cat. No. B261, one blue (size 7)
    and one red (size 6 1/2), at $3.25 each   6.50

1 bicycle mirror, Cat. No. M45, small (4 by 2),
    chrome-trimmed   4.75
                                                     $30.25

    I enclose a money order for $34.00 to cover the
cost of the order and the postal charge of $3.75.

                      Yours very truly,

                      Angela Green

                      Angela Green

An Order Letter

knives, with white handles, at $15.95. You are enclos-
ing a money order to cover the total cost as well as
an extra $2.80 for postage and handling.

Adjustment Letters

18f. **Write courteous adjustment letters.**

When filling an order, business people sometimes

```
                              R.F.D. 2
                              Cedar Falls, Iowa  50613
                              May 5, 1982


    Ajax Auto Supply
    6890 Clifton Road
    Dayton, Ohio   45410

    Gentlemen:

         In my letter of April 30, I ordered a pair of
    heavy-duty swimming fins with adjustable straps.
    Advertised on page 26 of your spring catalogue, these
    fins are numbered S20.  This morning, however,
    I received a yellow inflatable sea serpent, which I
    am returning to you by parcel post.  I'll appreciate
    your exchanging the sea serpent for the fins.


                              Yours truly,

                              Angela Green

                              Angela Green
```

An Adjustment Letter

make mistakes; and sometimes you make errors or leave out important information in your order letter. An adjustment letter is one that you write after an error has been made.

You should feel free to write to a company whose product you have purchased and are dissatisfied with. The only way for you, as consumers, to be sure that the quality of the products you buy remains high, is to express any dissatisfaction directly to the manu-facturer. Occasionally an individual product in a line of normally high-quality goods is made defectively. The manufacturer will usually replace the item for you and apologize for your inconvenience if you write. In your letter, be sure to mention specifics — how much you paid, exactly why you were unhappy with the product, and what you wish the manufacturer to do about it.

When you are trying to straighten out a mistake, by all means be courteous. Your adjustment letter should not include curt remarks like "Can't you read? Why didn't you send me what I ordered?" or "I'll never buy another thing from your store." Always be polite as you explain what happened and as you ask for an adjustment, but be insistent that some action be taken.

Also be very prompt about correcting a mistake. Don't wait two or three weeks before you exchange an article or complain about not receiving something that you ordered.

EXERCISE 6. Let's suppose that the Academy Novelty Company (see Exercise 5, page 454) failed to send you the six pencils that you ordered; more-over, you received blue shirts instead of green ones. It has been four days now since you received the package, and you still have had no word from the company about the missing pencils or a refund of your money. Write an adjustment letter.

THE ENVELOPE

18g. Fold your letter to fit your envelope.

There are two sizes of standard business envelopes, both of which are acceptable: $6\frac{1}{2} \times 3\frac{1}{2}$ inches and

$9\frac{1}{2} \times 4\frac{1}{2}$ inches. You should fold your business letter (on the standard $8\frac{1}{2} \times 11$-inch sheet) to fit the size of the envelope you are using.

For the large-size envelope, the letter is folded twice and inserted into the envelope. First fold the bottom third of the page up. Second, fold the top of the page down to about a half inch from the bottom, so that it will be easy to open. Place the letter in the envelope with the open end up.

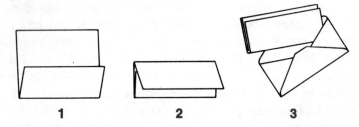

If your envelope is small, fold your letter up from the bottom to within a quarter of an inch of the top; then fold the right side over a third of the way; finally, fold the left side over, leaving about a fourth of an inch so that it can be opened easily.

If your letter is more than one page long, it is better to use the large envelope.

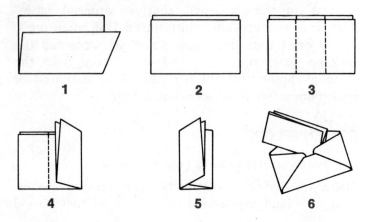

18h. Address your envelope correctly.

The envelope for a business letter is addressed in block form. Your name and address appear in the upper left-hand corner. Do not give yourself a title such as "Miss" or "Mr." You do, however, always use a title before the name of the person to whom you are writing. Except for titles, do not use abbreviations on the envelope. (Two-letter codes for states are frequently used. See the list on pages 461–62.)

```
Theodore Jonas
303 Clayton Street
Huntington, West Virginia 25703


                    Executive Secretary
                    Chamber of Commerce
                    Mystic, Connecticut 06355
```

Place the name and address of the person to whom you are writing on the lower half of the envelope. It should be identical to the inside name, title, and address.

EXERCISE 7. After drawing two envelopes on your paper, use the following information as you correctly address them. (You will not use every word given below.)

1. *Sender:* Ms. Ginny D'Espies, Point Pleasant, New Jersey, 08472, 1851 Riviera Parkway
   Receiver: Mr. Robert Cleveland, 1112 Rose Boulevard, Utah 84112, Salt Lake City

2. *Sender:* Mr. Thomas Flanders, New York City, 81 Waverly Place, New York State, zip code 10013

   Receiver: Department of Parks and Recreation, Commissioner, Grand Rapids, Michigan, zip code 49506, 336 East High Street

EXERCISE 8. Using an appropriate envelope, properly address the letter that you wrote for Exercise 3 (page 453). Be sure that the return address on the envelope is accurate. Also be sure that the address on the envelope is identical with the inside address in your letter. Fold your letter and place it in the envelope; do not seal the envelope.

CHECKLIST FOR WRITING LETTERS

1. Is my letter attractive? Is the form correct, with each of the parts correctly placed?
2. Does the heading give my complete address and the full date? Have I used commas to separate the city from the state and the day of the month from the year?
3. Is the inside address accurate, complete, and properly spaced?
4. Is the salutation appropriate? Is it followed by a colon?
5. In the body of my letter, are my sentences grammatically correct and accurately punctuated? Are all words correctly spelled? Have I used paragraphing properly?
6. Is the closing appropriate? Does the first word begin with a capital letter? Do the other words begin with a small letter? Does a comma follow the closing?
7. Have I been consistent in the use of block or semiblock style in the letter? Have I used block style on the envelope? Is the address on the envelope identical with the inside address in the letter?
8. Is the address on the envelope accurate, complete, and attractively placed?

9. Have I folded the letter to fit the envelope?
10. Have I remembered to put my return address on the envelope?

▶ **NOTE** The United States Postal Service recommends the use of two-letter codes for states, the District of Columbia, and Puerto Rico. The Service also recommends the use of nine-digit zip codes. When you use these codes, the address should look like this:

EXAMPLE   Ms. Mary Suarez
19 Battle Creek Drive
Wichita, KS   67208–1313

The two-letter code is in capital letters and is never followed by a period. Refer to the following list for two-letter codes.

Alabama	AL	Massachusetts	MA
Alaska	AK	Michigan	MI
Arizona	AZ	Minnesota	MN
Arkansas	AR	Mississippi	MS
California	CA	Missouri	MO
Colorado	CO	Montana	MT
Connecticut	CT	Nebraska	NE
Delaware	DE	Nevada	NV
District of Columbia	DC	New Hampshire	NH
Florida	FL	New Jersey	NJ
Georgia	GA	New Mexico	NM
Hawaii	HI	New York	NY
Idaho	ID	North Carolina	NC
Illinois	IL	North Dakota	ND
Indiana	IN	Ohio	OH
Iowa	IA	Oklahoma	OK
Kansas	KS	Oregon	OR
Kentucky	KY	Pennsylvania	PA
Louisiana	LA	Puerto Rico	PR
Maine	ME	Rhode Island	RI
Maryland	MD	South Carolina	SC

South Dakota	SD	Virginia	VA
Tennessee	TN	Washington	WA
Texas	TX	West Virginia	WV
Utah	UT	Wisconsin	WI
Vermont	VT	Wyoming	WY

REVIEW EXERCISE. Choose one of the following assignments. Use the checklist both *before* and *after* you write the letter. Properly address an envelope, and fold your letter to fit it. Do not seal the envelope or mail the letter.

1. Write to the Commissioner of Patents, Department of Commerce, Washington, D.C. 20025, asking for information regarding recent patents of interest to hunters. Request a copy of Patent 3,065,821 and mention that you are enclosing twenty-five cents to cover the cost.

2. Write to the Bureau of Information, *Popular Mechanics,* 224 West 57th Street, New York, New York 10019. Ask for the free "Where-to-Find-It List" for the current month and year.

3. Write the Forest Service, U.S. Department of Agriculture, Washington, D.C. 20250. Ask for information about America's national forests.

4. Read an editorial in a newspaper or an article in a magazine, and then write a letter to the editor clearly and courteously expressing your opinion about it.

Mechanics

PART FIVE

Chapter 19

Capital Letters

The Rules for Capitalization

In written or printed English, a capital letter at the beginning of a word not only serves as an important eye signal to the reader (indicating, for example, the beginning of a sentence) but also often marks a significant difference in meaning (for example, the difference between *march* and *March*). In your writing, then, you should use necessary capitals. Just as important, you should carefully avoid unneeded capitals. Learning the rules of capitalization in this chapter will help you develop this writing skill.

19a. Capitalize the first word in every sentence.

INCORRECT the home economics teacher told us, "by doing a simple experiment, you can find out whether or not coffee contains chicory. sprinkle a small amount of coffee into a glass of ice water. the coffee grounds will stay on top of the water. if chicory is present, it will not float but will sink and color the water."

CORRECT The home economics teacher told us, "By doing a simple experiment, you can find out whether or not coffee contains chicory. Sprinkle a small amount of coffee into a glass of ice water. The cof-

> fee grounds will stay on top of the water.
> If chicory is present, it will not float
> but will sink and color the water."

Traditionally, the first word of a line of poetry is capitalized.

EXAMPLE   A duck whom I happened to hear
          Was complaining quite sadly, "Oh, dear!
            Our picnic's today,
            But the forecasters say
          That the skies will be sunny and clear."

Some modern poets (E. E. Cummings, for example) do not follow this practice. They may capitalize only the first line or sometimes not even that. When you are quoting, use capital letters as they are used in the copy of the poem.

EXERCISE 1. Make a list of the ten words that should be capitalized in the following paragraph. Be sure to capitalize the words you list.

    work has begun on developing a new kind of laser radar this instrument would be especially useful for blind people how does the radar work a laser device, which is small enough to fit onto an eyeglass frame, emits invisible infrared light beams when the light strikes an object, it bounces back to a receiver placed in the blind person's ear the receiver, in turn, sounds a small tone with this sort of device, the blind person can "hear" any object nearby the device is very promising in fact it may one day replace the cane or the Seeing Eye dog as an aid for the blind there are few better examples of how beneficial laser research can be.

19b. Capitalize the pronoun *I* and the interjection *O*.

Although rarely used, *O* is always capitalized. Generally, it is reserved for invocations and is followed by the name of the person or thing being addressed. In your writing, you will probably find little opportunity to use *O.* You may, however, use the interjection *oh,* which is not capitalized unless it is the first word in a sentence.

EXAMPLES The play was a hit, but oh, how frightened I was!

"Exult **O** shores! and ring **O** bells!" is a line from Walt Whitman's poem "**O** Captain! My Captain!"

EXERCISE 2. Number 1–10 on your paper. If an item is correct, write *C* after the appropriate number. If there are errors in the use of capitals, copy the item on your paper, inserting capitals where needed and omitting unnecessary capitals.

1. oh dear! i think i've lost my watch.
2. yesterday i learned the psalm which begins, "Bless the Lord, o my soul."
3. why shouldn't i paint the chair pink?
4. I think I'll pass the test tomorrow, but Oh, how I dread taking it!
5. In the poem "The Fool's Prayer," the jester pleads, "O Lord, be merciful to me, a fool!"
6. walking in the woods, i almost stepped on a snake, and Oh, was i frightened!
7. Oh, Simone! I've won a trip to Europe!
8. Please listen carefully while i read the answer i received.
9. oh, for pity's sake! i wish you would stop saying, "o Romeo, Romeo, wherefore art thou, Romeo?"
10. My favorite lines from the play are

    "see how she leans her cheek upon her hand.
    oh, that i were a glove upon that hand,
    that i might touch that cheek!"

19c. Capitalize proper nouns and proper adjectives.

As you study the following words, observe (1) the difference between a common noun and a proper noun and (2) the ways adjectives (called *proper adjectives*) may be formed from proper nouns.

COMMON NOUNS	PROPER NOUNS
a poet	Homer
a country	Turkey
a goddess	Athena
a queen	Queen Elizabeth

PROPER ADJECTIVES
Homeric simile
Turkish border
Athenian wisdom
Elizabethan drama

Common nouns name a class or group. For example, *teacher* and *student* are common nouns because they name one of a group of people. Common nouns are not capitalized unless they begin a sentence or a direct quotation or are included in a title (see page 477). Proper nouns, such as *Mrs. Hersey* and *Paul Donahue,* name *particular* people, places, or things. They are always capitalized.

Some proper names consist of more than one word. In these names, short prepositions (generally, fewer than five letters) and articles are not capitalized.

EXAMPLES   Tomb of the Unknown Soldier
Society for the Prevention of Cruelty to Animals
Ivan the Terrible

Proper adjectives, adjectives formed from proper nouns, usually modify common nouns: *Spanish mackerel.* Sometimes, however, the proper adjective modifies a proper name (for example, *Victorian*

England) or is part of a proper name (for example, *Arctic Circle*).

► **NOTE** Proper nouns and adjectives sometimes lose their capitals through frequent usage; examples are *maverick* and *titanic*.

EXERCISE 3. Following is a list of common and proper nouns. For each proper noun, give its proper adjective. Use your dictionary if you wish. After the proper adjective, write an appropriate noun for the adjective to modify. For each common noun, give two proper nouns.

EXAMPLES   1. Mexico
                 1. *Mexican border*
                 2. city
                 2. *Chicago, New York*

1. France	4. Jefferson	7. pioneer	9. island
2. India	5. Spain	8. month	10. author
3. the Bible	6. continent		

(1) Capitalize the names of persons.

EXAMPLES

Sandra	Bobby Joe Franklin
Miss Willis	Mr. Kenji Hayashi
Margaret Love	Aunt Jean and Uncle Gordon

(2) Capitalize geographical names.

Towns, Cities   Georgetown, San Diego, Kansas City
Counties, Townships   Harrison County, Sheffield Township
States   Alaska, Florida, North Dakota, New Hampshire
Sections   the East, the North, the Southwest, the Middle West, New England

▶ **NOTE** The words *north, west, southeast,* etc., are not capitalized when they indicate direction: *driving through the Northwest* but *traveling northwest; states in the South* but *south of town.*

Countries the United States of America, Canada, New Zealand
Continents North America, Asia, Europe, Africa
Islands Philippine Islands, Long Island, the West Indies, the Isle of Palms
Mountains Rocky Mountains, Mount McKinley, the Alps, the Mount of Olives
Bodies of Water Pacific Ocean, Adriatic Sea, Red River, Lake of the Woods
Roads, Highways, Streets Route 66, Interstate 787, Pennsylvania Turnpike, Seneca Avenue, West Twenty-first Street, Walnut Drive
Parks Yellowstone National Park, Cleburne State Park

▶ **NOTE** In a hyphenated number, the second word begins with a small letter.

Notice that words like *City, Island, River, Street,* and *Park* are capitalized because they are part of the name. If words like these are not part of a proper name, they are common nouns and are therefore not capitalized. Compare the following lists.

PROPER NOUNS	COMMON NOUNS
life in New York City	life in a big city
Liberty Island	a faraway island
crossing the Spokane River	across the river
on State Street	on a narrow street
in Grant Park	in a state park

EXERCISE 4. Number 1–20 on your paper. In each of the following items you are to choose the correct one of the two forms. After the proper number on your paper, write the letter of the correct form (*a* or *b*).

1. a. Her store is on Front Street in Burlington.
   b. Her store is on front street in Burlington.
2. a. We crossed the Snake river.
   b. We crossed the Snake River.
3. a. He now lives in california.
   b. He now lives in California.
4. a. Did you fly over South America?
   b. Did you fly over south America?
5. a. She took a picture of Pikes peak.
   b. She took a picture of Pikes Peak.
6. a. City streets in the west are often wide.
   b. City streets in the West are often wide.
7. a. Yellowstone National Park has many geysers.
   b. Yellowstone national park has many geysers.
8. a. The city of Columbus is the capital of Ohio.
   b. The City of Columbus is the capital of Ohio.
9. a. The hurricane swept over the Gulf Of Mexico.
   b. The hurricane swept over the Gulf of Mexico.
10. a. Drive east on Interstate 35.
    b. Drive East on interstate 35.
11. a. We are proud of our State parks.
    b. We are proud of our state parks.
12. a. I live on Forty-Fifth Street.
    b. I live on Forty-fifth Street.
13. a. The headquarters are in Travis County.
    b. The headquarters are in Travis county.
14. a. The Vikings called the atlantic ocean the sea of darkness.
    b. The Vikings called the Atlantic Ocean the Sea of Darkness.
15. a. The states in the Midwest are referred to as the nation's breadbasket.
    b. The States in the midwest are referred to as the nation's breadbasket.
16. a. A three-lane Highway is dangerous.
    b. A three-lane highway is dangerous.
17. a. I have a map of the Hawaiian Islands.
    b. I have a map of the Hawaiian islands.
18. a. New York City is the largest city in the east.
    b. New York City is the largest city in the East.

19. a. The Great Salt Lake is near the Nevada border.
    b. The Great Salt lake is near the Nevada border.
20. a. Her address is 2009 Bell Avenue.
    b. Her address is 2009 Bell avenue.

EXERCISE 5. Write a paragraph of about 100 words telling about a town or city that you know well. Give its exact location (the county, state, section of the country), and name some of its streets. Also tell about the points of interest — parks, dams, lakes, mountains — that your state is proud of. Be sure to capitalize all of the geographical names that you use in your description.

(3) Capitalize names of organizations, business firms, institutions, and government bodies.

Organizations   United Fund, National Basketball Association, American Cancer Society

► NOTE   The word *party* is usually written without a capital letter when it follows a proper adjective: *Republican party, Democratic party, Federalist party.*

Business firms   Imperial Biscuit Company, Western Union, Academy Department Stores, Inc.
Institutions   United States Naval Academy, Tufts University, Radcliffe College, North High School, Bellevue Hospital

► NOTE   Do *not* capitalize words like *hotel, theater, college,* and *high school* unless they are part of a proper name.

Kenmore High School	a high school teacher
Waldorf-Astoria Hotel	a hotel in New York
Ritz Theater	to the theater

Government bodies Congress, Federal Bureau of Investigation, House of Representatives, State Department [Usage is divided on the capitalization of such words as *post office* and *courthouse.* You may write them either way unless the full name is given, when they must be capitalized: *Kearny Post Office, Victoria County Courthouse.*]

(4) Capitalize the names of historical events and periods, special events, and calendar items.

Historical events and periods French Revolution, Boston Tea Party, Middle Ages, World War II
Special events Interscholastic Debate Tournament, Gulf Coast Track and Field Championship, Parents' Day
Calendar items Saturday, December, Fourth of July, Mother's Day

► NOTE Do not capitalize the names of seasons unless personified: *summer, winter, spring, autumn,* or *fall,* but *"Here is Spring in her green dress."*

Names of seasons are, of course, capitalized when they are part of the names of special events: *Winter Carnival, Spring Festival.*

(5) Capitalize the names of nationalities, races, and religions.

Nationalities Canadians, an American, a Greek
Races Oriental, Caucasian
Religions Christianity, a Baptist, Mormons, Moslems, Buddhists

(6) Capitalize the brand names of business products.

EXAMPLES Tostitos, Frigidaire, Chevrolet

► NOTE Do not capitalize the noun that often follows a brand name: *Chevrolet truck.*

(7) Capitalize the names of ships, planets, monuments, awards, and any other particular places, things, or events.

Ships, Trains the *Mayflower,* the *Discovery,* the *Yankee Clipper,* the *Silver Meteor*

Aircraft, Spacecraft, Missiles F–18 *Hornet, Voyager 2, Titan II*

Planets, Stars Mars, Jupiter, the Milky Way, the Dog Star

► **NOTE** Planets, constellations, asteroids, stars, and groups of stars are capitalized; however, unless they are listed with other heavenly bodies, *sun, moon,* and *earth* are not capitalized.

Monuments, Memorials Washington Monument, Lincoln Memorial

Buildings Prudential Insurance Building, Rockefeller Center, Eiffel Tower

Awards Purple Heart, Distinguished Service Cross, Masquers' Dramatic Medal, Key Club Achievement Award

EXERCISE 6. Copy the following, using capitals wherever needed.

1. mars and saturn
2. on monday, march 20
3. a theater on west forty-third street
4. a hospital in albany, new york
5. carson park, near jefferson high school
6. laddie boy dog food
7. the sinking of the *lusitania*
8. world war I
9. the class play on thursday night
10. columbia university
11. an oriental rug
12. the union of soviet socialist republics
13. fuller brushes
14. on christmas eve
15. a presbyterian
16. new haven yacht club
17. ford motor company
18. toyota sedan
19. french and indian war
20. the united states supreme court

EXERCISE 7. Correctly use each of the following in a sentence of your own.

1. high school
2. High School
3. hotel
4. Hotel
5. building
6. Building
7. earth
8. Earth
9. south
10. South

19d. Do *not* capitalize the names of school subjects, except languages and course names followed by a number.

EXAMPLES   Next year I will study a foreign language and will take general science, history, and algebra.

At present I am taking English, Geography I, American History II, and home economics.

▶ **NOTE**   Do *not* capitalize the members of a class (*freshman, sophomore, junior, senior*) unless part of a proper noun: A *freshman* cannot attend the *Junior-Senior Banquet.*

REVIEW EXERCISE A. Copy the following sentences, using capitals wherever needed.

1. to begin with, ms. garcia mentioned the fact that mercury and venus are closer to earth than jupiter is.
2. all freshmen at jefferson high school know they will take at least three years of english and one year of mathematics.
3. while in the city of washington, we saw the ford theater, where lincoln was shot.
4. a methodist, a baptist, and a roman catholic conducted an interesting panel discussion.
5. since I plan to study medicine at northwestern university, I'm taking latin and biology I.

6. after I had gone to the grocery store at the corner of thirty-first street and stonewall avenue, I stopped at the twin oaks lumber company, which is two blocks south of cooper avenue.
7. vacationing in the west, we saw electric peak, which is on the northern boundary of yellowstone national park; we also saw devil's tower, which is in northeastern wyoming.
8. later we drove along riverside drive and saw the lincoln memorial, which is on the banks of the potomac river in potomac park.
9. in the spring, usually the first saturday after easter, the women's missionary society, a baptist organization, gives a picnic for our class.
10. leaving ecuador, in south america, on a banana boat named *bonanza,* they went through the panama canal and sailed through the caribbean sea to nassau in the bahama islands.

19e. Capitalize titles.

(1) Capitalize the title of a person when it comes before a name.

EXAMPLES   President Gaines   Mrs. Morrison
Principal Yates   Miss Chan
Dr. Hughes   Professor Jackson

(2) Capitalize a title used alone or following a person's name only if it refers to a high official or to someone to whom you wish to show special respect.

EXAMPLES   Can you name England's Prime Minister, the Prince of Wales, and the Queen of Sweden?

The General has written that he will be unable to attend.

I once saw the President jogging near the White House.

Andy Simmons, president of our science

club, announced that Marian had been elected secretary.

My brother Roger, a captain in the Marine Corps, is home on leave.

▶ **NOTE** When a title is used alone in direct address, it is usually capitalized.

EXAMPLES We are happy to see you, Doctor.
What is your decision, Superintendent?
Tell me, Coach, what are our chances?

(3) Capitalize words showing family relationship when used with a person's name but *not* when preceded by a possessive.

EXAMPLES Aunt Mabel, Cousin Enid, Uncle Stanley
my mother, your father, Clifford's sister

EXCEPTION When family-relationship words like *aunt* and *grandfather* are customarily thought of as part of a name, capitalize them even after a possessive noun or pronoun.

EXAMPLE My Uncle Stanley lives in Ohio.

▶ **NOTE** Words of family relationship may be capitalized or not when used in place of a person's name: I gave it to *Mother* or I gave it to *mother*.

(4) Capitalize the first and last words and all important words in titles of books, periodicals, poems, stories, movies, paintings, and other works of art.

Unimportant words in a title are *a, an, the,* and short prepositions (fewer than five letters) and coordinating conjunctions. Of course, if the last word in the title is a short preposition, it is capitalized.

The words *a, an,* and *the* written before a title are capitalized only when they are part of a title: the *Saturday Review, The Education of Henry Adams.*

Before the names of magazines and newspapers, *a, an,* and *the* are usually not capitalized in a composition: I was reading the *Denver Post.*

The Bible and the books of the Bible are always capitalized.

EXAMPLES   *I Know Why the Caged Bird Sings, The Sea Around Us, My Name Is Asher Lev* [books]

the *Ladies' Home Journal,* the *Riverton Gazette* [periodicals]

"The Charge of the Light Brigade" [poem]

"The Pit and the Pendulum" [story]

Star Wars, Gone with the Wind, The Black Stallion [movies]

Mona Lisa, Portrait in Gray and Black, The Thinker [works of art]

Treaty of Paris, Declaration of Independence, Bill of Rights [historical documents]

"Masterpiece Theater," "Good Morning America," "Nova," "Monday Night Football" [television programs]

"Missouri Waltz," "Love's Old Sweet Song," *The Marriage of Figaro,* "The Flight of the Bumblebee," Beethoven's *Ninth Symphony* [musical compositions]

(5) Capitalize words referring to the Deity.

EXAMPLE   God and His universe

► NOTE   The word *god* is not capitalized when it refers to the gods of ancient mythology: The Greek poet paid tribute to the god Zeus.

EXERCISE 8. Number on your paper 1–10. If the

capitalization in each of the following phrases and sentences is correct, write *C* (for *correct*) after the appropriate number on your paper. If the capitalization is incorrect, write the correct form.

1. superintendent adams
2. "Home On The Range"
3. the *Reader's Digest*
4. elected president of her class
5. the president of the United States
6. among the Roman gods
7. My Aunt Clare taught me to respect my parents.
8. my cousin's mother
9. N. Scott Momaday won the Pulitzer Prize
10. *the Mystery of Edwin Drood*

EXERCISE 9. Write two sentences of your own to illustrate each of the five rules for capitalizing titles. (You will have ten sentences in all.)

REVIEW EXERCISE B. Copy the following sentences, and use capitals wherever needed. In this exercise, apply all the rules you have learned in this chapter. Be prepared to give a reason for each capital that you use.

1. speaking to the seniors of lamar high school, mrs. carter praised *losing battles,* a well-known novel by eudora welty.
2. on the sunday before labor day, we drove as far as the murphy motel, a mile west of salem, virginia; the manager, mr. kelly, told us he was a member of the virginia tourist court association.
3. waiting for a city bus at the corner of twenty-first street and hemphill drive, we admired the westlake shirts in henson's window display.
4. mother and her sister, my aunt carlotta, told me about rockefeller center and about the shops on fifth avenue in new york city.

5. professor massey studied at the library of congress and the folger shakespeare library during july and august.
6. althea gibson's autobiography, *I always wanted to be somebody,* was published by harper & row.
7. I especially like the photographs — made by pan american world airways — of mount mckinley, in alaska.
8. in her junior year at sheridan high school, aunt selma studied latin, french, english, geometry, and art.
9. the reverend walker said that the greeks worshipped many gods, whereas it is our practice to worship only one god.
10. after the soldiers so bravely fought against the forces of general santa anna in 1836, the alamo became famous as the shrine of texas liberty, a symbol of american freedom, like the statue of liberty.

REVIEW EXERCISE C. Copy the following, using capitals wherever needed.

1. dr. deborah n. morgan
2. taking chemistry II
3. traffic on a main street
4. *the adventures of huckleberry finn*
5. merry christmas, mayor.
6. in history class
7. an assignment in english
8. a problem in mathematics
9. a park in the west
10. a mexican town
11. the washington monument
12. north of kansas city
13. on highway 80
14. the secretary of state
15. early christians and jews
16. the old testament in the bible
17. last thanksgiving
18. "song of the open road"
19. the boston tea party
20. the milky way and the north star

SUMMARY STYLE SHEET

Names of Persons

Augusta Savage	a sculptor
Mrs. Alfred E. Jones	a friend of the family
Mr. Stanley Fillmore	our family lawyer

Geographical Names

Mexico City	a city in Mexico
Shetland County	a county in North Carolina
the Canary Islands	some islands in the Atlantic
Great Smoky Mountains	climbing mountains
Pacific Ocean	across the ocean
Sixth Street	a narrow street
Abilene State Park	a state park
in the East, North, Midwest	traveling east, north, west

Organizations, Business Firms, Institutions, Government Bodies

Oakdale Garden Club	a club for gardeners
Safety First Moving Company	a company of movers
Rosedale High School	a small high school
Supreme Court	a traffic court
Department of Commerce	a department of government

Historical Events and Periods, Special Events, Calendar Items

War Between the States	a bitter war
Atomic Age	an age of progress
National Open Golf Tournament	a golf tournament
Labor Day	a national holiday
April, July, October, January	spring, summer, autumn, winter

Nationalities, Races, Religions

British	a nationality
Caucasian	a race

| Roman Catholic | a religion |
| God and His universe | the gods of ancient Rome and myths about them |

Brand Names

| Mercedes-Benz | a sports car |
| Zenith | a television |

Other Particular Places, Things, Events, Awards

Flying Cloud	a clipper ship
Metroliner	a streamlined train
Enterprise	a spacecraft
Polaris	a missile
North Star	a bright star
Earth, Mars, Jupiter, Saturn, Pluto	on the earth
Jefferson Memorial	a memorial to Jefferson
Washington Monument	a monument in Washington
Senior Class Picnic	a senior in high school
Congressional Medal of Honor	a medal for bravery

Specific Courses, Languages

Chemistry I	my chemistry class
Spanish	a foreign language
United States History II	the history book

Titles

Officer Wiley	a police officer
Hurry, Officer!	
the President of the United States	the president of the class
the Senator from West Virginia	a senator's duties
the King of Denmark	a king's subjects
Uncle Randolph	my favorite uncle
Harriett's Aunt Lucy	Harriet's aunt
A Wrinkle in Time	a novel
the New York Times	a daily newspaper
Holy Bible	a religious book

Chapter **20**

End Marks
and Commas

**Periods, Question Marks,
Exclamation Points, Commas**

In speaking, you use voice inflections and pauses to make your meaning clear. In writing, you use marks of punctuation such as end marks and commas as substitutes for these inflections and pauses.

Be sure to use proper marks of punctuation when you write or revise your compositions. If you learn the rules in this and in the following chapters and apply these rules, your compositions will be not only correct but also easier to understand.

END MARKS

End marks—periods, question marks, and exclamation points—indicate your purpose. For instance, if you intend to state a fact, you use a period to end your statement. (For a classification of sentences according to purpose, see Chapter 2, pages 75–76.)

20a. A statement is followed by a period.

Periods follow declarative sentences, sentences that

make statements. Notice in the second example directly below that a declarative sentence containing an indirect question is followed by a period.

EXAMPLES   Nancy Lopez won the tournament.
[declarative sentence]
Sarah asked what was the matter.

20b. A question is followed by a question mark.

Use a question mark after interrogative sentences.

EXAMPLES   What if an earthquake strikes?
How can a fish drown?
Was the bus on time?
Where is it? There?

A direct question may have the form or word order of a declarative sentence. Since it *is* a question, however, it is followed by a question mark.

EXAMPLES   A fish can drown?
The bus was on time?

Be sure to distinguish between a declarative sentence which contains an indirect question and an interrogative sentence, which asks a direct question.

INDIRECT QUESTION   He asked me **what kept her away.** [declarative]
DIRECT QUESTION   What kept her away? [interrogative]

20c. An exclamation is followed by an exclamation point.

EXAMPLES   Ouch!
Wow! What a game!
Look out!

Sometimes declarative and interrogative sentences show such strong feeling that they are more like exclamations than statements or questions. If so, the exclamation point should be used instead of the period or question mark.

EXAMPLES   I simply cannot solve this puzzle!
Can't you be quiet for a minute!

20d. An imperative sentence is followed by either a period or an exclamation point.

As with declarative and interrogative sentences, imperative sentences, particularly commands, may show strong feeling. In such cases, the exclamation point should be used. When an imperative sentence makes a request, it is generally followed by the period.

EXAMPLES   Close that door!
Please close that door.
Look at the clowns.

Sometimes, to be courteous, a writer will state a command or request in the form of a question. Because of the purpose, however, the sentence is really an imperative sentence and is therefore followed by a period or an exclamation point.

EXAMPLES   May I interrupt for a moment.
Will you stop that noise!

20e. An abbreviation is followed by a period.

EXAMPLES   A. E. Housman [Alfred Edward Housman]
Mr., Jr., Dr. [Mister, Junior, Doctor]
Calif., Mass. [California, Massachusetts]
B.C., A.D. [before Christ, *anno Domini*]
Ave., St., Rd. [Avenue, Street, Road]
lb., oz., in., ft. [pound or pounds, ounce or ounces, inch or inches, foot or feet]

If an abbreviation comes at the end of a statement, do not use an extra period as an end mark.

EXAMPLE Mrs. Valdez has never been to Brooklyn, N.Y.

BUT Have you ever been to Brooklyn, N.Y.**?**

Some frequently used abbreviations and abbreviation of government agencies and international organizations are correctly written without periods. Abbreviations in the metric system are often written without periods, especially in science books.

EXAMPLES TV, IQ, FM, UFO, ROTC, USAF, UN, rpm, km, cm, ml, kg

When in doubt about whether to use periods, consult your dictionary.

EXERCISE 1. Copy the following sentences, inserting periods, question marks, or exclamation points.

1. What a score
2. What is the score
3. I asked what the score was
4. Roman troops invaded Britain in 54 BC
5. By AD 800 Baghdad was already an important city
6. Dr Jonas E Salk developed the first effective polio vaccine
7. Why is absolute zero theoretically the lowest temperature possible
8. Please explain why absolute zero is theoretically the lowest temperature possible
9. Is there a complete absence of heat when the temperature is absolute zero
10. Yippee A color TV in our hotel room

EXERCISE 2. Correctly using periods, question marks, and exclamation points, write ten sentences as directed on the following page.

1. One sentence stating a fact
2. One sentence making a request
3. One exclamation
4. Two direct questions
5. Two declarative sentences containing indirect questions
6. One imperative sentence that shows strong feeling
7. One imperative sentence that does not show strong feeling
8. One courteous command in the form of a question

COMMAS

Like other marks of punctuation, commas are necessary for clear expression of ideas. As you read the following sentences aloud, notice how the placement of the comma affects the meaning of each sentence.

EXAMPLES   When your friends help, you stop working.

When your friends help you, stop working.

If you fail to use necessary commas, you may confuse your reader.

CONFUSING   My favorite cousins are Bonnie Gail Billy Joe Calvin Joan and Rana. [How many cousins?]

CLEAR   My favorite cousins are Bonnie Gail, Billy Joe, Calvin, Joan, and Rana.

The rules and exercises that follow will help you learn the correct use of commas.

20f. Use commas to separate items in a series.

Notice in the following examples that the number of commas in a series is only one less than the number of items in the series.

EXAMPLES   Students, teachers, parents, and visitors attended the picnic. [nouns]

The happy, carefree, enthusiastic picnickers thoroughly enjoyed the outing. [adjectives]

They swam, sunbathed, played games, ate, and chatted. [verbs]

They roamed over the hill, through the fields, down to the lake, and across the bridge. [prepositional phrases]

Suddenly a storm broke with a crashing of thunder, a flashing of lightning, and a downpouring of rain. [gerund phrases]

Those who had walked to the picnic, who had brought small children, who had no umbrellas or raincoats, or who had worn good clothes dashed to a nearby farmhouse. [subordinate clauses]

When the last two items in a series are joined by *and,* you may omit the comma before the *and* if the comma is not necessary to make the meaning clear.

CLEAR WITH COMMA OMITTED   Sugar, coffee and celery were on sale last Saturday.

NOT CLEAR WITH COMMA OMITTED   We elected our class officers: president, vice-president, secretary and treasurer. [How many officers were elected, three or four? Does one person serve as secretary and treasurer, or are two people needed for separate jobs?]

CLEAR WITH COMMA INCLUDED   We elected our class officers: president, vice-president, secretary, and treasurer.

Some writers prefer always to use the comma before the *and,* whether or not it is necessary for clarity. Follow your teacher's instructions on this point.

▶ **NOTE** Some words—such as *shoes and socks, rod and reel, needle and thread*—are used in pairs and may be set off as one item in a series: *For supper we had ham and eggs, lettuce and tomatoes, and ice cream and cake.*

(1) If all items in a series are joined by *and* or *or*, do not use commas to separate them.

EXAMPLES   I bought a tie and a shirt and a hat.
Hubert or Roy or Shirley can build the float.

(2) Independent clauses in a series are usually separated by semicolons. Short independent clauses, however, may be separated by commas.

EXAMPLES   The wind blew furiously through the trees; lightning flashed across the sky; thunder boomed and rolled; rain poured down.
The wind blew, lightning flashed, thunder boomed, rain poured down.

20g. Use a comma to separate two or more adjectives preceding a noun.

EXAMPLE   That is a rough, narrow, dangerous road.

When the last adjective in a series is thought of as part of the noun, the comma before the adjective is omitted.

EXAMPLES   I collect foreign postage stamps.
A vain, talkative disc jockey annoys me.

Pairs of words like *postage stamp, disc jockey, car key, movie star, stock market,* and *living room* are considered as single units—as though the two words were one word, a compound noun. In the previous sentences, *foreign* modifies the unit *postage stamp; vain* and *talkative* modify *disc jockey.*

A good test to determine whether the adjective and noun form a unit is to insert the word *and* between the adjectives. In the first sentence, *and* cannot be logically inserted: *foreign and postage stamps.* In the second sentence, *and* would be logical between the first two adjectives (*vain and talkative*) but not between the second and third (*talkative and disc*). If *and* fits sensibly between the adjectives, use a comma.

Another test is to change the order of the adjectives. *Talkative, vain disc jockey* would be correct, but not *postage foreign stamps* or *disc talkative jockey.* If the order of the adjectives cannot be reversed sensibly, no comma should be used.

EXERCISE 3. Number your paper 1–10. Copy each series below, inserting commas wherever needed.

EXAMPLE   1. Eva caught bass catfish and perch.
           1. *bass, catfish, and perch*
                  or
           1. *bass, catfish and perch*

1. George Washington Carver derived from the peanut such items as ink coffee beauty cream and pigments.
2. My little sister can read write add and multiply.
3. Sulfur is used for manufacturing matches plastics paper and insect sprays.
4. She lowered her long curled dark eyelashes.
5. It was an unusual attractive floor lamp.
6. Mosquitoes hummed crickets chirped mockingbirds sang and frogs croaked.
7. A wise monkey is supposed to hear no evil see no evil and speak no evil.
8. On the surface of the moon are round deep craters and steep rugged mountains.
9. Do you want French dressing mayonnaise or vinegar on your salad?

10. Robert Browning says that youth is good that middle age is better and that old age is best.

EXERCISE 4. Number your paper 1–10. Think of an appropriate series of words, phrases, or clauses for each blank below; then write each series, properly punctuated, after the corresponding number on your paper.

1. —— are among my classmates.
2. We noticed —— all along the highway.
3. The —— movie star attracted huge crowds on opening night.
4. Our teacher said that ——.
5. I want —— for my birthday.
6. The —— autumn leaves are beautiful indeed.
7. You can make high grades by ——.
8. A —— woman won the marathon.
9. Today symbols of success include ——.
10. A considerate person ——.

EXERCISE 5. Write ten sentences, each one containing a correctly punctuated series, as follows:

1. Two sentences with a series of nouns
2. Two sentences with a series of verbs
3. Three sentences with adjectives in a series
4. One sentence with a series of subordinate clauses
5. Two sentences with a series of phrases

20h. Use a comma before *and, but, or, nor, for,* and *yet* when they join independent clauses.

A comma goes before a coordinating conjunction when a completed thought is on *both sides* of the conjunction. Do not be misled by compound verbs, which often make a sentence look as though it contains two independent clauses. Compare the structures of the two sentences on the following page.

COMPOUND SENTENCE (two independent clauses)
Brian changed the oil, and Carla washed the car.

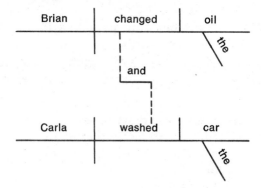

SIMPLE SENTENCE (one subject with a compound verb)
Brian changed the oil and washed the car.

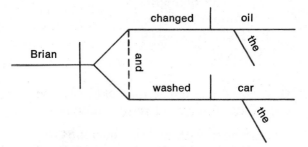

Study the following correctly punctuated compound sentences, noticing that independent clauses (with a subject *and* a verb) are on both sides of *and, but, or, nor, for,* and *yet.*

Into the garbage pail she flung the burned cake, **and** her mother helped her start another.

All of us were at the game, **but** Quincy was at the movies.

Either the gift was lost in the mail, **or** she has forgotten to thank me.

He did not come to my birthday party, **nor** did he even bother to answer the invitation.

Natalie Levy will no longer sell magazine sub-
scriptions to everyone in our neighborhood, **for**
she has finally saved enough money for college.
The critics hated the play, **yet** it ran for six
months.

► **NOTE** A comma always goes before *for* and *yet*
joining two independent clauses. The comma may be
omitted, however, before *and, but, or,* or *nor* when the
independent clauses are very short and when there is
no possibility of misunderstanding.

EXAMPLE The lights were off and the door was
         locked.

EXERCISE 6. Many sentences in this exercise contain clauses joined by the conjunctions *and, but, or,
nor, for, yet.* Do not copy the sentences. Number
your paper 1–20. Decide where the commas should
come, and write on your paper after the proper
number the word preceding each comma; add the
comma and the conjunction following it. If a sentence
is correct as it is written, write *C* (for *correct*) after the
proper number on your paper.

EXAMPLES 1. New York led in the first inning by
             two runs but Houston was leading in
             the third inning by a score of six to
             two.
          1. *runs, but*
          2. Ethan whispered something to Philip
             and quickly left the stadium.
          2. *C*

1. The long drought that had crippled the farmers
   and ranchers finally ended for day after day the
   rain came down in sheets.
2. The beds of streams that had long been dry came
   to life and the caked soil became green with grass.

3. For a time the ranchers rejoiced for their cattle began to grow fat.
4. There was plenty of water now for crops and livestock yet the rains did not stop.
5. Small streams turned into raging rivers and the rivers became large lakes greedily engulfing the countryside.
6. Frightened sheep huddled on the hilltops and the carcasses of many fat cows floated down the rivers.
7. The levees broke and water flooded the towns.
8. A levee broke in my hometown and torrents of water covered the city square.
9. Not only were places of business ruined as merchandise floated out broken doors and windows but several persons were drowned when their houses were washed away.
10. Soon the American Red Cross set up first-aid stations near the town and provided food and clothes for the homeless.
11. Neighboring cities began to chip in with their relief dollars and merchants pledged twenty percent of their sales receipts for the Flood Fund.
12. The state legislature passed an emergency appropriation bill to help the flood victims and the national government came forward with assistance for the disaster area.
13. At last the weather became more merciful and settled down to normal.
14. The bright sun and dry winds came forth to challenge the angry streams and rivers.
15. The clean-up job took tremendous courage and hard work yet stores soon opened for business.
16. Squads of rescue workers helped ranchers to clear away debris and farmers to replant crops.
17. Civic organizations did not fail to anticipate a possible typhoid epidemic nor did they forget to combat the hordes of mosquitoes infesting the once-flooded area.

18. There were some tragic consequences of the deluge but the flood had good psychological effects.
19. Both farmers and ranchers could now hope for good crops and green pastures for the first time in seven years.
20. People laughed as they gave credit to the new governor for breaking the drought or they moaned upon hearing someone mention the incoming "flood" of mail.

20i. Use a comma to set off nonessential clauses and nonessential participial phrases.

A nonessential (or nonrestrictive) clause or participial phrase adds information that is not necessary to the main idea in the sentence.

As you read the following sentences aloud, pause and lower your voice to indicate that each bold-faced clause or participial phrase is not essential to the basic meaning of the sentence.

NONESSENTIAL CLAUSES   Ella Riley, **who likes animals,** wants to be a veterinarian.

The National Bank and the Merchandise Mart, **which were firetraps,** were torn down.

I read about Sequoya, **whose invention of an alphabet aided other Cherokees.**

NONESSENTIAL PHRASES   Senator Stewart, **hoping for a compromise,** began a filibuster.

Alice's Adventures in Wonderland, **written by Lewis**

Carroll, has become a classic.

Each bold-faced clause or phrase above can be omitted because it is not essential to identify the word it modifies. For example, the first clause, *who likes animals,* does not identify Ella Riley; neither does the first phrase, *hoping for a compromise,* identify Senator Stewart. Each of them may be omitted without affecting the meaning of the main idea: *Ella Riley wants to be a veterinarian. Senator Stewart began a filibuster.*

However, when a clause or phrase is necessary to the meaning of a sentence, or when it tells *which one,* the clause or phrase is *essential* (or *restrictive*), and commas are *not* used.

Notice how the meaning of each sentence below changes when the essential clause or phrase is omitted.

ESSENTIAL CLAUSES Students **who pass the test** will have a day off.

All buildings **which were fire-traps** were torn down.

I'd like to throw every hat **that I buy on sale** into the garbage can.

► NOTE An adjective clause beginning with *that* is usually essential.

ESSENTIAL PHRASES Senators **hoping for a compromise** began a filibuster. [Not all senators; just the ones hoping for a compromise.]

A book **written by Lewis Carroll** has become a classic. [Not any book, but one by Lewis Carroll.]

EXERCISE 7. Seven of the following sentences contain nonessential clauses; copy and properly punctuate these sentences. Three sentences are correct as they are written; for these, write *C* (for *correct*) after the proper number on your paper.

1. Daisy Maude Snyder who is my second cousin will visit me next week.
2. We take the *Shreveport Times* which has especially good editorials.
3. Highways that have eight lanes are built for speed and safety.
4. You should know my father who likes to tinker with anything mechanical.
5. All people who travel often should learn how to pack properly.
6. Theodore Snead who has a short haircut seems friendly.
7. I attend Cottonwood High School which has an enrollment of 368.
8. All contestants who answer this difficult question will receive a prize.
9. The hognose snake which some people fear is not poisonous.
10. In "The Gift of the Magi" which is a very beautiful short story the two main characters who are deeply in love make sacrifices in order to buy gifts for each other.

EXERCISE 8. The following sentences contain participial phrases, some essential and some nonessential. If a sentence is correctly punctuated, write *C* (for *correct*) after the proper number on your paper. Copy the other sentences, punctuating them correctly.

1. All students, planning to attend the Student Council meeting, will be excused from class at two o'clock.

2. Louis Pasteur working hard in his laboratory took time out to treat people for rabies.
3. The fifty-story Civic Center, located on the corner of Main Street and Daniels Place, dominates the skyline of the city.
4. Every child, enrolling in school for the first time, must be vaccinated for polio.
5. Their youngest daughter loved by everyone is not at all spoiled.
6. Anyone seeing a suspicious character should notify the police.
7. A long-distance telephone call received on one's birthday is always welcome.
8. My left big toe, badly bruised by the blow, began to swell.
9. Mrs. Danby trying not to smile offered to help us put on the stage make-up.
10. The "House of Tiles" built in Mexico City during the sixteenth century is now famous as the "House of Sanborn."

EXERCISE 9. Number your paper 1–25. Many of the following sentences contain nonessential clauses or participial phrases and therefore require commas. The other sentences, however, require no commas and are correct. If a sentence is correctly punctuated, write *C* (for *correct*) after the proper number on your paper. If a sentence is incorrect, copy on your paper the word that should be followed by a comma and place the comma after it.

EXAMPLES   1. A novelist whose latest book is a best seller gave a talk at our school.
   1. *C*
   2. Betty Furness acclaimed as a consumer advocate gave a talk at our school.
   2. *Furness, advocate,*

1. Ellen Barnes who is captain of the basketball team is an honor student.
2. Players who are late for practice will be sent back to the locker room.
3. We are looking for high school students who are interested in a Saturday job.
4. My friends knowing how much I like crazy sweat shirts gave me several of them for my birthday last month.
5. Some members of the audience thinking the show was over left their seats.
6. The new library which is in the center of the campus is easy to get to.
7. Anyone looking for some good detective novels should consult Barry who collects them.
8. Last night's rock concert reviewed in this morning's newspaper was the best I ever heard.
9. A telephone directory that lists phone numbers by address rather than by name is used by telephone operators.
10. All crew members who were washed overboard swam to safety.
11. Panoramic views of the Grand Canyon can be seen from the South Rim which is open all year or from the North Rim which is closed in winter because of snow.
12. Barbara Jordan had been a member of the Congressional committee which examined the evidence against the President.
13. *Robert's Rules of Order* which is still a popular guide to parliamentary procedure was first published in 1876.
14. A few students having completed their assignment early were excused from class.
15. Psychokinesis which is otherwise known as PK is the influencing or moving of physical objects by willpower.
16. People who like people are usually well liked.
17. Some road signs and markings that may not seem

important to the daytime driver may be very important to the nighttime driver.

18. World population which is increasing faster than the food supply is a major concern.
19. Anyone believing in good-luck charms is superstitious.
20. The luxurious dirigible *Hindenburg* which was built in Germany in the 1930's exploded as it arrived in New Jersey killing thirty-six people.
21. Hurricanes that start in the eastern Caribbean usually follow a northwestward course toward the east coast of the United States.
22. Mr. Werler who is curator of the zoo says that television fascinates gorillas.
23. Windsurfing is a sport that requires balance, strength, and a knowledge of sailing.
24. Golf sometimes called the most frustrating sport is, nevertheless, surprisingly popular.
25. Since its publication about thirty years ago, *The Lord of the Flies* written by William Golding who was then an English schoolmaster has been read by millions of students.

20j. Use a comma after certain introductory elements.

(1) Use a comma after words such as *well, yes, no, why,* **etc., when they begin a sentence.**

EXAMPLES   **No,** I have not answered her letter.
                   Why, surely you haven't forgotten already!

(2) Use a comma after an introductory participial phrase.

EXAMPLES   **Pausing for a moment in the doorway,** the teacher smiled at the class.
                   Frightened by the noise, the pigeons flew from the roof.

(3) Use a comma after a succession of introductory prepositional phrases.

EXAMPLES   **Near the gate at the end of the lane,** I watched the wild stallion race out of the corral.

In paintings by modern artists, colors are often very bright.

A short introductory prepositional phrase does not require a comma unless the comma is necessary to make the meaning clear.

EXAMPLES   **In this state** we have a sales tax.

In this state, taxes are comparatively high. [The comma is necessary to avoid reading *state taxes.*]

(4) Use a comma after an introductory adverb clause.

EXAMPLES   **After Pablo Casals had played the cello recital,** the crowd gave him a standing ovation.

Until we found the source of the fire, everyone was searching nervously through closets and wastebaskets.

EXERCISE 10. The sentences in this exercise contain introductory elements. Decide where commas should be used. Copy on your paper the word preceding each comma, and place a comma after it. Number your answers to accord with the number of the sentences. If a sentence does not require a comma, write *C* (for *correct*) after the appropriate number.

EXAMPLES   1. Known in China four thousand years ago falconry is an ancient sport.
      1. *ago,*
      2. Like a hawk a falcon has a crooked beak.
      2. *C*

1. Although falconry is no longer a popular sport a small number of people still enjoy it.
2. Having sharp claws and hooked beaks falcons are by nature good hunters.
3. Instead of using guns or other modern weapons some hunters capture and train falcons.
4. After learning to fly a female falcon is taken from the nest and tamed.
5. Until the falcon becomes accustomed to living around humans it wears a hood.
6. Covering the eyes and most of the head this leather hood helps the hunter control the falcon.
7. When the falcon has the hood on the hunter carries the bird into a field.
8. In the field is the desired game.
9. When the hunter sees a crow or a pigeon and takes the hood off the falcon quickly attacks the game.
10. Besides a hood other equipment is used in falconry.
11. Attached to the falcon's legs jesses are short leather strips with bells.
12. If a falcon should bring down game out of sight these jesses help the hunter find the spot.
13. During the hunt falconers usually wear heavy leather gloves.
14. When they are training a young falcon to hunt they also use lures.
15. Used properly lures teach falcons to attack certain birds.
16. Containing pieces of meat and the wings of a bird the lures quickly attract falcons.
17. Within seconds a hungry falcon usually pounces upon the lure.
18. Yes falcons become trained in a short time.
19. Since a falcon's speed and accuracy are tremendously effective guns are unnecessary.
20. In the field with a trained falcon hunters often use a dog to flush and retrieve the game.

20k. Use commas to set off elements that interrupt the sentence.

Two commas are used around an interrupting element — one before and one after.

EXAMPLES   He, of course, won't be there.
Linda, by the way, sends her regards.

Sometimes an "interrupter" comes at the beginning or at the end of a sentence. In these cases, only one comma is needed.

EXAMPLES   Nevertheless, I think we should go.
Therefore, the answer is wrong.
I don't know why, however.

(1) Appositives and appositive phrases are usually set off by commas.

EXAMPLES   Everyone, even his enemies, respects him.
An extremely talented dancer, Chita Rivera received an ovation.
I often play tennis, a lively game.

Sometimes an appositive is so closely related to the word preceding it that it should not be set off by commas. Such an appositive usually has no modifiers; that is, there is no appositive phrase.

EXAMPLES

my sister **Elizabeth**   we **girls**
the poet **Countee Cullen**   us **students**

EXERCISE 11. Number your paper 1–20, and copy (1) the word preceding the appositive (if any), (2) the appositive or appositive phrase, and (3) the word following the appositive or appositive phrase (if any). Correctly punctuate the appositives; not all of the sentences will need commas.

EXAMPLE   1. My sister Helen discussed air pollution
with Mr. Mays the owner of a garage
and with Hiram a car dealer.
1. *sister Helen discussed*
Mays, the owner of a garage, and
Hiram, a car dealer

1. "Ecology" an obscure word not many years ago
has become a popular term today.
2. The word's origin is *oikos* the Greek word for
"house."
3. Ecology is the study of an enormous house the
world of all living things.
4. Ecologists study the bond of a living organism
to its environment the place in which it lives.
5. Humans one kind of living organism affect their
environment in both beneficial and harmful ways.
6. My sister Helen is worried about the environment.
7. She and many of her friends attended Earth Day
a festival devoted to ecology.
8. An amateur photographer my sister prepared a
slide show on soil erosion in Grant Park.
9. One of many displays at the Earth Day festival
my sister's presentation attracted wide attention.
10. The mayor a member of the audience soon promised to appoint a committee to correct the problem.
11. The folk-singing group The Travelers gave a short
concert during the festival.
12. Among other displays was a set of graphs illustrated charts that showed the condition of air,
land, water, and animals in the United States.
13. Air quality a major concern of environmentalists
showed improvement.
14. The charts showed that automobile emissions the
greatest cause of air pollution have decreased.
15. Land development in the past fifty years has reduced the total acreage of coastal wetlands the
home for millions of animals.
16. Insecticides are being produced in greater quantity
than ever before an alarming statistic.

17. More than two hundred varieties of wildlife creatures in all parts of the United States are threatened by extinction.
18. Mr. Lewis the compiler of all these statistics talked with me briefly about the environment.
19. The ecologist Professor Blake joined us.
20. We all agreed that the community the place where we live and work is the environment we can help the most.

EXERCISE 12. Use each of the following items as an appositive in a sentence of your own. Be sure to use commas if necessary.

1. Linda
2. a nuisance
3. my neighbor
4. a good teacher
5. Bernice and Maggie
6. the life of the party
7. a girl sitting near me
8. the candidate to elect
9. a book for young people
10. the man that you should meet

(2) Words used in direct address are set off by commas.

EXAMPLES That program, **Florence,** has been changed.
Miss Nelson, may I leave class early?
Please answer the doorbell, **Elsie.**

EXERCISE 13. Copy and correctly punctuate the following sentences.

1. Do you remember Patty what Romeo's last name is?
2. Mr. President I move that we adjourn.
3. Please let me go to the movies Dad.
4. Yes, Mrs. O'Neill, I shall be glad to help you.
5. What is the answer to the riddle my wise friend?

(3) Parenthetical expressions are set off by commas.

Parenthetical expressions are side remarks adding information or relating ideas. When writing, you should ordinarily use commas to set off parenthetical matter.[1]

The following expressions are commonly used parenthetically: *consequently, however, moreover, nevertheless, therefore, after all, as a matter of fact, at any rate, for example, for instance, in fact, in my opinion, in the first place, of course, on the contrary, on the other hand, generally speaking, I believe (guess, know, hope, think, suppose), to tell the truth.*

EXAMPLES   He did not**,** **however,** keep his promise.
After all, I couldn't have known.
People prefer dark clothes in winter**,** **generally speaking.**

Some expressions may be used both parenthetically and not parenthetically. Compare the following pairs of correctly punctuated sentences; read the sentences aloud.

PARENTHETICAL
However, did you do that?
To tell the truth, he tries.
Mom**,** **I think,** will approve.

NOT PARENTHETICAL
However did you do that?
He tries **to tell the truth.**
I think Mom will approve.

▶ **NOTE** A contrasting expression introduced by *not* is parenthetical and must be set off by commas.

EXAMPLE   It is the spirit of the giver**,** **not the gift,** that counts.

---

[1] For the use of parentheses and dashes to set off parenthetical matter, see pages 557–58.

EXERCISE 14. Number your paper 1–10. Copy the following: (1) the word (if any) preceding each interrupter, (2) the interrupter itself, and (3) the word (if any) following it. Supply the necessary punctuation.

EXAMPLE   1. However your plan in my opinion might work.
          1. *However, your*
             plan, in my opinion, might

1. To tell the truth I have never seen a flying fish.
2. I do know however that some birds can swim.
3. No person of course can see everything in existence; everybody has to depend upon the word of authorities.
4. My father is I believe an authority about fish that can fly.
5. In fact he has seen a Catalina fish fly as high as twenty feet in the air.
6. Having large fins not wings this fish skips along the top of the water and then suddenly leaps skyward.
7. This fish generally speaking is about a foot or a foot-and-a-half long.
8. There are other animals that fly without wings however.
9. Some squirrels for example can glide from one tree to another; they fly about at night not in the daytime.
10. On the contrary I am sticking to the truth; these squirrels use their tails as rudders and their skin as built-in parachutes.

EXERCISE 15. Use each of the following items as a parenthetical or an interrupting element in a correctly punctuated sentence of your own.

EXAMPLE   1. our new drama coach
          1. *The main speaker was Mrs. Wilkins, our new drama coach.*

1. the umpire	6. Michigan
2. for instance	7. my friend
3. well	8. no
4. as a matter of fact	9. I think
5. therefore	10. on the contrary

20l. Use a comma in certain conventional situations.

(1) Use a comma to separate items in dates and addresses.

EXAMPLES   My family moved to Knoxville, Tennessee, on Monday, May 4, 1981.

On May 4, 1981, I changed my address to 645 Commerce Street, Knoxville, Tennessee 37902.

Notice that no comma divides *May 4* (month and day) or *645 Commerce Street* (house number and street name) because each is considered one item. The zip code is not separated from the name of the state by a comma: Racine, Wisconsin 53401.

(2) Use a comma after the salutation of a friendly letter and after the closing of any letter.

EXAMPLES   Dear Aunt Edith,   Sincerely yours,
            My dear Cynthia,   Yours very truly,

(3) Use a comma after a name followed by *Jr., Sr., M.D.,* etc.

EXAMPLES

Allen Davis, Jr.   Ens. Charles Jay, U.S.N.
Carol Ferrara, M.D.   Martin Luther King, Jr.

EXERCISE 16. Copy and correctly punctuate any of the following sentences that need commas. If a sentence is correct as it stands, write *C* (for *correct*) after the proper number on your paper.

1. On Sunday September 13 1981 I visited friends who live at 234 Oakdale Drive Birmingham Alabama 35223.
2. Were you in St. Louis during May or June in 1979?
3. This letter is addressed to Mr. M. K. Cranberry Jr. 4608 Cherry Blossom Lane Appleton Wisconsin 54911.
4. The Constitution of the United States was signed on September 17 1787 eleven years after the adoption of the Declaration of Independence on July 4 1776.
5. The letter ended, "Yours truly Joanna H. Fleming M.D."

20m. Do not use unnecessary commas.

Too much punctuation is just as confusing as not enough punctuation. This is especially true of commas.

CONFUSING   Cora, hurt my feelings, and then, apologetically, said, she was cross, because of an aching, wisdom tooth.

CLEAR   Cora hurt my feelings and then apologetically said she was cross because of an aching wisdom tooth.

Have a *reason* (either a definite rule or a matter of meaning) for every comma or other mark of punctuation that you use. When there is no rule requiring punctuation and when the meaning of the sentence is clear without it, do not insert any punctuation mark.

SUMMARY OF USES OF THE COMMA

20f.   Use commas to separate items in a series.
   (1) If all items in a series are joined by <u>and</u> or <u>or</u>, do not use commas to separate them.
   (2) Independent clauses in a series are usually separated by semicolons. Short independent clauses are sometimes separated by commas.

20g. Use a comma to separate two or more adjectives preceding a noun.

20h. Use a comma before <u>and, but, or, nor, for,</u> and <u>yet</u> when they join independent clauses.

20i. Use a comma to set off nonessential clauses and nonessential participial phrases.

20j. Use a comma after certain introductory elements.
(1) Use a comma after words such as <u>well, yes, no, why,</u> etc., when they begin a sentence.
(2) Use a comma after an introductory participial phrase.
(3) Use a comma after a succession of introductory prepositional phrases.
(4) Use a comma after an introductory adverb clause.

20k. Use commas to set off sentence interrupters.
(1) Appositives and appositive phrases are usually set off by commas.
(2) Words used in direct address are set off by commas.
(3) Parenthetical expressions are set off by commas.

20l. Use a comma in certain conventional situations.
(1) Use a comma to separate items in dates and addresses.
(2) Use a comma after the salutation of a friendly letter and after the closing of any letter.
(3) Use a comma after a name followed by <u>Jr., Sr., Ph.D.,</u> etc.

20m. Do not use unnecessary commas.

REVIEW EXERCISE A. Select from the following sentences all words which should be followed by a comma. List these words on your paper, placing a comma after each one. Number your answers according to sentences.

EXAMPLE 1. No Madge I did not talk to Mr. Huey the manager of the bookstore.
1. *No, Madge, Huey,*

1. Looking for the lost car keys we searched under

the car in the house on the porch and among the weeds.
2. Well I guess that Stan likes raisins not prunes.
3. Among the synonyms are *humor wit sarcasm* and *irony.*
4. After we had placed an advertisement in the evening paper we found the owner of the puppy.
5. This letter which is dated July 14 1981 is addressed to Mr. Nicholas Walters Sr. R.F.D. 3 Culver City California 90230.
6. I sold three tickets Caleb sold four Jill sold ten and Myrna sold twelve.
7. About ten o'clock on the morning of Saturday February 23 we entered the city limits of Hartford Connecticut.
8. Phyllis you know of course that Archie hates teas receptions and formal dinners.
9. We left Moravia which is a resort town in New York and drove on to Owasco Lake which is near Syracuse.
10. Wanting to be noticed the baby jumped up and down in her crib and shook the railings and whimpered piteously.

REVIEW EXERCISE B. Using the Summary of Uses of the Comma (pages 509–10), write sentences of your own to illustrate the rules, as follows:

1. Three sentences illustrating rule 20f (illustrating both subrules)
2. Two sentences illustrating rule 20g
3. Three sentences illustrating rule 20h
4. Two sentences illustrating rule 20i, one containing a nonessential clause and the other containing a nonessential participial phrase
5. Four sentences illustrating rule 20j (one sentence for each subrule)
6. Three sentences illustrating rule 20k (one sentence for each subrule)

7. Three sentences illustrating rule 20l (one sentence for each subrule)

Write before each sentence the number of the rule it illustrates.

REVIEW EXERCISE C. Copy the following sentences, inserting end marks and commas where necessary.

1. When Mr. Charles Chatham Jr. my geography teacher visited West Lafayette Indiana he toured the campus of Purdue University
2. Reading that book I learned that Ottawa not Montreal is the capital of Canada
3. Vera will you write to me at 237 Candona Drive Boulder Colorado   80303
4. That plant is I think a kind of cactus that is commonly called a prickly pear
5. Yes Acadia National Park which is on the Atlantic coast is only a short drive from Bangor Maine
6. In the second sentence on page 23 notice the lively vivid action verbs the introductory prepositional phrases and the two subordinate clauses
7. Libby leave the room shut the door and be quiet
8. Mrs. Hood assured me that she didn't mind my breaking the cup but I am going to see what I can do about finding her another one
9. Look out Jack That big angry Doberman pinscher almost bit you
10. Oh didn't you know that on March 5 1981 my family left Reidsville North Carolina and moved to Highland Park a suburb of Chicago Illinois

Chapter 21

Semicolons and Colons

SEMICOLONS

A semicolon looks like what it is: part period and part comma. It says to the reader, "Stop here a little longer than you stop for a comma but not so long as you stop for a period."

Semicolons are used primarily in compound sentences. Since most writers depend largely upon simple and complex sentences to express their ideas, the semicolon is not often used. As you study the rules in this chapter regarding semicolons, follow the lead of professional writers; use the semicolon correctly and effectively but sparingly.

21a. Use a semicolon between independent clauses in a sentence if they are not joined by *and, but, or, nor, for, yet.*

Notice in the following pairs of sentences that the semicolon takes the place of the comma and the conjunction joining the independent clauses.

EXAMPLES   First I washed the dishes and swept the kitchen**, and** then I went to the grocery store.

First I washed the dishes and swept the kitchen; then I went to the grocery store.

Lillian enjoys reading detective stories, **but** her brother prefers science fiction.

Lillian enjoys reading detective stories; her brother prefers science fiction.

Similarly, a semicolon can take the place of a period between two complete thoughts (independent clauses) that are closely related.

EXAMPLE   Wilma listened attentively to the joke. Her half smile gradually changed into an ear-to-ear grin. [two simple sentences]

Wilma listened attentively to the joke; her half smile gradually changed into an ear-to-ear grin.

As you study the sentences below (taken from the works of professional writers), observe that each semicolon has a complete thought on *both* sides of it and that the two independent clauses are not joined by *and, but, or, nor, for,* or *yet.* Since the thoughts of the independent clauses in each sentence are very closely related, a semicolon is better than a period.

EXAMPLES   The clock was stopped with two seconds remaining in the game; the fans were tensed and sitting on the edge of their seats.

In one city a fur dealer was giving merchandise certificates as prizes in a radio contest; in another a sewing machine distributor gave credit certificates to winners (and losers) of contest promotions.

A huge tie results; to break the tie entrants must pay another, often higher, fee and solve more difficult puzzles.

EXERCISE 1. Read the following sentences and decide where semicolons may be used. Copy on your paper the following: (1) the word before each semicolon, (2) the semicolon itself, and (3) the word that comes after it. In some instances, you may prefer to use a period. If so, write the word before the period, the period itself, and the word (capitalized) following the period.

EXAMPLES 1. Great earthquakes usually begin gently only one or two slight shocks move the earth.
1. *gently; only*
2. In minutes, however, violent shocks begin to tear the earth apart there are few natural forces as destructive as earthquakes.
2. *apart. There*

1. Pressure often builds along faults, or cracks, in the earth's crust the weight of this pressure causes earthquakes.
2. The San Andreas fault extends the entire length of California earthquakes often occur along this fault.
3. During an earthquake, huge chunks of the earth's crust begin to move the San Francisco earthquake of 1906 was one of the most destructive earthquakes recorded in history.
4. Energy released during an earthquake is tremendous it can equal the explosive force of 180 metric tons of TNT.
5. Scientists study the force of earthquakes they measure this force on a scale of numbers called the Richter scale.
6. An earthquake measuring less than 5 on the Richter scale is not serious more than 1000 earthquakes measuring 2 or less occur daily.

7. In 1906 one of the most powerful earthquakes in history occurred in the Pacific Ocean near Ecuador its Richter measurement was 8.9.
8. Tidal waves are a dangerous result of earthquakes geologists use the Japanese word *tsunami* for these destructive waves.
9. Predicting when earthquakes will take place is not yet possible predicting where they take place is somewhat more certain.
10. Earthquakes seem to strike in a regular time sequence in California', for example, a major earthquake usually occurs every 50–100 years.

21b. Use a semicolon between independent clauses joined by such words as *for example, for instance, that is, besides, accordingly, moreover, nevertheless, furthermore, otherwise, therefore, however, consequently, instead, hence.*

These words are often transitional expressions linking independent clauses. When used in this way, they are preceded by a semicolon, not a comma. They are, however, usually followed by a comma.

INCORRECT Janet did as she was told, however, she grumbled ungraciously.

CORRECT Janet did as she was told**; however,** she grumbled ungraciously.

INCORRECT I did not go to the movies, instead, I worked on my project.

CORRECT I did not go to the movies**; instead,** I worked on my project.

Caution: When the expressions listed in the rule appear *within* a clause, not as a transition *between* clauses, they are usually punctuated as interrupters (set off by commas). The two clauses are still separated by a semicolon: *We are going ahead with plans for the picnic; everyone,* **however,** *will not attend.*

21c. A semicolon (rather than a comma) may be needed to separate the independent clauses of a compound sentence if there are commas within the clauses.

This use of the semicolon often helps to make a sentence clear.

CONFUSING   She will invite Irene, Beth, and Eunice, and Graham will ask Leslie and Val.

CLEAR   She will invite Irene, Beth, and Eunice; and Graham will ask Leslie and Val.

CONFUSING   After the fire, Lionel stood in the middle of the lot, now covered with charred debris, and, not tired and discouraged, he began to scrape through the ashes as if he were trying to uncover something of value.

CLEAR   After the fire, Lionel stood in the middle of the lot, now covered with charred debris; and, not tired and discouraged, he began to scrape through the ashes as if he were trying to uncover something of value.

EXERCISE 2. Follow the directions for Exercise 1 as you show where to use semicolons in the following sentences.

1. Traveling through the countryside last summer, we decided not to follow any schedule, for example, we took side roads if we found any that looked interesting.
2. One quiet road, many miles from the main highway, wound narrowly through the hills, at times it seemed to disappear altogether under the bushes growing along it.
3. As Dad steered the car carefully, the conversation that Mother and I had been having died out,

impressed by the stillness of our surroundings, we became strangely silent.

4. There were no houses nearby, but, seeing the remains of a few old rock chimneys, we knew that someone must have lived here many years ago.
5. After traveling about ten miles along this road, we noticed a small, square area fenced around with iron rails, inside the fence, all overgrown with grass and wildflowers, were old graves.
6. A few of the graves, dating back to the early 1800's, had crude stone monuments with traces of names that the elements had not yet scratched out, but others, having only two stones marking the site, had no names.
7. As we looked at the little cemetery, we wondered what stories these people could have told about early settlements, about the hardships of pioneers, or about the terrors of the wilderness, perhaps they had lived through wars, epidemics, and blizzards.
8. A famine, according to our history books, had struck this lonely area, therefore, we assumed that some of these people had died during a time of severe food shortage.
9. We continued to stand there for some time, each of us deep in thought, finally we walked slowly back to the car.
10. On the way back to the highway, we continued to be very quiet, furthermore, each of us seemed relieved when we finally drove into a bright, lively town.

21d. Use a semicolon between items in a series if the items contain commas.

EXAMPLES   The examinations will be held on Wednesday, June 26; Thursday, June 27; and Friday, June 28.

There were two representatives from
Pittsburgh, Pennsylvania; four from
Buffalo, New York; and three from
Cleveland, Ohio.

EXERCISE 3. All of the following sentences contain
items in a series. If the items should be separated by
semicolons, copy the sentence, adding the needed
semicolons. If a sentence needs no semicolons, write
C (for *correct*) after the corresponding sentence number on your paper.

1. In the sixteenth century there were centers of
   learning in France, Italy, and Germany.
2. Western culture was enriched by centers of learning in Paris, France, Rome, Italy, and Mainz,
   Germany.
3. The Aztecs in Mexico had constructed dams to
   irrigate cornfields, had made mirrors and razors
   out of stone, and had devised effective war weapons.
4. The Incas in Peru planted crops, such as corn,
   domesticated animals, such as the llama, and developed crafts, such as weaving.
5. Mrs. Healy discussed the importance of people
   like Gutenberg, inventor of movable type, Galileo,
   inventor of the first complete astronomical telescope, and Newton, discoverer of the laws of
   gravity.

REVIEW EXERCISE A. Read the following sentences
and decide where semicolons should be used. Do not
copy the sentences. Instead, write on your paper the
sentence number; after it, copy the word preceding
the needed semicolon, write the semicolon, and then
copy the word following the semicolon. If a sentence
needs no semicolon, write *C* (for *correct*) after the
appropriate number on your paper. (*Caution:* Re-

member that when a semicolon and quotation marks come together, the semicolon goes *outside* the quotation marks.)

EXAMPLE 1. Unfortunately, many superstitions are not dead they survive in our conversations and sometimes influence our behavior.
1. *dead; they*

1. Our conversations frequently mirror old superstitions we "interpret" ordinary events strangely and illogically almost every day.
2. Generally speaking, these interpretations are virtual synonyms for events for example, *my burning ears* means "somebody is talking about me."
3. Other examples include *Friday 13,* "an unlucky day," *open umbrellas indoors,* "bad luck," and *gifts of knives,* "cut or severed friendships."
4. Many customs have their roots in superstitions for instance, when you cover your yawns with your hand, you are not only being polite but also paying respect to superstition.
5. People used to think that horned devils sat in trees or on high buildings and passed the time of day by shooting poisoned arrows into the hearts of unfortunate persons walking below.
6. Since the air seemed to be infested with hordes of devils, many people believed that these imps would seize every opportunity to enter the body and corrupt the person's soul.
7. To yawn was to create the opening that the devils were seeking people who covered the yawn with their left hand could stop the invisible invaders from entering their bodies.
8. When someone sneezes in our presence, we often say "Bless you" very quickly this custom is also based upon ancient lore about devils.
9. Although a sneeze is no more than a noisy spray

of moisture, it seems to call for a special and an immediate blessing.

10. Long ago it was believed that demons were continually trying to put spells on people however, when a person sneezed, the curse was shaken off and thus the person deserved a blessing.

11. My friend Gloria often brags about something like never missing a word on a spelling test nevertheless, she then suddenly freezes with fearful anticipation of failure and adds quickly, "Knock on wood."

12. In order to be sure that she will make a perfect score on the next test, Gloria finds a piece of wood and knocks on it vigorously I do the same thing.

13. This custom hinges on an old idea that demons lived in trees and that they would occasionally help by bringing a person good luck.

14. As Shakespeare's Iago tells us in plain language, devils have to *appear* good at times otherwise they could not lure people away from goodness.

15. These tree-dwelling devils were not fools they knew how to use "good luck" for their own evil purposes.

16. They also expected people to perform certain rituals one of these was a kind of thanksgiving ceremony.

17. A person enjoying a run of good fortune was obligated to show gratitude by knocking on a tree the devils living inside the tree not only heard the thank-you knocks but also extended the period of good luck.

18. After people had moved from the country to large cities, no tree was convenient therefore, any piece of wood became an appropriate substitute.

19. The superstitious fear of walking under a ladder is more sensible a ladder could fall and injure you.

20. I imagine that our grandchildren will go on knock-

ing on wood, blessing a person who sneezes, and covering their yawning mouths but these customs are rather foolish actions for people living in an enlightened age.

REVIEW EXERCISE B. Using semicolons and commas where appropriate, write two sentences of your own (ten sentences in all) to illustrate each of the following patterns of punctuation.

1. PATTERN An independent clause; an independent clause.

   EXAMPLE Glenda made a basket just before the final buzzer of the game; we won by a score of 78 to 76.

2. PATTERN Independent clause, coordinating conjunction, independent clause.

   EXAMPLE Glenda made a basket just before the final buzzer of the game, and we won by a score of 78 to 76.

3. PATTERN Introductory element, independent clause; independent clause.

   EXAMPLE Just before the final buzzer of the game, Glenda made a basket; we won by 78 to 76.

4. PATTERN Independent clause; transitional word, independent clause.

   EXAMPLE The score was tied for the last three minutes of the quarter; however, Glenda made a basket just before the buzzer.

5. PATTERN Independent clause with commas; coordinating conjunction, independent clause.

   EXAMPLE Oscar is bringing ham sandwiches, potato salad, and deviled eggs; and I am baking cookies and making lemonade.

COLONS

Generally, the colon is used to call the reader's attention to what comes next.

21e. Use a colon to mean "note what follows."

(1) Use a colon before a list of items, especially after expressions like *as follows* and *the following*.

EXAMPLES The equipment that you will need is **as follows:** a light jacket, heavy boots, a rifle, several cartons of shells, and a sharp hunting knife.

That summer we traveled through **the following** states: Arkansas, Kentucky, Tennessee, North Carolina, and Virginia.

The principal's desk was cluttered with all kinds of papers: unopened letters, absence reports, telephone messages, and unpaid bills.

I have three hobbies: sewing, cooking, and painting.

In the last two examples, the items before which the colon is used are appositives. If a word has a list of appositives following it, the colon is used to make the sentence clear.

▶ **NOTE** When a list follows immediately after a verb or preposition, do not use a colon.

INCORRECT My three hobbies are: sewing, cooking, and painting.

CORRECT My three hobbies are sewing, cooking, and painting.

INCORRECT That summer we traveled through: Arkansas, Kentucky, Tennessee, North Carolina, and Virginia.

CORRECT That summer we traveled through Arkansas, Kentucky, Tennessee, North Carolina, and Virginia.

(2) Use a colon before a long, formal statement or quotation.

EXAMPLE Horace Mann had this to say about dealing with those who disagree with you: "Do not think of knocking out another person's brains because he differs in opinion from you. It would be as rational to knock yourself on the head because you differ from yourself ten years ago."

21f. Use a colon in certain conventional situations.

(1) Use a colon between the hour and the minute when you write the time.

EXAMPLES 7:30 A.M.   3:15 P.M.

(2) Use a colon between chapter and verse in referring to passages from the Bible.

EXAMPLES Genesis 27:28   Ruth 1:16

(3) Use a colon after the salutation of a business letter.

EXAMPLES Dear Sir: Dear Mrs. Roberts:
Gentlemen: Dear Professor Stanton:

EXERCISE 4. Number your paper 1–10. Decide where colons should appear in the following sentences. If a sentence does not need a colon, write *C* (for *correct*) after its number. If a colon is required after a word, copy the word and write a colon after it. If a colon is needed to divide numbers, copy the numbers and add the needed colon.

EXAMPLE 1. At 9 01 A.M., Miss Blake wrote on the board this line from Kipling's speech "Words are the most powerful drug used by humanity."

1. *9:01*
   speech:

1. Reading Proverbs 3 13, the minister supported his main point with the following quotation "Happy is the man that findeth wisdom, and the man that getteth understanding."
2. In science class we have to learn the meaning of the following words *amphibian, chromosome, neutron, oxidation,* and *vertebrate.*
3. Ms. Thompson invited Meredith, Natalie, and Samantha.
4. The farmer explained the uses of the various parts of the plow landslide, clevis, jointer, and beam.
5. Experts can identify a fingerprint by observing the nature of the following arches, whorls, loops, and composites.
6. At 10 45 the teacher closed the lesson by reading Exodus 20 12 "Honor thy father and thy mother, that thy days may be long upon the land which the Lord thy God giveth thee."
7. At 8 20 the agent told us that the 6 10 train would not arrive before 9 15 P.M.
8. Along the midway were several kinds of rides a roller coaster, a whip, two merry-go-rounds, and a Ferris wheel.
9. There were sandwiches, cold drinks, and candy on our television tables.
10. At an airport I like to listen to the many noises engines roaring during takeoff, loudspeakers announcing departures and arrivals, passengers dropping quarters into insurance machines, telephones ringing at every counter, and skycaps greeting incoming passengers.

REVIEW EXERCISE C. Using commas, semicolons, and colons, copy and correctly punctuate the following sentences.

1. A scrawny friendly stray dog wandered out onto the field and the umpire stopped the game temporarily.
2. Because they do not conduct electricity the following materials can be used as insulators rubber glass cloth and plastics.
3. There are only three primary colors in painting red blue and yellow.
4. Other colors are mixtures of primary colors for instance purple is a mixture of red and blue.
5. The ten-gallon hat of the cowboy was used as a protection from the sun a dipper for water and a pan for washing his hands and leather chaps protected him from thorny bushes.
6. The minister began the sermon by quoting these verses from the Bible Matthew 23 37 and John 16 27.
7. In his speech to the Sock and Buskin our dramatic club Mr. Henry Stevenson Jr. quoted from several Shakespearean plays *Romeo and Juliet The Tempest Macbeth* and *Julius Caesar.*
8. Harriet Tubman was a leader of the Underground Railway she rescued more than 300 slaves.
9. From 1851 to 1864 the United States had four presidents Millard Fillmore a Whig from New York Franklin Pierce a Democrat from New Hampshire James Buchanan a Democrat from Pennsylvania and Abraham Lincoln a Republican from Illinois.
10. From 1 15 to 1 50 P.M. I was so sleepy that my mind wandered completely tuning out the lesson I rested my head on my right palm and let my eyelids sag to half-mast.

Chapter **22**

Italics and Quotation Marks

ITALICS

Italics are printed letters that lean to the right, *like this.* When you write or type, you indicate italics by underlining the words you want italicized. If your composition were to be printed, the typesetter would set the underlined words in italics. For example, if you type

> Daniel Defoe wrote <u>Robinson Crusoe</u>.

the sentence would be printed like this:

> Daniel Defoe wrote *Robinson Crusoe.*

22a. Use underlining (italics) for titles of books, plays, movies, periodicals, works of art, long musical compositions, ships, and so on.

EXAMPLES <u>Great Expectations</u> [a novel]
<u>Romeo and Juliet</u> [a book-length play]
<u>St. Louis Post-Dispatch</u> [a newspaper]
<u>Reader's Digest</u> [a magazine]
<u>Madame Butterfly</u> [an opera]
<u>Haydn's Surprise Symphony</u> [a long musical composition]
<u>Venus de Milo</u> [a statue]
<u>Flying Cloud</u> [a ship]
<u>Spirit of St. Louis</u> [a plane]

The words *a, an,* and *the,* written before a title, are italicized only when they are part of the title. Before the names of newspapers and magazines, however, they are not italicized, even if they are capitalized on the front page of the newspaper or on the cover of the magazine.

EXAMPLES I am reading Pearl Buck's *The Good Earth.*

In the museum we saw Edmonia Lewis' statue *The Death of Cleopatra.*

My parents subscribe to the *Wall Street Journal* and the *Atlantic.*

Magazine articles, chapter headings, and titles of short poems, short stories, and short musical compositions, when referred to in a composition, should be placed in quotation marks, not italicized. See page 536 for this rule.

22b. Use underlining (italics) for words, letters, and figures referred to as such and for foreign words.

EXAMPLES The word <u>existence</u> has three <u>e</u>'s.

Because my <u>7</u> looked like a <u>9</u>, I lost five points on the math test.

Is your knowledge of foreign expressions limited to <u>faux pas</u> and <u>bon voyage</u>?

EXERCISE 1. List on your paper all words and word groups in the following sentences which should be italicized; underline each. Before each word or word group, write the number of the sentence in which it appears.

1. Christopher Columbus and his crew sailed on three ships: the Santa María, the Niña, and the Pinta.

2. Some foreign phrases, like faux pas and qui vive, can often express ideas more clearly than English words can.

3. I just got back my book report on Charlotte Brontë's novel, Jane Eyre.

4. The margin is full of red ink saying that William Penn's last name has two n's, that the word bland does not adequately describe the author's style, and that I should always cross my t's and dot my i's.

5. After her long lecture Mrs. Reece asked me to comment on Bach's beautiful Brandenburg Concertos and Mozart's opera The Marriage of Figaro.

6. Since I was reading an article in the March issue of the Reader's Digest, I did not hear her lecture on musicians.

7. I had, however, just learned two new words, reverberate and venerable; therefore, I solemnly answered, "Their venerable melodies have reverberated through the centuries."

8. Upon hearing my learned comment, Consuela, who had been reading the Chicago Tribune, dropped her newspaper in amazement.

9. Stunned by my reply, Mrs. Reece began to stammer something about Michelangelo and the beauties of his works of art, such as his Kneeling Angel and his David.

10. After the bell had rung, she told us to become familiar with such books as Lives of the Composers and Art Through the Ages.

QUOTATION MARKS

When writing a composition, you may wish to report the exact words of a conversation, to copy a passage from a book, or to refer to the title of a song or magazine article. You should, therefore, learn how to use quotation marks correctly.

22c. Use quotation marks to enclose a direct quotation—a person's exact words.

EXAMPLES   Gwen said, "The last feature has started."

"Let's go for a swim," suggested Sue.

Do not use quotation marks for *indirect* quotations.

DIRECT QUOTATION   Jacqueline said, "I am going to Trenton on Saturday." [the speaker's exact words]

INDIRECT QUOTATION   Jacqueline said that she was going to Trenton on Saturday. [not the speaker's exact words]

Caution: Be sure to place quotation marks at both the beginning and the end of a direct quotation.

INCORRECT   She whispered, "Please don't tell the coach.

CORRECT   She whispered, "Please don't tell the coach."

22d. A direct quotation begins with a capital letter.

EXAMPLE   According to Albert Einstein, "Imagination is more important than knowledge."

Miss March said, "All of Unit 7 and the first chapter in Unit 8." [Although this is not a sentence, it is apparently Miss March's complete remark.]

EXCEPTION   If the direct quotation is obviously a fragment, it may begin with a small letter.

EXAMPLE   Are our ideals, as Scott says, mere "statues of snow" that soon melt? [The quotation is obviously only a part of Scott's remark.]

22e. When a quoted sentence is divided into two parts by an interrupting expression such as *he said* or *Mother*

asked, **the second part begins with a small letter.**

EXAMPLES "I believe," she said, "that Franny is telling only part of the truth."
"I'm sorry," I replied, "but I can't possibly go to your party."

If the second part of the quotation is a new sentence, a period (not a comma) follows the interrupting expression; and the second part begins with a capital letter.

EXAMPLE "A folk ballad usually has many stanzas," explained the teacher. "Each stanza has four lines."

Caution: Remember that an interrupting expression is not a part of a quotation and therefore should not be inside quotation marks.

INCORRECT "Please don't tell me, I said, how the movie ends."
CORRECT "Please don't tell me," I said, "how the movie ends." [Two pairs of quotation marks are needed for the broken quotation.]

When two or more sentences are quoted together, use only one set of quotation marks.

INCORRECT Joseph said, "In the spring I like to work in the yard." "I hate to wash windows and mop floors."
CORRECT Joseph said, "In the spring I like to work in the yard. I hate to wash windows and mop floors."

22f. A direct quotation is set off from the rest of the sentence by commas or by a question mark or exclamation point.

EXAMPLES Margaret announced, "I really must be

going," then stayed for another hour.
The crowd yelled, "Hold that line!" as
the visiting team threatened to score.

22g. **Other marks of punctuation when used with quotation marks are placed according to the following rules:**

(1) Commas and periods are always placed inside closing quotation marks.

EXAMPLES   "I haven't seen the movie," remarked
Jeannette, "but I understand it's excellent."

As I feared, Mr. Watkins announced,
"Close your books for a pop quiz."

He read aloud "Ode to the End of
Summer," a poem by Phyllis McGinley.

(2) Colons and semicolons are always placed outside closing quotation marks.

EXAMPLES   Socrates once said, "As for me, all I
know is that I know nothing"; I wonder
why everyone thinks he was such a wise
man.

The following actresses were cited for
"best performance in a leading role":
Sally Fields, Bette Midler, Marsha Ma-
son, Jane Fonda, and Jill Clayburgh.

(3) Question marks and exclamation points are placed inside the closing quotation marks if the quotation is a question or an exclamation; otherwise, they are placed outside.

EXAMPLES   "Is the pain unbearable?" the dentist
asked as I squirmed and grunted.

"Not yet!" I exclaimed. "But it
could be after you start drilling!"

Is his motto still, "Stay in the game and pitch"?

How I laughed when he called me a "budding genius"!

EXERCISE 2. Number your paper 1–10. If a sentence below contains an indirect quotation, change it to a direct quotation, correctly punctuated. If a sentence contains a direct quotation, change it to an indirect quotation, correctly punctuated.

EXAMPLES
1. Mr. Anderson said that he would pay me well.
1. *Mr. Anderson said, "I will pay you well."*
2. "What's the trouble?" she asked.
2. *She asked what the trouble was.*

1. My brother said that he would miss the rehearsal.
2. "What is your excuse?" asked the principal.
3. "Sam," asked Claudette, "why aren't you playing football this year?"
4. The thief finally admitted stealing the furs.
5. I told my parents that I needed fifteen dollars.
6. "How is it possible?" asked my teacher.
7. Sharon yelled that the score was tied again.
8. Granddad says two rings around the moon mean rain within two days.
9. Ellen said she thought she could win.
10. "That," Ms. Turner confessed facetiously, "is the first mistake I've made in ten years."

22h. When you write dialogue (two or more persons having a conversation), begin a new paragraph every time the speaker changes.

EXAMPLE
"You have just come down?" said Mr. Drummle, edging me a little away with his shoulder.

"Yes," said I, edging *him* a little away with *my* shoulder.

"Beastly place," said Drummle. "Your part of the country, I think?"

"Yes," I assented. "I am told it's very like your Shropshire."

"Not in the least like it," said Drummle.[1]

EXERCISE 3. Write a page of dialogue that will show your ability to use quotation marks correctly. Perhaps you would like to retell a favorite anecdote in your own words and let the dialogue of the speakers carry the action forward. Better still, report the exact words of a real conversation that will entertain your classmates. You can get ideas for interesting dialogues if you will remember definite situations—for example, arguing about a play on the baseball diamond, apologizing for a social blunder, trying to make an escape from a determined salesperson, or mistaking a stranger for an old friend.

22i. When a quoted passage consists of more than one paragraph, put quotation marks at the beginning of each paragraph and at the end of the entire passage. Do not put quotation marks after any paragraph but the last.

EXAMPLE   "At nine o'clock this morning," said the newscaster, "someone entered the Mill Bank by the back entrance, broke through two thick steel doors guarding the bank's vault, and escaped with sixteen bars of gold.

"No arrests have been made, but state police are confident the case will be solved within a few days."

---

[1] From *Great Expectations* by Charles Dickens.

► **NOTE** A long passage (not dialogue) from a book or other printed source is often set off from the rest of the text so as to be easily recognizable as quoted matter. The entire passage may be indented; in printed matter it may be set in small type; and in typewritten copy it may be single-spaced instead of double-spaced. When a passage taken from another source has been identified by one of these devices, no quotation marks are necessary.

22j. **Use single quotation marks to enclose a quotation within a quotation.**

EXAMPLES　　Exasperated, Joanne reported, "Then she remarked innocently, 'I was only trying to help.' "

Mrs. Hull answered, "The phrase 'Injustice anywhere is a threat to justice everywhere' is from one of Martin Luther King's letters."

"Why did you shout 'ouch!'?" I asked.

"Did you hear me ask 'Where's the money?' " she inquired.

EXERCISE 4. Write eight sentences of your own, as instructed below. Check over your sentences to make sure quotation marks are correctly placed.

1. Two quoted sentences, each interrupted by an expression such as *she said*
2. One sentence containing a quoted fragment or part of a sentence
3. Two sentences, each containing an indirect quotation
4. One sentence containing a quoted question
5. One interrogatory sentence ending with a quotation that is not a question
6. One sentence containing a quotation within a quotation

REVIEW EXERCISE A. Rewrite each of the following short passages, inserting quotation marks where necessary. Remember to begin a new paragraph each time the speaker changes.

1

Race-car driver Janet Guthrie, said Chet, reading from his notes, is a trained physicist who has spent many years working in an important job for an aircraft corporation.

2

I interviewed the next great movie star for my entertainment column, said George. Who is it? I asked. My sister, George replied. She is taking acting lessons at night and on weekends. With such dedication, I replied, you may be right about her future as a movie star.

3

Who shot that ball? Coach Larsen wanted to know. I did, came the reply from the small, frail-looking player. Good shot, the coach informed him, but always remember to follow your shot to the basket. I tried but I was screened, said the player.

4

The *Brownsville Beacon,* the editorial began, will never support a candidate who tells the taxpayers, Vote for me and I will cut taxes.

The reason is simple. Taxes, just like everything else in this inflationary society, must increase. Any candidate who thinks otherwise is either a fool or a liar.

22k. Use quotation marks to enclose titles of articles, short stories, poems, songs, chapters, and other parts of books or periodicals.

EXAMPLES   Review Chapter 24, "Your Inborn Behavior."

The title of the article, "What Every Adolescent Should Know," caught my attention.

I have not read "More Alarms by Night," though I have read many other short stories by James Thurber.

Do you really think that "Medusa" is Louise Bogan's best poem?

Mom was singing "On Top of Old Smoky."

Remember that long, book-length poems and long musical compositions are italicized, not quoted. (See page 527.)

EXAMPLES   She assigned Chapter VIII, "The Food You Need," beginning on page 125 of *Your Health and Safety.*

Have you read the short story called "The Ambitious Guest" in Nathaniel Hawthorne's book *Twice-Told Tales?*

"Figures – Freckles – Foresight," an article in *Good Housekeeping,* is interesting.

You may wonder how to decide whether to italicize a title or to put it in quotation marks. In general, you italicize the title of a book-length poem, one long enough to be published in a separate volume. Such poems are usually divided into titled or numbered sections – cantos, parts, books, etc. Examples are Milton's *Paradise Lost,* Tennyson's *Idylls of the King,* and Lowell's *Life Studies.*

Long musical compositions, the titles of which should be italicized, include operas, symphonies, ballets, oratorios, and concertos.

EXAMPLES In my report on Samuel Taylor Coleridge, I plan to quote from *Lyrical Ballads,* from Part VII of *The Rime of the Ancient Mariner,* and from the second stanza of "Kubla Khan."

Mr. Hurley sang "The Last Rose of Summer" from the opera *Martha.*

My favorite song is "Tonight" from *West Side Story.*

REVIEW EXERCISE B. Copy the following, correctly using italics and quotation marks.

1. At the party Ellen sang Tomorrow from the Broadway musical Annie.
2. The Latin term summa cum laude appeared on the valedictorian's diploma.
3. I have never seen the opera Carmen, said Joanna, but I have often heard the Toreador Song.
4. After reading Welty's story A Worn Path, I wrote an essay entitled Phoenix Rises; but at one point I omitted the o in the word Phoenix.
5. My favorite story by Arthur Conan Doyle is The Adventure of the Dying Detective, which is included in the anthology The Complete Sherlock Holmes.
6. The San Francisco Chronicle, in reviewing the ballet Swan Lake, stated, Last night's performance was the highlight of the season.
7. Have you ever seen the play Waiting for Godot? asked Marian. If not, you should certainly see the production by the senior class next Friday in the school auditorium.
8. Mr. Meyers announced, Since you students did so well in today's discussion of Shakespeare's Henry V, I will assign no homework. Needless to say, this news delighted me.
9. Oh, look! exclaimed Jean as we looked through

the old magazines. This 1963 issue of Life has an article entitled Loch Ness Secret Solved.
10. Miss Charles asked, What did the Nurse mean when she exclaimed, Ah, welladay!?

REVIEW EXERCISE C. This exercise covers all marks of punctuation that you have studied so far. Copy and correctly punctuate the following sentences.

1. In 1831 a man named Michael Faraday my history teacher began experimented with a magnet and a copper disk
2. Oh I read about Faraday in the book You and Science Helen said
3. Faraday's important discovery continued Mr McCall is described in yesterday's assignment
4. I then remembered the chapter entitled Science Is Applied to Industry and Agriculture
5. Was it Michael Faraday who wrote I have at last succeeded in magnetizing and electrifying a ray of light
6. When I said that Faraday turned magnetism into electricity Mr McCall exclaimed Good for you Stephanie
7. I thought sir Ada interrupted that Faraday invented the radio
8. The radio in 1831 Helen asked in astonishment
9. No the radio came in the early twentieth century Mr McCall went on Ada Faraday's linking of light and electricity did lead to the radio Faraday however invented the dynamo not the radio
10. Although it's true that a dynamo is a universally recognized symbol of power Mr McCall concluded I quote exact words from your textbook The dynamo does not itself create power but changes the power of heat or falling water into electricity

Chapter 23

Apostrophes

Possessive Case, Contractions, Plurals

Apostrophes are necessary for expressing meaning clearly in written English. For instance, the difference in meaning between *shell* and *she'll* or *shed* and *she'd* is indicated in writing by the apostrophe (and, of course, the context in which the word appears).

If you sometimes forget to use apostrophes, or if you use them incorrectly, the rules in this chapter will prove helpful.

The possessive case of a noun or pronoun shows ownership or relationship. The nouns and pronouns printed in bold-faced type below are in the possessive case.

OWNERSHIP   I borrowed **Martha's** mitt.

Julia's canoe needs painting.

Have you seen **my** scrapbook?

RELATIONSHIP   **Lydia's** cousin is in town.

Cleaning up was a **day's** work.

I appreciate **your** sending the gift.

23a. To form the possessive case of a singular noun, add an apostrophe and an *s*.

EXAMPLES

Mom's car

Nell's baseball

the governor's speech

Mrs. Jones's briefcase

a hard day's work

this morning's paper

a quarter's worth

a dollar's worth

EXCEPTION A proper name ending in *s* may add only an apostrophe if the name consists of two or more syllables or if the addition of *'s* would make the name awkward to pronounce. Example: *Ulysses'* (not *Ulysses's*) *plan; Mrs. Rawlings'* (not *Rawlings's*) *car.*

EXERCISE 1. Form the possessive case of each of the following singular words. After each possessive word, write an appropriate noun.

EXAMPLE 1. Carol

1. *Carol's idea*

1. dime
2. week
3. child
4. cousin

5. friend
6. Ruth
7. Aunt Margaret
8. fox

9. Eloise
10. Mr. Ross

23b. To form the possessive case of a plural noun ending in *s*, add only the apostrophe.

EXAMPLES both girls' behavior

two weeks' vacation

five dollars' worth

families' efforts

knives' edges

heroes' stories

Most plural nouns do end in *s*. Some nouns, however, form their plurals somewhat irregularly. (See page 657.) To form the possessive case of a plural noun that does not end in *s*, add an apostrophe and an *s*.

EXAMPLES **women's** gloves **teeth's** cavities

EXERCISE 2. Write the possessive case of each of these plural words.

1. mice
2. magazines
3. people
4. galaxies
5. deer
6. quarters
7. novels
8. dictionaries
9. geese
10. children

Caution: Do not use an apostrophe to form the *plural* of a noun. Remember that the apostrophe shows ownership or relationship; it is nearly always followed by a noun.

INCORRECT Two girls' forgot their coats.

CORRECT Two girls forgot their coats. [simple plural]

CORRECT Two **girls'** coats are hanging in the hall. [The apostrophe shows that the coats belong to the two girls.]

EXERCISE 3. Revise the following phrases by using the possessive case.

EXAMPLE 1. the meetings of the athletes
    1. *the athletes' meetings*

1. a lunch for sergeants
2. absences of students
3. the shoes for women
4. salaries of teachers
5. textbook for sophomores
6. duty of the voters
7. food for invalids
8. the work of actors
9. uniforms for nurses
10. spirit of the players

SUMMARY

The following examples illustrate rules 23a and 23b:

Singular	Singular Possessive	Plural	Plural Possessive
friend	friend's home	friends	friends' homes
month	month's work	months	two months' work

dollar	dollar's worth	dollars	three dollars' worth
enemy	enemy's attack	enemies	enemies' attack
box	box's lid	boxes	boxes' lids
thief	thief's loot	thieves	thieves' loot
woman	woman's purse	women	women's purses
sheep	sheep's wool	sheep	sheep's wool
ox	ox's yoke	oxen	oxen's yoke

23c. Possessive personal pronouns do not require an apostrophe.

Possessive personal pronouns are

my, mine	our, ours
your, yours	their, theirs
his, her, hers, its	

Caution: The possessive form of *who* is *whose,* not *who's* (meaning "who is"). Similarly, do not write *it's* (meaning "it is") for *its,* or *they're* (meaning "they are") for *their.*

My, your, her, its, our, and *their* are used before a noun. *Mine, yours, hers, ours,* and *theirs,* on the other hand, are never used before a noun; they are used as subjects, complements, or objects in sentences. *His* may be used in either way.

EXAMPLES   That is **my** book. That book is **mine.**
Her answer was correct. **Hers** was the correct answer.
Sandra has **your** hat. Sandra has a hat of **yours.**
Janet has **our** tickets; Sally has **theirs.**
Here is **his** report. Here is a report of **his.**

23d. Indefinite pronouns in the possessive case require an apostrophe and *s*.

EXAMPLES   everyone's ideas   neither's fault
somebody's pencil   another's answer

EXERCISE 4. Number 1–10 on your paper. Choose the correct word in parentheses, and write it after the corresponding number.

1. The mistake is probably (ours, our's).
2. (Who's, Whose) dog is that?
3. (Yours, Your's) is more appropriate than mine.
4. Were (anyone's, anyones') boots left in the locker room yesterday?
5. That old car of (their's, theirs) has two flat tires.
6. The team was proud of (its, it's) good sportsmanship.
7. (Everybodys, Everybody's, Everybodys') suggestions will be considered.
8. Ms. Parker, (who's, whose) mother is a senator, takes part in all the campaigns.
9. (Eithers, Either's, Eithers') costume may win the prize.
10. (Ones, One's, Ones') emotions should not take the place of careful judgment.

REVIEW EXERCISE A. Using the following words, make four columns on your paper. Head the columns *Singular, Singular Possessive, Plural,* and *Plural Possessive,* and write those forms of each word. Add a suitable noun to follow each word in the possessive case. If you do not know how to spell the plural form of any of these words, use your dictionary.

1. cousin   6. woman
2. lady   7. jockey
3. salmon   8. penny
4. doctor   9. umpire
5. guard   10. her

REVIEW EXERCISE B. Some of the words in each of the following sentences are incorrect. After the number of each sentence, write correctly the incorrect words in the sentence.

EXAMPLE   1. Marie's mother is one of the judge's in
the Art Museums' contest.
1. *judges, Museum's*

1. Mrs. Macmillan, my best friends mother, is a
member of NOW, the National Organization for
Women.
2. Who's turn is it to read aloud Elinor Wylie's
poem "Velvet Shoes"?
3. Jill's mother bought twenty dollar's worth of
camera equipment.
4. The firefighters' actions held the damage in yes-
terdays' fire to a minimum.
5. Everybodys' suggestions seem better than our's.
6. The childrens' report cards were signed by all
their teachers'.
7. In six month's time, those student's behavior has
greatly improved.
8. Mrs. Smiths' banquet honored her employees'
wives and husbands.
9. One of Hercules' labors was to capture Diomedes'
mares.
10. My oldest sisters' twin daughters say that the
new reading room is a favorite meeting place of
their's.

**23e. In compound words, names of organizations and
business firms, and words showing joint possession,
only the last word is possessive in form.**

Compound words	school **board's** decision
	nobody **else's** business
	mother-in-**law's** house
	secretary-**treasurer's** report
Organizations	American Medical **Association's** endorsement
Business firms	Wizard Freight **Company's** moving vans
Joint possession	Bess and **Marie's** room

parents and **teachers'** aims
Rodgers and **Hart's** musical *Pal
Joey*

EXCEPTION   When one of the words showing joint possession is a pronoun, both words must be made possessive in form: **Marie's and my room** [not *Marie and my room*].

► NOTE   Use the *of* phrase to avoid awkward possessive forms.

AWKWARD   the manager of the Greenville Appliance Center's daughter

BETTER   the daughter of the manager of the Greenville Appliance Center

AWKWARD   the Society for the Prevention of Cruelty to Animals' advertisement

BETTER   the advertisement of the Society for the Prevention of Cruelty to Animals

23f. When two or more persons possess something individually, each of their names is possessive in form.

EXAMPLES   **Mrs. Wheeler's** and **Mrs. Stuart's** children [the children of two different mothers]
Edith's and **Gwen's** shoes [individual, not joint, possession]

EXERCISE 5. Revise the following phrases by using the possessive case.

EXAMPLE   1. The boat owned by Sarah and Evan
1. *Sarah and Evan's boat*

1. the secret of Alison and Mary
2. the policy of Procter and Gamble
3. the feet of Alice and June
4. letters written by the editor in chief
5. the secrets of everybody else

6. the cooking of his brother-in-law
7. the party given by Acme Life Insurance Company
8. the car belonging to Mr. Montgomery and the one owned by Mrs. Osborn
9. the equipment shared by Leslie and me
10. the employees of the Kurtz Novelty Corporation

REVIEW EXERCISE C. Copy and correctly punctuate the following phrases. If a phrase does not need an apostrophe, write *C* (for *correct*) after its number on your paper.

1. Vickys car keys
2. the keys to the car
3. a womans career
4. the firefighters dance
5. an hours drive
6. forty cents worth
7. worth forty cents
8. letters from friends
9. several friends advice
10. Sandy and Ellens bicycle
11. a months salary
12. last weeks score
13. six weeks vacation
14. Jessicas and Beryls posters
15. Randolph Companys sale
16. the men at work
17. childrens wisdom
18. from the mouths of babes
19. in two years time
20. suggestions of theirs

REVIEW EXERCISE D. From the following sentences, list in order on your paper all words requiring apostrophes, and insert the apostrophes. After each word, write the thing possessed or related. Number your list by sentences.

1. One Saturday afternoon, coming out of Millers Shoe Store on my way to Hardin and Crawfords Cafe, I saw two little girls selling the next mornings paper. 2. One girls name was Mona, and the others name was Clara.
3. "Read tomorrows news tonight!" yelled Mona. 4. "Read all about Colorados blizzard, the

Mayors operation, the high schools champion-ship swimmers, and the Charity Funds progress!" 5. All the while, Clara was silently watching the suns disappearance behind dark clouds overhead; she made no effort to catch a customers attention. 6. Monas yelling, however, was not getting much better results than Claras silence; neither girl had sold one cents worth of the Cloverville Publishing Companys newspapers. 7. In fact, everyone rushed past the two girls newsstand as though neither girl was there.

8. Angry because of her partners attitude, Mona scolded, "Clara, are you going back to Mrs. Longs office without selling any of the companys papers? 9. Ones job out here is to advertise each days news and to sell at least three dollars worth in an hours time." 10. Claras face was still turned upward; she seemed indifferent to her friends anxiety.

11. Walking back and forth, Mona waved her papers under cab drivers noses and pedestrians chins. 12. Trying to get the peoples interest, she yelled, "Read about your citys crime wave! Robbery at Rich and Thompsons stationery store! Arson in Baileys hardware store! 13. Buy your childrens favorite comics — Brenda Starrs adven-tures, Supermans victories, Dennis the Menaces crazy doings, Lucys wise words!" 14. The girls words sold only thirty cents worth of news; no one cared about "tomorrows news tonight."

15. In a few minutes time it began to rain, and Monas hopes for good sales completely van-ished. 16. But Claras hopes were high! 17. Dash-ing forward, she had in an instant every passerbys full attention. 18. "Step right this way, folks!" she barked. "Umbrellas for sale! Buy yourselves fifteen cents worth of umbrella. 19. These eight sections of Sundays paper can cover your heads!" 20. In ten minutes time Mona and Claras news-

stand had sold all its papers, and two very wet little girls were happily racing toward Mrs. Longs office.

23g. Use an apostrophe to show where letters or numbers have been omitted in a contraction.

A contraction is a shortened form of a word or figure (*can't* for *cannot*, *'81* for *1981*) or of a group of words (*she'll* for *she will*, *let's* for *let us*, *o'clock* for *of the clock*). Contractions are used chiefly in conversation and in informal writing. The apostrophes in contractions indicate where letters have been left out.

EXAMPLES   She is not here.   She isn't here.
               You are right.   You're right.
               Marian is late.   Marian's late.
               She has gone home.   She's gone home.
               I had forgotten.   I'd forgotten.

Ordinarily, the word *not* is shortened to *n't* and added to a verb without any change in the spelling of the verb:

is not	isn't	were not	weren't
are not	aren't	has not	hasn't
does not	doesn't	have not	haven't
do not	don't	had not	hadn't
did not	didn't	would not	wouldn't
was not	wasn't	should not	shouldn't

EXCEPTIONS   will not   won't
                 cannot   can't

Remember: do not confuse contractions with possessive pronouns. Study the following lists.

CONTRACTIONS	POSSESSIVE PRONOUNS
Who's playing? [*Who is*]	**Whose** play is it?
It's growing. [*It is*]	Watch **its** growth.
You're the boss. [*You are*]	**Your** boss telephoned.

There's a fish. [*There is*]   That fish is **theirs.**
They're white cats. [*They*   **Their** cats are white.
   are]

EXERCISE 6. Write ten sentences of your own, using correctly each of the words listed below.

1. it's   6. there
2. you're   7. whose
3. their   8. its
4. who's   9. they're
5. your   10. theirs

EXERCISE 7. Number 1–10 on your paper. If a sentence below has a contraction without an apostrophe, copy the contraction and add a correctly placed apostrophe. If a sentence is correct as it stands, write *C* after the number.

1. Well be there on time.
2. Well, be there on time.
3. Didnt you know that?
4. "Schools out!" she yelled.
5. Schools were notified.
6. She lets us win.
7. Lets win this game.
8. Its four oclock.
9. Whos calling, please?
10. The gold rush was in 49.

EXERCISE 8. Number 1–10 on your paper. Choose the correct word in parentheses, and write it after the corresponding number.

1. (*It's, Its*) is a contraction of *it is* or *it has.*
2. (It's, Its) been lost for months.
3. (*Who's, Whose*) is a contraction of *who is* or *who has.*
4. (Who's, Whose) that beautiful girl?

5. (Who's, Whose) bracelet is this?
6. (Your, You're) my best friend.
7. (There, Their, They're) not very happy.
8. Our speaker is Dr. Morgan, (whose, who's) just returned from France.
9. (Theirs, There's) no time like the present.
10. I think that (theirs, there's) is the best exhibit.

23h. Use the apostrophe and *s* to form the plural of letters, numbers, signs, and of words referred to as words.

EXAMPLES   The word *grammar* has two *r*'s, two *a*'s, and two *m*'s.
Grades on this test ran from the low 70's to the upper 90's.
Circling the *&*'s in my composition, the teacher said to spell out all *and*'s.

EXERCISE 9. Number 1–10 on your paper. Correctly form the plural of each of the following italicized items:

1. learning her *ABC*
2. cross your *t*
3. no *if* about it
4. *+* and *−*
5. *p* and *q*
6. writing *Z*
7. to pronounce the *r*
8. the early *1980*
9. no *6* or *7* in the answer
10. his *oh* and *ah*

REVIEW EXERCISE E. List in order the words that require apostrophes in the following sentences. Be sure that you insert the apostrophes exactly where omissions occur in contractions and after the *s* in possessives of plural words.

1. Im still working on todays assignment. 2. After two hours hard work, Im not through revising it, although Ive certainly taken time to dot my *i*s and cross my *t*s. 3. Now Ill need to go back

and strike out some *and*s and *so*s. 4. If Id followed my teachers instruction, Id have added some action verbs to replace too many weak *were*s. 5. Its a job to write a composition on "My Familys Most Remarkable Character."

6. My papers purpose is to describe my dog Frodos main characteristics. 7. To begin with, hes remarkably clever in devising ways to get my sisters or my attention so that well play ball with him. 8. If were busy, hell roll the ball under the furniture with his nose and stand there growling or whining until weve retrieved it. 9. One day we thought wed found a way to prevent this: we blocked up all openings with strips of wood. 10. No doubt Frodos first thoughts were, "This wont do at all. 11. Ill just have to find some other method." 12. So he carried the ball to the bathroom and dropped it into the tub, convinced hed found a new opening. 13. I thought Id break this habit by drenching him with shower water as I put him into the tub near his ball, but no luck. 14. Now hes frantic to take showers with me.

15. Frodos ability to learn new commands depends on what he feels he should or should not be expected to do: hell roll over, sit up, talk, even walk backwards at a moments notice for a mere toss of the ball. But he considers it beneath a dogs dignity to walk slowly and in a straight line when hes taken out at eight oclock for his mornings walk. 16. Hes determined to explore the delights of the citys streets, always chasing leaves, sniffing cars tires, and examining passersby, human and canine. 17. Though Ive told him often he shouldnt chase cars, hes still in the habit of barking at passing autos. 18. The walks weve shared have sometimes been harrowing experiences. 19. Im convinced, however, of Frodos charmed life. 20. Hes been nearly hit by several cars, but Frodo still dashes down the streets center lane, hotly pursuing the car thats nearest to him.

Chapter 24

Other Marks of Punctuation

Hyphens, Dashes, Parentheses

HYPHENS

As you know, some compound words are hyphenated (*attorney-general*); some are written as one word (*carport*); some are written as two or more words (*real estate*). As our language grows, new compound words enter the vocabulary, bringing writers the problem of choosing the correct form.

Whenever you need to know whether a word is hyphenated, consult your dictionary. In addition, learn to use the hyphen in the following situations.

24a. Use a hyphen to divide a word at the end of a line.

If you will look at the right margins of pages in this book, you will see that hyphens are often used to divide words at the ends of lines. *A word must always be divided between syllables.*

INCORRECT

She spoke, but it was obvious that she didn't recognize me.

CORRECT

She spoke, but it was obvious that she didn't recognize me.

If you need to divide a word and are not sure about its syllables, look it up in your dictionary. Keep in mind these rules for syllable division:

1. Since words are divisible between syllables only, do not divide one-syllable words.

INCORRECT

Do you know how much that big kettle weighs?

CORRECT

Do you know how much that big kettle weighs?

CORRECT

Do you know how much that big kettle
weighs?

2. You should try to avoid dividing capitalized words.

INCORRECT

Jane's aunt works at the Smithsonian Institution.

CORRECT

Jane's aunt works at the Smithsonian
Institution.

3. If a word is already hyphenated, divide it *only* at a hyphen.

INCORRECT

Tonight I am going to meet my new mother-in-law.

CORRECT

Tonight I am going to meet my new mother-
in-law.

4. Do not divide a word so that one letter stands alone.

INCORRECT

The utility company built a dam to generate e-
lectricity.

CORRECT
The utility company built a dam to generate electricity.

EXERCISE 1. Suppose that you are considering dividing the following words at the ends of lines. If necessary, check your dictionary for the proper syllabication. Then copy each word and use a hyphen to indicate where you would make the division. If a word should *not* be divided, write "carry forward" after the corresponding number on your paper.

EXAMPLES 1. monument
          1. *monu-ment (or mon-ument)*
          2. month
          2. *carry forward*

1. swimming
2. method
3. panorama
4. special
5. impartial
6. inside
7. French
8. Indo-Chinese
9. unhappy
10. whose
11. questionnaire
12. spectacular
13. Vera
14. cross-reference
15. hyphen
16. strength
17. cameo
18. traction
19. galaxy
20. oboe

24b. Use a hyphen with compound numbers from twenty-one to ninety-nine and with fractions used as adjectives.

EXAMPLES thirty-five students
          a two-thirds majority [but *two thirds* of the votes]

24c. Use a hyphen with the prefixes *ex-, self-, all-,* and with the suffix *-elect,* and with all prefixes before a proper noun or proper adjective.

EXAMPLES ex-champion   mid-September
          self-confident   trans-Pacific
          all-star   anti-Communist
          President-elect pre-Revolutionary

EXERCISE 2. In the following sentences, ten hyphens are needed. List the words that should be hyphenated, correctly punctuated, on your paper.

1. The exstudents hoped that the proposal would pass by a two thirds majority.
2. About three fourths of the club members are under twenty one years of age.
3. The expresident told us about events that took place during the preRenaissance era.
4. An all American quarterback last year, Mac boasts of being a self made star.
5. December and January have thirty one days; but February has only twenty eight, except during leap year, when it has twenty nine.

DASHES

As you have learned, many words and phrases are used *parenthetically,* that is, they break into the main thought. They are explanations, qualifications, or just "side remarks." They do not affect the grammatical construction of the sentences in which they occur.

Most parenthetical elements are set off by commas (see page 505) or parentheses (see page 557). Sometimes, however, words or phrases or clauses used parenthetically may demand a stronger separation. In such instances, you use a dash.

24d. Use a dash to indicate an abrupt break in thought.

EXAMPLES   Stephens▬Ms. Stephens, I mean▬ was waiting for me in her office.

Julia Stowe▬her nickname is "Peanuts" ▬has moved into my neighborhood.

"Then what▬what shall I say?" Sara faltered.

"I hope▬" Audrey began and then stopped.

EXERCISE 3. Copy the following sentences (adapted from the work of professional writers who used the dash correctly and effectively) and insert dashes where they are appropriate.

1. "It it's not right," she stammered.
2. Suddenly and don't ask me how it happened the conviction came to me that she was right.
3. My sister's engagement this is supposed to be a secret will be announced Sunday.
4. The climate there winters sometimes last for eight months will be quite a change from Florida.
5. The valedictorian that is, the student having the highest average will receive a special award.

PARENTHESES

Parentheses are used to set off parenthetical elements that serve as explanations or qualifications. Since parentheses are *enclosing* marks, they are used in pairs.

24e. Use parentheses to enclose matter which is added to a sentence but is not considered of major importance.

EXAMPLES　Next Monday night (of course, I'll see you before then) we will meet at the stadium.

During the Middle Ages (from about A.D. 500 to A.D. 1500), Moslems and Vikings invaded Europe.

Mrs. Clement Nelson (formerly Miss Valerie Kirk) was the guest of honor.

North Carolina's Senator Jordan (Democrat) led the debate on the proposal.

There are several poems by Sara Teasdale (1884–1933) in this book.

As you see from the examples above, the material enclosed in parentheses may range from a single word or number to a short sentence. In the first example, the sentence in parentheses is part of the main sentence. Sometimes an entire sentence, standing alone, can be placed in parentheses.

EXAMPLE   Correct the spelling errors in these sentences. (Do not write in your book.)

Notice that the period for the enclosed sentence is placed inside the parentheses. Punctuation marks are used within parentheses when they belong with the parenthetical matter, as above. Do not, however, place a punctuation mark within parentheses if it belongs to the sentence as a whole.

EXAMPLE   She plans to rehearse at least twenty hours (probably longer); moreover, she must know her part before the first rehearsal.

In general, follow these two rules when you are considering using parentheses:

1. Always be sure that any material enclosed in parentheses may be omitted without changing the basic meaning and construction of the sentence.

2. Commas, dashes, and parentheses are frequently interchangeable, especially for setting off incidental words or phrases. Commas are more common than dashes; dashes are more common than parentheses.

EXERCISE 4. Decide where parentheses may be used in the following sentences (adapted from the works of professional writers who used parentheses). Copy the sentences, adding the parentheses and punctuating the parenthetical elements correctly.

EXAMPLE   1. These three powers formed the Triple

> Entente which means "triple under-
> standing."
> 1. *These three powers formed the Triple
>   Entente (which means "triple under-
>   standing").*

1. Bake the meat in an oven set at 450° F 232° C for about forty minutes.
2. For shallow containers, buy Oasis a spongelike, moisture-retaining block from a florist.
3. Around her neck she wore a shabby furpiece whether mink, muskrat, or alley cat I could not determine.
4. Having learned something do not eat old turtles I was now determined to explore the whole subject.
5. Beginning with her book of poems *A Street in Bronzeville* and including her marvelous *Annie Allen* which was awarded the Pulitzer Prize for Poetry in 1950 the work of Gwendolyn Brooks has received well-deserved praise from critics.
6. She frets about the heavy expenses of being on the tour $15,000 a year.
7. A sperm whale the kind Moby Dick was grows to eighty feet.
8. The architect later he designed the Woolworth Tower in New York became dissatisfied and threatened to sue.
9. I am only against the fake or in a kinder term the exaggerated advertising claim.
10. The game State vs. Eastern was nothing but an endless series of fumbles at midfield.

REVIEW EXERCISE A. Copy the following sentences, and punctuate them by using hyphens, dashes, or parentheses. (Do not add commas in this exercise.) When you have a choice between dashes and parentheses, be prepared to give a reason for your choice.

EXAMPLE   1. In my history book there are several maps see page 716, for example that clearly show the proximity of Cuba to the United States.

       1. *In my history book there are several maps (see page 716, for example) that clearly show the proximity of Cuba to the United States.*

1. During the next ten years 1970–1980 my aunt worked for Throckmorton Brothers, Inc.
2. Senator Varner Republican, New York voted against the proposal; nevertheless, it passed by the required two thirds majority.
3. In April of 1980 the President's policy a boycott of the Summer Olympics was supported by the U.S. Olympic Committee.
4. The ex president of the club he always seemed too self confident and all knowing was fond of quoting Shakespeare in any situation.
5. These symptoms dizziness, headaches, fever often indicate the beginning of an infectious disease.
6. One of my New Year's resolutions to do my homework on time has been difficult to keep.
7. Twenty seven members of the Glee Club lucky people! have been invited to sing at the Governor's Ball.
8. Althea either Althea or her twin Lucille will doubtless make the All State team this year.
9. I am definitely going to the beach probably in mid July and I can hardly wait!
10. In "The Secret Sharer," Joseph Conrad 1857–1924 links Leggatt to Cain with the phrase "a fugitive and a vagabond." See Genesis 4:14.

REVIEW EXERCISE B. This exercise covers capitalization and all marks of punctuation (Chapters 19–24).

Copy and correctly punctuate the following sentences, using capitals where necessary. You may divide sentences if you wish.

1. Early suffragists women like lucy stone elizabeth cady stanton and susan b anthony campaigned to get the vote for women
2. Rod evans sailing over the last hurdle easily won the race roger evans his brother came in a slow second
3. Hurrah shouted Sylvia I knew youd make it Rod When are you heading for the olympics your mother said last night my son rod is going to be all american this year
4. Rosemary is knitting her first sweater a pink soft wool one with no sleeves whatever according to directions in the May 81 issue of seventeen magazine
5. Well he does I believe still live at 268 fairway lane des moines iowa   50318
6. Fathers day comes on the third sunday in june mothers day comes on the second sunday in may
7. Elena dreams of working at the brookhaven national laboratory at upton new york
8. Ive carefully studied chapter 20 end marks and commas in our textbook english grammar and composition as well as the other chapters on punctuation therefore I use commas for appositives and for series quotation marks to enclose titles of chapters and semicolons to separate independent clauses not joined by and but or nor for or yet
9. Jimson weed was named after jamestown virginia and wisteria was named after caspar wistar 1696–1752 an anatomist
10. A devilfish doesnt have a forked tail and a sand dollar wont buy an ice-cream cone or a ticket to the play annie but an electric eel can shock you

REVIEW EXERCISE C. This exercise covers capitalization and all marks of punctuation (Chapters 19–24). Copy and correctly punctuate the following sentences, using capitals where necessary.

1. Get your big feet out of the aisle John Linda muttered stumbling over them on her way to the chalkboard
2. What a great story exclaimed José who I remembered usually finishes his reading assignments very quickly
3. Mr. Sanchez a kindly generous man in our neighborhood distributes gum fruit and small toys to the children in brooks hospital
4. When she comes home from work my mother always asks me where is your sister
5. In an editorial entitled which way is up the editor of our school paper the cumberland news wrote As our school's athletic record improves school spirit declines
6. This salad requires the following lettuce tomato cucumber and onion in addition of course there is the dressing an important part of any salad.
7. I agreed with Mrs Guth my guidance counselor that I had better apply early for summer jobs for there are only a limited number of positions available.
8. E M Treanor jr was taken by ambulance to dade county emergency center where he was treated by dr henry and dr su
9. Samuel Clemens 1835–1910 who used the pen name Mark Twain wrote the novel the adventures of tom sawyer and patterned one of its characters becky thatcher after laura hawkins a neighbor who lived across the street from clemens in hannibal missouri
10. As an international language english has some drawbacks for example it has many words with more than one meaning and the spelling of many of its words is confusing

Aids to
Good English

PART SIX

Chapter **25**

The Library

Location and Arrangement of Facilities

Anyone who can read and who has a desire to learn can become educated in a library. Books on every known subject are found in the library. One of the greatest values of a library is that it puts all its resources at your disposal in such a way that you can find information quickly.

KNOW YOUR LIBRARY

25a. Know your library so that you can make effective use of it.

No doubt there is a library in your school, and there is probably a library in your community. You should be familiar with both, so that you don't wander around aimlessly or have to ask the librarian for help each time you go there. Learn the location of the reading room, the fiction and nonfiction books, the card catalogue, the reference books, the newspapers and magazines, and the circulation desk.

25b. Observe the rules of your library.

Remember, first of all, that the library is a quiet place, a place where people read or study or sometimes just relax. You may be able to think clearly with the radio blaring, your phonograph playing, or even a television program going, but many people cannot. Study requires concentration, and concentration demands quiet. There is little talk in libraries; all necessary conversation should be in whispers. There is little movement in libraries, for people are sitting and reading or writing. Remember these things when you are in the library, and be considerate of others who are there.

The librarian is there to help you, but not you alone. Be courteous when you ask for assistance, appreciative when you receive it, and thoughtful enough not to demand unnecessary time.

Take care of the books you use. You may mark passages in books you own but not in those belonging to the library. When you take a book home, be sure that it does not fall into the hands of your baby sister or into the teeth of the dog. Return books when they are due. If they are overdue, pay your fine; and if by some misfortune you have damaged a book, pay for it willingly.

The library deserves your cooperation in return for the services it offers you. Chief among these services is its simple, practical arrangement of books for your convenience.

ARRANGEMENT OF BOOKS

Library books are arranged in two ways, depending on whether the book is fiction or nonfiction. You probably know that the two kinds of books are kept in different parts of the library.

Fiction

25c. A separate section of the library is set aside for books of fiction.

Books of fiction are placed together in one section and are arranged in alphabetical order according to the last name of the author. If there are several books by the same author, these are further arranged alphabetically by the first word of the title (not counting *A, An,* or *The*).

For example, suppose you want to find Robert Louis Stevenson's *The Master of Ballantrae.* Having located the fiction section, you move to the *S*'s, to find authors whose last name begins with *S.* You need not be concerned with titles just yet. You may see books by Sabatini, Sayers, Scott, Shippen, Spark, Steinbeck, and Stevens before you come to Stevenson. You may then find books by Dorothy Stevenson and Janet Stevenson before you come to Robert Louis Stevenson. When you find his books, you then begin to look at titles. Perhaps you will see *The Black Arrow* and *Kidnapped* before you find *The Master of Ballantrae; Treasure Island* may follow your book.

▶ **NOTE** Books by authors whose names begin with *Mc* are arranged as though the name were spelled *Mac; St.* is arranged as though spelled out (*Saint*).

EXERCISE 1. Arrange the following fiction books in the order that you would find them on the library bookshelf. Remember, the alphabetical order is first for authors' names, and then for titles by the same author.

1. *Trap-Lines North,* Stephen W. Meader
2. *Pride and Prejudice,* Jane Austen
3. *Emma,* Jane Austen

4. *Agent in Place,* Helen MacInnes
5. *Invisible Man,* Ralph Ellison
6. *Coming into the Country,* John McPhee
7. *The Good Earth,* Pearl Buck
8. *The Call of the Wild,* Jack London
9. *Show Boat,* Edna Ferber
10. *So Big,* Edna Ferber

Nonfiction

25d. Nonfiction books are arranged according to the Dewey decimal system.

The Dewey decimal system was developed by Melvil Dewey, an American librarian. Under this system, all books are numbered and grouped according to ten subject classes. The classifications with the numbers that stand for them are as follows:

000–099   General Works (encyclopedias, periodicals, book lists, books about the library). Since many of these are reference books, some libraries use the letter *R* before the number.

100–199   Philosophy (psychology, conduct, personality)

200–299   Religion (bibles, theology, mythology)

300–399   Social Sciences (communication, economics, education, etiquette, folklore, government, law)

400–499   Philology or Language (grammars, dictionaries, foreign languages)

500–599   Science (animals, astronomy, biology, botany, chemistry, geology, general science, mathematics, physics)

600–699   Technology (agriculture, aviation, business management, engineering, health, home economics, medical science, pollution control)

700–799	The Arts (motion pictures, music, painting, photography, sculpture, recreation, sports)
800–899	Literature (poetry, drama, essays, criticism, history of literature)
900–999	History (archaeology, geography, travel)

Biographical works dealing with the lives of several persons (collective biography) are marked 920. However, individual biographies (the life of one person) are handled somewhat differently. Like fiction, they are generally kept in a separate section. In most libraries they are marked **B,** but in some they are given the number 92. Under the **B** (or the 92) comes the initial of the last name of the subject of the biography, since you are more likely to be thinking of the name of the person whose life interests you than the name of the person who wrote the biography. Thus, a biography of Franklin D. Roosevelt would be marked:

$\dfrac{B}{R}$ – Biography, Roosevelt.

All the books about Roosevelt are then arranged alphabetically by author on the same shelf. You can then find a *particular* biography of Roosevelt.

Nonfiction books other than individual biographies are marked on the spine of the book with their proper number. Each of the main subject groups is divided into ten subgroups, and each of the subgroups is further divided. Still more specific subdivisions are made by using decimals. For example, if you are looking for a play by Shakespeare, the general subject is Literature, which is numbered 800–899. The exact number for English drama is 822, and the number for Shakespeare is 822.3. Though at first glance this may appear quite complicated, in practice it makes it simple for you as a library user to find any book you are looking for—once you know its number.

This does not mean that you have to memorize the Dewey decimal system; it simply means that you should understand how it works.

EXERCISE 2. In which Dewey number range will you find each of the following?

1. a book on farming
2. lives of sports figures
3. the Encyclopædia Britannica
4. a play
5. a French-English dictionary
6. a collection of humorous essays
7. gods of ancient Greece
8. a book on child psychology
9. a book on the War of 1812
10. a book about North American flowers
11. a civics text
12. a cookbook
13. a book on chess
14. a book about Victorian literature
15. a book on cancer research
16. a history of the movies
17. a book on the care of dogs
18. a book on diet and nutrition
19. a history of religious art
20. a book about Buddhism

THE CARD CATALOGUE

Every book in the library has a Dewey decimal system number of its own. It is not necessary, however, to search through the shelves to find the number and the book. The number appears on any one of several cards arranged in a cabinet of small drawers. This cabinet, called the *card catalogue,* is usually conveniently located in the front of the library near the circulation desk. On cards in the card catalogue you will find the number that leads you to the shelf where books in that number category are kept. This number is called the *call number.*

25e. Every nonfiction book has a call number which appears on its catalogue card.

The call number appears in the upper left-hand corner of the catalogue card. For example, a nonfiction travel book on Germany may have the number 941.3. Fiction books may be marked **F** or may have no number at all.

In a very large library, books are kept in "stacks," and you cannot look for a book yourself. Instead, you give the call number to the librarian, who sends for the book.

For each book in the library's collection, the card catalogue contains a *title card,* an *author card,* and, if the book is nonfiction, a *subject card.*

25f. The card catalogue lists books by title, author, and subject.

The cards in the card catalogue are filed in alphabetical order in drawers. The drawers are labeled like the volumes of an encyclopedia, for example A – AMY, AN – AZ, B – BIO, BIP – BUL, and so on.

The Title Card

The simplest way to find a particular book is to look for the title card. At the top of the title card is the title of the book. Its position in the alphabetical order is determined by the first word of the title, unless the first word is *A, An,* or *The,* in which case the book will be listed under the second word of the title. For example, *The Last of the Mohicans* will be listed under **L.**

The Author Card

Occasionally you may know the name of the author but not the title of the particular book you want. Or perhaps you have read one of the author's books and would like to read another. On the author card, the author's name appears at the top. All books by the same author will then be arranged in alphabetical order according to the title. For example, the author card for *The Master of Ballantrae* will precede the card for *Treasure Island,* also by Stevenson, in the card catalogue, with "Stevenson, Robert Louis" printed at the top of the card. As with the arrangement of books on the shelves, names beginning with *Mc* are listed as if they were spelled *Mac; St. George* would be filed as if it were spelled *Saint George.*

The Subject Card

Sometimes you are not looking for a particular book by a particular author but are merely interested in a book on a certain subject. Nonfiction books are also catalogued according to the subject with which they deal. If, for example, you're an amateur photographer and want to learn how prints are developed, you look for cards under "Photography." Under this large subject classification there may be further divisions, such as "Photography — Print Developing."

Often books may be listed under more than one subject heading. A book about baseball may be listed under "Sports," "Athletics," "Baseball," and even "Games."

"See" and "See Also" Cards

A "see" or "see also" card refers you to another section of the catalogue; they are cross-reference cards. Suppose you want to find some books by Mark Twain. You might look for the author card under **T.** Instead of finding cards for his books there, you possibly would find under "Mark Twain" a card saying, "See Clemens,

Samuel Langhorne" (Twain's real name). The "see" card, then, directs you to a different part of the catalogue, in this case the **C** file.

"See also" cards refer you to other subjects closely related to the one in which you are interested. If you are looking under "Newspapers," you may find a card saying "See also Journalism." Looking up "Journalism," you will find more books on your subject.

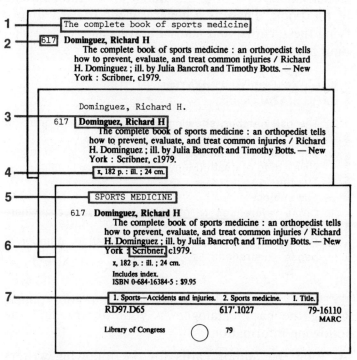

Top to bottom: title, author, and subject cards

1. Title heading
2. Call number
3. Author
4. Physical description of the book
5. Subject heading

6. Publisher and date of publication
7. Other headings under which the book is listed (In some libraries this book is shelved with books on sports accidents and injuries.)

In addition to the title, author, and subject, the catalogue card also tells you the publisher of the book, the place and date of publication, the number of pages, whether the book has illustrations or maps, and occasionally it gives a brief statement about the contents of the book. There is a general trend toward simplifying these cards, and many libraries use cards which omit place of publication.

SUMMARY OF INFORMATION IN THE CARD CATALOGUE

1. The **call number,** showing the location of the book on the library shelves
2. The **author,** full name, date of birth, and—if no longer alive—date of death (Many libraries omit the dates.)
3. The **title**
4. The **subject**
5. **Cross references** to other books or subjects, where appropriate
6. **Publisher,** place and date of publication, number of pages, illustrations

EXERCISE 3. Number from 1–20 on your paper. Using the card catalogue in your library, find the following information:

A. Find the author cards for the following writers and list one book for each. If there is no card, put "not in our library" after the proper number.
   1. Robert Frost
   2. James Thurber
   3. Willa Cather
   4. Erma Bombeck

B. Look up these title cards to see if these books are in your library. If they are, list the author and biographical dates; if not, write "not in our library."

5. *Anne Frank: The Diary of a Young Girl*
6. *I Knock at the Door*
7. *To Kill a Mockingbird*
8. *Shane*

C. Find a book in your library on each of these subjects:

9. nuclear energy
10. exploration of space
11. running
12. water pollution

D. List the title, author, call number, and date of publication for the following:

13. a book of essays or articles
14. a book on careers
15. a book of poetry
16. a book of short stories

E. List the title and author of a book *about* the following:

17. Virginia Woolf
18. Walt Whitman
19. John F. Kennedy
20. Golda Meir

REFERENCE BOOKS

Your library may have a special reference room where reference books are kept and where people using these books may work. In any case, all reference books will be kept in one section of the library. Some may be on closed shelves, and you must ask the librarian for them. Others are usually on open shelves or on tables. Since reference books are in such constant demand, they must be used only in the library; they may not be checked out.

Every library has several main types of reference books: (1) dictionaries, (2) encyclopedias, (3) biographical dictionaries, (4) atlases, (5) almanacs, (6) books on specific subjects such as literature, authors, etc., and (7) reference guides showing where information may be found. You should familiarize yourself with the kinds of information they offer you.

The *Readers' Guide*

25g. To find a magazine article, use the *Readers' Guide*.

The *Readers' Guide to Periodical Literature* may be regarded as the card catalogue for magazines. It indexes all the articles, poems, and stories in more than a hundred magazines; the magazines are listed in the front of each volume.

The *Readers' Guide* appears in a paperback edition twice a month (except for July and August, when it appears once a month). Each issue lists articles that were published two to four weeks previously. From time to time these issues are combined into single volumes covering periods of several months. Clothbound cumulations appear at two-year intervals.

As you can see from the sample entries on page 577, magazine articles are listed by subjects (SOLVENTS) and by authors (SOLOWEY, E. M.). Except for stories, magazine articles are not listed by title in the *Readers' Guide*. The subject and author entries appear in a single alphabetical list; the subject SOLVENTS is followed by the the author entry SOLZHENITSYN, Aleksandr. The first word of the subject entry and the author's last name in the author entry are printed in capital letters. Each entry lists the title of the article, the name of the magazine, and the pub-

SOLOTAROFF, Theodore   — author entry
Rukeyser: poet of plenitude. Nation 230:277-8
 Mr 8 '80

SOLOVIOFF, Nicholas
Monumental relics of abandoned technology — title of article
[reproductions of paintings] Fortune 101:88-
95 Ja 28 '80

SOLOWEY, E. M.
Land reclamation in the Arava: Kibbutz date of
Ketura. il BioScience 30:112-14 F '80 magazine

SOLUBILITY
How electric fields modify alkane solubility in
lipid bilayers. S. H. White, bibl f il Science — author's name
207:1075-7 Mr 7 '80

SOLVENTS   — subject entry
Printmaking: solvents. J. A. Waller and L.
Whitehead. Am Craft 40:81 F/Mr '80

SOLZHENITSYN, Aleksandr Isaevich
Nobeliana [excerpt from The oak and the calf;
tr by H. Willetts] il por New Repub 182:23-5 — volume number
Mr 22 '80
Solzhenitsyn on Communism [tr by A. Klimoff]
por Time 115:48-9 F 18 '80   — magazine
Writer underground [excerpt from The oak and
the calf; tr by H. Willetts] N Y Times Bk R — page reference
85:3+ F 10 '80

SOMALIA
    Defenses
 See also
United States—Navy—Forces in Somalia division of
    Foreign relations   main subject
    Ethiopia
 See Ethiopia—Foreign relations—Somalia
    Native races
 See also
Somalis

lication date. The subject entry also lists the author
of the article. The *Readers' Guide* employs in its
entries a system of abbreviations; a key to these abbreviations appears in the front of the *Readers' Guide.*
Most names of magazines are also abbreviated (*Bsns
W* for *Business Week*); these are noted in the list of
magazines which also appears at the front.

You will observe that "see" and "see also" references are also given in the *Readers' Guide;* for example under SOMALIA, "*See also* Somalis."

Of course, finding out what articles have been
published on a certain topic or by a certain author
will be of little help to you unless you can obtain the
magazines in which the articles appear. Usually you

will find near the *Readers' Guide* a list of the magazines to which your library subscribes and a notation
on which back issues are available. If there is no list,
the librarian can supply the information.

EXERCISE 4. Referring to the "Key to Abbreviations" and to the "List of Periodicals Indexed" at
the front of the *Readers' Guide,* give the meaning of
each of the following:

1. Sci N L	5. v	8. abr
2. cond	6. Je	9. +
3. 54:320–56	7. Sch & Soc	10. por
4. Atlan		

EXERCISE 5. Find in the *Readers' Guide* one article
listed under any five of the following subjects. For
each article, give the title, author (if given), magazine,
date, and page numbers.

EXAMPLE   1. Solar energy

· (Looking in the *Readers' Guide,* you
might find the following entry: What's
ahead for solar energy? Latest size-up
[interview] D. Hayes. il por U.S. News
88: 53–4 Mr 3 '80)

1. *"What's Ahead for Solar Energy? Lat-*
est Size-up," an interview written by
D. Hayes, illustrated, contains a por-
trait. U.S. News and World Report,
Volume 88, pages 53–54, March 3,
1980

1. Lasers	6. Astrology
2. Television	7. Boats
3. National parks	8. Space exploration
4. Computers	9. Leisure
5. United Nations	10. Music

EXERCISE 6. Select someone you want to know more about — a personality in the entertainment world, a great pilot or explorer, a government official — *or* something that interests you — a hobby, cooking, outer space, stars. Then look through several volumes of the *Readers' Guide* and find five magazine articles about the topic you chose. List these articles, giving complete information about each one, as in Exercise 5.

The Vertical File

25h. To find a pamphlet, use the vertical file.

Much valuable information is published in pamphlet form. The Division of Public Documents of the U.S. Government Printing Office alone publishes hundreds of pamphlets each year; many industrial concerns and educational organizations also issue pamphlets regularly. Your librarian files these materials in a vertical file. Sometimes newspaper clippings of special interest will also be included. Each pamphlet or clipping is placed in a folder and filed away in a cabinet. For up-to-the-minute material, you will find the vertical file very useful. Consult your librarian to see whether a file folder is available on a topic you are studying.

Dictionaries of Synonyms

There is a different kind of dictionary with which you may not be acquainted and which can be of great help to you in your writing: the dictionary of synonyms. The most famous of these is *Roget's Thesaurus of English Words & Phrases. Thesaurus* means "treasury," in this instance a treasury of words. If, for example, you have overused the adjective "good" in the first draft of a composition, you can find in the *Thesaurus* over a hundred synonyms for "good," as well as many antonyms and cross references to related words.

Originally the arrangement of the *Thesaurus* was rather complicated, but now there is an edition called *Roget's Thesaurus in Dictionary Form*. All entries are arranged in alphabetical order, with synonyms grouped according to meaning. If you know how to use the dictionary, you can use this edition of the *Thesaurus*.

Similar to the *Thesaurus* is *Webster's New Dictionary of Synonyms*. Either of these books will help you to avoid needless repetition and, incidentally, to enlarge your vocabulary.

Encyclopedias

While you may own a dictionary, you may not have an encyclopedia, which generally appears in many volumes and is therefore more costly. Encyclopedias are made up of a collection of articles, alphabetically arranged, on almost all subjects. There are also many valuable illustrations. As you proceed with your education, you will find that the encyclopedia is more and more valuable to you. It is usually the first source you use in obtaining information on a subject. If you are writing a long paper or giving a report, you will turn to the encyclopedia for general information and an overall view of your subject before proceeding to books and periodicals.

To find information on a particular subject in the encyclopedia, you may use first the guide letters on the spine of each volume and then the guide words at the top of the pages. If you depend wholly upon this method of finding material, however, you may overlook other important information. It is better to look in the index, usually the last volume of the set. Here you may find that your subject is discussed in several different articles which may appear in several different volumes. By using the index you can find *all* the material on your topic that the encyclopedia contains.

Although encyclopedias are rewritten and revised continuously, you may find (by looking on the title page) that the encyclopedias in your library were published several years ago. For up-to-date information, you should check the annual or yearbook which many encyclopedia companies publish every year. These yearbooks will give the most recent events and latest developments in your subject field.

The following well-known encyclopedias are usually available in most libraries:

Compton's Encyclopedia
    26 volumes
    Fact index (which itself gives information) at end
        of each volume
    Publishes a yearbook and an annual supplement
Encyclopedia Americana
    30 volumes
    Index in Volume 30
    Publishes *Americana Annual*
Encyclopædia Britannica
        Propædia — a guide to the Britannica–1 volume
        Micropædia — brief subject and reference infor-
            mation–10 volumes
        Macropædia — extensive treatment of major topics
            – 19 volumes
World Book Encyclopedia
    22 volumes
    Index in Volume 22
    Publishes an annual

Compton's Encyclopedia and *World Book Encyclopedia* are written for younger readers.

Shorter encyclopedias of one or two volumes include *The New Columbia Encyclopedia, The Random House Encyclopedia,* and the *Lincoln Library of Essential Information.*

Biographical Reference Books

Although encyclopedias include biographical articles, there are several special books devoted entirely to accounts of the lives of famous people.

The *Dictionary of American Biography* contains articles about famous Americans who are no longer living. The set includes sixteen volumes. Similar to the *D.A.B.* is the *Dictionary of National Biography,* which presents the lives of distinguished English people who are no longer living.

Current Biography is the best source of information about currently prominent persons. It is published monthly in pamphlet form and bound in an annual volume. By using the cumulative index in each issue, you can locate biographies of persons in the news in previous months. Frequently photographs of the persons discussed are included in *Current Biography.*

Another important reference book is *Who's Who,* which contains essential facts — parentage, important biographical dates, positions held, achievements and awards, publications, present address — about distinguished international figures. This book is published annually. Since biographies of English people predominate in *Who's Who,* you may find that *Who's Who in America* is more useful to you. Similar to *Who's Who,* although published only every two years, this work contains data about famous Americans only. Remember that both *Who's Who* and *Who's Who in*

America deal only with living persons and give only essential biographical information.

A valuable series of reference works by Stanley Kunitz is composed of biographies of authors. Unlike the two *Who's Who* books, Kunitz' works give much "human-interest" information and also include photographs.

Stanley J. Kunitz and Howard Haycraft:
British Authors of the Nineteenth Century
American Authors 1600–1900
Stanley J. Kunitz and Vineta Colby:
European Authors 1000–1900

Interesting profiles of modern writers are contained in:
Contemporary Authors and *Contemporary Authors: First Revision*

Other biographical reference books are *Webster's Biographical Dictionary, World Biography,* and *American Men of Science.*

Atlases

An atlas is much more than just a book of maps. It contains a vast amount of information about the cities and countries of the world—facts about population, resources, industries, natural wonders, climate, exports and imports, history. You should know where the atlases are located in your library and should familiarize yourself with some of them. Especially useful are the following:

National Geographic Atlas of the World
Goode's World Atlas
Ambassador World Atlas
The New York Times Atlas of the World

Almanacs

Almanacs are full of information on current events. They also contain much of historical interest: facts, dates, statistics, sports records, etc. The two most useful almanacs are the *World Almanac and Book of Facts* and the *Information Please Almanac.* Both are published annually. Remember to use the index to find information quickly; it is found in the front of the *World Almanac* and in the back of the *Information Please Almanac.*

Reference Books About Literature

There are several collections of quotations, the most famous of which is Bartlett's *Familiar Quotations.* Bartlett's book is useful when you want to know the following:

(1) The author of a quotation
(2) The literary work in which the quotation appeared
(3) The complete quotation when you know only a part
(4) A few famous lines by any author
(5) Quotations by various authors on a particular subject

Bartlett's is arranged chronologically by author. Under each author's name, the quotations are further arranged chronologically according to the date on which they were said or written. Two separate indexes are included in the back of the book. One lists the authors alphabetically; the other is an alphabetical listing of subjects or key words from the quotations. You can use the author index to find the number of the page that contains quotations from a particular author's works. If you know the quotation or a part of it, you can use the index to find its author or the full quotation. Suppose, for instance, that you want to find out who wrote

> Ring out the thousand wars of old,
> Ring in the thousand years of peace.

If you look under either *ring* or *peace,* both key words in the quotation, you will find the page given where the quotation appears, along with references to other quotations containing the same key words.

In addition to Bartlett's, Stevenson's *Home Book of Quotations* is especially useful if you want a quotation on a certain subject. The quotations in Stevenson's book are arranged alphabetically by subject. There are also many cross references. If, for example, you are looking under *Freedom,* you will find several entries there and also a note, *see also Liberty,* with five subheads.

Other good indexes of quotations include the following:

Flesch's *New Book of Unusual Quotations*
Mencken's *A New Dictionary of Quotations*
Oxford Dictionary of Quotations

Granger's *Index to Poetry* tells you *where* to find a poem or popular prose passage, but it does not *quote* these. Granger's book lists poems and prose passages according to subject, title (or first line), and author. You can use it to learn where you can find a certain literary work, who wrote a certain work, and what poems and passages have been written on a particular subject. Again, you will not find the poem or passage itself in Granger's *Index.*

If you are looking for a poem, however, you will probably find it in Stevenson's *Home Book of Verse* or *Home Book of Modern Verse.* These large collections contain many well-known poems, classified under general headings such as "Love Poems" or

"Familiar Verse." Three additional excellent poetry anthologies are Van Doren's *An Anthology of World Poetry* (arranged by countries) and Untermeyer's *Modern American Poetry* and *Modern British Poetry* (arranged in chronological order; also available in a single volume). All five books have indexes by title, author, and first line.

Other useful reference books on literature are

Oxford Companion to American Literature
Cambridge History of American Literature (3 volumes)
Burke & Howe's *American Authors and Books*
Oxford Companion to English Literature
Cambridge History of English Literature (15 volumes)
Harper's Dictionary of Classical Literature
Brewer's Dictionary of Phrase and Fable
Benét's *Reader's Encyclopedia*
Book Review Digest
Short Story Index
Essay & General Literature Index (7 volumes)
Oxford Companion to the Theatre
Logasa's *Index to One-Act Plays*

Other Special Reference Books

Among other reference books, you might find the following of interest, according to the subject which you are researching:

Dictionary of American History (companion to the *Dictionary of American Biography*)
Encyclopedia of American Facts and Dates
Encyclopedia of the Social Sciences
Encyclopedia of Sports
Encyclopedia of Religion
The International Cyclopedia of Music and Musicians, ed. Oscar Thompson

Grove's *Dictionary of Music and Musicians*
McGraw-Hill *Encyclopedia of Science and Technology*
Murphy's *How and Where to Look It Up*
Webster's New Geographical Dictionary (companion to *Webster's Biographical Dictionary*)

EXERCISE 7. Go to the library and locate the encyclopedias, atlases, and almanacs. After you have looked up each of the following items, write after the appropriate number on your paper the name of the reference work you used. Do not use the same book twice.

1. a list of national parks
2. a portrait of Margaret Bourke-White and reproductions of her photographs
3. a chart of Archimedes' principle of specific gravity
4. a list of points of interest in Kansas
5. types of cosmetic make-up used for motion pictures
6. the origin and development of polo
7. a discussion and illustrations of three kinds of mosquitoes
8. last year's major league baseball statistics
9. the population of Vermont
10. a map of Sweden

EXERCISE 8. Disregarding unabridged and abridged dictionaries, as well as encyclopedias, decide what reference book would be best to use for looking up each of the following. Number your paper 1–10. After the corresponding number, write the title of the reference book.

1. a picture and biography of Jim Rice, a baseball player
2. the names of the five states that border on Nevada
3. a list of quotations about science and beauty

4. a quotation from the works of Emily Dickinson
5. a biography of the American author Sinclair Lewis
6. a book listing synonyms for *creative*
7. a brief list of facts about Lorraine Hansberry, the American playwright.
8. a list of facts about Martha Graham, the American dancer
9. the complete poem "Song of the Open Road"
10. a book containing the limerick by Edward Lear beginning "There was an Old Man in a boat"

EXERCISE 9. Suppose that you have been assigned reports on the following subjects. Give for each subject the names of at least two reference books that you might use.

1. DNA, the genetic code
2. fluoridation of water
3. Marianne Moore, poet
4. the climate of Puerto Rico
5. Robert Redford, movie star

EXERCISE 10. Referring to the proper reference book, answer the following questions. Give your sources.

1. What is the Pulitzer Prize? Name the most recent Pulitzer prizewinning (a) novelist, (b) poet, (c) playwright. Cite the work for which each won the award.
2. What is the Nobel Prize? Who was the first American to win the Nobel Prize for literature? What other Americans have won it?
3. Identify each of the following and give the most recent winner of each: Walker Cup, Stanley Cup, Davis Cup.
4. Who won the Academy Awards for best actor and best actress last year?

5. What television show won the Emmy award for best comedy series last year?

EXERCISE 11. Find the author of the following quotations. Remember to look under a key word. A short quotation like "leave no stone unturned" (Euripides), for example, may be cited under *leave, stone,* and *unturned.*

1. I'll tell the world.
2. As good as gold.
3. What fools these mortals be!
4. Beauty is in the eye of the beholder.
5. All that glisters is not gold.
6. Early to bed and early to rise
   Makes a man healthy, wealthy, and wise.
7. Uneasy lies the head that wears a crown.
8. The almighty dollar.
9. To thine own self be true.
10. To strive, to seek, to find, and not to yield.
11. The fault . . . is not in our stars, but in ourselves. . . .
12. They also serve who only stand and wait.
13. A little learning is a dangerous thing.
14. With malice toward none, with charity for all.
15. The only thing we have to fear is fear itself.

Chapter 26

The Dictionary

Arrangement and Content of Dictionaries

The reference book that you will use most often from now on is the dictionary. In addition to giving the spelling and meaning of words, a good dictionary tells you how a word is pronounced, what its part of speech is, how it is used in speech and writing, and many other things as well.

If all of the information contained in a dictionary is to be of any use to you, you must know that it is there and know how to find it. You should also know that, even though it is customary to speak generally of "the dictionary," there are in fact many different kinds of dictionaries, each with its special uses. Skillful users of dictionaries know enough about each major type to enable them to go to the one that best suits their purposes. This chapter is intended to show you the differences between kinds of dictionaries and to suggest in a general way what you may expect to find in each of them.

KINDS OF DICTIONARIES

There are so many special kinds of dictionaries — crossword puzzle dictionaries, scientific dictionaries, rhyming dictionaries, and so on — that it would take a much longer chapter than this to describe all of them. Here we will consider the three kinds of dictionaries that you will be making most use of right now: the unabridged dictionary, the abridged or "college-size" dictionary, and the school dictionary.

The Unabridged Dictionary

The unabridged dictionary is probably a familiar sight to you from your visits to the reference section of your library. It usually has a stand of its own and looks big enough to contain all the words there are. Although an unabridged dictionary may contain upwards of 450,000 words, it does not list all the English words in daily use; but it does list most of them. Because new words come into the language every day, no dictionary can be completely up-to-date. The word "unabridged" merely means that a dictionary is not a shorter version of some larger dictionary.

There are several unabridged dictionaries in print. Undoubtedly the best known is *Webster's New International Dictionary,* which has been kept up-to-date through succeeding editions. The word "international" means that this dictionary contains information about words as they are used throughout the English-speaking world. It therefore has some entries and spellings that are mainly used in Scotland, Australia, Canada, and so on. It is, however, mainly an American dictionary, and the great majority of its entries deal with meanings, pronunciations, and usages that are current in the United States. The newest unabridged dictionary is the *Random House Dictionary of the English Language: Unabridged Edition.*

You will be hearing more about unabridged dictionaries and their use as you go on in high school. For now, it is enough that you have an idea of the

kind of information included in this kind of dictionary.
Below you will find three entries for the word *funnel*
reproduced from *Webster's Third New International
Dictionary.*

¹**fun·nel** \'fən²l\ *n* -s *often attrib* [ME *fonel, funel,* fr. OProv
fonilh, fr. ML *fundibulum,* short for L *infundi-
bulum,* fr. *infundere* to pour in, fr. *in* +
fundere to pour — more at IN, FOUND]
1 a : a utensil that has typically the shape of
a hollow cone with a tube extending from the
point, is designed to catch and direct a down-
ward flow of liquid or some other substance,
and is sometimes fitted or combined with a
strainer or filter — see SEPARATORY FUNNEL
b : something shaped like a funnel (as a
conical part, passage, or hole); *specif :* the
swimming funnel of a cephalopod **c :** one
that serves as a constricted channel or central
agent or organization through which some-

funnel 1a

thing passes or is transmitted **2 :** a stack or flue for the escape
of smoke or for ventilation; *specif :* the stack of a ship **3 :** a
cylindrical band of metal; *esp :* one around the top of an upper
mast around which the rigging fits **4 :** RUNNING GATE
5 : FUNNEL CLOUD **6 :** a black usu. cylindrical metal hood
attached to a spotlight to prevent the spill of light outside the
illuminated area of a stage
²**funnel** \"\ *vb* **funneled** *also* **funnelled; funneled** *also*
funnelled; funneling *also* **funnelling; funnels** *vi* **1 :** to
have or take the shape of a funnel **:** NARROW, WIDEN ⟨a shallow, rounded valley bottom ∼s into a miniature gorge with
steep bluffs —*Jour. of Geol.*⟩ **2 :** to move to or from a focal
point or into a central channel ⟨the gang ... ∼ed onto the end
of the jetty off the slope —R.O.Bowen⟩ ⟨orders were ∼ing out
to the ships from the flagship —Alexander Griffin⟩ **3 :** to
pass through or as if through a funnel; *specif :* to move
through a constricted passage or central medium ⟨the fierce
winds which ∼ed up the valley center —John Steinbeck⟩
⟨through the great port ∼s much of the overseas commerce
—*Newsweek*⟩ ⟨thousands of pictures ... ∼ed back to the
press and public through the public-relations division —Robert
Moora⟩ **∼** *vt* **1 :** to cause to funnel: **a :** to form into the
shape of a funnel ⟨∼s his hands and shouts through them⟩
b : to cause to move to or from a focal point or into a central
channel ⟨traffic is ∼ed into consolidation stations ... and
fanned out to destinations —*Distribution Age*⟩ ⟨airlift's traffic
pattern ∼s planes from widely separated ... bases into two
20-mile-wide corridors —*Nat'l Geographic*⟩ **c :** to direct to
a single recipient or distribute from a single source ⟨impurities
∼ed into the air by automobiles, backyard bonfires, and fac-
tory chimneys —*N.Y. Times*⟩ ⟨∼ the kerosine into the tank⟩
d : to send or direct through a narrow passage or central
medium ⟨pass ... through which were ∼ed troops and supplies —F.T.Chapman⟩ ⟨cupped her hands over the lens of the
flashlight, ∼ing the light through a small opening —E.S.
Gardner⟩ ⟨if a bank ∼s its news through a public-relations
firm —*Banking*⟩ **2 :** to serve as a means for the transmission
or direction of ⟨accused the press of ∼ing secret military information to Soviet Russia —*Newsweek*⟩ ⟨∼ ... high-caliber
young people to the agency business —*Printers' Ink*⟩
³**fun·nel** \'fün²l, 'fən-\ *n* -s [origin unknown] *dial Eng*
: HINNY

By comparing this page with the entry for the same
word in the sample column on page 593, you will be
able to see how the treatment of a common word
differs in an unabridged dictionary from that in a
smaller dictionary. Notice the many examples of

guide word ——— | **funky**

entry word ——— **funk·y**[1] (fung'kē), *adj.*, **funk·i·er, funk·i·est. 1.** *Informal.*
overcome with fear; terrified. **2.** depressed. [FUNK[1] + -Y[1]]
funk·y[2] (fung'kē), *adj.*, **funk·i·er, funk·i·est.** *Slang.* **1.** evil-
smelling; foul. **2. a.** earthy; down-to-earth. **b.** pleasantly
unconventional or offbeat. **c.** excellent; fine. **d.** sexy or
sensual. —**funk'i·ness,** *n.* [*funk* stench (akin to ONF

alternate
spelling ——— *funkier* < LL *fūmicāre;* see FUME) + -Y[1]]
fun·nel (fun'³l). *n.. v.* **-neled, -nel·ing** or [*esp. Brit.*)
-nelled, -nel·ling. —*n.* **1.** a cone-shaped utensil with a
tube at the apex, for conducting liquid or other substance
through a small opening, as into a bottle, jug, or the like.
2. a smokestack, esp. of a steamship or a locomotive. **3.** a

word
derivation ——— flue, tube, or shaft, as for ventilation. —*v.t.* **4.** to concentrate, channel, or focus. [late ME *fonel,* < MF **founel* <
OPr *fonilh* < LL **fundibul(um),* aph. var. of L *infundibulum*
< *infund(ere)* (to) pour in] —**fun'nel·like',** *adj.*

pronunciation ——— **fun'nel cloud',** tuba (def. 2).
fun·ny (fun'ē), *adj.,* **-ni·er, -ni·est,** *pl.* **-nies.** —*adj.* **1.**
providing fun; amusing; comical: *a funny remark; a funny
person.* **2.** attempting to amuse; facetious. **3.** warranting
suspicion; deceitful; underhanded: *He won't stand for any
funny stuff.* **4.** insolent; sassy. **5.** *Informal.* curious;
strange; peculiar; odd: *Her speech has a funny twang.* —*n.*
6. funnies, *U.S.* **a.** comic strips. **b.** Also called **funny
paper.** the section of a newspaper containing comic strips,
word games, etc. —**fun'ni·ly,** *adv.* —**fun'ni·ness,** *n.*

synonyms
and ——— —**Syn. 1.** diverting, comic, farcical, absurd, ridiculous,
incongruous, droll, witty, facetious, humorous. FUNNY,
antonyms LAUGHABLE, LUDICROUS refer to that which excites laughter.
FUNNY and LAUGHABLE are both applied to that which
provokes laughter or deserves to be laughed at: *a funny
story, scene, joke; a laughable incident, mistake.* That which is
LUDICROUS excites laughter by its incongruity and foolish
absurdity: *The monkey's attempts to imitate the woman were
ludicrous.* —**Ant. 1.** solemn, sad, melancholy.
fun'ny bone', the part of the elbow where the ulnar
nerve passes by the internal condyle of the humerus, which
when struck causes a peculiar, tingling sensation in the arm

usage label ——— and hand; crazy bone.
fun'ny busi'ness, [*Slang.*] improper or unethical conduct,
as deception, trickery, etc.
fun'ny mon'ey, *Slang.* **1.** counterfeit currency. **2.**
money from undisclosed or questionable sources, esp. for
political purposes. **3.** warrants, convertible securities, and
the like issued by a company as a means for acquiring
another company or companies.

spelling of
verb form ——— **fun'ny pa'per,** funny (def. 6b).
fur (fûr). *n.. adj.. v.* [**furred, fur·ring.**] —*n.* **1.** *Zool.* the fine,
soft, thick, hairy coating of the skin of a mammal. **2.** such

numbered
definitions ——— a coat, as of sable, ermine, or beaver, used for lining, trimming, or making garments. **3.** Often, **furs.** a garment made
of fur. **4.** any coating resembling fur, as matter on the
tongue. **5. make the fur fly, a.** to cause a scene or disturbance, esp. of a violent nature; make trouble. **b.** to do
things quickly. —*adj.* **6.** of or pertaining to fur, animal
skins, dressed pelts, etc. —*v.t.* **7.** to line, face, or trim with
fur, as a garment. **8.** *Building Trades.* to apply furring to
(a wall, ceiling, etc.). **9.** to clothe (a person) with fur. **10.**
to coat with foul or deposited matter. [ME *furre* < MF
fourr(er) (to) line a garment. OF *forrer,* orig. to encase < *fuerre*

part of
speech ——— sheath < Gmc; akin to OE *fōdder* case, sheath, Icel *fōthr,*
Gk *pōma*] —**fur'less,** *adj.*
fur.. furlong; furlongs.
fu·ran (fyŏŏr'an, fyŏŏ ran'), [*n.*] *Chem.* a liquid heterocyclic

primary and
secondary ——— compound, C₄H₄O, used chiefly in organic synthesis. Also
accents called **furfuran.** [aph. form of FURFURAN]
fur·be·low (fûr'bə lō'), *n.* **1.** a festooned flounce, as on a
woman's gown. **2.** any bit of showy trimming or finery.
—*v.t.* **3.** to ornament with or as with furbelows. [var. of
FALBALA]
fur·bish (fûr'bish), *v.t.* to restore to freshness of appearance or condition. [ME *furbish(en)* < MF *forbiss-,* long s.
of *forbir* to polish, clean < Gmc; cf. OHG *furban*] —**fur'-
bish·er,** *n.*
fur·cate (*adj.* fûr'kāt, -kit; *v.* fûr'kāt), *adj., v.,* **-cat·ed,
-cat·ing.** —*adj.* **1.** forked; branching. —*v.i.* **2.** to form a
fork; divide into branches. [< ML *furcāt(us)* cloven. See
FORK, -ATE[1]] —**fur·ca·tion** (fər kā'shən), *n.*

actual uses included in the entry in the unabridged dictionary. These illustrative quotations are set off in angle brackets (< >).

The College Dictionary

A "college-size" dictionary is shorter and less detailed than an unabridged dictionary. It may contain from 125,000 to 150,000 words, but less is likely to be said about each of these words than in an unabridged dictionary. College dictionaries are designed for the convenience of students, secretaries, letter writers, and everyone else who has occasion to look up a spelling, meaning, pronunciation, or point of usage. The sample column on page 593 reproduces a number of entries more or less typical of college dictionaries.

One college dictionary differs from another in its methods of presenting information. You will be hearing more about such differences later. However, if you use such a dictionary in school or at home, it is essential that you find out for yourself the arrangement and method of presentation used in that book. All dictionaries have introductory notes that explain such matters. Read them. You would not try to use a new camera or amplifier without reading the instructions; or, if you did, the results would almost certainly be unfortunate. To use your dictionary well, you have to know how it is meant to be used.

The School Dictionary

The dictionary that you probably know best is the *school dictionary*—one designed with students of your age and background specifically in mind. Such dictionaries, particularly the one you are likely to be using this year, are much like college dictionaries. The difference is that the school dictionary contains fewer words, and these are defined with a younger student's experience in mind.

School dictionaries also differ one from the other. The method of each one is carefully explained in its introductory section, and again, it is essential that you study this material carefully. This part of a school dictionary usually gives a simpler and more detailed account of dictionary features than the introduction in a college dictionary. In addition, exercises are often included. The sample column on page 597 will give you an idea of the treatment of words in a school dictionary.

EXERCISE 1. Study the table of contents at the front of your dictionary. Notice where the introductory notes are to be found, where the definitions start, and where special tables, charts, or other features may be found. Then write on your paper the part of your dictionary in which you think each of the following items of information can be found. Use *front* for anything that comes before the actual definitions, *main part* for the alphabetical listing of entries, and *back* for anything that comes later. If you think an item might be in two places, give both.

EXAMPLE   1. The pronunciation of the word *naïve*
            1. *main part*

1. An explanation of the way syllables are divided in the dictionary entries
2. The meaning of the abbreviation *F.O.B.*
3. The population of Tokyo
4. The capital of Alaska
5. The life dates (birth and death) of George Washington
6. The number of centimeters in a cubic inch

7. The meaning of the abbreviations *n., adj.,* and *v.t.*
8. The meaning of *prism*
9. An explanation of the meaning of *vowel* and *consonant*
10. An explanation of the treatment of prefixes in the dictionary

EXERCISE 2. Now find each of the items of information in Exercise 1, giving the number of the page on which it appears. Check your answers in Exercise 1, correcting those that turn out to be wrong.

EXERCISE 3. Judging from your study of the sample columns (592, 593, and 597) and from descriptions of the different kinds of dictionaries, indicate in which kind of dictionary you would expect to find the following items. (Use *unabridged, college,* or *school* in your answers. If two or more of the kinds would be likely to have it, give two or more answers. Use a question mark for a doubtful case.)

EXAMPLE   1. The meaning of the British word *windscreen*
    1. *unabridged, college (?)*

1. The meaning of the abbreviation *etc.*
2. The pronunciation of a word used mainly in Scotland
3. A pronunciation key
4. Five different ways to pronounce *Algonquin*
5. A detailed explanation of the way alphabetical order is used in a dictionary
6. A list of major colleges and universities in the United States
7. Two dozen definitions for the word *get*
8. A chart showing the Indo-European languages
9. An extended list of words using the *non*-suffix
10. The date on which Guy Fawkes Day is celebrated in Great Britain

Oneida

Onei·da \ō-'nīd-ə\ *n* : a member of an Iroquoian people originally of what is now central New York [Iroquois *Oné yóde'*,
literally, "standing rock"]

onei·ric \ō-'nīr-ik\ *adj* : of or relating to dreams : DREAMY
[Greek *oneiros* "dream"]

one·ness \'wən-nəs\ *n* 1 : the quality, state, or fact of being
one (as in thought, spirit, or purpose) 2 : IDENTITY 1

oner·ous \'än-ə-rəs, 'ō-nə-\ *adj* : being difficult or burdensome
⟨an *onerous* task⟩ [Middle French *onereus*, from Latin *onero-
sus*, from *oner-, onus* "burden"] — **oner·ous·ly** *adv* — **oner-
ous·ness** *n*

one·self \wən-'self, ,wən-\ *also* **one's self** \wən-, ,wən-,
,wənz-\ *pron* 1 : a person's self : one's own self — used re-
flexively as object of a preposition or verb or for emphasis in
various constructions 2 : one's normal, healthy, or sane condition or self

one–sid·ed \'wən-'sīd-əd\ *adj* 1 : lacking in objectivity
: BIASED ⟨take a *one-sided* view of a problem⟩ 2 : decided or
differing by a wide margin ⟨a *one-sided* game⟩ ⟨a *one-sided*
score⟩

one–step \'wən-,step\ *n* : a ballroom dance marked by quick
walking steps backward and forward in $2/4$ time — **one–step**
vi

one·time \'wən-,tīm\ *adj* : FORMER ⟨a *onetime* teacher⟩

one–to–one \,wən-tə-'wən, -də-\ *adj* : pairing each element of
a set with one and only one element of another set ⟨a *one-to-
one* correspondence⟩

one–track *adj* : obsessed or seemingly obsessed with one thing
or one idea

one–way *adj* : that moves in, allows movement in, or functions in
only one direction ⟨*one-way* traffic⟩ ⟨a *one-way* ticket⟩

on·go·ing \'ȯn-,gō-ing, 'än-\ *adj* 1 : being in process 2 : making progress

on·ion \'ən-yən\ *n* : a widely grown Asian herb of the lily family
with pungent edible bulbs; *also* : its bulb [Middle French *oig-
non*, from Latin *unio*]

on·ion·skin \-,skin\ *n* : a thin strong translucent paper of very
light weight

on·look·er \'ȯn-,lùk-ər, 'än-\ *n* : SPECTATOR — **on·look·ing**
\-,lùk-ing\ *adj*

¹on·ly \'ōn-lē\ *adj* 1 : unquestionably best : PEERLESS ⟨the
only dog for me⟩ 2 : alone in its class or kind : SOLE ⟨the *only*
survivor⟩ [Old English *ānlīc*, from *ān* "one" + *-līc* "-ly"]

²only *adv* 1 **a** : JUST, MERELY ⟨worked *only* in the morning⟩ **b**
: EXCLUSIVELY, SOLELY ⟨known *only* to me⟩ 2 : at the very least
⟨it was *only* too true⟩ 3 **a** : in the final outcome ⟨will *only* make
you sick⟩ **b** : with nevertheless the final result being ⟨won the
battles, *only* to lose the war⟩ 4 **a** : as recently as ⟨*only* last
week⟩ **b** : in the immediate past ⟨*only* just talked to them⟩

³only *conj* 1 : with this sole restriction ⟨you may go, *only* come
back early⟩ 2 : were it not that ⟨would play tennis, *only* I'm too
tired⟩

KINDS OF INFORMATION IN DICTIONARIES

26a. Learn what your dictionary tells you about words.

Refer often to the sample entries from the unabridged and abridged dictionaries (pages 592, 593, and 597) as you study the following.

Spelling

When you don't know the spelling of a word, you can look it up in the dictionary, which is the authority on correct spelling. If a word may be spelled two ways—like *oneself* or *one's self*—the dictionary usually gives the more common spelling first.

If there is a spelling problem connected with forming the plural of a word or with adding a suffix (like *–ed, –ing, –ness*), the dictionary shows you how to spell these words. Examples are *fur, furred* and *funnier, funniest.*

EXERCISE 4. Number your paper 1–10. Find the answers to the following questions in your dictionary.

A. Which is the more common spelling for the following?
  1. neighbor, neighbour
  2. flunkey, flunky
  3. lodestar, loadstar
  4. draught, draft
  5. catalogue, catalog

B. Correctly add the suffix listed on the right to the word on the left:
  6. lonely   est
  7. refer   ed
  8. usual   ly
  9. happy   ness
  10. travel   ing

Capital Letters

If you are not sure about capitalizing a word, the dictionary will help you. Notice on page 597 the capital in *Oneida*. Some words, like *democratic,* may or may not have a capital, depending upon how you use the word. Usually, *democratic* is listed as an uncapitalized common adjective; however, when the particular party is designated in the list of definitions, then a capital is used — *Democratic party*. Sometimes when a word refers to a particular product, it is listed with a capital — for example, *Jell-O*. When the word refers to any product like *Jell-O*, it is uncapitalized.

EXERCISE 5. Check your dictionary to find out whether (or when) the following words are capitalized. If the words may be used both ways, write sentences illustrating both uses.

1. arab	6. mumbo jumbo
2. bible	7. president
3. escalator	8. republican
4. god	9. scot
5. mercury	10. state

Syllables

Whenever you need to divide a word at the end of the line, you should split it between syllables only. The dictionary divides all words into syllables: for instance, *ac cu rate* is divided into three syllables.

If your dictionary should use a small dot or dash to show the breaks between syllables, *do not confuse this dash or dot with the hyphen.* Be sure that you know what the hyphen looks like in your dictionary by looking up such words as *mother-in-law* or *ack-ack*.

EXERCISE 6. Divide the following words into syllables. Check your work in the dictionary.

1. forevermore
2. impractical
3. old-fashioned

4. preliminary
5. recognize

Pronunciation

To show how a word is pronounced, the dictionary uses *diacritical marks,* which indicate the sounds of vowels, and it respells the word using certain consonants to mean certain sounds. Dictionaries differ somewhat in the marking systems they use. As you learn to master your dictionary's method of showing the correct pronunciation of a word, you will need to refer to the pronunciation key (usually given at the bottom, or the top, of each page).

Your teacher may wish to have you learn the common pronunciation markings now so that in your dictionary practice you will be able to understand how to pronounce any word you look up. If so, you should turn to pages 606–14, where you will find further explanation and exercises.

Part of Speech

A part-of-speech label is given for every word listed in your dictionary. The label is likely to be one of the following abbreviations:

n.	noun	*pron.*	pronoun
v. or *vb.*	verb	*prep.*	preposition
adv.	adverb	*conj.*	conjunction
adj.	adjective	*interj.*	interjection

In addition, most dictionaries label those verbs that take objects *v.t.* (for *transitive verb*) and those that do not *v.i.* (for *intransitive verb*). Many verbs that can be used with or without an object have some of their meanings labeled *v.i.* and some labeled *v.t.* The distinction between transitive and intransitive verbs is discussed on pages 16–17 of this book.

Dictionary practices differ in the placing of the part-of-speech label. The label may appear immediately after the pronunciation respelling (as in the samples in this chapter) or it may appear at the end of the entry.

EXERCISE 7. Look up these words in your dictionary, and classify each one according to its part of speech. (If a word may be used as three or four parts of speech, write each use after the proper number on your paper.)

1. base	5. jerk	8. play
2. beside	6. not	9. regular
3. court	7. out	10. row
4. forward		

Derivation

Your dictionary also tells you the derivation or the origin of a word. To indicate the languages from which a word has come, abbreviations like *L.* (Latin) and *F.* (French) are used. The meanings of these and other abbreviations are given in the key to the abbreviations at the front of the dictionary. Look on page 592 and notice the origin of *funnel*. Knowing the derivation of a word can sometimes help you remember its meaning.

EXERCISE 8. Write after the proper number on your paper the origin of each word listed below. If your student dictionary does not give the derivations, go to an unabridged or college dictionary. If a word is unfamiliar to you, learn its meaning when you look up its origin.

1. chlorophyll
2. exorbitant
3. kaleidoscope
4. phosphorus
5. pince-nez

6. procrastinate
7. quixotic
8. sponsor
9. sporadic
10. sympathy

Meaning

Of course, you know that a dictionary defines words. But do you make full use of its definitions? When a word has many different meanings, do you seek out the particular definition that you are looking for? Notice on page 592 the different meanings for *funnel* as a noun. There is a difference between a *funnel* for liquid and a stage *funnel*. Again, as you can see on page 597, there are two meanings for the adjective *one-sided*. These are indicated by numbers.

Some dictionaries place the oldest meaning first; others list the meanings in the order of their use, the most common meaning being given first. Either way, you will need to look over the many definitions until you find the one that fits the sentence in which you have found the word.

EXERCISE 9. Number your paper 1–10. Look up the exact meaning of each italicized word in these sentences, and write the meaning after the corresponding number.

1. Now I will *pose* for a snapshot.
2. His attitude seems to be a *pose*.
3. On the counter was a novelty key *ring*.
4. The *rings* indicated that the tree was twenty years old.
5. The *kite* lives on snails.
6. When the breezes are not too strong, sailors use *kites.*
7. The third *volume* in the series is the most useful.

8. The *volume* control on my radio is broken.
9. Government employees must pass a *civil* service test.
10. She wasn't even *civil*.

Labels Showing Usage Levels

Most dictionaries give some indication as to levels of usage. Words or meanings may be labeled *Slang, Colloq.* (colloquial) *Obs.* (obsolete, no longer in common use), etc. Not all dictionaries use the same labels, and even when they do, the labels may not mean the same thing. It is therefore essential that you read the introductory section of your dictionary to find out what the usage labels mean. Words and meanings that are not labeled are understood to be *standard:* in general use by the majority of English-speaking people.

EXERCISE 10. Look up the following words in your dictionary to see whether or not they are standard English. If you find no label anywhere in the definitions of a word, write "standard" on your paper after the proper number. If you find a label indicating a special classification, write the label on your paper, using the abbreviation found in your dictionary.

1. blob	5. stool pigeon	8. pep
2. bug	6. hydrogen	9. smithereens
3. case	7. note	10. snooze
4. cosmos		

Synonyms and Antonyms

A synonym is a word having almost the same meaning as the word being defined: *calm, serene.* An antonym is a word having the opposite meaning: *hot, cold.* Frequently, you will find a small paragraph set aside not only listing synonyms but also showing the distinctions of meanings. When you want to choose the exact word for your meaning, your dictionary, with its listings of synonyms and its cross references, will help you find the word.

EXERCISE 11. Look up the following words in your dictionary, and make a list of the synonyms given for each word.

1. freedom
2. laughable
3. shrewd
4. rough
5. loud

Illustrations

If the meaning of a word can best be shown by a picture, the dictionary may give an illustration. If, for example, you are studying gauges or the ancient pyramids, the chances are that you can find these illustrated in your dictionary.

26b. Find out what your dictionary tells you about people and places.

In your dictionary the names of people and places are either listed in a special biographical, geographical, or "proper names" section, or listed in the main body along with all other words. You can easily discover which method your dictionary uses.

To learn what your dictionary can tell you about a person, look up *Gabriela Mistral* under *M*. First of all, you find her name correctly spelled, and you can see how to pronounce it. In parentheses you find 1889–1957, the dates of her birth and death. Next is information about her nationality, which is Chilean. Finally, you learn why she became famous, that she was a Chilean poet. Should you happen to look up the name of a President, you would find the dates the person was in office. Your dictionary also has interesting information about people in the Bible (Moses, Lazarus) as well as about mythological and literary characters (Diana, Maid Marian).

Now look up the name of a place — say *Hwang Ho, Patmos,* or *Richmond* — in your dictionary. Notice that you can find out (1) how to spell and pronounce the word; (2) what it is (city, river, island); (3) where it is; (4) how big it is; (5) why it is important. Very frequently information about history and government is given.

EXERCISE 12. When your teacher gives the signal, look up the answers to the following questions in the dictionary you have. Write the answers on your paper. Accuracy is more important than speed, but speed *is* important. Your speed shows to some extent your knowledge of the dictionary.

1. Where is Madagascar?
2. In what year did Christopher Columbus die?
3. How high is Mount Everest?
4. When was Ralph Bunche born?
5. What is the Hydra?
6. How large is Lake Huron?
7. What was the nationality of Nellie Melba?
8. How long is the Rio Grande?
9. Who was Merlin?
10. Where is the Gatun Dam?

REVIEW EXERCISE. Number your paper 1–10. By using your dictionary, correctly answer each of the following questions.

1. What is the correct syllable division of the word *hypochondriac?*

2. Which is the more usual spelling—*pretence* or *pretense?*
3. When, if ever, is the word *army* capitalized?
4. What part of speech is *please?*
5. Is *nincompoop* slang?
6. What is the origin of the word *jujitsu?*
7. What is the meaning of the word *ossify?*
8. What is the meaning of *NCO?*
9. Who was Alfred Bernhard Nobel?
10. Is it correct to use the word *swell* as an adjective in formal writing?

PRONUNCIATION

26c. Use your dictionary for pronunciation.

The regular way of learning to pronounce a word is to listen to the pronunciation of your parents, teachers, and friends. The dictionary gives pronunciations for all of its entry words, but you will use it mainly for the pronunciation of words that you have never heard or do not hear often. Dictionary makers try to give the standard pronunciation, but since words are pronounced differently in different places, it is not always possible to give a single pronunciation that is suitable for Boston, Chicago, Houston, and Atlanta. For this reason, you may sometimes find that your dictionary tells you one thing about the sound of a word and that you hear it spoken quite differently in your part of the country. When this happens, you may wish to ask your teacher about the acceptable pronunciation of that word in your area. You should not, however, assume that a pronunciation you hear is wrong just because the dictionary does not give it.

Because the actual spelling of many English words does not clearly indicate how they are pronounced, dictionaries use simplified respellings to indicate the sound of a word. Moreover, since there are more sounds in English than there are letters to represent them, special symbols called *diacritical marks* must be used to show different speech sounds represented by the same letter. The following pair of words illustrates both respelling and the use of diacritical marks:

bit (bit)   bite (bīt)

Notice that *bite* is respelled without the silent *e* and that the different sounds of *i* are distinguished, the *i* in *bit* being unmarked and the one in *bite* being written with a straight line above it.

Indicating pronunciation is one of the dictionary maker's most difficult tasks, and it is not surprising that there is some disagreement as to how it should be done. The systems used in various dictionaries differ in a number of details. You will see some of these differences in this chapter. However, when you have need of a pronunciation, you will not need to know all the different ways of indicating it. What you will need to know is how to interpret the pronunciation given in your own dictionary. To do this you must familiarize yourself with the explanatory notes dealing with pronunciation and with the pronunciation key. Most dictionaries explain the system they use in the introductory pages. A full key is usually given inside the front cover. Many dictionaries print a shorter key on each page or each set of facing pages. The key illustrates the use of each letter and symbol used by means of simple examples that everyone knows how to pronounce.

Consonant Sounds

The sounds that a speaker makes by squeezing or

cutting off the stream of breath are called *consonants*. The last sounds in *with, this,* and *have* are made by forcing the breath through a narrowed passage at one point or another between the throat and the lips. The last sounds in *first, wasp,* and *break* are made by cutting off the breath momentarily.

Consonants present few problems in representing pronunciation because most of them are pronounced in essentially the same way in all words. In a few cases, ordinary English spelling uses one letter for two different consonant sounds. For example, the letter *c* stands for two quite different sounds in *cake* and *cell*. In giving the pronunciation of these words, the dictionary would spell the first with a *k* and the second with an *s*.

Two closely related sounds, the first one in *thin* and the first one in *then,* are distinguished in different ways in different dictionaries. For example:

	WSD[1]	NCD	T−B	SCD
thin	/thin/	/thin/	(thin)	(thin)
then	/then/	/then/	(ꝼHen)	(then)

Notice that all of these dictionaries use plain "th" for the sound of the consonant in *thin* and that they differ only in the symbol they use for the related sound in *then*. Whichever dictionary you use, the sound represented by the plain letters will be the one in *thin, thimble,* and *thank*.

Vowel Sounds

The sounds that are made when a speaker does not squeeze or stop the flow of breath are called *vowels*.

[1] The abbreviations stand for *Webster's School Dictionary, New Collegiate Dictionary, Thorndike-Barnhart High School Dictionary,* and *Standard College Dictionary,* respectively.

Although we use five letters (*a, e, i, o, u*) and sometimes a sixth (*y*) in representing vowel sounds in writing, there are actually nine different vowels that are used by most speakers of English in America. To indicate these sounds, dictionary makers use the letters above in combination with diacritical marks.

Long Vowels

The long straight mark over a vowel is called the *macron*. When the macron appears over a vowel, the vowel is said to have the sound of its own name. Such vowels are called *long vowels*.

EXAMPLES   **fate** (fāt)
                  sleep (slēp)
                  side (sīd)
                  lone (lōn)
                  fuse (fūz)

Short Vowels

The vowels in the words *cat, beg, dig, odd,* and *up* are called *short vowels*. Dictionaries differ in their methods of showing the sound of short vowels.

One method uses this symbol (˘), called a breve (brĕv) over the vowel. Another method is to leave short vowels unmarked.

EXAMPLES   **add**   (ăd) or (ad)
                  bed   (bĕd) or (bed)
                  big   (bĭg) or (big)

Sometimes, when all that we say in an unaccented syllable is the sound of the consonant, the pronunciation respelling in certain dictionaries may omit the short vowel altogether.

EXAMPLES   **localize** (lōk′ l īz)
                  pagan (pāg′ n)

The Schwa

If your dictionary is a recent one, you are probably already familiar with the symbol (ə), called the *schwa* (shwä). This upside-down *e* is used to represent the blurred, unclear sound of "uh" in such words as

alone	(ə·lōn′)
nickel	(nik′ əl)
Hannibal	(han′ ə·bəl)
collect	(kə·lect′)
support	(sə·pôrt′)

Most modern dictionaries use the schwa, but some use it more than others. Dictionaries prepared by the G. & C. Merriam Company (*Webster's School Dictionary,* the *New Collegiate Dictionary,* and others) use this symbol in respelling one-syllable words and other words in which the schwa appears in an accented syllable. Most other dictionaries use the schwa only for unaccented syllables. The examples that follow illustrate this difference:

	WSD[1]	NCD	T–B	SCD
bun	ˈbən	ˈbən	bun	bun
color	ˈkəl-ər	ˈkəl-ər	kul′ər	kul′ər
supper	ˈsəp-ər	ˈsəp-ər	sup′ər	sup′ər

EXERCISE 13. Look up the pronunciation of each of the following words in your dictionary and copy it after the appropriate number on your paper. Follow the practice of your dictionary in using parentheses or slant lines to enclose the pronunciation.

1. acknowledge
2. aghast
3. athletic
4. choir
5. generous
6. phonograph

[1] The abbreviations stand for *Webster's School Dictionary, New Collegiate Dictionary, Thorndike-Barnhart High School Dictionary* and *Standard College Dictionary,* respectively.

7. pressure   9. these
8. suppose   10. thought

Accent Marks

In words of more than one syllable, one syllable is always spoken louder than the others. The syllable stressed in this way is said to be accented, and it is marked in the pronunciation in one of several ways, depending again on the dictionary you are looking at.

	WSD[1]	NCD	T–B	SCD
battery	'bat-ə-rē	'bat er-ē	bat'ər i	bat'ər ē

In some words, the placing of the accent makes a great deal of difference. For example, if we accent the first syllable of *rebel,* we have a noun meaning "a rebellious person," while if we accent the second, we have a verb meaning "to rise up or battle against authority."

For certain words of three or more syllables, the dictionary gives two accents. The first, as shown above, is called the *primary accent;* the second is called the *secondary accent.* Dictionaries handle accent marks in different ways. Some put accent marks before the syllable being stressed; some after. Some use a light mark for the secondary accent; some place the secondary accent to the left and below the stressed syllable. Notice how it is done in four dictionaries for the word *elevator.*

	WSD[1]	NCD
elevator	'el-ə-ˌvāt-ər	'el-ə-ˌvāt-ər

	T–B	SCD
	el'ə vāt'ər	el'ə·vāt'ər

---

[1] The abbreviations stand for *Webster's School Dictionary, New Collegiate Dictionary, Thorndike-Barnhart High School Dictionary,* and *Standard College Dictionary,* respectively.

EXERCISE 14. Look up the pronunciation of each of the following words in your dictionary and copy it after the appropriate number. Be sure to include accent marks and diacritical marks. Indicate syllable division in whatever way your dictionary does.

1. appropriate (adjective)
2. appropriate (verb)
3. establish
4. foreground
5. fraternity
6. instrumental
7. lighthouse
8. promote
9. serpent
10. wheelbarrow

EXERCISE 15. Rewrite each italicized word, showing the accented syllable and the part of speech as in your dictionary.

EXAMPLE
1. What can his *object* be?
   I don't know, but I *object* to his method.
1. (*ob'ject*), *n.*
   (*ob·ject'*), *v.*

1. What is your favorite *subject?*
   You should not *subject* him to ridicule.
2. Many people *protest* against war.
   Their *protest* is objected to by others.
3. No one is *perfect,* but people do try to *perfect* themselves.
4. I do not *suspect* her of malice, but her attitude is *suspect.*
5. All young people *rebel,* but she remained a *rebel* all her life.
6. I *reject* your hypothesis.
   This one is a *reject* because it is defective.
7. We cannot *refuse* to help those in need.
   All *refuse* should be thrown into the proper receptacle.
8. Do you like this *console* table?
   No one could *console* him in his grief.

Words Commonly Mispronounced

Using the key below, practice saying the following commonly mispronounced words correctly.

accept (ak·sept')
alias (ā'lē·as)
almond (ä'mənd,
  am'ənd)
architect (är'kə·tekt)
athlete (ath'lēt)
attacked (ə·takt')
auxiliary (ôg·zil'yər·ē,
  ôg·zil'ər·ē)

bade (bad)
because (bi·kôz')
bicycle (bī'sik·əl)
blackguard (blag'ərd,
  blag'ärd)

café (ka·fā', kə·fā')
candidate (kan'də·dāt,
  kan'də·dit)
cello (chel'ō)
cement (si·ment')
champion (cham'pē·ən)
chasm (kaz'əm)
children (chil'drən)
column (kol'əm)
comparable (kom'pər·ə·
  bəl)
contrary (kon'trer·ē)

curiosity (kyo͞or'ē·os'
  ə·tē)

demonstrative (di·mon'
  strə·tiv)
discretion (dis·kresh'ən)
docile (dos'əl)
drowned (dround)

elm (elm)
everybody (ev'rē·bod'ē,
  ev'rē·bud'ē)

faucet (fô'sit)
film (film)
finale (fi·nä'lē, fi·nal'ē)
forbade (fər·bad',
  fôr·bad')
further (fûr'thər)
futile (fyo͞o'təl)

genuine (jen'yo͞o·in)
geography (jē·og'rə·fē)
geometry (jē·om'ə·trē)
gesture (jes'chər)
gigantic (jī·gan'tik)
grimy (grī'mē)

PRONUNCIATION KEY: add, āce, câre, pälm; end, ēven; it, īce; odd, ōpen, ôrder; to͝ok, po͞ol; up, bûrn; ə = a in *above*, e in *sicken*, i in *flexible*, o in *melon*, u in *focus*; yo͞o = u in *fuse*; oil; pout; check; go; ring; thin; this; zh, vision.

"Pronunciation Key" from *Funk and Wagnall's Standard College Dictionary.* Copyright © 1977 by Harper & Row, Publishers, Inc. Reprinted by permission of the publisher.

handkerchief (hang′
  kər·chif)
height (hīt)
hundred (hun′drid)

impious (im′pē·əs)
indicted (in·dīt′id)
infamous (in′fə·məs)
influence (in′floō·əns)
introduce (in′trə·doōs′)
irreparable (i·rep′ər·ə·
  bəl)
Italian (i·tal′yən)
italics (i·tal′iks)

just (just)

length (lengkth, length)
library (lī′brer·ē,
  lī′brə·rē)

mischievous (mis′chi·
  vəs)
municipal (myoō·nis′ə·
  pəl)
museum (myoō·zē′əm)

perform (pər·fôrm′)
perhaps (pər·haps′)
perspiration (pûr′spə·
  rā′shən)

piano (pē·a′nō)
poem (pō′əm)
preferable (pref′ər·ə·
  bəl)
prescription (pri·skrip′
  shən)
probably (prob′ə·blē)

quantity (kwon′tə·tē)

recognize (rek′əg·nīz)
remonstrate (ri·mon′
  strāt)
reputable (rep′yə·tə·
  bəl)
rinse (rins)

strength (strengkth,
  strength)
suite (swēt)
superfluous (soŏ·pûr′
  floō·əs)

telegraphy (tə·leg′rə·fē)
theater (thē′ə·tər)

vehicle (vē′ə·kəl)
victual (vit′l)

wrestle (res′əl)

Chapter 27

Vocabulary

Context Clues, Synonyms, Word Analysis

The best way to increase your vocabulary is to read widely and to remember a good deal of what you have read. This may seem like an old-fashioned method, but there are really no shortcuts. There are, however, ways of improving your efficiency in learning the new words that you encounter. Knowing how to find clues to the meaning of a word elsewhere in the sentence and knowing something about the ways words are formed will help.

This chapter is intended to help you develop skills that will be useful in building a better vocabulary. But before you begin, take the following test on the meanings of words that appear in books commonly read by students of your age. What percentage of these words do you know now?

Diagnostic Test

Number your paper 1–25. After the proper number, write the letter of the word which is nearest in meaning to the italicized word at the left.

1. *absolve*   a. forget   c. pardon
                   b. accuse   d. figure out

2. *allusion*   a. reference   c. mistaken idea
                  b. criticism   d. disappoint-
                                        ment

3. *anarchy*   a. dictatorship   c. entryway
                  b. lawlessness   d. country ruled
                                        by a queen

4. *benevolence* a. laziness   c. rudeness
                  b. mysterious-   d. kindliness
                     ness

5. *bizarre*   a. childish   c. strange
                  b. poorly   d. common
                     chosen

6. *candid*   a. small   c. hidden
                  b. straight-   d. unjust
                     forward

7. *competent*   a. capable   c. incapable
                  b. aggressive   d. sane

8. *discrepancy* a. difference   c. dislike
                  b. dishonesty   d. noise

9. *docile*   a. stupid   c. easily misled
                  b. easily tired   d. easily man-
                                        aged

10. *exasperated* a. irritated   c. puzzled
                  b. undecided   d. overjoyed

11. *flaunt*   a. betray   c. show off
                  b. point out   d. give in

12. *grueling*   a. questioning   c. exhausting
                  b. frightening   d. stubborn

13. *haven*   a. paradise   c. shelter
                  b. town   d. small river

14. *immune*   a. in bad health   c. healthy
                  b. alone   d. protected

15. *incomprehen-* a. startling   c. not under-
    sible   standable
                  b. too expensive   d. not flam-
                                        mable

16. *ingenious*   a. dishonest   c. simple-
                                       minded
                  b. clever   d. frank

17. *jaunty*   a. light-hearted c. nervous
                  b. strolling   d. yellowish

18. *lethal*   a. deadly   c. criminal
                  b. explosive   d. warlike

19. *meander*   a. walk rapidly   c. examine
                  b. untie   d. wander

20. *mediocre*   a. ignorant   c. ill-tempered
                  b. ordinary   d. boring

21. *ominous*   a. altogether   c. threatening
                  b. disappearing   d. hungry

22. *retrieve*   a. recover   c. make up
                  b. hunt   d. overlook

23. *skeptical*   a. doubting   c. cruel
                  b. unfriendly   d. untrust-
                                       worthy

24. *tawdry*   a. cute and   c. tattered and
                     charming   worn
                  b. showy and   d. ill-fitting
                     tasteless

25. *wary*   a. trusting   c. tired
                  b. cowardly   d. cautious

27a. List new words with their meanings in your note-book, and use them in speech and writing.

When you learn a new word, list it in your notebook with its meaning. Use it in speech and writing as often as you can in order to make it a permanent part of your vocabulary. Begin now by listing any words that were new to you in the diagnostic test. Keep a special section of your notebook for this purpose; after each exercise in this chapter, add to the list all words you did not know. Add any other words you learn from day to day.

WAYS TO LEARN NEW WORDS

Context

The total situation in which a word is used is called its *context*.

27b. Learn new words from their contexts.

The words that surround a particular word are one part of the context; the circumstances in which it is used are another part.

Verbal Context

The other words in the sentence are the *verbal context* of a word. They often supply clues to meaning. For example, if you did not know the meaning of the word *pedestrians,* you would probably be able to guess it from the surrounding words in the following sentence:

> Because there were no sidewalks, **pedestrians** had to be careful to avoid cars.

Sidewalks are intended for people to walk on. Since the absence of sidewalks makes this street or road dangerous for *pedestrians,* the word probably has something to do with "walking people" or "people who are on foot." Of course, guesses based on context turn out to be wrong sometimes, but they are well worth making. In fact, you have learned most of the words you know by making guesses of this kind.

Physical Context

The actual situation being discussed is the *physical context.* Suppose that you happen to hear someone say "At last she's got a strike." This time the other words in the sentence are not much help if you do not know what *strike* means. What does help is knowing what the speaker is talking about. If she is watching a baseball game, *strike* means one thing; it means quite another if she is talking about fishing or bowling. We call this *physical context* because the surroundings—in this case, a baseball park, a boat, or a bowling alley—usually give us the clue we need.

Since the two kinds of context work together to help you discover the meaning of unfamiliar words, it is not important that you be able to distinguish one kind from the other. What is important is that you remain alert to all possible clues that a situation may provide to the meaning of a new word.

EXERCISE 1. Number your paper 1–10. For the italicized word in each of the sentences, select the definition from the list below that is closest in meaning. Write its letter beside the proper number. When you have finished, check in your dictionary the meaning of any words you are not sure of. You will not need all of the definitions in the list.

a. warn gently
b. youthful
c. able to float
d. having little resistance to
e. trace
f. one who is too enthusiastic
g. expert
h. frighten
i. good-natured
j. burdensome
k. proverbial saying
l. repeat
m. showing good judgment
n. injury to repay injury

1. The people threatened to revolt unless the queen repealed the *oppressive* new tax.
2. Not a *vestige* of the old path remained to guide the explorers.
3. Life jackets are necessarily made from *buoyant* materials.

4. The state police will *reiterate* their earlier warnings to motorists about to set out on holiday trips.
5. People in public life are expected to be *discreet* in both their private and public affairs.
6. Some people seem to be more *susceptible* to colds than others.
7. Jane is so *amiable* that people sometimes take advantage of her.
8. Mr. Collins, who never could remember an *adage* exactly, was fond of saying, "The early worm gets eaten."
9. The announcer occasionally had to *admonish* the children to stop eating the prizes.
10. The general of the occupying army threatened to make *reprisals* unless the townspeople cooperated with his troops.

EXERCISE 2. Number your paper 1–10. Copy each italicized word in the following passage, and write next to it what you think it means. Write either a definition or a *synonym*. When you have completed the exercise, check with dictionary meanings, rewrite those you had wrong, and restudy the context which you missed. Add new words to your notebook list.

Although our team had played a good game, the second half of the ninth inning found our (1) *adversaries* holding a three-run lead, and this seemed too big for us to (2) *surmount*. Our hope (3) *diminished* further when our first batter flied out to center, but it revived a little when Frank, our pitcher, hit a double. Our opponents decided to use (4) *strategy*, and they gave an (5) *intentional* base on balls to George, our third batter. Excitement reached a (6) *climax* when Eddie, the fourth man up, hit a sharp grounder which the second baseman was unable to (7) *intercept*. (8) *Subsequent* events were almost too quick to follow. With the bases full, Joe, our catcher, hit a home run, and the (9) *frenzied* spectators rushed out on the field and carried him with wild (10) *acclaim* to the clubhouse.

27c. Learn to find the meaning you want in the dictionary.

Although there are some words in English, like *carbon dioxide,* that have only one meaning or only a few very closely related meanings, most common words have many. The word *point,* for example, may mean "a place," "the tip of a pencil," "a unit of scoring in a game," "the main idea that someone is trying to express," and many other things as well. Since dictionaries define all of the important uses of a word, it is important not to settle for the very first definition that is listed for an entry word.

The best way of testing definitions in context is to keep in mind the context in which you read or heard the word. You can then try the various meanings until you find the one that fits. Take this sentence, for example:

The general **dispatched** the captives quickly and painlessly.

The meaning of the sentence depends upon the meaning of *dispatched.* Keeping the whole sentence in mind will help you to choose the right meaning for *dispatched* in this sentence. Of the three definitions your dictionary is certain to give — (1) to send away; (2) to put to death; (3) to dispose of quickly, as business — only the second really fits. The sentence means that the general put the captives to death in a quick and painless way.

To make the differences between a word's various meanings clear, dictionary makers often provide sample contexts as part of the definition. The same context for meaning (1) of *dispatch* might be "to dispatch a messenger." When such illustrative examples are given, you can easily compare your context with this one to make sure you have found the meaning you want.

EXERCISE 3. The italicized words in the following sentences all have a number of different meanings. Using your dictionary, find the meaning that fits best and write it after the proper number on your paper. Be sure to test each meaning given in the context of the sentence before making your choice.

1. Both of the candidates appeared to tire in the last *hectic* days of the campaign.
2. The modest hero of "The Great Stone Face" *ascribes* to others all of the excellent qualities he does not recognize in himself.
3. The courts of the dictator made a *farce* of justice.
4. Occasionally one of Judy's friends would *impose* on her generosity.
5. Many of Shirley Jackson's most famous short stories have distinctly *morbid* themes.
6. It was like Harry never to think of the *orthodox* solution to a problem.
7. Having been wiped out by her partner's treachery, Ms. Marple merely shrugged and set about *retrieving* her fortune.
8. The lost party of explorers found only muddy water to *slake* their thirst.
9. Only the pilot's coolness in the face of danger prevented a *tragedy*.
10. It was soon evident that the ruthless leader's civilized manners were only a *veneer*.

Determining the Part of Speech

Many words in English can be used as different parts of speech. Since these words do different jobs in sentences, the meanings have to be stated differently if they are to fit into the proper kinds of context. For example, a dictionary would list all of the meanings for *seal* illustrated by the following sentences:

That is the **seal** of the State of New York.
Christmas **seals** raise money to fight tuberculosis.
The sailors desperately **sealed** the leak.
The notary **sealed** the document to make it official.

In the first two sentences, *seal* is used as a noun; in the second two, it is used as a verb. Most dictionaries indicate in some way the part of speech of each meaning they define. Some group the noun meanings, the verb meanings, etc., together, and others show the part of speech of each meaning at the end of the entry. However your dictionary does it, it will save you time to know the part of speech of the meaning you are looking up. (If you are not clear how dictionaries indicate the part of speech, review page 600.)

EXERCISE 4. Look up *root* and *iron* in your dictionary. List as many parts of speech as you can find for each entry and indicate the number of meanings given for each.

EXERCISE 5. Use each of the following words in a sentence of your own as the part of speech indicated.

EXAMPLE 1. seal [as a noun]
    1. *The queen signed the paper and affixed her seal.*

1. affront [as a noun]
2. alien [as an adjective]
3. epic [as a noun]
4. intrigue [as a verb]
5. moor [as a verb]
6. plot [as a noun]

7. tutor [as a verb]
8. solvent [as an adjective]
9. testimonial [as a noun]
10. wrangle [as a verb]

EXERCISE 6. Follow these instructions for each of the ten sentences following. (1) Write the italicized word after the proper number. (2) After the word, write its part of speech in this sentence. (3) Then write a synonym or a short definition. Be sure that you give the appropriate meaning for words that have more than one definition.

EXAMPLE 1. Cross-country racing demands great *stamina.*
　　　　　1. *stamina, noun, endurance*

1. Comedians who imitate well-known people have to be excellent *mimics.*
2. The barons *wrested* power from the tyrannical King John at Runnymede.
3. Many movie stars attended the *premiere.*
4. Despite the evidence against her, the defendant continued to *aver* her innocence.
5. There was a *perceptible* improvement in assembly attendance after the principal's short speech.
6. A winter of terrible hardship and constant rumors of the enemy's strength had *demoralized* the troops.
7. Although the general never rode horses when he could help it, he is the subject of many *equestrian* statues.
8. No one ever thought of offering them any but the most *menial* jobs.
9. A duel between the two warriors *climaxed* the action in the third scene.
10. There is little room for *dissent* in a country ruled by a dictator.

REVIEW EXERCISE A. The words in this exercise have been chosen from those you have studied so far in this chapter. Number your paper 1–20. After the proper number, write the letter of the word which is nearest in meaning to the italicized word at the left.

1. *admonish*
   a. warn gently
   b. punish
   c. prohibit
   d. applaud

2. *adversary*
   a. reversal
   b. bearer of bad news
   c. opponent
   d. spy

3. *ascribe*
   a. tell about
   b. give as a cause
   c. envy
   d. speak ill of

4. *dispatch*
   a. receive
   b. command
   c. send away
   d. punish

5. *hectic*
   a. calm
   b. feverishly excited
   c. noisily cheerful
   d. angry

6. *impose*
   a. take advantage
   b. show off
   c. pretend
   d. reveal

7. *intrigue*
   a. plot
   b. entertain
   c. slander
   d. imitate

8. *menial*
   a. cruel
   b. servantlike
   c. ordinary
   d. by hand

9. *mimic*
   a. show
   b. imitate
   c. envy
   d. perform

10. *morbid*
    a. gloomy
    b. fatal
    c. imaginative
    d. ordinary

11. *oppressive*
    a. respected
    b. burdensome
    c. unfair
    d. unfriendly

12. *orthodox*
    a. religious
    b. public
    c. conventional
    d. unusual

13. *perceptible*
    a. slight
    b. proverbial
    c. noticeable
    d. frightening

14. *retrieve*   a. search for   c. follow
               b. locate   d. bring back

15. *stamina*   a. ability to   c. endurance
                     reason   d. part of a
               b. speed   flower

16. *strategy*   a. planning   c. sport
               b. warfare   d. rules

17. *subsequent*   a. less impor-   c. coming be-
                      tant   fore
                  b. hidden   d. something
                                      that follows

18. *surmount*   a. climb on   c. give up
                b. overcome   d. tower

19. *veneer*   a. thin coating   c. fault
              b. locality   d. decoy

20. *vestige*   a. trace   c. ceremony
             b. honor   d. secret

Using the Right Word

27d. Select the word that conveys the precise meaning and impression you want to give.

There is little point in knowing a large number of words unless you make some use of them. While many of the new words you learn from now on will be more useful to you in your reading than in your own writing and speaking, you will certainly find that some of them will help you to express your thoughts with greater clarity and precision.

The English language is rich in synonyms — words that have the same general meaning but that have subtle shades of difference between them. Choosing the right synonym can mean a great deal when you are trying to write clearly and effectively.

EXERCISE 7. Number your paper 1–10. For each

sentence in this exercise, select the most appropriate synonym for the word *walk* from the following list. Use a different word in each sentence. You may use any tense needed to fit the structure of the sentence. Write that word next to the number, and be prepared to explain in class why each word is most appropriate. If you are in doubt, use your dictionary.

amble	stride
march	stroll
pace	tramp
plod	tread
promenade	wander

1. The referee picked up the ball, —— back five yards, and put it on our thirty-yard line.
2. Over a thousand veterans —— in the Memorial Day parade.
3. —— the deck of a large ocean liner is an exhilarating experience.
4. In her haste she —— ahead of her companions through the crowded street.
5. The horse —— slowly along the path as its rider enjoyed the scenery.
6. Unaware of the surroundings, the blissful couple —— slowly, arm in arm.
7. The cows had —— a path to the stream.
8. The happy boy on his vacation —— idly along beside the brook.
9. Hoping to make up the lost time, the hikers —— resolutely through the woods.
10. The weary hiker, lifting each foot with obvious effort, —— up the hill.

EXERCISE 8. Number your paper 1–10. Refer to the dictionary for the exact meaning of each adverb. Then answer each of the questions by writing the most appropriate adverb next to the number of the question which the adverb answers.

barbarously	grotesquely
comprehensively	nocturnally
defiantly	reluctantly
ferociously	reverently
genially	ungraciously

1. How did the tiger bare its teeth at the visitors in the zoo?
2. How did the tourists stand at the Tomb of the Unknown soldier?
3. How did the Goths and Vandals act when they sacked and burned the city of Rome?
4. How did the nervous patient approach the dentist's chair?
5. How did the captured heroine stare at her enemy?
6. How did the announcer smile as she greeted the contestant in the quiz contest?
7. How was the unnatural-looking clown dressed?
8. How did the weary couple greet the unexpected guests at dinnertime?
9. How did the well-prepared student answer the examination questions?
10. When do owls hunt for prey?

EXERCISE 9. Number your paper 1–15. Next to each number, write the letter of the correct synonym for the italicized word. Refer to your dictionary whenever necessary.

1. *abate*
   a. help b. lessen c. return
2. *aloof*
   a. awkward b. scared c. standoffish
3. *durable*
   a. lasting b. tired c. hard
4. *encounter*
   a. meet b. reach c. reckon
5. *falter*
   a. need b. hesitate c. misplay

6. *futile*
   a. old   b. frail   c. useless
7. *gaudy*
   a. general   b. useful   c. showy
8. *intricate*
   a. complicated   b. interior   c. pretty
9. *laconic*
   a. slow   b. funny   c. terse
10. *manifest*
    a. strengthen   b. reveal   c. displace
11. *poise*
    a. composure   b. beauty   c. pride
12. *potency*
    a. pretense   b. strength   c. view
13. *requisite*
    a. necessary   b. late   c. early
14. *turbulent*
    a. ancient   b. young   c. violent
15. *ultimate*
    a. final   b. aged   c. reliable

27e. Learn to understand and use literary terms.

High school students are frequently asked to discuss books or plays. The words in the following exercises will help you to carry on a literary discussion with intelligence and clarity.

EXERCISE 10. Number your paper 1–10. Use your dictionary to look up any unfamiliar words in column A. Write the letter from column B which is appropriate for the numbered word in column A.

	A	B
1.	atmosphere	a. the main story
2.	comedy	b. the main character
3.	foreshadowing	c. an unchanging conventional
4.	plot	character

5. protagonist
6. setting
7. soliloquy
8. stereotype
9. theme
10. tragedy

d. the main subject or idea of a literary work
e. a hint of something to come
f. speech by a character to him- or herself
g. the color or feeling pervading a literary work
h. a play making fun of something
i. a serious play having an unhappy ending
j. a historical literary work
k. a play with a happy ending
l. the place and time of a literary work

EXERCISE 11. Number your paper 1–10. Use your dictionary to look up any unfamiliar words in column A. Write the letter from column B which is appropriate for the numbered word in column A.

A

1. biographical
2. didactic
3. farcical
4. fictitious
5. hackneyed
6. melodramatic
7. poignant
8. realistic
9. romantic
10. satirical

B

a. painfully moving or touching
b. freely imaginative and fanciful
c. appealing to emotion by sensationalism and exaggeration
d. marked by broad or boisterous humor
e. ornate in style
f. attacking or ridiculing a custom, habit, or idea
g. of a person's life
h. overused, commonplace, stale
i. clear and simple
j. representing in literature life as it actually is
k. intended to instruct, teacher-like
l. not real, imaginary, made up

PREFIXES AND ROOTS

When you look up a word in the dictionary, you often find older words listed as the origin. English has borrowed words from almost all languages, but particularly from Latin and Greek. Sometimes one Latin or Greek word element is found in many English words. Knowing the meaning of a Greek or Latin word element gives you an understanding of a great many English words.

These word elements may be the part of a word that comes first, called the *prefix;* they may be the main part, called the *root;* they may be the part added at the end, called the *suffix.* Many words have only one or two of these parts, but some have three. Consider the word *semiannual.* This word is composed of the prefix *semi-,* meaning "half" in Latin; the root *-annu-,* meaning "year" in Latin; and the suffix *-al,* from a Latin suffix meaning "pertaining to." The word *semiannual* means "pertaining to an event that occurs every half year." (The same root may show a vowel change in different words. In *biennial,* for example, *-enni-* is the same root as *-annu-* although two of its letters are changed.)

27f. Learn some of the common Latin prefixes and roots.

LATIN PREFIX	MEANING	LATIN ROOT	MEANING
ad–	to, toward	–cis–	cut
bi–	two	–fid–	faith
con–	with	–ped–	foot
in–	into	–spec–	look
intro–	within	–voc–	call

The word parts from Latin listed above are commonly used in English words. If you learn the meaning of these prefixes and roots, you will be able to figure out the meaning of a great many words in which they occur.

EXERCISE 12. Number your paper 1–5. Write the prefix and its meaning and the root and its meaning for each word in the numbered list below. Then write the meaning of the whole word. Use your dictionary if necessary.

EXAMPLE   1. submarine
              1. *sub (under) + mare (sea) = underwater*
                                        boat

1. biped   4. advocate
2. incise   5. introspect
3. confide

Here are some other commonly used Latin prefixes and roots. Before you do the exercise below them, try to think of words in which these parts appear. Can you see a relationship between the meaning of the part and the meaning of the whole word?

LATIN PREFIX	MEANING	LATIN ROOT	MEANING
ab–, abs–	off	–cid–	kill
re–	back, again	–cogn–	know
sub–	below, under	–dic–, –dict–	say, speak
		–hom–	man
		–pond–	a weight
		–prob–	prove
		–sed–	seat
		–ten–, –tens–	stretch
		–tract–	draw
		–vert–, –vers–	turn

EXERCISE 13. Number your paper 1–10. For each italicized word, write the part or parts derived from Latin and their meanings. Then write the meaning of the word as it is used in the phrase. Use your dictionary if necessary. Ignore the suffixes in this exercise.

EXAMPLES 1. *dictate* letters
1. *dict* (*speak*) = *speak a message for someone to write down*
2. *subtract* the balance
2. *sub* (*below*) + *tract* (*draw*) = *withdraw or take away the balance*

1. to *recognize* a friend
2. a detective from the *homicide* division
3. faultless *diction*
4. act of *subversion*
5. a *ponderous* elephant

6. on *probation*
7. *retract* the statement
8. a *tenuous* conclusion
9. a *versatile* musician
10. a *sedentary* job

27g. Learn some of the common Greek prefixes and roots.

There are many words in English which are derived from Greek words. Study the following list of common prefixes and roots.

GREEK PREFIX	MEANING
auto–	self
eu–	good
hydr–	water
micro–	small
ortho–	right, straight
sym–	together
tri–	three

GREEK ROOT	MEANING
–astr–, –aster–	star
–chir–	hand
–dox–	opinion
–geo–	earth
–graph–	write
–log–	speech, science of (something)
–nomy–	law

GREEK ROOT	MEANING
–phobia–	dread of
–phon–	sound
–pod–	foot

EXERCISE 14. Number your paper 1–10, skipping a line after each number. Copy the italicized words that follow. After referring to your dictionary, write the part or parts derived from Greek and their meaning. Then write the meaning of the word as it is used in the phrase. Ignore the suffixes in this exercise.

EXAMPLE 1. a case of *hydrophobia*
1. *hydro (water) + phobia (dread)* = *a case involving a dread of water*

1. marked by an *asterisk*
2. an *autograph* collector
3. granted *autonomy*
4. treated by a *chiropodist*
5. a flattering *eulogy*
6. studying *geology*
7. examining a *microphone*
8. an *orthodox* believer
9. a flutist in the *symphony*
10. standing on a *tripod*

EXERCISE 15. As your teacher dictates them, write the meaning of each of the following Latin and Greek prefixes. Then write a word in which the prefix appears. Be prepared to explain the relationship between the meaning of the prefix and the meaning of the word.

1. ab–
2. ad–
3. auto–
4. bi–
5. con–
6. di–, dia–
7. hydr–
8. in–
9. intro–
10. micro–
11. ortho–
12. re–
13. sub–
14. sym–
15. tri–

EXERCISE 16. As your teacher dictates them, write the meaning of each of the following Latin and Greek roots. Then write a word in which the root appears. Be prepared to explain the relationship between the meaning of the root and the meaning of the word.

1. –astr–	10. –graph–	19. –prob–
2. –cogn–	11. –hom–	20. -sed–
3. –chir–	12. –log–	21. –ten–, –tens–
4. –cid–	13. –nomy–	22. -tract–
5. –cis–	14. –ped–	23. –vers–
6. –dict–	15. –phobia–	24. –vert–
7. –dox–	16. –phon–	25. –voc–
8. –fid–	17. –pod–	
9. –geo–	18. –pond–	

27h. Learn the origins of words as an aid to remembering meaning.

(1) Words with interesting histories

Study the origin of each word when you look it up in the dictionary. For example, in the entry for the word *candidate* you will find the following: [L. *candidatus,* clothed in white]. *L.* means "Latin," and *candidatus* is the Latin word from which *candidate* comes. The explanation of this word origin is that in ancient Rome candidates wore white robes. Many other words, like the ones in the following exercise, have interesting stories connected with them.

EXERCISE 17. Number your paper 1–10. Next to the appropriate number, write the italicized word. By referring to the dictionary, write the definition of each word and the language of its origin. Be prepared to explain the origin orally in class.

1. The *assassination* of the Austrian Archduke touched off the explosion of World War I.
2. Digital computers now do in a few seconds

calculations which would take mathematicians months or years to complete.

3. Exhibits of armor in museums remind us of the days of *chivalry*.
4. Diogenes, a famous *cynic,* used a lantern in daylight as he searched for an honest man.
5. The engineer *detonated* the explosive, and the rock split.
6. Yellow fever has been *eradicated* through the work of Walter Reed.
7. The disloyal citizen was *ostracized* by his fellow townspeople.
8. The *supercilious* senior ignored the freshmen.
9. *Tantalizing* odors from the kitchen made the hungry girls' mouths water.
10. The gypsy fortuneteller was decked out in heavy, *tawdry* jewelry.

(2) Foreign words in English

You have seen that many English words have a foreign origin. In addition to these, many foreign expressions have become part of the English language. Sometimes their pronunciation becomes "Anglicized," while their spelling remains as it was in the original language. Examples of such expressions are *en masse,* meaning "in a group," *joie de vivre,* meaning "joy in living," and *tête à tête,* meaning "a private conversation between two people." If you are alert to such expressions in your reading and listening, you will find that your vocabulary is growing in this direction.

EXERCISE 18. Ten familiar foreign expressions are given below in column A. Number your paper 1–10. Refer to the dictionary and copy next to each number the letter of the appropriate meaning from column B. Write the name of the language from which the expression comes.

	A		B
1.	cliché	a.	the best people
2.	deluxe	b.	the masses
3.	elite	c.	witty replies
4.	hoi polloi	d.	a midday rest
5.	incognito	e.	a meal at a fixed price
6.	patio	f.	a marble floor
7.	repartee	g.	with name concealed
8.	siesta	h.	timeworn expression
9.	table d'hôte	i.	never satisfied
10.	terra firma	j.	a terrace
		k.	solid earth
		l.	elegant

REVIEW EXERCISE B. The words in this exercise have been chosen from all those you have studied in this chapter. Number your paper 1–33 and write the correct synonym next to each number.

1. *acclaim*
   a. acquisition
   b. applause
   c. desire
   d. land

2. *aver*
   a. assert
   b. evade
   c. compare
   d. approach

3. *benevolence*
   a. kindliness
   b. sensation of flying
   c. health
   d. wealth

4. *biped*
   a. animal with two feet
   b. bison
   c. pedigree
   d. three-footed stand

5. *cynic*
   a. criminal
   b. sneerer
   c. picturesque
   d. tourist

6. *didactic*
   a. tightened
   b. knocking
   c. teacherlike
   d. flowerlike

7. *discreet*
   a. sly
   b. having good judgment
   c. hypocritical
   d. rounded

8. *exasperated*
   a. arranged
   b. annoyed
   c. decorated
   d. enervated

9. *falter*
   a. fail
   b. hesitate
   c. rise
   d. transport

10. *frenzied*
    a. wearied
    b. carried
    c. excited
    d. with carved edges

11. *gaudy*
    a. strange
    b. gay and showy
    c. elegant
    d. wicked

12. *hectic*
    a. feverish
    b. colorful
    c. stout
    d. emphatic

13. *incise*
    a. look into
    b. cut into
    c. sharpen
    d. intend

14. *intricate*
    a. complicated
    b. clever
    c. ingenious
    d. interesting

15. *intrigue*
    a. entertain
    b. plot
    c. gossip
    d. give alms

16. *meander*
    a. walk rapidly
    b. examine
    c. wander
    d. untie

17. *mimic*
    a. argue
    b. assert
    c. exhibit
    d. imitate

18. *morbid* .
    a. cheerful
    b. strict
    c. fatal
    d. gloomy

19. *ominous*
    a. altogether
    b. hungry
    c. threatening
    d. disappearing

20. *ostracized*
    a. banished
    b. enrolled
    c. combined
    d. distracted

21. *patio*
    a. terrace
    b. Spanish food
    c. tower
    d. hinged box

22. *perceptible*
    a. advisable
    b. noticeable
    c. stunning
    d. slight

23. *poise*
    a. gem
    b. composure
    c. intelligence
    d. reflection

24. *premiere*
    a. leader
    b. opening performance
    c. youth
    d. winner

25. *probation*
    a. connection
    b. decision
    c. courage
    d. trial period

26. *reiterate*	a. remember	c. warn
	b. protest	d. repeat
27. *retrieve*	a. reconcile	c. combine
	b. overlook	d. recover
28. *soliloquy*	a. dock	c. separate
	b. diamond	d. speech alone
29. *stamina*	a. endurance	c. startle
	b. part of a flower	d. a stone wall
30. *strategy*	a. planning	c. leveling
	b. tiling	d. pitcher
31. *supercilious*	a. high-ranking	c. youthful
	b. generous	d. haughty
32. *tawdry*	a. showy	c. bashful
	b. arid	d. friendly
33. *vestige*	a. honor	c. inheritance
	b. trace	d. secret

Word List

The following list of 360 words has been selected from books generally read by students your age. It should form the basis of your vocabulary study for the year. When you have mastered the exercises in this chapter, you will know most of these words.

abate	admonish	amends
abject	adroit	amiable
absolve	adversary	anarchy
abstain	advocate	animated
abstract	affected	antagonize
abstruse	affront	apathy
accessible	agility	apparition
acclaim	agitation	appraisal
acute	alien	
adage		arbitrary
	allusion	aroma
addicted	aloof	ascribe

assassin
assimilate
asterisk
atmosphere
augment
autonomy
aver

barbarism
benevolence
biographical
biped
bizarre
blithe
brusque
buoyant
cadence
calculation

caliber
callous
candid
centrifugal
chagrin
charlatan
chivalry
citadel
civility
cliché

clientele
climax
collaborate
comedy
commendable
commodious
competent
complement
compliance
comprehensive

confide
congeal
connive
connoisseur
contagious
controversy
cosmopolitan
culmination
cynic
debris

deduce
deficient
defile
defraud
demoralize
denounce
despot
destitute
detonate
dialogue

didactic
digress
diminish
dingy
discord
discreet
discrepancy
discrimination
disintegrate
dispatch

disperse
disrupt
dissect
dissent
docile
drastic
durable

dwindle
edifice
elegy

elite
embellish
emulate
encounter
epic
equation
equestrian
equilibrium
eradicate
erroneous

ethical
evacuate
exasperate
expedite
exploit
extol
extort
fallacy
falter
fantastic

farce
farcical
fervent
fictitious
figurative
filial
fissure
flaunt
formidable
fortitude

fossil
frenzied
futile

gallery
gaudy
gauntlet
geology
glean
glib
gloat

grotesque
grueling
guise
habitat
hackneyed
haven
havoc
hectic
herald
heretic

hilarious
homicide
horde
hydraulic
idiomatic
imbibe
immaterial
immune
impose
impulsive

incessant
incise
inclination
incomprehensible
indelible
indolence
indomitable
indulgent
inevitable
infamous

infringe
ingenious
innovation
intact
intelligible
intentional
intercept
intricate
intrigue
invoke

irrelevant
jaunty
laconic
larceny
lax
lethal
liability
livid
ludicrous
luxurious

malinger
manifest
manipulate
meander
mediocre
melodramatic
menial
metaphor
mimic
monotonous

moor
morbid
mottled
murky
navigator
nether
nimble

nominal
nondescript
obsession

obtuse
officious
omen
ominous
opaque
opportune
oppressive
optimistic
orthodox
ostracize

palatial
panorama
paramount
passive
patio
patriarch
perceptible
perennial
peruse
pervade

pessimistic
plaintive
plot
poach
poignant
poise
ponderous
portend
portly
potency

potion
precedent
predatory

premature
premier
premiere
presume
probation
procrastinate
proficient

promenade
prospective
protagonist
prowess
pungent
quaint
radiate
rapt
ravenous
realistic

realm
reconcile
redress
reiterate
reluctant
repast
replica
repress
reprimand
reprisal

requisite
resilient
resourceful
retract
retrieve
rigorous
romantic
ruthless
sable

satirical

sector
sedentary
seethe
sequel
setting
shrew
simile
sinister
skeptical
slake

smug
soliloquy
solvent
somber
sordid
spacious
spurn
stamina
statute
stereotype

sterile
strategy
submission
subsequent
subversion
sundry
supercilious
surmount
susceptible
symbol

taciturn
tantalizing
tawdry
tawny

terra firma
terse
testimonial
theme
thwart
tragedy

transcribe
transpire
treatise
tripod
trite
trivial
turbulent
tutor
tycoon
ultimate

unkempt
urban
veneer
venerable
versatile
vestige
vigilant
vilify
virtual
vogue

volatile
vulnerable
wan
wary
wistful
wrangle
wrest
wry
yearn
zodiac

Chapter 28

Spelling ~~MOTHERFUCKER~~

Improving Your Spelling

No one is a born speller. Everybody must work to learn to spell words correctly. If you really want to improve your spelling, you can do so by making a sustained effort. No one else can do this for you. The suggestions and rules in this chapter are designed to help you help yourself to learn to spell better.

GOOD SPELLING HABITS

As you read the italicized rules below, keep in mind that these are not merely rules to be learned now and forgotten later. They are suggestions for forming good habits that will help you spell words now and in the future, in school and out of school.

1. Keep a list of your spelling errors.
Whenever you misspell a word, find out immediately what the correct spelling is. Then list the word on a special page in your notebook. Although this does take time, it will not in the long run take as much time as you would use later trying to learn the same word after you had misspelled it for years.

One way to record your words is to prepare a spelling page with four columns. In the first column, correctly spell the word you missed. (Never enter a misspelled word on your spelling page.) In the second column, write the word again, this time divided into syllables and accented. In the third column, write the word once more, circling the spot that gives you trouble. In the fourth column, give the reason for your mistake, or set down any comment that will help you to learn the word.

EXAMPLES

probably	prob'a·bly	pro(babl)y	Pronounce correctly.
usually	u'su·al·ly	usua(lly)	*usual* + *ly* (Study rule 28d.)
tragedy	trag'e·dy	tra(ged)y	Keep *g* and *d* straight; *tragedy* has *raged* in it.

2. Use the dictionary as a spelling aid.

In order to keep an accurate word list (the only kind of any value), you will need to look up your misspelled words in the dictionary. Don't guess about the correct spelling. (You have already guessed and missed; another guess may lead to a further distortion of it. Play safe; use your dictionary.) The very experience of looking up the word helps you to fix it in your mind so that you will remember it longer.

3. Learn to spell by syllables.

A syllable is a word part which can be pronounced by itself. For instance, the word *thor' ough* has two syllables; the word *sep'a·rate* has three syllables; the word *par·tic'u·lar* has four syllables.

When you divide a long word into its syllables, you make a number of shorter parts out of it. Since short words are easy to spell, you make spelling easier. The word *superintendent,* for example, is a long word that may prove hard to spell unless you divide it into syllables. Then it becomes much easier: *su·per·in·ten·dent.*

EXERCISE 1. Look up the following words in your dictionary, and divide each one into syllables. Pronounce each syllable correctly, and learn to spell the word by syllables. Be prepared to make a perfect score on a spelling test on these words.

1. representative	5. apparent	9. acquaintance
2. fascinate	6. similar	10. awkward
3. candidate	7. benefit	
4. temperature	8. definition	

4. Avoid mispronunciations that lead to spelling errors.

Since you often spell words according to the way you pronounce them, mispronunciation causes misspelling. For instance, if you say *mis·chie'vi·ous* instead of *mis'chie·vous,* you will spell the word incorrectly by adding an extra syllable.

EXERCISE 2. *Oral Drill.* After carefully studying the correct pronunciations in parentheses below, read each word aloud three times, stressing the correct pronunciation of the italicized letters. Be prepared to spell these words from dictation.

1. at*hl*ete (ath'lēt)
2. chil*dr*en (chil'drən)
3. drow*n*ed (dround)
4. *es*cape (ə·scāp', e·scāp')
5. every*b*ody (ev'rē·bod'ē)
6. iden*ti*ty (ī·den'tə·tē)
7. in*tr*oduce (in'trə·dōos', –dyōos')
8. *j*ust (just)
9. li*br*ary (li'brer·ē, –brə·rē)
10. ligh*tn*ing (līt'ning)
11. p*er*haps (pər·haps')
12. p*r*efer (pri·fûr')
13. pro*b*a*b*ly (prob'ə·blē)
14. qui*et* (kwī'ət)
15. re*cog*nize (rek'əg·nīz)
16. su*r*prise (sər·prīz')
17. tha*n* (than)
18. the*n* (then)
19. um*b*rella (um·brel'ə)
20. us*ua*l*l*y (yōo'zhōo·əl·ē)

5. Revise your papers to avoid careless spelling errors.
Although rereading takes only a few minutes, it makes a great difference in the correctness of your work. As you find and revise your spelling errors, be sure to eliminate all botchy handwriting. When you carelessly dot closed *e*'s, make your *o*'s look like *a*'s and your *g*'s like *q*'s, or hurriedly write over letters, you will make twice as many spelling errors as you would if you were more careful about your handwriting. Remember, too, that careless mistakes in handwriting can distort your meaning. For instance, an undotted *i* looks like an *e,* and an uncrossed *t* may be interpreted as an *l.* There is a big difference between the meaning of *foot* and *fool,* for example.

6. To master the spelling of a word, pronounce it, study it, and write it.
When you are trying to learn how to spell a word, first *pronounce the word,* noting its syllables. As you know, thinking of a word syllable by syllable makes the spelling easier.

Second, *study the word,* noticing especially any letters which might make the spelling hard. Notice, for example, that *doctor* has two *o*'s, that *where* has *here* in it, and that *across* has only one *c,* being composed of two little words: *a + cross.*

Third, *write the word.* Spelling is of use only in writing. The movement of your hand in making the letters will help to fix the spelling in your mind.

EXERCISE 3. To gain practice in recognizing commonly misspelled words and in writing them, copy each of the following words. Carefully observe the italicized silent letters as you write. Then have a friend dictate the words to you (or your teacher may wish to do this in class).

1. answer	9. mortgage	17. meant
2. awkward	10. condemn	18. aisle
3. whole	11. column	19. tonight
4. toward	12. rhythm	20. discipline
5. know, knew	13. subtle	21. surely
6. knowledge	14. used to	22. though
7. written	15. before	23. through
8. often	16. instead	24. ninety

7. Learn lists of commonly misspelled words.

Most spelling errors made by students are made in relatively few frequently written words. Lists of such words appear on pages 673–76.

EXERCISE 4. If you miss any of the little words in the following list, you will make a serious error in spelling. Although many of these words may look easy to you, study each one carefully. If you misspell any word, put it on your spelling list.

across	color	hoping	speak
again	coming	laid	speech
all right	country	later	straight
almost	dear	likely	surely
always	doesn't	making	tear
among	eager	many	thing
any	early	minute	think
began	February	none	through
belief	forty	off	tired
bigger	friend	once	together
built	grammar	paid	truly
business	guess	raise	Tuesday
busy	half	really	very
buy	having	safety	wear
can't	heard	shoes	Wednesday

8. Learn to spell by association.

Make any kind of association that will help you to remember a difficult word. For example, the word *earnest* has two words in it, *ear* and *nest; delivery* has *liver*. You can link rhyming words, putting an easy word with a hard one: *ear, hear; truly, unruly; loose, noose.*

EXERCISE 5. Find the words within words in order to fix in your memory the correct spelling.

EXAMPLE   1. laboratory
              1. *Laboratory* has both *labor* and *orator*.

1. bulletin	6. courteous	11. excellent
2. ninety	7. explanation	12. apparent
3. meant	8. immediately	13. handkerchief
4. copies	9. attacked	14. apologize
5. opportunity	10. attention	15. permanent

SPELLING RULES

Although most spelling is learned by memorizing words, you can "figure out" the correct spelling of many words after you have mastered the rules given on the following pages.

ie and *ei*

28a. Write *ie* when the sound is long *e*, except after *c*.

EXAMPLES   achieve   deceit   receive
                    believe   field   relief
                    brief   grief   shield
                    ceiling   niece   thief
                    chief   piece   yield
EXCEPTIONS   either, leisure, neither, seize, weird

Write *ei* when the sound is not long *e*, especially when the sound is long *a*.

EXAMPLES   neighbor   counterfeit

rein	foreign
reign	forfeit
veil	height
weigh	heir

EXCEPTIONS   friend, mischief, kerchief

EXERCISE 6. Write the following words, supplying the missing letters (*e* and *i*) in the correct order. In class, be prepared to explain how the rule applies to each word. When you have determined the correct answers, memorize the list.

1. f . . . ld	8. conc . . . ve	15. pr . . . st
2. p . . . ce	9. fr . . . ght	16. . . . ther
3. f . . . nd	10. h . . . ght	17. n . . . ther
4. ch . . . f	11. w . . . ght	18. dec . . . ve
5. c . . . ling	12. rel . . . f	19. s . . . ze
6. bel . . . ve	13. conc . . . t	20. r . . . gn
7. rec . . . ve	14. ach . . . ve	

–cede, –ceed, and *–sede*

28b. Only one English word ends in *–sede: supersede;* **only three words end in** *–ceed: exceed, proceed,* **and** *succeed;* **all other words of similar sound end in** *–cede.*

EXAMPLES	precede	recede	secede
	intercede	concede	accede

Adding Prefixes and Suffixes

A *prefix* is one or more than one letter or syllable added to the beginning of a word to change its meaning.

28c. When a prefix is added to a word, the spelling of the word itself remains the same.

Take, for example, the word *do*. By adding the prefixes *un–* or *over–*, you have the words *undo* and *overdo*. The spelling of the word *do* does not change. Study the following examples:

il + literate = **il**literate
in + numerable = **in**numerable
im + mortal = **im**mortal
un + certain = **un**certain
dis + approve = **dis**approve
mis + step = **mis**step
re + organize = **re**organize
over + rule = **over**rule

A *suffix* is one or more than one letter or syllable added to the end of a word to change its meaning.

28d. When the suffixes *–ness* **and** *–ly* **are added to a word, the spelling of the word itself is not changed.**

EXAMPLES

sure + ly = sure**ly**
real + ly = real**ly**
usual + ly = usual**ly**
useful + ness = useful**ness**
polite + ness = polite**ness**
stubborn + ness = stubborn**ness**

EXCEPTIONS   Words ending in *y* usually change the *y* to *i* before *–ness* and *–ly:* empty – emptiness; easy – easily.

One-syllable adjectives ending in *y*, however, generally follow rule 28d: *dry – dryness; sly – slyly.*

True and *due* drop the final *e* before *–ly: truly, duly.*

EXERCISE 7. Number 1–20 on your paper. Correctly spell each word below as you add the prefix or suffix indicated.

1. un + necessary
2. re + commend
3. plain + ness
4. actual + ly
5. il + legal
6. im + mature

7. real + ly
8. sure + ly
9. dis + appear
10. dis + solve
11. occasional + ly
12. keen + ness
13. cleanly + ness
14. mis + spell
15. over + run
16. mean + ness
17. practical + ly
18. dis + appearance
19. in + adequate
20. dis + ease

EXERCISE 8. Number 1–10 on your paper. First, correctly add the suffix –*ly* to these words: *hungry, true, necessary, noisy, sleepy.* Then add the suffix –*ness* to *tardy, happy, saucy, flighty, heavy.*

28e. Drop the final *e* before a suffix beginning with a vowel.

EXAMPLES

hope + ing = hoping
care + ing = caring
share + ing = sharing
love + able = lovable

fame + ous = famous
imagine + ary = imaginary
admire + ation = admiration
force + ible = forcible

EXCEPTIONS
1. mile + age = mileage
2. The final *e* is kept in some words to avoid confusion with other words: *dyeing* and *dying, singeing* and *singing*
3. The final *e* is kept in words ending in *ce* or *ge* to retain the soft sound when adding suffixes beginning with *a* or *o: peaceable, advantageous*

EXERCISE 9. Write correctly the words formed as indicated.

1. become + ing
2. guide + ance
3. continue + ous
4. surprise + ed
5. shine + ing
6. ridicule + ous
7. please + ant
8. believe + ing
9. courage + ous
10. determine + ation

28f. Keep the final *e* before a suffix beginning with a consonant.

EXAMPLES

nine + ty = ninety   entire + ly = entirely
hope + ful = hopeful   awe + some = awesome
care + less = careless   pave + ment = pavement

EXCEPTIONS

due + ly = duly   nine + th = ninth
true + ly = truly   awe + ful = awful
whole + ly = wholly   argue + ment = argument
acknowledge + ment   judge + ment = judgment
  = acknowledgment

EXERCISE 10. Apply rules 28e and 28f as you add each designated suffix, and decide whether or not to keep or drop the final *e*. (In this exercise there are no exceptions to the rules.)

1. announce + ment
2. use + age
3. treasure + er
4. imagine + ary
5. definite + ly
6. care + ful
7. sincere + ly
8. write + ing
9. virtue + ous
10. desire + able
11. white + ness
12. revere + ent
13. sure + ly
14. hope + less
15. arrange + ment
16. have + ing
17. complete + ly
18. safe + ty
19. lose + ing
20. nine + ty

28g. With words ending in *y* preceded by a consonant, change the *y* to *i* before any suffix not beginning with *i*.

EXAMPLES

fifty + eth = fiftieth
lazy + ness = laziness
worry + ed = worried
mystery + ous = mysterious
hasty + ly = hastily

beautify + ing = beautifying
terrify + ing = terrifying
worry + ing = worrying
verify + ing = verifying
imply + ing = implying

EXCEPTIONS　(1) some one-syllable words:
shy + ness = shyness
spry + ly = spryly
sky + ward = skyward

(2) *lady* and *baby* with suffixes: *lady-
like, ladyship; babyhood*

Observe that words ending in *y* preceded by a vowel usually do not change their spelling before a suffix:

joy + ful = joyful　　boy + hood = boyhood
array + ed = arrayed　gay + est = gayest

EXERCISE 11. Apply rule 28g as you add each designated suffix and decide whether or not to change the final *y* to *i*. (In this exercise, there are no exceptions to the rule.)

1. extraordinary + ly
2. gratify + ing
3. modify + cation
4. try + ing
5. ally + ance
6. cry + ing
7. necessary + ly
8. fortify + cation
9. deny + al
10. carry + ed
11. glorify + ed
12. secretary + al
13. purify + ing
14. apply + cation
15. defy + ant
16. likely + hood
17. satisfy + ed
18. supply + er
19. rely + able
20. ply + ant
21. amplify + er
22. certify + cate
23. comply + ing
24. merry + ment
25. multiply + cation

28h. Double the final consonant before a suffix that begins with a vowel if both of the following conditions exist:

(1) the word has only one syllable or is accented on the last syllable, and

(2) the word ends in a single consonant preceded by a single vowel.

EXAMPLES

drop + ing = dropping   occur + ence = occurrence
plan + ed = planned   propel + er = propeller
sit + ing = sitting   control + ed = controlled

If both of these conditions do not exist, the final consonant is not doubled before a suffix:

jump + ed = jumped
appear + ance = appearance
tunnel + ing = tunneling
travel + er = traveler

EXERCISE 12. Apply rule 28h as you add each designated suffix.

1. run + er   11. expect + ation
2. defer + ed   12. open + ing
3. swim + ing   13. inform + ed
4. begin + er   14. number + ing
5. expel + ed   15. hit + er
6. control + ed   16. travel + ing
7. hot + est   17. riot + ous
8. flirt + ing   18. exist + ence
9. permit + ed   19. color + ation
10. compel + ing   20. stop + age

REVIEW EXERCISE A. All of the following words are spelled correctly, according to rule. Number 1–20 on your paper. After the appropriate number, write the number of the rule that applies to the correctly spelled word.

EXAMPLE   1. *niece 28a*

1. receive
2. concede
3. hoping
4. immortal
5. eight
6. defenseless
7. thief
8. dissatisfy
9. forlornness
10. tiresome
11. forfeit
12. definitely
13. serenity
14. patrolled
15. unnecessary
16. improvement
17. inquiring
18. capitalization
19. forbidden
20. merciless

The Plural of Nouns

Changing a singular noun to a plural noun sometimes presents problems. The rules on the following pages will help you solve these problems.

28i. Observe the rules for spelling the plural of nouns.

(1) The regular way to form the plural of a noun is to add an *s*.

SINGULAR	boat	nickel	teacher	house
PLURAL	boats	nickels	teachers	houses

(2) The plural of nouns ending in *s, x, z, ch,* or *sh* is formed by adding *es*.

The addition of *es* to the words below makes them pronounceable because of the extra syllable *es* creates.

SINGULAR	PLURAL
glass	glasses
Mrs. Jones	the Joneses
box	boxes
waltz	waltzes
beach	beaches
dish	dishes

EXERCISE 13. Correctly write the plural of each of the following words:

1. guess	6. cafeteria
2. ax	7. watch
3. tongue	8. branch
4. wall	9. speech
5. dollar	10. amateur

(3) The plural of nouns ending in *y* preceded by a *consonant* is formed by changing the *y* to *i* and adding *es*.

SINGULAR	sky	army	story	baby
PLURAL	skies	armies	stories	babies

EXCEPTION   Plurals of proper nouns: *the Hardys, the Carys.*

(4) The plural of nouns ending in *y* preceded by a *vowel* is formed by adding an *s*.

SINGULAR	delay	key	boy	guy
PLURAL	delays	keys	boys	guys

EXERCISE 14. Write the plural of the following words:

1. lady	5. butterfly	8. quantity
2. relay	6. ally	9. day
3. donkey	7. lullaby	10. jalopy
4. copy		

(5) The plural of some nouns ending in *f* or *fe* is formed by changing the *f* to *v* and adding *s* or *es*.

As you study the formation of the plurals in the following words, notice the way the words are pronounced.

SINGULAR	roof	belief	leaf	wife	calf
PLURAL	roofs	beliefs	leaves	wives	calves

EXERCISE 15. Write the plural of each of these words:

1. thief   4. knife
2. chef   5. giraffe
3. life

(6) The plural of nouns ending in *o* preceded by a vowel is formed by adding *s;* the plural of nouns ending in *o* preceded by a consonant is formed by adding *es.*

SINGULAR radio   rodeo   echo   hero   tomato
  PLURAL radios rodeos echoes heroes tomatoes
EXCEPTIONS Nouns ending in *o* preceded by a consonant and *referring to music* form the plural by adding *s*.

SINGULAR alto   solo   piano
  PLURAL altos solos pianos

EXERCISE 16. Write the plurals of these nouns:

1. shampoo   4. hobo
2. soprano   5. veto
3. torpedo

(7) The plural of a few nouns is formed in irregular ways.

SINGULAR foot man ox   mouse child   tooth
  PLURAL feet men oxen mice   children teeth

(8) The plural of compound nouns written as one word is formed by adding *s* or *es.*

SINGULAR spoonful   smashup   icebox
  PLURAL spoonfuls smashups iceboxes

(9) The plural of compound nouns consisting of a noun plus a modifier is formed by making the noun plural.

SINGULAR	PLURAL
sister-in-law	sisters-in-law
notary public	notaries public
attorney-at-law	attorneys-at-law

(10) Some nouns are the same in the singular and the plural.

SINGULAR AND PLURAL   deer, trout, Japanese, sheep

EXERCISE 17. Write the plural form of the following words:

1. woman	6. armful
2. ox	7. mouse
3. foot	8. man-of-war
4. son-in-law	9. deer
5. maid of honor	10. Chinese

(11) The plural of some foreign words is formed as in the original language.

SINGULAR	crisis	datum	analysis	alumnus
PLURAL	crises	data	analyses	alumni

► NOTE   A few words taken from a foreign language have an alternate plural form, regularly formed as in English: *appendix: appendices* or *appendixes.* Sometimes the English plural is the preferred one; the plural of *formula* is preferably *formulas,* not *formulae.* Consult your dictionary to determine the preferred spelling of the plural of such words.

(12) The plural of numbers, letters, signs, and words considered as words is formed by adding an apostrophe and *s.*

EXAMPLES   Put the *g*'s and the *6*'s in the second
column.
Change the *&*'s to *and*'s.

REVIEW EXERCISE B. Try to make a perfect score on this exercise, which covers the rules for forming the plural of nouns. Number your paper 1–33, and write the plural form of each of the following nouns.

After each one, write the number of the subrule that applies.

1. shelf
2. paper
3. gas
4. joy
5. echo
6. radio
7. cuff
8. elf
9. solo
10. woman
11. trout
12. hero
13. library
14. church
15. *A*
16. lieutenant colonel
17. handful
18. handkerchief
19. tornado
20. index
21. *13*
22. ox
23. maid of honor
24. Chinese
25. armful
26. roof
27. trio
28. history
29. man-of-war
30. potato
31. datum
32. knife
33. glass

WORDS OFTEN CONFUSED

If you will master both the meaning and the spelling of the words in the lists on the following pages, you can eliminate many errors in your compositions. Study only a few at a time, and really master them.

advice	[noun] *counsel* He gave me some excellent *advice*.
advise	[verb] *to give advice* She *advised* me to finish high school.
all ready	[pronoun plus adjective] *everyone ready* When he arrived, we were *all ready* to go.

already   [adverb] *previously*
       Sharon has *already* gone.

---

affect   [verb] *to influence*
       What he said did not *affect* my final
       decision.

effect   [verb] *to accomplish;* [noun] *conse-*
       quence or *result*
       The senator has *effected* many changes
       during her administration. The *effect*
       of these changes has been most bene-
       ficial.

---

all right   [This is the only acceptable spelling. Al-
       though it is in the dictionary, the spelling
       alright has not yet come into standard
       usage.]

---

all together *everyone in the same place*
       When we were *all together*, we opened
       the gifts.

altogether *entirely*
       He was *altogether* wrong.

---

brake   *stopping device*
       The *brakes* on our car are good.

break   *shatter, sever*
       The last straw *breaks* a camel's back.

---

capital   [noun] *city* or *money used by business;*
       [adjective] *punishable by death* or *of*
       major importance or *excellent*
       Raleigh is the *capital* of North Caro-
       lina.
       Mrs. Dawson will need more *capital* to
       modernize her equipment.

Killing a police officer is a *capital* crime.
She made a *capital* error in preparing the report.
This is a *capital* detective story.

capitol   [noun] *building; statehouse*
In Raleigh, the *capitol* is on Fayetteville Street.

---

choose   [used for present and future tense] *select*
You may *choose* your own partner.

chose   [past tense—rhymes with *hose*]
Yesterday she *chose* to postpone the meeting.

---

coarse   *rough, crude*
The *coarse* material is very durable.
He never uses *coarse* language.

course   *path of action or progress; unit of study; track or way;* also used with *of* to mean *as was to be expected*
The airplane lost its *course* in the storm.
I am taking a *course* in algebra.
She is at the golf *course*.
Of *course*, you have met Ellen.

EXERCISE 18. Number your paper 1–20. Write after the proper number the correct one of the words given in parentheses in the sentences below.

1. Betty has (all ready, already) handed in her paper.
2. (All right, Alright), I'll wrap the package now.
3. What was the coach's (advice, advise) to you players at half time?

4. Are you taking a (coarse, course) in sewing?
5. This poison is supposed to have a deadly (affect, effect).
6. Last night we (choose, chose) our leader.
7. She did not, of (coarse, course), remember me.
8. The mechanic adjusted the (brakes, breaks).
9. You should have known that Sacramento, not Los Angeles, is the (capital, capitol) of California.
10. You can (choose, chose) your own music.
11. They were (all together, altogether) at dinner.
12. The newspaper strike seriously (affected, effected) sales in department stores.
13. I'm sure that the baby will be (all right, alright).
14. His (coarse, course) manners offended everyone.
15. A fragile piece of china (brakes, breaks) easily.
16. The beautiful (capital, capitol) of our state is built of limestone and marble.
17. May we (choose, chose) between a dance and a picnic?
18. She was not (all together, altogether) satisfied.
19. Are they (all ready, already) to go now?
20. In *Hamlet*, Polonius gives the following (advice, advise) to his son Laertes: "This above all: to thine own self be true."

EXERCISE 19. Write twenty original sentences correctly using the seventeen words you have just studied. Use each word at least once.

---

complement   *something that completes or makes perfect; to complete or make perfect*
Linking verbs are followed by subject *complements.*
The office now has a full *complement* of personnel.
The yellow rug *complemented* the warm-looking room.

compliment	*a remark that says something flattering about a person; to say something flattering* I was not impressed by her flowery *compliments*. I must *compliment* you on that lovely flower arrangement.
consul	*the representative of a foreign country* The French *consul* was guest of honor at the banquet.
council	*a group called together to accomplish a job* The city *council* will debate the proposed bond issue tonight.
councilor	*a member of a council* At the council meeting Mother plans to introduce Dr. Watkins, the new *councilor*.
counsel	*advice; the giving of advice* I am deeply grateful for your *counsel*.
counselor	*one who gives advice* I do not think I am qualified to act as your *counselor*.
des′ert	*a dry region* Be sure to fill the gas tank before you start across the *desert*.
desert′	*to leave* She *deserted* her comrades.
dessert′	*the final course of a meal* What do you plan to have for *dessert* this evening?

EXERCISE 20. Number your paper 1–10, and write the correct one of the words in parentheses after the appropriate number.

1. Congress appropriated funds for a new irrigation project in the (desert, dessert).
2. The Security (Consul, Council, Counsel) of the United Nations consists of eleven members.
3. The new hat will effectively (complement, compliment) my fall outfit.
4. Besides teaching English, Miss Patton also serves as a guidance (councilor, counselor).
5. With my brother away at college, our house seems (deserted, desserted).
6. You should pay more attention to your parents' (consul, council, counsel).
7. I passed on your charming (complement, compliment) to Isabel.
8. At their meeting, all the members of the city (council, counsel) agreed that the tax proposal was unworkable.
9. Baked Alaska is my favorite (desert, dessert).
10. In the opera *Madame Butterfly,* Sharpless is the American (consul, counsel) in Japan.

EXERCISE 21. Write ten original sentences, each using one of the words you have just studied.

---

formally   *properly, according to strict rules*
Should he be *formally* introduced?

formerly   *previously, in the past*
The new consul was *formerly* a member of Congress.

---

hear   *to receive sounds through the ears*
Did you *hear* the President's speech?

here	*this place* Come *here*, Rover.
its	[possessive of *it*] The bird stopped *its* singing.
it's	*it is* *It's* an easy problem.
lead	[present tense, pronounced lēd] *to go first* I'll *lead* the way.
led	[past tense of *lead*] Last week she *led* us to victory.
lead	[pronounced led] *a heavy metal;* also *graphite* in a pencil The *lead* on my line was too heavy for the cork.
loose	[rhymes with *noose*] *free, not close together* The string on the package is too *loose*. The car swerved out of the *loose* gravel.
lose	[pronounced lōoz] *to suffer loss* Do not *lose* our lunch money.
moral	having to do with *good* or *right;* also *a lesson of conduct* It is a *moral* question. These fables all have a *moral*.
morale	*mental condition, spirit* The *morale* of the citizens is low.
passed	[verb, past tense of *pass*] He *passed* us in the corridor.
past	[noun or adjective or preposition]

I didn't inquire about his *past*.
Her *past* experience got her the job.
I went *past* the house.

peace   opposite of *strife*
After the long war, *peace* was welcome.

piece   *a part of something*
Do you care for a *piece* of pie?

EXERCISE 22. Number your paper 1–20. Write after the proper number the correct one of the words given in parentheses in the sentences below.

1. Sitting in the back row, we could hardly (here, hear) the speaker.
2. The class is proud of (its, it's) progress.
3. The commander praised the division's high (morale, moral).
4. It is already (passed, past) nine o'clock.
5. Facing defeat, he did not (lose, loose) courage.
6. The searchers hoped that the dog would (lead, led) them to the lost skier.
7. Mother told us to stay (hear, here).
8. The hard-driving fullback (led, lead) the team to victory.
9. I have more interest in my work than I (formally, formerly) had.
10. Molly (passed, past) all her examinations.
11. We couldn't decide what the (moral, morale) of the story was.
12. I like a pencil that has soft (led, lead).
13. Everyone was (formally, formerly) dressed at the dance.
14. (It's, Its) too late to catch the early train.
15. There Benito found true (peace, piece) of mind.
16. June shouted, "I'll give you a (peace, piece) of my mind!"

17. When my shoelace came (lose, loose), I tripped and fell.
18. Mrs. Hogan just (past, passed) me in the hall.
19. This (peace, piece) of chicken is bony.
20. Clara never seems to (lose, loose) her temper.

EXERCISE 23. Write twenty original sentences correctly using the words you have just studied. Use each word at least once.

plain	*not fancy;* also *a flat area of land;* also *clear* Steven wears very *plain* clothes. The storm lashed the western *plains*. She made her point of view *plain*.
plane	*a flat surface, a level;* also *a tool;* also *an airplane* Are you taking *plane* geometry? The debate was conducted on a high *plane*. Martin made the wood smooth by using a *plane*. The *plane* arrived at the airport on time.
principal	*head of a school;* also, as an adjective, *main* or *most important* Ted had a long talk with the *principal*. Winning is not our *principal* goal.
principle	*a rule of conduct;* also *a law* or *a main fact* We live by certain *principles*. They don't know the first *principles* of physics.
quiet	*silent, still* The library should be a *quiet* place.
quite	*to a great extent or degree; completely*

My little brother is *quite* clever for his age.
I *quite* understand your reasons for not attending.

---

shone [past tense of *shine*]
The sun *shone* this morning.

shown *revealed*
Laurie has not *shown* me her scrapbook.

---

stationary *in a fixed position*
The chairs were not *stationary*.

stationery *writing paper*
Use white *stationery* for business letters.

---

than [a conjunction, used for comparisons]
Jimmy enjoys swimming more *than* golfing.

then [an adverb or conjunction indicating *at that time* or *next*]
I polished my shoes; *then* I combed my hair.
Did you know Barbara *then?*

---

their [possessive of *they*]
The girls gave *their* opinions.

there *a place* [also used to begin a sentence (see page 49)]
I'll be *there* on time.
There aren't any cookies left.

they're *they are*
They're at the station now.

EXERCISE 24. Number your paper 1–25. Write the

correct one of the words in parentheses after the corresponding number.

1. Please be as (quiet, quite) as possible in the corridors.
2. Mrs. Carver is the (principal, principle) of our school.
3. The last reel of the movie was not (shone, shown).
4. The deer froze in its tracks, remaining (stationary, stationery) for nearly a minute.
5. He said that not paying debts is against his (principals, principles).
6. Dr. Palmer was (quiet, quite) pleased with the results of the experiment.
7. That night the big moon (shone, shown) brightly.
8. Did you buy a box of blue (stationary, stationery)?
9. (Than, Then) he erased the board and started over.
10. Melissa knows how to use a (plain, plane) in shop class.
11. Your (principal, principle) problem is learning to spell.
12. What did you do (than, then)?
13. A coyote was crossing the (plain, plane).
14. Do you still live (their, they're, there)?
15. Alice has mastered the basic (principals, principles) of grammar.
16. Do you drink your coffee (plain, plane) or with cream and sugar?
17. I can work much faster (than, then) he can.
18. All of the freshmen invited (their, there, they're) parents to the party.
19. (Their, There, They're) coming here tomorrow.
20. (Their, There) are two *s*'s in *omission* and in *possible*.
21. No matter what game you are playing, do not let your opponent know your (principal, principle) objectives.
22. Two years ago my parents bought a (stationary, stationery) store with their savings.

23. This summer my mother has decided that I am going to improve myself rather (than, then) enjoy myself.
24. (Their, There, They're) books are still here.
25. As we landed, we saw the wide, green (plain, plane) below.

EXERCISE 25. Write twenty original sentences correctly using the words you have just studied. Use each word at least once.

---

threw	*hurled* Freddy *threw* three strikes.
through	*in one side and out the opposite side* The fire truck raced *through* the heavy traffic.

---

to	[a preposition; also part of the infinitive form of a verb] She told us *to clean* the windows. [infinitive] They have gone *to the store.* [prepositional phrase]
too	[adverb] *also; more than enough* I like soccer, and Ted does, *too.* He was *too* tired to think clearly.
two	*one + one* I noticed *two* packages on the sofa.

---

waist	*the middle part of the body* This dress is too large in the *waist.*
waste	*unused material;* also, *to squander* During the war, children collected *waste* fats. Please do not *waste* money on that.

weak	*feeble; lacking force;* opposite of *strong* The fawn is too *weak* to walk yet. We could not hear his *weak* voice.
week	*seven days* Carol has been gone a *week*.
weather	*conditions outdoors* [no *h* sound] The *weather* suddenly changed.
whether	indicates alternative or doubt [pronounce the *h*] She didn't know *whether* or not to enter the contest.
who's	*who is, who has* I can't imagine *who's* at the door now. *Who's* been marking in my book?
whose	[possessive of *who*] *Whose* bicycle is this?
your	[possessive of *you*] What is *your* idea?
you're	*you are* Joe, *you're* the best friend I have.

EXERCISE 26. Number your paper 1–20. Write after the proper number the correct one of the words given in parentheses in the sentences below.

1. The (weather, whether) in Mexico City was pleasant.
2. Dad (threw, through) the skates into my closet.
3. Sally is going to the concert. Are you going (to, too, two)?
4. Next (weak, week) the Bears will play the Packers.

5. We were in Boston a (weak, week).
6. The ball crashed (threw, through) the window.
7. Those children are (to, too, two) tired to study.
8. (Your, You're) trying too hard, Tommy.
9. (To, Too, Two) of the puppies are brown.
10. I don't remember (weather, whether) I signed the check or not.
11. I became (weak, week) in the knees when she announced my entrance.
12. (Your, You're) sleeve is torn.
13. Each majorette wore a gold sash around her (waist, waste).
14. (Whose, Who's) bat is it?
15. Tell me (weather, whether) or not we won.
16. The water seeped (threw, through) the basement window.
17. (Whose, Who's) going to be first?
18. I forgot (to, too, two) address the envelope.
19. You should not consider this a (waist, waste) of time.
20. I couldn't decide (weather, whether) or not to agree.

REVIEW EXERCISE C. Write a sentence correctly using each of the following words.

1. your	10. chose	18. stationary
2. who's	11. breaks	19. principle
3. to	12. you're	20. plain
4. waist	13. too	21. shown
5. through	14. whose	22. their
6. week	15. its	23. whether
7. loose	16. there	24. led
8. weak	17. then	25. piece
9. moral		

REVIEW EXERCISE D. Number your paper 1–20. After the appropriate number, write the correctly spelled word in parentheses in the phrases following.

1. a (brief, breif) talk
2. (neither, niether) one
3. (course, coarse) cloth
4. three (solos, soloes)
5. now and (then, than)
6. more (then, than) that
7. going (threw, through)
8. a few (weeks, weaks)
9. (surely, surly) on time
10. many (heros, heroes)
11. on the (cieling, ceiling)
12. two (copies, copys)
13. (loosing, losing) weight
14. some good (advice, advise)
15. four (cupsful, cupfuls)
16. may (choose, chose)
17. chocolate cake for (desert, dessert)
18. driving (passed, past) the theater
19. (to, too) energetic
20. (weather, whether) or not to stay

50 Spelling Demons

Here are fifty simple words which cause many people trouble. It is wise to be aware of them. You will learn them most easily if you study them five at a time.

ache	cough	guess	once	tired
again	could	half	ready	tonight
always	country	hour	said	trouble
answer	doctor	instead	says	wear
blue	does	knew	shoes	where
built	don't	know	since	which
busy	early	laid	sugar	whole
buy	easy	meant	sure	women
can't	every	minute	tear	won't
color	friend	often	though	write

300 Spelling Words

absence	accidentally	accomplish
absolutely	accommodate	accurate
acceptance	accompany	accustomed

achievement

acquaintance
actually
administration
affectionate
agriculture
amateur
ambassador
analysis
analyze
anticipate

apology
apparent
appearance
approach
approval
arguing
argument
assurance
attendance
authority

available
basically
beginning
believe
benefit
benefited
boundary
Britain
calendar
campaign

capital
category
certificate
characteristic

chief
circuit
circumstance
civilization
column
commissioner

committees
comparison
competent
competition
conceivable
conception
confidential
conscience
conscious
consistency

constitution
continuous
control
cooperate
corporation
correspondence
criticism
criticize
cylinder
debtor

decision
definite
definition
deny
description
despise
diameter
disappearance
disappointment
discipline

disgusted
distinction
distinguished
dominant
duplicate
economic
efficiency
eighth
elaborate
eligible

embarrass
emergency
employee
encouraging
environment
equipped
essential
evidently
exaggerate
exceedingly

excellent
excessive
excitable
exercise
existence
expense
extraordinary
fascinating
fatal
favorably

fictitious
financier
flourish
fraternity
frequent
further

glimpse
glorious
grabbed
gracious

graduating
grammar
gross
gymnasium
happiness
hasten
heavily
hindrance
humorous
hungrily

hypocrisy
hypocrite
icy
ignorance
imagination
immediately
immense
incidentally
indicate
indispensable

inevitable
innocence
inquiry
insurance
intelligence
interfere
interpretation
interrupt
investigation
judgment

knowledge

leisure
lengthen
lieutenant
likelihood
liveliness
loneliness
magazine
maneuver
marriage

marvelous
mechanical
medieval
merchandise
minimum
mortgage
multitude
muscle
mutual
narrative

naturally
necessary
negligible
niece
noticeable
obligation
obstacle
occasionally
occurrence
offense

official
omit
operations
opportunity
oppose
optimism
orchestra

organization
originally
paid

paradise
parallel
particularly
peasant
peculiar
percentage
performance
personal
personality
perspiration

persuade
petition
philosopher
picnic
planning
pleasant
policies
politician
possess
possibility

practically
precede
precisely
preferred
prejudice
preparation
pressure
primitive
privilege
probably

procedure
proceed

professor
proportion
psychology
publicity
pursuit
qualities
quantities
readily

reasonably
receipt
recognize
recommendation
referring
regretting
reign
relieve
remembrance
removal

renewal
repetition
representative
requirement
residence
resistance
responsibility
restaurant
rhythm

ridiculous

sacrifice
satire
satisfied
scarcely
scheme
scholarship
scissors
senate
sensibility
separate

sergeant
several
shepherd
sheriff
similar
skis
solemn
sophomore
source
specific

sponsor
straighten
substantial
substitute
subtle

succeed
successful
sufficient
summary
superior

suppress
surprise
survey
suspense
suspicion
temperament
tendency
thorough
transferring
tremendous

truly
unanimous
unfortunately
unnecessary
urgent
useful
using
vacancies
vacuum
varies

Speaking
and
Listening

PART SEVEN

Chapter  **29**

Speaking Before Groups

Preparing for and Delivering Various Kinds of Speeches

The ability to speak easily and naturally will help you to succeed in school and, later, in a career. Speaking before groups is easy if you have some training and experience. In this chapter, you will learn how to handle some of the most common speech situations you will meet in school.

PREPARING A SPEECH[1]

29a. Choose an appropriate topic.

A good speech requires careful preparation. Trying to make a speech without planning it is like approaching a test in a new subject without studying for it. This section will guide you through the necessary steps in preparing a speech for delivery.

Sometimes the subject of your speech will be given to you, or you may be given a choice among several subjects. If the choice of topic is left to you, you should be guided by two principles:

---

[1] Since preparing a speech is in many ways like preparing a composition, you will find additional, detailed suggestions for choosing a topic and organizing content in Chapter 13, page 332.

(1) Choose a topic that is well known to you.

If your hobby is raising pigeons, talk about their care and breeding. If you have used a sailboat or motorboat, explain how to handle it. If you have gone on an overnight hike, tell about your experiences.

When you talk from firsthand experience, you are not at a loss for ideas, you speak fluently, and you convey enthusiasm. Your listeners will be attentive because they are aware that you know what you are talking about.

(2) Choose a topic that is interesting to you and your audience.

Suppose you act as a volunteer at a local hospital. Your experience there has helped you decide to become a doctor. Preparing a talk about careers in medicine will certainly be interesting to you. Ideas about what to say and how to say it will come naturally to you because you care about the topic.

When thinking about your topic, think about your audience. Obviously, medical careers can be interesting to students because students are often concerned about choosing an occupation. If your audience is made up of adults, however, you might change your focus—emphasizing, for example, your local hospital's need for new doctors.

EXERCISE 1. List five subjects that you feel able to speak about because of your experience. In a sentence or two for each, write what your experience is.

EXAMPLE   *How to Collect Stamps. My grandmother is a stamp collector, and she taught me how to sort, identify, and store stamps.*

EXERCISE 2. Reflect on a speech you have recently heard, perhaps in a school assembly, in church, or on television. Discuss the following questions in class.

1. Was the speech based on firsthand experience?
2. Did the speaker have a genuine interest in the subject?
3. Was the subject interesting to the audience? Why, or why not?

29b. Have a definite purpose when you speak.

Have an aim for your speech. Know beforehand *why* you are speaking. Your purpose may be

    a. To inform
    b. To convince
    c. To entertain
    d. To move to action

Suppose, for example, you are going to speak to your English class on the topic of automobiles. What you say depends largely on your purpose.

If your purpose is *to inform,* you may discuss what a buyer should keep in mind before purchasing a secondhand car, how a carburetor works, or what the proper method of waxing or polishing a car is.

If your purpose is *to convince,* you may discuss why pollution controls should be in every car.

If your purpose is *to entertain,* you may talk about a travel adventure you have had.

If your purpose is *to move to action,* you may suggest ways to conserve gasoline. People can, for example, form car pools or use public transportation whenever possible.

Once you determine your purpose, always keep it in mind when preparing your talk.

EXERCISE 3. Suppose you were asked to speak to your classmates on one of the topics listed below. Decide on a purpose for your talk and list three points your talk will cover.

1. Baseball
2. The gasoline crisis
3. School regulations
4. Volunteer action
5. Rock music

6. Pollution
7. Backpacking
8. Solar energy
9. Earning money
10. My neighborhood

29c. Gather material for your speech.

After you have settled on your topic and purpose, your next step is to gather material. Follow these steps:

1. Explore your own background. You may know more about your subject than you think. Examine your information and ideas. What do they suggest for further exploration?

2. Observe. Keep your eyes and ears open for material related to your topic. You may learn from conversations, newspapers, or television programs.

3. Question. Ask someone who knows a great deal about your topic to give you additional information.

4. Read. When you have completed the preceding three steps, it is time to use the library. Consult encyclopedia articles, books, and magazines. Record pertinent information on note cards for easy reference.[1]

5. Reflect. Choose a subject well in advance of the scheduled speaking date. You will then have ample time to think about your speech, adding and discarding ideas. Jot down new thoughts as they occur to you. This kind of preparation is a slow process, but

---

[1] See instructions on taking notes in Chaptes 15, pages 391–94.

it results in thorough knowledge of your subject matter that, in turn, will contribute to self-confidence as you talk.

EXERCISE 4. Select a topic for a three-minute talk to your class. Make a list of the sources of information you intend to consult, using the following headings.

1. Your own experience (describe it)
2. Situations you may observe for information
3. People you are going to question, and what you will ask them
4. Books and periodicals (name of the book, magazine, or newspaper, title of chapter or article, page number)

Use one of the topics listed below, or choose one of your own.

1. How to earn money
2. Should television commercials be shown to young children?
3. Why study history?
4. The man or woman I most admire
5. My hobby
6. Cats and cat lovers
7. Stock car races
8. Origami
9. The best vacation in the world
10. Protect the whales!

29d. Prepare an outline for your talk.

Your final step in preparation is to arrange the material you have gathered. If you have jotted down your notes on index cards with each idea on a separate card, you can easily put them in sequence. Lay aside those that do not seem to fit logically into your plan. If it seems that your speech will be too long, decide which sections to exclude and remove those cards.

Do not attempt to write your speech. Preparing an outline helps you arrive at the best arrangement of main and supporting ideas and fixes them in your memory. Later you can develop your wording from it.[1]

An outline for a short speech should usually cover only one side of a page and should include only your main points. The following example illustrates the form and content of an outline for a short speech.

MODEL OUTLINE

TRAINING A DOG

Purpose: To inform

I. The importance of training
   A. Value to dog
   B. Value to owner

II. Basic training
   A. Housebreaking
   B. Walking on a leash
   C. Responding to owner's call

III. Advanced training
   A. Further training in obedience
   B. Training for hunting

IV. Things to avoid
   A. Coddling
   B. Overfeeding

EXERCISE 5. Using the topic and the sources you chose for Exercise 4, prepare an outline for a three-minute speech.

29e. Make a strong introduction and conclusion.

---

[1] For a full discussion of outlining, see pages 349–51.

Prepare your introduction carefully. A good speaker catches the audience's attention at the very beginning with something that will pique their interest. Begin with an unusual fact or observation, a question, or even an exaggeration; then develop your topic.

EXAMPLES State champions! Is that too wild a dream for our baseball team this year?

Boxing, button collecting, bookbinding, and beetles — all these are hobbies that people enjoy. But I'm here to speak in praise of bowling.

A common problem for speakers is knowing how to stop. They often drift to a halt weakly like a motorboat that has run out of gas. The conclusion is your last chance to drive home main ideas. It is important enough for you to prepare carefully.

Conclude by summarizing your major points.

EXAMPLES Our ball team should have a good season. Most of last year's players are back; we have some promising newcomers; the pitching staff is strong; and we have the best coach in Staunton County.

If you're looking for an interesting hobby, take up bowling. It's good exercise because it develops every muscle in the body. It's good fun because you can join our school bowling club. It's inexpensive because the local alley has a reduced rate for high school students. You may become a champion!

DELIVERING A SPEECH

If you have gone through the preparatory steps in the earlier part of this chapter, you are almost ready to deliver your speech. You may feel that you need some pointers.

29f. Prepare for delivering a speech.

Probably you feel somewhat nervous before beginning to speak before a group. You should! Nervousness is a sign that your body is keyed for action. Experienced actors and actresses readily admit that they are tense before stepping on the stage.

What you must guard against is *excessive* nervousness, which prevents free movement or coherent thinking.

Here are some practical suggestions for delivering a speech.

1. Know your subject thoroughly. Begin your preparation well in advance of the day on which you are scheduled to speak. Mull over your topic, talk about it with your parents and friends, and read as much as you can about it. When you know your material thoroughly, you will gain self-confidence.

2. Practice. Rehearse your talk aloud, preferably before a full-length mirror. Do not try to memorize the speech. (You may, however, memorize the first and last sentences so that you can get off to a smooth start and finish gracefully.)

3. Keep your purpose in mind. Think of what you want your listeners to believe, feel, or do. Concentrate on *why* you are speaking.

4. Relax. Yawn, breathe deeply, and let yourself go limp for a moment or two before you face your audience. These actions reduce tension.

Nonverbal Communication

Body movements and gestures are types of nonverbal communication. They are often used during a speech.

For example, if you are describing something very tall, you might gesture by raising your hand above your head. If you are expressing doubt about something, you might shrug your shoulders.

29g. Use nonverbal communication effectively.

When speaking, look at your audience. Eye contact can do two important things: (1) It can hold your audience's attention and (2) it can tell you the audience's reaction to your talk. Some of your listeners may be confused. Others may be unable to hear. Only by looking at the faces of the audience will you know.

Keep your gestures under control. A good comedian uses gestures to get laughs. A good speaker uses gestures to emphasize words. Gestures can show anger, surprise, disgust, and many other feelings. They are a type of sign language.

Exaggerated gestures, however, only distract an audience. A nervous speaker might gesture uncontrollably. Since audiences read gestures as they listen to words, choose gestures with care.

Pause between parts of your speech. Short pauses during your talk can relieve tension and signal your audience that a new topic is about to begin.

EXERCISE 6. Deliver the three-minute speech for which you prepared in Exercises 4 and 5.

Pronunciation and Enunciation

Learn to use standard pronunciation and to enunciate words correctly. These skills will be an asset in all your speaking, formal and informal.

29h. Learn to pronounce words correctly.

(1) Listen to good speakers.

Radio and television announcers, public speakers, actors and actresses, and teachers are generally good models to imitate in pronunciation.

(2) Refer to the dictionary.

You should have a dictionary in your home so that you can check the pronunciation of unfamiliar words. If this is not possible, jot down any word that you are not sure how to pronounce, and look it up when you get to school.

EXERCISE 7. With the aid of a dictionary, learn the pronunciation of the following words.

absolutely	faucet	khaki
admirable	February	laboratory
alloy	final	orchestra
ally	finale	parliamentary
alternate	finance	particular
banquet	forehead	penalize
champion	formerly	positively
chastisement	gesture	recipe
column	grievous	romance
comfortable	hearth	salve
corps	hospitable	secretive
coupon	influence	solemnity
decade	interesting	usually

EXERCISE 8. Write ten sentences using words in Exercise 7. Try saying the sentences casually as you would in conversation, but be sure you use standard pronunciation.

EXAMPLES We decided in February to conduct our meetings according to parliamentary procedure.

Did the official penalize the champion?

(3) Do not omit sounds or syllables.

Speakers sometimes omit essential sounds. Pronounce each of the following words with particular attention to the sound represented by the bold-faced letter:

accept	length	probably
asked	library	recognize
exactly	picture	strength

Be sure to include the sound of *h* when you pronounce these words:

hue	humane	humid
huge	humanity	humor
human	humble	humorous

Be careful not to leave out a syllable when you use these words in public speaking.

accidentally	electric	history
actually	family	jewel
average	finally	mathematics
champion	generally	memory
chocolate	geography	mystery
company	giant	poetry
cruel	grocery	suppose

EXERCISE 9. *Oral Drill.* Read the following sentences aloud, making sure you pronounce each word correctly.

1. Poetry is no longer a mystery to me.
2. History and geography are both concerned with humanity.
3. Where is the library?
4. Susie asked whether it is humid in Costa Rica.
5. I don't see the humor in this grocery list.
6. Bill generally whistles while he does mathematics.
7. The mystery concerns the missing family diamonds.

8. This electric cord is exactly nine feet in length.
9. That giant dog has great strength.
10. The champion did not see the humorous picture.
11. Thank you; I shall accept your offer of chocolate.
12. I suppose Mel upset the vase accidentally.
13. I have a different memory of that incident.
14. The company finally left on Saturday.
15. What is the average length of your swims?

(4) Do not add sounds or syllables.

Each of the following words has only one syllable.

bale	film	known
blown	gale	male
down	grown	realm
elm	helm	sale

Study the following words to be sure you do not add a syllable or a sound when you pronounce them.

athlete	grievous	lightning
burglar	hindrance	ticklish
chimney	idea	translate
draw	laundry	umbrella

(5) Do not transpose sounds.

There are some words in which sounds are often transposed. Speakers may say, for example, *calvary* for *cavalry, modren* for *modern*. Be careful of the following:

cavalry	performance
children	perspiration
hundred	poinsettia
irrelevant	prescription
larynx	prodigy
modern	tragedy

EXERCISE 10. *Oral Drill.* Read the following sentences aloud, making sure you pronounce each word correctly.

1. That elm tree must have been blown down in the gale.
2. The lightning seemed to touch the chimney.
3. The Colemans have four modern paintings for sale.
4. Paula hopes to make a name for herself in the realm of music.
5. Do you think in French, or do you translate each sentence?
6. Slight stature is no hindrance to some athletes.
7. It was a ticklish situation.
8. Will my umbrella fit into your suitcase?
9. These hundred bales of cotton came from Mississippi.
10. The burglar must have come down the fire escape.
11. Can you draw any ideas from Shakespeare's tragedy?
12. Maggie's performance makes her a prodigy.
13. Jerry did not know what kind of film he had been using.
14. The horse cavalry has grown irrelevant in warfare.
15. Did you see the red poinsettia in the laundry room?

29i. Improve your enunciation by sounding your words clearly.

To enunciate means to speak clearly and distinctly. A speaker may use standard pronunciation but mumble or mouth words so that no one can hear.

To enunciate clearly, you must move your lips, tongue, and jaw. Practice nonsense phrases and sentences such as the following to develop clear enunciation.

Betty Botta bought a bit of butter.
"But," said Bet, "this butter's bitter.
If I put it in my batter,
It will make my batter bitter."
Prunes and prisms, prunes and prisms.
The big black bug bit the big black bear.
Truly rural, truly rural.

When speaking, be careful not to link each sentence with the one before by saying *and*. At the end of each sentence, stop! Begin each new sentence cleanly.

Another common fault is the use of *ur*. Avoid using this sound between words or sentences.

EXERCISE 11. People often substitute *n'* for *ng*, as, for example, *swimmin'* for *swimming*. List twenty words ending in *-ng* and check your pronunciation of each word.

EXERCISE 12. *Oral Drill.* The final consonant combinations in the following words are difficult to pronounce. Practice until you can say each word clearly and easily.

1. breadth	10. lengths	19. twelfths	28. faiths
2. width	11. respects	20. months	29. myths
3. hundredth	12. acts	21. folds	30. accepts
4. lifts	13. sects	22. fields	31. precepts
5. wafts	14. facts	23. builds	32. depths
6. shifts	15. tracts	24. adjusts	33. precincts
7. crafts	16. mists	25. masks	34. tastes
8. tufts	17. tests	26. desks	35. asks
9. hyacinths	18. fifths	27. youths	36. tenths

EXERCISE 13. *Oral Drill.* Practice saying the following pairs of words, being careful not to substitute *d* for *t*, or *t* for *th*.

1. riding	writing	10. true	through
2. medal	metal	11. taught	thought
3. bidden	bitten	12. tinker	thinker
4. pedal	petal	13. boat	both
5. madder	matter	14. tent	tenth
6. padding	patting	15. tick	thick
7. beading	beating	16. tree	three
8. boding	boating	17. tow	throw
9. biding	biting	18. tie	thigh

KINDS OF SPEAKING SITUATIONS

The pages that follow describe three kinds of speaking assignments you should be prepared to fulfill.

Talking About an Experience or Telling a Story

Beginning speakers are often asked to speak about a personal experience or tell an interesting story. You should learn to do this smoothly and entertainingly.

29j. Relate experiences and stories by using dramatic effects.

(1) Begin with action.

Long, explanatory openings are usually unnecessary and dull. Start in the middle of things. Give your listeners credit for being able to fill in the background. Read the following examples of openings.

1

When I awoke one night in camp and found a snake coiled at the foot of my bed, I was a bit upset.

2

I did not stop to think when I saw smoke pouring out of the window of my neighbor's house. I rushed to the phone and shouted, "I want to report a fire!"

3

Walking home from the movies late one night, I was startled when two men dashed out of a store and scrambled into a waiting car. Then I heard someone inside the store scream, "Help!"

(2) Use direct conversation.

The exact words of a speaker are more interesting and lively than an indirect statement. Compare these two versions of the same incident.

In March, 1775, Patrick Henry stood before the Virginia Legislature. He said he would rather die than live under British rule. His speech is one of the most famous in American history.

In March, 1775, Patrick Henry stood before the Virginia Legislature and delivered these ringing words:

"Is life so dear, or peace so sweet, as to be purchased at the price of chains and slavery? . . . I know not what course others may take, but as for me, give me liberty or give me death!"

Patrick Henry's call to battle is one of the most famous speeches in American history.

(3) Maintain suspense.

Include details and episodes that keep your listeners in suspense. Lead to a climax. Do not reveal the ending too soon.

(4) Use action-packed verbs.

A good storyteller chooses verbs that are specific rather than general because they help a listener to see, feel, and hear.

GENERAL   Alice walked into the classroom.
SPECIFIC   Alice strolled [sidled, limped, burst, dashed, slouched] into the classsoom.

EXERCISE 14. Briefly relate an unusual experience you have had or have heard about. It may be exciting, amusing, or both, but the incident or its outcome should be unusual. Be sure you begin with action, use conversation and specific verbs, and maintain suspense.

EXERCISE 15. Relate an unusual incident in the life of a famous man or woman. Use the library to get your facts; then retell the incident in your own words. The following list is suggestive only.

1. Barbara Jordan
2. Amelia Earhart
3. Martin Luther King, Jr.
4. Chris Evert Lloyd
5. Thomas Edison
6. N. Scott Momaday
7. Marie Curie
8. Muhammad Ali
9. John F. Kennedy
10. Sen. Daniel Inouye

Talking About Current Events

Current happenings of local, state, national, or international significance are suitable subjects for talks before groups. So, too, are events in the fields of business, science, music, art, sports, education, and literature.

29k. Choose current events to talk about that are important to you and your audience.

Your talk should be more than a restatement of a news item. It should express a fresh and original viewpoint — your own.

A current-events talk may be divided into two parts: (1) a statement of the facts and (2) an interpretation of the facts.

Where can you obtain the facts? Accounts in reputable newspapers or news magazines provide a source of material. So do radio and television broadcasts. For background information consult histories, encyclopedias, and atlases in your school or local library.

You cannot expect, of course, to interpret fully all of the complex events of our complex world. Many brilliant analysts devote their careers to such matters. When you select a current event to talk about, keep a few guiding principles in mind:

(1) Limit your topic.

TOO BROAD	The energy crisis
SUITABLE	How a midwestern town has put solar energy to use
TOO BROAD	Forest conservation
SUITABLE	Congress votes for six new national parks

Do not select a topic about which you can do nothing but parrot what you have read. Choose one that has some significance for you and your listeners and about which you have done some thinking.

(2) Choose a topic about which you know enough to talk intelligently.

Many current happenings are so involved and so puzzling that there are honest differences of opinion about them. Thorough study often leaves one uncertain about what to think of an event. Do not feel that you *must* express an original opinion about your topic if you do not have one. Instead, show that you have thought about the event — and tell what some of your thoughts are.

For example, a student may report on a speech in favor of preserving a local wilderness area. Without giving an opinion, the student can raise some questions that bear on the issue: Has the speaker ever visited the area? Is it valuable for use by the public? How would it be protected? The report will be a stimulating one even though personal "interpretation" has been in the form of questions.

EXERCISE 16. Deliver a three-minute talk on an important current event. Prepare an outline to guide you when speaking.

Talking About Books, Movies, and Television Shows

Reporting on books and dramatic programs helps to sharpen your own appreciation of them and gives your listeners ideas and suggestions for their own entertainment.

29l. Make a report on a book, movie, or television program by describing and evaluating your subject.

Your purpose in a book report is to tell enough about the book so that your listeners may decide whether they want to read it. A book report includes at least two elements: (1) a description of the plot or contents and (2) your evaluation.

When discussing fiction, do not reveal the entire plot, because you may give away the ending for your audience. Tell just enough to build interest. You may describe an exciting or amusing part of the book in detail or, if you wish, read it aloud when it is short. Your listeners can then judge for themselves whether the book has merit.

Always remember to begin your review by giving the title and author. (If you are reviewing a movie, you may choose to give the director's name.)

In discussing fiction or drama, describe the appearance and traits of the main characters. Show how they act under certain circumstances, and indicate how they change during the course of the story.

In addition to giving the title and author and touching upon the plot and characters, discuss some of the following topics in your report. Do not try to include them all.

1. Setting (time and place)
2. Climax
3. Style (vocabulary, narrative or descriptive skill)
4. Humor (Illustrate by reading a few paragraphs aloud.)
5. An incident that reveals character
6. A brief account of the author's life
7. The theme

Your listeners will want to hear your opinion of the book or movie. Do not be satisfied with a statement such as, "I enjoyed the book immensely" or "I thought the movie was dull." Explain why you found it interesting or boring. Was it because of the style, plot, vocabulary, or setting? Was the story too fanciful or too realistic?

In reporting on nonfiction, consider such topics as

1. Title and author
2. Scope (What are the main topics?)
3. Style (Are the explanations interesting? clear?)
4. Usefulness (What useful information have you learned from reading it? Discuss an event, discovery, problem, or topic in detail.)

EXERCISE 17. Read and report orally to your class on a novel, biography, drama, or work of nonfiction that your teacher has approved in advance. Prepare an outline to guide you when speaking.

EXERCISE 18. Orally review a good movie or television play that you have recently seen.

Chapter 30

Listening

Sharpening Listening Skills

Each day you spend a large part of your time listening. You listen more than you speak, you speak more than you read, and you read more than you write. If you are an average student, you spend 63 percent of your day listening. By learning to listen more effectively, you can improve your performance at school and in a career.

PURPOSEFUL LISTENING

Know why you are listening and keep your purpose always in mind. Are you listening to become informed, to understand and follow directions, or to form a judgment?

30a. Keep in mind your purpose for listening.

(1) Listen to gain information.

Forgetting sets in immediately after learning. You may forget something less than an hour after hearing it. To retain the important parts of what you hear, pay close attention to what is said and review it immediately. If you listen attentively, you will remember more.

EXERCISE 1. Compose five questions similar to the following. Read them aloud, pausing about five

seconds between each question to allow your classmates time to jot down their answers. When you have
finished, your classmates will check their answers to
determine how accurately they have listened.

1. In the series of numbers $7 - 2 - 5 - 4 - 3$, the fourth
   number is ———.
2. In the list of words $in - on - up - at - of$, the third
   word is ———.
3. In the list of words $and - off - but - for - how$, the
   word beginning with o is ———.
4. In the announcement, *"Send your entries together
   with 25¢ to Music Contest, Post Office Box 119,
   New York, N.Y. 10006,"* the post office box number is ———.
5. In the statement, *"Ed and Linda will make the
   campfire, Bea and Paula will set up the tent, and
   Charlie will cook the food,"* what is Bea's job?

EXERCISE 2. Compose an explanation or announcement in which certain essential information is omitted.
Read your announcement to the class. Your classmates will show their mental alertness by telling what
information is missing.

EXAMPLE   "To make pancakes, put milk, egg, and
           shortening in a bowl. Mix lightly. Grease
           the griddle. Turn the pancakes when the
           edges look cooked and when the tops are
           covered with bubbles." [This statement
           omits mention of amounts, of flour or pan-
           cake mix, and of pouring the batter onto
           the griddle.]

(2) Listen to instructions.

As you listen to instructions, follow these guides:

a. Ask questions if you don't understand something.

b. Take notes if the instructions are long or complicated or if they are to be carried out at some later time.
c. Don't let your attention wander; you may miss an essential detail.

EXERCISE 3. Orally give travel directions from school to your home. Call upon students to repeat your directions.

EXERCISE 4. Describe how to do or make something, taking care that each step of the process is in correct order. Give your classmates a chance to ask questions before calling on them to repeat your instructions.

30b. Listen carefully during discussions.

Give each speaker in a discussion your full attention. If someone asks you a question, be sure you understand the question exactly before giving an answer. Rephrase the question in your own words or ask the speaker to repeat the question if you are not sure you understand.

Sometimes in a discussion a question may come into your mind as you listen. Be sure the question is a good one—perhaps the speaker has already answered your question or is about to answer it.

EXERCISE 5. Invite one of your classmates to lead a group discussion. This leader will begin the discussion by giving a short oral report. (See page 682 for a list of possible topics.) Each member of the class will then ask the leader one question. Be careful not to repeat questions or to ask something not related to the talk.

LISTENING TO SPEECHES

During speeches, a good listener uses special skills to remember and evaluate the speech.

30c. Listen accurately to speeches.

There is no point in listening if you fail to understand the speaker's message. Listening for certain aspects of a talk will help you.

(1) Notice the structure of a speech or lecture.

A good speaker prepares an outline of a formal speech and sticks to this prearranged plan. A good listener can discern the structure of a prepared talk by asking such questions as these:

    a. What is the speaker's topic?
    b. What are the main points?
    c. What facts are offered as proof?
    d. What does the speaker want me to feel, believe, or do?

To perceive a speaker's plan is not always easy. Making a mental outline as you listen or jotting down notes in the form of an outline may help you to follow the speaker's points.

(2) Listen for transitional words, phrases, and sentences.

A speaker will sometimes give an audience clues by telling what the main points will be, by signaling them with transitional devices, and by summarizing the message.

MAIN POINTS   I want to speak to you about George Washington as a surveyor, soldier, and President.

There are three reasons why I am opposed to increasing our membership dues this year.

TRANSITIONAL
DEVICES

Next . . .
In the second place . . .
There is still another reason . . .
In conclusion . . .
Finally . . .

SUMMARIES

A high school education, therefore, is necessary if you want to lead a satisfying and useful life.

I conclude as I began: Everyone should be trained to help heart attack victims.

(3) Pay attention to nonverbal clues.

A speaker may communicate with more than words. Unspoken, or nonverbal, messages include the speaker's postures, gestures, and facial expressions. Do gestures mark the main points? Does a shrug or other movement indicate details that can be forgotten? Also pay attention to whatever props, such as diagrams, charts, or models, the speaker uses.

EXERCISE 6. Borrow a book of speeches from the library. Ask a teacher or a classmate to read a short speech from it. The rest of the class should observe the structure of the speech, making a rough outline from notes that they take as they listen. When the outlines are compared, how closely do they resemble one another? Analyze the ways in which students were guided (or perhaps misled) to perceive the structure of the speech.

30d. Evaluate what you hear in speeches.

As a listener, always think about what you are hearing.

(1) Distinguish main ideas from details.

Facts are important as a foundation for ideas. If you try to recall all the facts a speaker mentions, however, you may miss the main point.

In the following paragraph, notice the detailed facts that are given. What is the main idea?

> Cigarette smoking produces many harmful effects and shortens life. For almost four years the American Cancer Society studied approximately 200,000 men between the ages of fifty and sixty-nine. In that time 7,316 of the regular cigarette smokers died. During the same time 4,651 non-smokers of the same age died. The difference of 2,665 can be regarded as the number of excess deaths associated with smoking. Most of the excess deaths resulted from coronary-artery disease. Some were caused by lung cancer and others by diseases of the arteries, bladder, and liver. The death rate from all causes was higher among smokers than nonsmokers.

EXERCISE 7. Compose a paragraph that states detailed facts to prove a point. (See pages 303–04 for help in writing this type of paragraph.) Read your paragraph aloud and ask your classmates to repeat the main idea. To find your facts, use an encyclopedia, a science or history book, or some other reliable source.

(2) Distinguish facts from opinions.

A fact is a statement that can be proved to be either true or false. An opinion cannot be proved true or false; it represents someone's belief. Of the statements below, which are facts and which are opinions?

Water boils at 100° Celsius.
Everyone should study a foreign language.
To find the area of a rectangle, multiply the length by the width.
The opening of the Panama Canal was the most important event in history.
My political party has the better candidate.

EXERCISE 8. Analyze the following paragraph. On a separate piece of paper, list which ideas are facts and which are opinions.

The 1920's were the years of the "Harlem Renaissance," when black writers, poets, and performers captured the mood and imagination of the entire nation. The best poet of this age was Langston Hughes, who wrote of the joys, sorrows, and hopes of black Americans. The most famous performer was Bessie Smith, the blues singer, who recorded hundreds of memorable songs.

(3) Watch out for propaganda devices.

Sometimes speakers attempt to persuade listeners by using propaganda devices. Among the most common such devices are the following:

Name-calling. When a speaker attempts to defeat an opponent by unfair personal attacks, do not believe what you hear until the person under attack has had a full opportunity to reply or until you have examined the evidence.

Slogans. Although slogans are simple, catchy, and easily remembered, they can be dangerous. Don't accept slogans as substitutes for your own thinking. Slogans *oversimplify* by reducing a chain of arguments to a few words.

EXAMPLES   They just don't make them like they used
            to.
            America for Americans.

The testimonial. Well-known personalities are often used to persuade you to vote a certain way, buy a certain product, or adopt a certain belief. Ask yourself: Is the speaker an authority in the field? Is the speaker unbiased? Knowing something about the speaker's background and reputation will help you judge the value of any testimonial.

The bandwagon. Most people like to do what others are doing and believe as others believe. Propagandists know and capitalize on this human tendency. You need willpower and the ability to think for yourself to resist hopping on the bandwagon. Do not be fooled into joining a movement simply because others are doing it.

EXERCISE 9. Find an example of each of the preceding propaganda devices. You may use radio and television commercials or newspaper and magazine advertisements. For each example, tell how an alert listener should respond.

Index

A

Abbreviations
  for states, 461
  in dictionaries, 600–01
  in letters, 449
  in *Readers' Guide,* 576–77
  punctuation after, 485–86
  rules for using, 372–73
Accent marks, in dictionaries, 611
Accept, except, 220–21
Action, in a story, 405
Action verb, defined, 16
Active voice, defined, 166
Address, direct, commas with, 505
Addresses, commas with, 508
Addressing envelopes, 459
Adjective clause
  combining sentences by using, 270
  defined, 109
  diagramed, 116
  introduced by adverb, 110–11
  relative pronouns in, 109–11
Adjective phrase
  combining sentences by using, 260–61
  defined, 81–82
  diagramed, 85–86
  punctuation of, 501
Adjectives
  after linking verb, 12, 18
  articles as, 12
  comparison of, 202–09
  defined, 10–11
  diagramed, 58–60
  ending in *-ly,* 25
  function of, 10–12
  in sentences, 12
  introductory, for sentence variety, 280

nouns used as, 11–12
position of, in sentences, 12–13
predicate, 66
pronominal, 11
proper, capitalization of, 468–69
separated from word it modifies, 13
telling *which one, what kind, how many,* 10–11
Adjustment letters, 455–57
Adverb clause
  combining sentences by using, 271–72
  commas with, 501
  defined, 113
  diagramed, 119
  subordinating conjunction in, 114
Adverb phrase
  combining sentences by using, 260–61
  defined, 83–84
  diagramed, 85–86
Adverbs
  comparison of, 202–09
  defined, 22
  diagramed, 58–60
  distinguished from *-ly* adjective, 26
  distinguished from prepositions, 30
  form of, 26
  introductory, for sentence variety, 280
  modifying an adjective, 23–24
  modifying an adverb, 25
  modifying a verb, 22–23
  telling *when, where, how, to what extent,* 22
Advice, advise, 659

Affect, effect, 221, 660
Agreement of pronoun and antecedent, 147–49
  antecedents joined by *and,* 149
  antecedents joined by *or, nor,* 149
  gender, 147
Agreement of subject and verb
  after *here is, there is,* 143
  collective nouns, 142
  doesn't, don't, 140–41
  each, everyone, etc., 134
  intervening phrases, 132
  predicate nominative, mistaken agreement with, 143
  several, few, both, many, 134
  some, any, none, all, most, 134–35
  subjects joined by *and,* 137
  subjects joined by *or, nor,* 138–39
Ain't, 221
All, number of, 134–35
All ready, already, 659–60
All right, 660
All the farther, all the faster, 221
All together, altogether, 660
Almanacs, 584
Ambassador World Atlas, 583
American Authors 1600–1900, 583
American Men of Science, 583
Among, between, 221, 222
And etc., 221
Antagonist, 404
Antecedent
  agreement of pronouns with, 147–49
  defined, 7
Anthology of World Poetry, 586
Antonyms, 603–04
Any, number of, 134–35
Anybody, number of, 134
Anyone, number of, 134

Anywheres, 221
Apostrophe
  in contractions, 549–50
  it's, its, 543
  misuse of, with possessive pronouns, 543
  to form plural letters, numbers, etc., 551
  to form plural possessives, 541
  to form possessive of compound words, words showing individual or joint possession, etc., 545–46
  to form singular possessives, 541
Appositive
  as sentence fragment, 251
  commas with, 103, 503
  defined, 102
  diagramed, 104
Appositive phrase, 103
  combining sentences by using, 264
Appropriate words, 435
Article
  capitalization in titles, 477–78
  defined, 12
Articles, magazine (*Readers' Guide*), 576–78
As, case of pronoun after, 197
As, like, 222, 229
As if, 222, 229
At, 222
Atlases, 583
Author card, 571–72
Authors, reference books about, 582–83
Auxiliary verb = Helping verb

B

Bad, comparison of, 205
Bartlett's *Familiar Quotations,* 584–85

Base of sentence, 62–63
Be, list of forms of, 18
Begin, principal parts of, 156
Beside, besides, 222
Better, best, 205
Between, among, 222
Biographical dictionaries, 582–83
Blow, principal parts of, 156
Blowed, 156
Body
  of a business letter, 450
  of a composition, 356
Both, number of, 134
Brake, break, 660
Break, principal parts of, 156
Breve, 609
Bring, principal parts of, 156
Bring, take, 223
British Authors of the Nineteenth Century, 583
Burst, principal parts of, 156
Bursted, 156
Business letter
  adjustment letter, 455–57
  appearance, 446
  arrangement on page (*illustration*), 447
  body, 450
  checklist for, 460–61
  closing, 450
  envelope, 457–58
  folding, 457–58
  form, 447–48
  heading, 448
  inside address, 448
  model of, 451
  order letter, 454
  parts of, 447–52
  punctuation in, 447–49, 524
  request letter, 453
  salutation, 449–50, 524
  signature, 451–52
  stationery, 446
Bust, busted, 223
But, in double negative, 236

C

Call number, 571, 573
Can't hardly, 236
Can't scarcely, 236
Capital, capitol, 660–61
Capitalization
  dictionary as guide to, 599
  of business firms and products, 472, 473
  of calendar items, 473
  of course names with numbers, 475
  of first word in line of poetry, 466
  of first word in sentence, 465–66
  of first word in direct quotation, 530
  of geographical names, 469–70
  of government bodies, 472–73
  of historical events, 473
  of *I* and *O,* 466–67
  of institutions, 472
  of languages, 475
  of names of particular places, things, and events, 474
  of names of persons, 469
  of nationalities, 473
  of proper adjectives, 468–69
  of proper nouns, 468–69
  of races and religions, 473
  of school subjects, 475
  of seasons, 473
  of special events, 473
  of titles of persons, 476–77
  of titles of publications, works of art, etc., 477–78
  of words referring to Deity, 478
  of words showing family relationship, 477
  rules for, 465–78
  summary style sheet for, 481–82

Card catalogue, 570–74
-cede, -ceed, -sede, 649
Characterization, in narrative writing, 404
Checklist
for determining parts of speech, 35
for information in card catalogue, 574
for letter writing, 460–61
for style of manuscript, 481–82
for uses of apostrophe, 542–43
for uses of comma, 509–10
for writing compositions, 366–67
for written reports, 397
Choose, chose, 661
Choose, principal parts of, 156
Chronological order of details, in paragraphs, 311–12
Clause
adjective, 109–11
adverb, 113–14
defined, 106
diagramed, 118–20, 121–23
distinguished from phrase, 106
essential, 496
independent, 106–07
introductory, for sentence variety, 283
main = independent
misplaced, 216–17
nonessential, 495–96
nonrestrictive = nonessential
noun, 115–16
restrictive = essential
subordinate, 107–11
Clichés, 436
Climax, in a story, 405
Closing, of a business letter, 450
Coarse, course, 661
Coherence
in the composition (linking expressions), 358–61
in the paragraph (order of details, connectives), 311–19
Collective nouns
list of, 142
number of, 142
College dictionaries, 594
Colloquial words, dictionary label for, 603
Colon
after salutation of business letter, 524
before a list, 523–24
before a long formal statement or quotation, 524
in writing Biblical chapters and verses, 524
in writing the time, 524
position of, outside closing quotation marks, 532
Combining sentences
inserting adjectives, adverbs, or prepositional phrases, 260–61
using appositive phrases, 264
using compound subjects and verbs, 266–67
using participial phrases, 262–63
writing a complex sentence, 270–74
writing a compound sentence, 268
Come, principal parts of, 156
Comma
after closing in letters, 508
after introductory elements, 500–01
after salutation in friendly letters, 508
between parts of a compound sentence, 491–93
in a series, 487–89
in direct address, 505
in letters, 508
rules for, 487–509

Comma, *continued*
summary of uses, 509-10
to set off nonessential phrases and clauses, 495-96
unnecessary use of, 509
with appositives, 503
with coordinate adjectives, 489-90
with dates and addresses, 508
with interrupters, 503
with parenthetical expressions, 505-06
with quotation marks, 531-32
Comma splice = Run-on sentence
Common noun, 4-5
Comparative degree
correct use of, 205-09
defined, 203
rules for forming, 202-09
Comparison of modifiers
double, 207-08
illogical, 206-07
irregular, 205
regular, 203-04
Complement, compliment, 662-63
Complements
after linking verb, 18
compound, 66
defined, 62
diagramed, 71-73
function of, 62-63
subject, 66
Complete predicate, defined, 41
Complete subject, defined, 41
Complex sentence
combining sentences by writing, 269-74
defined, 122
diagramed, 122
Complimentary close, in business letter, 450
Composition
adapting subject to readers, 342

arranging ideas in order, 347
checklist for, 366-67
choosing a subject for, 333-35, 336
coherence in, 358-62
determining the purpose, 343-44
emphasis in, 363-64
grouping related ideas, 346
introduction, body, conclusion, 353-58
limiting the subject, 340-41
linking expressions in, 358-61
listing ideas in, 345
materials for, 333-40
outlining, 348-51
paragraphing, 358-62
summary of steps in writing, 364-65
Compound-complex sentence
defined, 122
diagramed, 122
Compound direct object, 70, 73
Compound indirect object, 70, 73
Compound noun, 6
Compound prepositions, 30
Compound sentence
combining sentences by writing, 268
comma in, 491-93
defined, 121
diagramed, 121
Compound subject
combining sentences by using, 266-67
defined, 51
diagramed, 56-57, 58
number of, 137
Compound subject complement, 66
diagramed, 72
Compound verb
combining sentences by using, 266-67

Compound verb, *continued*
  defined, 52
  diagramed, 56–57, 58
Compton's Encyclopedia, 581
Conclusion, of a composition,
  356–58
  of a talk, 684–85
Conflict in a story, 404–05
Conjugation of verbs, 163–64
Conjunctions
  coordinating, 31–32
  correlative, 31–32
  defined, 31
  subordinating, list of, 114,
  272
Connectives
  between paragraphs, 358–62
  within a paragraph, 316–19
Connotation of words, 428–30
Consistency of tense, 164–65
Consonants
  defined, 607–08
  dictionary markings for, 608
Consul, council, 663
Contemporary Authors, 583
*Contemporary Authors: First
  Revision,* 583
Context, as clue to word mean-
  ing, 34, 618–19
Contractions, use of apostro-
  phe in, 549–50
Coordinating conjunctions, list
  of, 31
Copulative verb = Linking verb
Correlative conjunctions, list of,
  31
Could of, 224–25
Course, coarse, 661
Current Biography, 582

D

Dangling modifiers, 210–12
Dangling participle, examples
  of, 212

Dashes, 556
Dates, commas with, 508
Declarative sentence, defined,
  75
Demonstrative pronouns, 9
Denotation of words, 428–30
Dependent clause = Subordinate clause
Derivation of words, 424–26,
  601
Description, in writing stories,
  416–17
Descriptive paragraph, 327
Desert, dessert, 639
Details, in paragraph development, 303–05
  arranged chronologically,
  311–12
  arranged in order of importance, 313–15
  arranged spatially, 312–13
Dewey decimal system, 568–
  70
Diacritical marks
  accent, 611
  breve, 609
  explained, 600, 606–11
  macron, 609
  vowel sounds, 576, 608–09
Diagraming
  adjectives and adverbs, 58–
  60
  appositives, 104
  complements, 71
  complex sentences, 122
  compound-complex sen-
  tences, 122
  compound objects, 73
  compound sentences, 121
  compound subject and compound verb, 57, 58
  compound subjects, 56–57
  compound verbs, 57
  direct and indirect objects,
  72–73
  nouns of direct address, 56

Diagraming, *continued*
  predicate adjective and predicate nominative, 72
  prepositional phrases, 85–86
  simple sentences, 121
  subject and verb, 55–56
  subordinate clauses, 117–20
  there beginning a sentence, 56
  understood subject, 56
  verbals and verbal phrases, 99–102
  with correlatives, 58
Dialogue
  paragraphing of, 533–34
  punctuation of, 529–33
  writing, 412–14
Dictionaries
  abbreviations in, 576–77
  accent marks in, 611
  arrangement of information in, 598–604
  as guide to capitalization, 599
  as guide to pronunciation, 600, 606–11
  as guide to spelling, 598, 644
  as guide to usage, 603
  biographical, 582–83
  college, 594
  derivations, 601
  diacritical marks in, 607–11
  guide words in, 593
  illustrations in, 604
  information in, 598–604
  kinds of, 590–95
  macron in, 609
  parts of speech in, 600–01
  school, 594–95
  schwa in, 610
  syllable division in, 599
  synonyms and antonyms in, 603–04
  unabridged, 591–94
  usage labels in, 603
Dictionaries, of synonyms, 579–80

Dictionary of American Biography, 582
Dictionary of National Biography, 582
Direct address, commas with, 505
Direct object
  compound, 70
  defined, 67
  diagramed, 72–73
Direct quotations, punctuation of, 530–33
Direct references as connectives, 316–17
Discover, invent, 225
Discussions, listening to, 702
Dividing words, 553–55
Do, principal parts of, 153, 156
Doesn't, agreement with subject, 140–41
Don't
  agreement with subject, 140–41
  for *doesn't*, 225
Double comparison, 207–08
Double negative, 235–37
Double subject, 228
Draft, for report, 395–96
Drive, principal parts of, 156
Drownded, for *drowned*, 155

E

Each, number of, 134
Eat, principal parts of, 156
Effect, affect, 221, **660**
Either, number of, 134
Emphasis in compositions, 363–64
Encyclopaedia Britannica, 581
Encyclopedia Americana, 581
Encyclopedias, use of, 580–82
End marks, 483–86
Enunciation, 691–92

Envelope, of business letter, 457–59
Essential clause, 496
Etymology, defined, 424
Every, number of, 144
Everybody, number of, 134
Everyone, number of, 134
Everywheres, 221
Except, accept, 220–21
Exclamation point, 484–85, 531–32, 532–33
Exclamatory sentence, defined, 76
Expository paragraph, 328

F

Fact and opinion, distinguishing, 705–06
Fall, principal parts of, 156
Familiar Quotations, Bartlett's, 584–85
Famous people, dictionary information about, 604–05
Few, number of, 134
Fewer, less, 225
Fiction, library arrangement of, 567
Folding a business letter, 457–58
Foreign words, underlining, 528
Formal words, 432–33
Formally, formerly, 664
Fractions, hyphens with, 555
Fragment = Sentence fragment
Freeze, principal parts of, 156

G

Gender, 147
Geographical names, capitalization of, 469–70

Gerund
  defined, 93
  diagramed, 100
Gerund phrase, defined, 95
Give, principal parts of, 156
Go, principal parts of, 156
Good, comparison of, 205
Good, well, 225–26
Good usage, special problems in, 220–26, 228–37
  all the farther, all the faster, 221
  beside, besides, 222
  between, among, 222
  double negative, 235–37
  double subject, 228
  hisself, 9
  its, it's, 665
  less, fewer, 225
  of, with *inside, off*, etc., 229–30
  theirselves, 9
  them, used incorrectly for *these, those*, 232
  this here, that there, 232–33
  way, ways, 233
  when, where, used incorrectly in definitions, 233
Goode's World Atlas, 583
Granger's *Index to Poetry and Recitations*, 585
Greek prefixes and roots, 633–34

H

Had of, 228, 230
Had ought, hadn't ought, 228
Haven't but, haven't only, 236
He, she, etc., as double subject, 228
Heading, of business letter, 448
Hear, here, 664–65
Helping verbs

Helping verbs, *continued*
  defined, 20
  list of, 20
Here is, number of subject after,
  143
Hisself, theirselves, 9
Home Book of Modern Verse,
  Stevenson's, 585
Home Book of Quotations,
  Stevenson's, 585
Home Book of Verse, Steven-
  son's, 585
Hyphen, uses of, 553–55

I

ie, ei, spelling rule for, 648
Illustrations in the dictionary,
  604
Imperative sentence
  defined, 76
  punctuation of, 76, 485
Incidents, in developing paragraphs, 307
Indefinite pronouns, list of, 9
Independent clause, 106–07
Index to Poetry, Granger's, 585
Indirect object
  compound, 70, 73
  defined, 69
  diagramed, 73
Indirect quotation, 530
Infinitive
  defined, 97
  distinguished from preposi-
    tional phrase, 97
  with *to* omitted, 98–99, 102
Infinitive clause, 98
Infinitive phrase
  defined, 98
  diagramed, 101–02
  introductory, for sentence
    variety, 281–82
Informal words, 432–34

Information Please Almanac,
  584
Inside address of business let-
  ter, 448
Interjection, defined, 33
Interrogative pronoun, 9
Interrogative sentence, defined,
  76
Interrupters, commas with, 503
Intransitive verbs, 16–17
Introduction
  of a composition, 353–55
  of a story, 410–12
  of a talk, 684–85
Introductory expressions, for
  variety, 278–83
  punctuation with, 500–01
Invent, discover, 225
Irregular comparison, 205
Irregular verbs
  defined, 155
  list of, 156
Italics (underlining), 527–28
  compared with quotation
    marks for use with titles,
    537–38
  for foreign words, etc., 528
  for titles, 527
  uses of, 527–28
Its, it's, 665
It's me, 183

J

Joint possession, use of apostrophe in, 545–46

K

Kind, sort, type, 228
Know, principal parts of, 156
Knowed, 156

L

Latin prefixes and roots, 631–
32
Lay, lie, 168–70
Lead, led, lead, 665
Learn, teach, 228
Least, in comparisons, 204
Leave, let, 229
Less, in comparisons, 204
Less, fewer, 225
Let, leave, 229
Letter writing
business, 444–61
checklist for, 460–61
five tips on, 444–45
order, 454–55
request, 453
Library
arrangement of books, 566–
70
card catalogue, 570–74
Dewey decimal system, 568–
70
fiction, 567
finding magazine articles
(*Readers' Guide*), 576–78
nonfiction, 568–74
organization of, 565–70
reference books, 575–87
vertical file, 579
Library paper = Report
Lie, lay, 168–70
Like, as, 229
Like, as if, 229
Limiting the subject for composition, 340–41
Linking expressions
between paragraphs, 359
lists of, 317, 359
within paragraphs, 316–19
Linking verb
complements of, 18
defined, 17
Listening
distinguishing fact from opinion, 705–06

during discussions, 702
evaluating nonverbal cues,
704
for main ideas, 705
for propaganda devices, 706–
07
to gain information, 700
to instructions, 701–02
to speeches, 703–07
Literary terms, 629
Literature, reference books on,
584–86
Loaded words, 431
Loose, lose, 665

M

Macron, 609
Magazine articles listed in
Readers' Guide, 576–78
Main clause = Independent
clause
Manuscript, defined, 371
Manuscript form
abbreviations, rules for, 372–
73
dividing words at end of a
line, 374
rules for writing numbers,
373–74
standard correction symbols,
374–75
standards in preparation,
371–72
Many
comparison of, 205
number of, 134
Many a, number of, 144
Meaning of a word, dictionary
definition of, 602, 621–22
Misplaced modifiers, 214–17
Models for letter writing
adjustment, 456
business, 451

Models for letter writing, *continued*
  envelope for business letter, 459
  order, 455
  request, 451
Modern American Poetry, 586
Modern British Poetry, 586
Modifiers
  comparison of, 202–09
  dangling, 210–12
  defined, 202
  misplaced, 214–17
Modify, meaning of, 10–11, 202
Moral, morale, 665
Most, number of, 134–35
Much, comparison of, 205

N

Narrative paragraph, 325
Narrative writing, 403–16
National Geographic Atlas of the World, 583
Negative, double, 235–37
Neither, number of, 134
New Book of Unusual Quotations, 585
New Dictionary of Quotations, 585
New words, 427–28
New York Times Atlas of the World, 583
No, in double negative, 236–37
No one, number of, 134
Nobody, number of, 134
Nominative case
  for predicate nominative, 183
  for subject of verb, 181–82
None, in double negative, 236–37
  number of, 134–35
Nonessential clause, 493–94

Nonfiction, library arrangement of, 568–70
Nonrestrictive clause = Nonessential clause
Nonstandard English, 130
Note card, in writing reports, 392–94
Note-taking, for written reports, 391–94
Nothing, in double negative, 236–37
Noun
  common, 4–5
  compound, 6
  defined, 4
  plurals, formation of, 655–58
  proper, 4–5
  singular, but plural in form, 145
  used as adjective, 11–12
Noun clause
  combining sentences by using, 294
  defined, 115–16
  diagramed, 119–20
Nowheres, 221
Number, defined, 129
Numbers, hyphens with, 555
Numbers, rules for writing, 373–74

O

Object
  direct, defined, 67
  indirect, defined, 69
  never in a phrase, 70
  of verb, case of, 184–85, 186
Object of preposition
  case of, 188
  defined, 79–80
Objective case
  object of preposition in, 188–89

Objective case, *continued*
  object of verb in, 184–85,
    186
Of, with *inside, off,* etc., 229–30
*Official Associated Press Al-
    manac,* 584
One, number of, 134
Onomatopoeia, 419–20
Order letter, 454–55
Outcome, in a story, 405–06
Outlining, for compositions,
    348–51
  for talks, 683–84
Opinion and fact, distinguish-
    ing, 705–06
*Oxford Dictionary of Quota-
    tions,* 585

P

Paragraph
  choosing a topic for, 299–300
  coherence in, 311–25
  connectives in, 316–19
  defined, 293–94
  descriptive, 327
  developed by contrast or
    comparison, 308–09
  developed by detail or ex-
    ample, 303–05
  developed by incident, 307
  developed by reasons, 308
  direct references in, 316–19
  expository, 328
  narrative, 325
  plan for, 301–02
  specific details in, 303–05
  topic sentence, 294–95
  transitional devices in, 316–
    19
  unity in, 296–97
  unrelated ideas in, 296–97

Paragraphing a composition,
    356–62
Parentheses, 557–58
  rules for, 558
Parenthetical expressions
  commas with, 505–06
  dashes with, 556
Part of speech, dictionary labels
    for, 600–01
Participial phrase
  as dangling modifier, 210–12
  as sentence fragment, 247
  combining sentences by us-
    ing, 262–63
  commas with, 495–96, 500
  defined, 92
  diagramed, 100
  introductory, for sentence
    variety, 281–82
  nonessential, 495–96
Participle
  dangling, 210–12
  defined, 88
  introductory, for sentence
    variety, 280
Parts of speech
  adjective, defined, 10–11
  adverb, defined, 22
  conjunction, defined, 31
  determined by use, 34
  interjection, defined, 33
  noun, defined, 4
  preposition, defined, 29
  pronoun, defined, 6
  summary of uses, 35
  verb, defined, 16
Passed, past, 655
Passive voice, defined, 166
Past participle, defined, 89–90
Peace, piece, 666
People, dictionary information
    about, 604–05
Period
  after abbreviation, 485–86
  as end mark, 483–84
  position of, inside parenthe-
    ses, 558

Period, *continued*
  position of, inside quotation
    marks, 532
Personal pronouns
  case of, 180–86, 188–93,
    196–97
  defined, 8
Phrase
  adjective, 81–82
  adverb, 83–84
  appositive, 103, 251
  defined, 20, 78
  distinguished from clause,
    106
  gerund, defined, 95
  infinitive, defined, 98
  nonessential, 495–96
  nonrestrictive = nonessential
  participial, defined, 92
  prepositional, 79
  to begin sentence, 281–82
  verb, 20–21
  verbal, 88–102, 248–49
Piece, peace, 666
Places, dictionary information
  about, 604–05
Plain, plane, 667
Planning
  a composition, 344–51
  a paragraph, 301–02
  a story, 406–09
Plot of a story, 405–06
Plural number, defined, 129
Plurals, formation of, 655–58
  compound nouns, 657
  foreign words, 658
  letters, 551, 658
  nouns, irregular method, 657
  nouns, regular method, 655
  nouns, same in plural and
    singular, 658
  nouns ending in *f, fe,* 656
  nouns ending in *o,* 657
  nouns ending in *s, x, z,* etc.,
    655
  nouns ending in *y,* 656
  numbers, 551, 658

signs, 551, 658
  words as words, 551
Point of view of story, 409–10
Positive degree of comparison,
  203–05
Possessive case, 179, 540–46
Predicate
  complete, defined, 41
  compound, defined, 52
  simple, defined, 43
Predicate adjective
  compound, 66
  defined, 66
  diagramed, 72
Predicate nominative
  compound, 66
  defined, 66
  diagramed, 72
  mistaken agreement with, 143
Prefixes
  defined, 631
  Greek, 633–34
  hyphen with, 555
  Latin, 631–32
  spelling of words with, 649–
    54
Prefixes and roots, as aids to
  word meaning, 631–34
Prepositional phrases
  combining sentences by us-
    ing, 260–61
  defined, 79
  diagramed, 85–86
  examples of, 79
  introductory, for sentence
    variety, 281–82
  used as adjective, 81–82
  used as adverb, 83–84
Prepositions
  compound, list of, 30
  defined, 29
  distinguished from adverbs,
    30
  list of, 29–30
  object of, 79–80, 184–85, 186
Present participle
  defined, 89

Present participle, *continued*
distinguished from verb
phrase, 89
Principal, principle, 667
Principal parts of verbs
defined, 153-54
irregular, 155-57
regular, 154-55
Pronominal adjective, 11
Pronoun
after *than, as,* 197
agreement with antecedent,
147-49
case of, 179-89
defined, 6
demonstrative, 9
in an incomplete construction, 196-97
indefinite, 9
interrogative, 9
personal, 8, 180-81
possessive, 8
reflexive, 9
relative, 9
unacceptable forms of, 9
unnecessary, in double subject, 228
who, which, that, distinguished, 233
who and *whom,* 190-93
Pronunciation
as an aid in spelling, 645, 646
dictionary indications of, 600,
606-11
in speaking, 687-90
reading diacritical marks,
607-11
words commonly mispro-
nounced, 613-14
Proper adjective
capitalization of, 468-69
defined, 12
Proper noun
capitalization of, 468-69
defined, 4-5
Protagonist, 404

Punctuation
after an abbreviation, 485-86
apostrophe, 540-51
colon, 523-24
comma, 487-510
dashes, 556
end marks, 483-86
exclamation point, 484-85
hyphen, 553-55
in letters, 447-50
italics (underlining), 527-28
parentheses, 557-58
period, 483-84
question mark, 484
quotation marks, 529-38
semicolons, 513-19
Purpose, in composition writing, 343-44

Q

Question mark, 484
position of, in quotation, 532-
33
Quiet, quite, 667-68
Quotation marks
compared with italics for
titles, 537-38
dialogue, paragraphing of,
533-34
for direct quotations, 530-33
quotation within a quotation,
535
single, 535
to enclose titles of chapters,
articles, etc., 536-38
with other marks of punctuation, 531-33

R

Raise, rise, 173

*Rand McNally New Cosmo-
politan World Atlas,* 583
*Random House Dictionary of
the English Language: Un-
abridged Edition,* 591
*Readers' Guide to Periodical
Literature,* 576–78
Reference books
about authors, 582–83
about literature, 584–86
almanacs, 584
atlases, 583
biographical, 582–83
description and use of, 575–
86
dictionaries, 587–88, 590–
611
encyclopedia, use of, 580–82
for finding quotations, 584–
85
special, 586–87
Reflexive pronouns, 8–9
Regular comparison, 203–04
Regular verb, 154
Relative pronoun
case of, 190–93
defined, 109–110
list of, 9
who, which, that, distinguished, 233
who and *whom,* 190–93
Report writing
acknowledging sources, 396
bibliography, 390
checklist, 397
developing preliminary outline, 391–92, 395
length of summary, 378, 387
main ideas in articles, 376–77
model, 397–401
rough draft, 395–96
source materials, 389–90
subject selection, 387–89
taking notes for, 377–78,
391–94
using own words, 377, 396

Request letter, 453
Restrictive clause = Essential
clause
Ride, principal parts of, 156
Ring, principal parts of, 156
Rise, raise, 173
*Roget's Thesaurus of English
Words & Phrases,* 579
Roots and prefixes, as aids to
word meaning, 631–34
Run, principal parts of, 156
Run-on sentence, 254–55

S

Said, same, such, 231
Salutation, in a business letter,
449–50
School dictionary, 594–95
Schwa, 610
See, principal parts of, 156
"See" card, 572–73
Semicolon
between independent clauses
containing commas, 517
between independent clauses
joined by *for example, that
is,* etc., 516
between independent clauses
not joined by *and, but,* etc.,
513–14
between items in a series,
518–19
position of, outside closing
quotation marks, 532
Sentence
base of, 62–63
classified by purpose, 75–76
classified by structure, 120–
22
combining, 259–76
complements, 62–64, 66–73
complex, 122
compound, 121

Sentence, *continued*
compound-complex, 122
declarative, 75
defined, 39
diagraming, 55-60, 71-73, 121-22
distinguishing from fragment, 39, 243-45
exclamatory, 76
fragment, 243-53
imperative, 76
interrogative, 76
kinds of, 75-76, 120-22
parts of a, 38-76
run-on, 254-55
simple, 121
stringy, 277
subject and predicate (verb), 40-54
variety in, 278-87
Sentence combining, *see*
Combining sentences
Sentence fragment
common types of, 246-53
defined, 243
distinguished from sentence, 39, 243-45
Sentence variety, 278-87
Series, commas in, 487-89
Set, sit, 171-72
Setting, in narratives, 404
Several, number of, 134
Shall, will, 231-32
Shone, shown, 668
Shrink, principal parts of, 156
Signature, of business letter, 451-52
Simple predicate, 43
Simple sentence, 121
Simple subject, 42
Single quotation marks, use of, 535
Singular number, defined, 129
Sit, set, 171-72
Slang, use of in writing, 433-34
So, for *so that, therefore,* 232

Some, number of, 134
Some, somewhat, 232
Somebody, number of, 134
Someone, number of, 134
Sounds and meanings of words, 421-22
Spatial order of details, in paragraphs, 312-13
Speak, principal parts of, 156
Speaking before groups
choosing a topic, 679-80
conclusion, 684-85
delivery, 685-92
enunciation, 691-92
gathering material, 682-83
introduction, 684-85
nonverbal communication, 686-87
outline, 683-84
preparation, 679-85, 686
pronunciation, 687-90
purpose for, 681
relating experiences, 693-95
talking about books, movies, and television shows, 697-98
talking about current events, 695-97
Speeches, listening to, 703-07
Spelling
demons, list of, 673
dictionary as guide to, 598, 644
doubling final consonant, 653-54
final *e* before suffix, 651
good habits, 643-48
ie, ei, 648-49
plurals, 655-58
pronunciation and, 645, 646
rules, 648-58
words commonly misspelled, list of, 673-76
words often confused, list of, 659-71
words with prefixes, 649-50

Spelling, *continued*
  words with suffixes, 650–54
Standard correction symbols, 374–75
Standard English, 130
Standards in manuscript preparation, 371–72
State-of-being verb = Linking verb
States, abbreviations for, in addresses, 461
Stationary, stationery, 668
Stationery, business letter, 446
Steal, principal parts of, 156
Stevenson's *Home Book of Modern Verse,* 585
  Home Book of Quotations, 585
  Home Book of Verse, 585
Story writing
  action, 405
  arousing reader's interest, 410–12
  characters, 404
  climax, 405
  conflict, 404–05
  description in, 415–16
  dialogue, 412–14
  finding material, 406–07
  outcome, 405–06
  planning for, 406–09
  plot, 405–06
  point of view, 409–10
  setting, 404
  situation, 404–05
Stringy sentences, 277
Subject (of sentence)
  after *there* or *here,* 48
  agreement with verb, 130–45
  case of, 181
  complete, defined, 41
  compound, 51, 137
  defined, 40
  how to find, 45–46
  in questions, 48
  in unusual position, 48–49

never in a phrase, 47, 132
simple, defined, 42
understood, 50–51
Subject card, 572
Subject complement, 66
Subordinate clause
  as a sentence fragment, 246–47
  defined, 107
  diagraming, 117–20
  noun, 115–16
  introductory, for sentence variety, 283
  relationship to independent clauses, 107–08
  relative pronouns in, 109–11
  uses of, 108–11
Subordinating conjunctions, list of, 114, 272
Suffixes
  defined, 650
  final *e* before (spelling), 651
  hyphens with, 555
  spelling of words with, 649–54
Summary, writing, 376–401
Summary, *see also* Checklist
Superlative degree of comparison, 203–04, 205–06
  correct use of, 205–09
  rules for forming, 203–04
Swim, principal parts of, 156
Syllables
  as an aid in spelling, 644
  dictionary marking of, 599
Synonyms, 603–04, 626
  degrees of formality among, 434–35

T

Take, bring, 223
Take, principal parts of, 156
Teach, learn, 228
Tense, consistency of, 164–65

Than, pronoun after, 197
Than, then, 232, 668
That, which, who, distinguished, 233
That there, this here, 232–33
Their, there, they're, 668
Theirselves, hisself, 9
Them, for *these* or *those,* 232
Then, than, 232
There, beginning a sentence, diagramed, 56
There, their, they're, 668
There is, number of subject after, 143
Thesaurus of English Words & Phrases, Roget's, 579
This here, that there, 232–33
Threw, through, 670
Throw, principal parts of, 156
Throwed, 156
Tired words = Clichés
Title card, 571, 573
Titles
  of persons, capitalization of, 476–77
  of publications, capitalization of, 477–78
  of works of art, number of, 144
  use of italics and quotation marks with, 527–28, 537–38
To, too, two, 670
Topic outline, 348–49
Topic sentence, 294–305
  defined, 294
  development of, 299–305
Topics for composition, list of, 367–70
Transitive verbs, 16–17, 166

U

Unabridged dictionary, 591–94
Underlining (italics), 527–28
  See Italics

Understood subject, 50–51
Unity in the paragraph, 296–97
Unless, without, 233
Usage, special problems in, *see* Good usage

V

Variety in sentences
  beginning with a phrase, 281–82
  beginning with a subordinate clause, 283
  beginning with single-word modifiers, 281
  varying kinds of sentences, 286–87
  varying length of sentences, 277
  varying sentence beginnings, 278–83
Verb phrase, defined, 20–21
Verbal phrases, 88–102, 248–49
Verbals
  gerund, defined, 93
  infinitive, defined, 97
  participle, defined, 88
Verbs
  action, 16–17
  active voice, 166–67
  agreement with subject, 130–45
  as simple predicate, 43
  be, forms of, 18
  compound, 52
  conjugation of, 163–64
  consistency of tense, 164–65
  correct use of, 153–73
  defined, 15
  helping, list of, 20
  intransitive, 16–17
  irregular, 155–57
  linking, 17–19
  passive voice, 166–67
  principal parts, 153–64

Verbs, *continued*
  regular, 154–55
  special problems, 168–73
  specific, 440–43
  state-of-being, 17
  tenses, 162–64
  transitive, 16–17
Vertical file, use of, 579
Vocabulary
  diagnostic test, 615–17
  exact words, 626
  meanings in context, 618–19
  notebook, 617
  prefixes, 631–34
  right word, using the, 626
  roots, 631–34
  ways to learn new words, 618–29
  word list, 639–42
Voice, active and passive, 166
Vowel sounds
  defined, 608–09
  dictionary markings for, 609–10

W

Waist, waste, 670
Ways, for *way,* 233
Weak, week, 671
Weather, whether, 671
Webster's Biographical Dictionary, 583
Webster's New Dictionary of Synonyms, 580
Webster's New International Dictionary, 591
Week, weak, 671
Well, comparision of, 205
Well, good, 225–26

When, misused in writing a definition, 233
Whether, weather, 671
Which, that, who, 233
Who, whom, 190–93
Who's whose, 671
Who's Who, 582–83
Who's Who in America, 582–83
Will, shall, 231–32
Without, unless, 233
Word histories, 424–26
Word origins, 424–26, 635
Words
  beauty in, 423–24
  commonly mispronounced, 613–14
  dividing at end of a line, 374
  formal and informal, 432–33
  general and specific, 438–39
  often confused (spelling), 659–71
  sound and meaning in, 421–22, 423
  stating amount, number of, 144
World Almanac and Book of Facts, 584
World Biography, 583
World Book Encyclopedia, 581
Worse, worst, 205
Write, principal parts of, 156

Y

Your, you're, 671

Z

Zip code, 462

Tab Key Index

GRAMMAR

1 The Parts of Speech

1a noun, 4
1b pronoun, 6
1c adjective, 10
1d verb, 16
1e adverb, 22
1f preposition, 29
1g conjunction, 31
1h interjection, 33
1i determining parts of speech, 34

2 The Parts of a Sentence

2a sentence defined, 39
2b subject & predicate, 40
2c simple subject, 42
2d simple predicate, or verb, 43
2e subject never in a prepositional phrase, 47
2f compound subject, 51
2g compound verb, 52
2h complement defined, 62
2i subject complement, 66
2j direct object, 67
2k indirect object, 69
2l sentences classified by purpose, 75–76

3 Phrases

3a phrase defined, 78
3b prepositional phrase, 79
3c object of a preposition, 79
3d participle defined, 88–89
3e participial phrase, 92
3f gerund defined, 93
3g gerund phrase, 95
3h infinitive defined, 97
3i infinitive phrase, 98
3j appositive defined, 102
3k appositive phrase, 103

4 The Clause

4a clause defined, 106
4b independent clause, 106
4c subordinate clause, 107
4d adjective clause, 109
4e adverb clause, 113
4f noun clause, 115
4g sentences classified by structure, 121–22

USAGE

5 Agreement

5a singular & plural defined, 129
5b agreement in number, 131
5c phrase between subject & verb, 132
5d singular pronouns, 134
5e plural pronouns, 134
5f other indefinite pronouns, 134
5g-i compound subjects, 137–39
5j *don't* & *doesn't*, 140
5k collective nouns, 142
5l subject & verb agreement, 143

5m	subject after verb, 143
5n	words stating amount, 144
5o	titles singular in number, 144
5p	*every* & *many a,* 144
5q	singular nouns plural in form, 145
5r	pronoun & antecedent agreement, 147–49

6 The Correct Use of Verbs

6a	principal parts, 153
6b	regular verbs, 154
6c	irregular verbs, 155
6d	unnecessary change in tense, 164

7 The Correct Use of Pronouns

7a-b	nominative case, 181, 183
7c-e	objective case, 184, 186, 188
7f	*who* & *whom,* 191
7g	incomplete constructions, 197

8 The Correct Use of Modifiers

8a	comparison, 203–04
8b	comparative & superlative degrees, 206
8c	*other* & *else,* 206
8d	double comparison, 207
8e	clear comparisons, 208
8f	dangling modifiers, 210
8g	placement of modifiers, 214

9 Glossary of Usage

SENTENCE STRUCTURE

10 Writing Complete Sentences

10a	fragment defined, 243
10b-d	types of fragments, 246, 248, 251
10e	avoiding fragments, 252
10f	run-on sentence, 254

11 Sentence Combining and Revising

11a	inserting adjectives, adverbs, or prepositional phrases, 260
11b	using participial phrases, 262
11c	using appositive phrases, 264
11d	using compound subjects and verbs, 266
11e	compound sentence, 268
11f	complex sentence, 270–74
11g	varying the beginnings of sentences, 278–83
11h	varying the kinds of sentences, 286

COMPOSITION

12 Writing Paragraphs

12a	paragraph defined, 293
12b	topic sentence, 294
12c	unity in a paragraph, 296
12d-j	paragraph development, 299, 300, 301, 303, 307, 308
12k	coherence in a paragraph, 311–13

12l transitional devices, 317–18

13 **Writing Compositions**

13a choosing a subject, 333
13b limiting the subject, 340
13c adapting the subject, 342
13d determining the purpose, 343
13e planning the composition, 344–46
13f outlining, 349–51
13g parts of a composition, 353–56
13h-i linking expressions, 358, 361

14 **Manuscript Form**

14a accepted standards, 371
14b abbreviations, 372
14c writing numbers, 373
14d dividing words, 374
14e correction symbols, 374

15 **Writing Summaries and Reports**

15a reading carefully, 377
15b taking notes, 377
15c length of summary, 378
15d comparing summary with article, 379
15e choosing & limiting the subject, 387–88
15f locating sources, 389
15g preliminary outline, 391
15h note cards, 392
15i revising the outline, 395
15j writing the rough draft, 395–96
15k writing the final draft, 396

16 **Writing Stories**

16a planning the story, 407
16b point of view, 409
16c arousing interest, 410
16d using dialogue, 412
16e using description, 415

17 **Making Writing Interesting**

18 **The Business Letter**

18a choosing stationery, 446
18b making letters attractive, 446
18c proper form, 447
18d letters of request, 453
18e order letters, 454
18f adjustment letters, 455
18g folding the letter correctly, 457
18h addressing the envelope, 459

MECHANICS

19 **Capital Letters**

19a first word in a sentence, 465
19b I & O, 466
19c proper nouns & adjectives, 468–74
19d school subjects, 475
19e titles, 476–78

20 **End Marks and Commas**

20a period, 483
20b question mark, 484
20c exclamation point, 484
20d imperative sentences, 485

20e	period after abbreviation, 485
20f-g	commas in a series, 487–89
20h	comma between parts of compound sentence, 491
20i	commas to set off nonessential parts, 495
20j	comma after introductory elements, 500–01
20k	commas to set off interrupters, 503–05
20l	conventional uses of comma, 508
20m	unnecessary commas, 509

21 Semicolons and Colons

21a-c	semicolon between parts of compound sentences, 513–17
21d	semicolons in a series, 518
21e	colon to mean "note what follows," 523–24
21f	conventional uses of colon, 524

22 Underlining and Quotation Marks

22a	underlining titles, 527
22b	italics for words, letters, and figures, 528
22c	quotation marks for direct quotation, 530
22d	quotation begins with capital letter, 530
22e	quotation marks with interrupted quotation, 530–31
22f-g	quotation marks & other punctuation, 531–32

22h-i	quotation marks & paragraphs, 533, 534
22j	single quotation marks, 535
22k	quotation marks for titles, 536

23 Apostrophes

23a-d	apostrophe to form possessives, 541–43
23e	possessive of compound words, 545
23f	multiple possession, 546
23g	apostrophe in contractions, 549
23h	apostrophe to form plurals of letters, numbers, etc., 551

24 Other Marks of Punctuation

24a	hyphen to divide words, 553
24b	hyphen with compound numbers, 555
24c	hyphen with prefixes & suffixes, 555
24d	dash in break of thought, 556
24e	parentheses & parenthetical material, 557

AIDS TO GOOD ENGLISH

25 The Library

25a	knowing the library, 565
25b	library rules, 566
25c	fiction, 567

25d	Dewey decimal system, 568
25e	call number, 571
25f	card catalogue, 571
25g	the *Readers' Guide,* 576
25h	the vertical file, 579

26	**The Dictionary**
26a	information about words, 598
26b	people & places, 604
26c	pronunciation, 606

27	**Vocabulary**
27a	vocabulary notebook, 617
27b	meaning from context, 617
27c	using the dictionary, 621
27d	using the exact word, 626
27e	literary terms, 629
27f-g	prefixes & roots, 631, 633
27h	word origins, 635–36

28	**Spelling**
28a	*ie & ei,* 648
28b	*-sede, -ceed,* & *-cede,* 649
28c	prefixes, 649
28d-h	suffixes, 650–54
28i	plurals of nouns, 655–58

29b	determining the purpose, 681
29c	gathering material, 682
29d	preparing an outline, 683
29e	introduction and conclusion, 684
29f	preparing to deliver a speech, 686
29g	using nonverbal communication, 687
29h	learning correct pronunciation, 687–90
29i	improving enunciation, 691
29j	relating experiences, 693–94
29k	choosing important current events, 695–96
29l	making a report on a book, movie, or television show, 697

30	**Listening**
30a	purpose for listening, 700–01
30b	listening during discussions, 702
30c	listening to speeches, 703–04
30d	evaluating speeches, 705–06

SPEAKING AND LISTENING

29	**Speaking Before Groups**
29a	choosing a topic, 679

Key to
English Workshop Drill

To supplement the lessons in *English Grammar and Composition, Third Course,* there is additional practice in grammar, usage, punctuation, composition, vocabulary, and spelling in *English Workshop, Third Course.* The following chart correlates the rule in the textbook with the appropriate lesson in *English Workshop.*

Text Rule	Workshop Lesson	Text Rule	Workshop Lesson	Text Rule	Workshop Lesson
1a	1	5e	77, 81	13e–g	129
1b	2	5f	77		
1c	3	5g–i	78	15e	119
1d	5, 6	5k	79	15g	129
1e	7, 8	5m	79		
1f	9	5r	81	17	116, 117
1g	10				
1h	10	6a	86	18a–h	133, 134
1i	11	6b	86		
		6c	86–91	19c	54
2a	15, 20	6d	92	19d	55
2b	15			19e	56
2c	17	7a–b	97, 98		
2d	16	7c–e	99, 100	20a–d	48
2e–g	18	7g	102	20f–g	62
2h	26			20h	66
2i	26	10a	44	20i	67
2j	27	10b–d	44, 45	20j	67
2k	28	10e	44, 45	20k	64, 65
		10f	48, 49	20l	65
3a	33, 34, 35	11a	108	22c–f	68
3b	33	11b	110	22h	68
3c	33	11c	110		
3d–k	44	11d	109	23a–d	69
		11e	109	23g	70
4a–c	36	11f	111, 112, 113		
4d	37			27b	14, 96
4e	38	12a	118	27d	75
4f	39	12b	119, 120	27f–g	53
		12c	121		
5a	76	12g–j	122	28c	74, 84
5b	76	12k	123	28d–f	31, 42, 52
5c	77	12l	124		
5d	77, 81				

Correction Symbols

ms	error in manuscript form or neatness
cap	error in use of capital letters
p	error in punctuation
sp	error in spelling
frag	sentence fragment
ss	error in sentence structure
k	awkward sentence
nc	not clear
ref	error in pronoun reference
rs	run-on sentence
gr	error in grammar
w	error in word choice
¶	You should have begun a new paragraph here.
t	error in tense
∧	You have omitted something.

4
E 5
F 6
G 7
H 8
I 9
J 0